THE A-Z OF
West Bromwich Albion

THE A-Z OF
West Bromwich Albion

by **TONY MATTHEWS**

with assistance from
COLIN MACKENZIE

The Breedon Books
Publishing Company
Derby

First published in Great Britain by
The Breedon Books Publishing Company Limited
Breedon House, 44 Friar Gate, Derby, DE1 1DA.
1996

Acknowledgements

I would like to thank the following for their assistance and
support in helping me to compile this latest book on one of
England's finest football clubs:
Firstly, a huge thank you to my good friend and fellow Albion
fanatic, Colin Mackenzie, who has been such a huge help with
regards to the updating of many of the sections in the book – and
who certainly worked overtime with the proof-reading!
Thanks also to Albion supporters Glenn Willmore and Dave
Holloway, for supplying factual information, and Kevin Grice,
Barry Marsh and Lawrie Rampling, who loaned many
photographs; to Anton Rippon and the staff of Breedon Books
Limited, Derby; to the staff of the British Library (London) and to
the staff at both the Birmingham and West Bromwich Public and
Reference Libraries, all of whom had to suffer both mine and
Colin's presence over the last few years as we've busily turned
page after page, checking facts and figures appertaining to the
Albion. Last, but by no means least, thanks to my wife Margaret,
who has once again backed me every inch of the way with regards
to keeping to a strict schedule.

ISBN 1 85983 064 1

Printed and bound by Butler & Tanner Ltd., Selwood Printing
Works, Caxton Road, Frome, Somerset.

Colour separations by Colour Services, Wigston, Leicester.

Jackets printed by Lawrence-Allen, Weston-Super-Mare, Avon

Foreword

by Tony Hale
Chairman,
West Bromwich Albion FC

I was delighted to pen the foreword to this new book on West Bromwich Albion, a club with a great tradition.

This 'A-Z' is a veritable mine of information, not only for the avid supporter of the Baggies, but also for those statistically-minded football enthusiasts, like me, who simply love to read this kind of book.

Tony Matthews, our historian and museum curator, has collated many intriguing and fascinating stories. There are hundreds of facts and figures, portraits of all the star players, interesting in-depth coverage of several historical events in which Albion have been involved, and, of course, a collection of tremendous photographs, some of which go back a long time, and a few of which have not been seen in print before.

It was in 1878-79 that a group of young men formed a football team which was soon to become known as West Bromwich Albion. Ten years later the club had one of the finest teams in the country, winning the coveted English Cup and becoming founder members of the Football League.

Since then Albion have had their ups and downs. They went on to win the FA Cup a further four times, clinching the First Division championship in 1920, lifting the Football League Cup in 1966 and playing in four European competitions, as well as visiting countries all over the world, including prestigious tours to Russia in 1957, and China and Hong Kong in 1978.

On the down side, the club has come near to folding on a couple of occasions, relegation has been suffered many times and for two seasons Albion played in the old Third Division.

But despite all these highs and lows, the support for the club has always been there and now Albion have fans all over the globe who follow the club through thick and thin, and will continue to do so for many years to come.

We are entering a new era with Albion. The club is now a public limited company – and with such a super stadium waiting to be filled week in, week out, I am sure that in the future there are going to be some great times again at The Hawthorns.

Enjoy the book, enjoy your football and here's looking ahead to the Premiership – come on you Baggies!

Tony Hale

Introduction

AS far as I am aware, the information contained in this book is the most comprehensive statistical record ever produced on any football club, in this country or anywhere in the world.

There is considerably more data in this 1996 publication than there was in the *Centenary A-Z of West Bromwich Albion* which was published in 1979.

The information in this 'encyclopaedia' has been obtained from numerous sources with frequent reference being made to the club's official programme – the *Albion News* – which was first published in 1905, and also to the *History of West Bromwich Albion Football Club* which was serialised in the programme from 1911 to 1930. The latter source of material is, on the whole, the accurate account of the club's earlier years.

A variety of local and national newspapers have also been consulted, including the *Sports Argus, Free Press, Weekly News, Birmingham Daily Gazette, Saturday Night, Midland Athlete, Express & Star, Sporting Star, Birmingham Evening Mail, Sunday Mercury, Sports Mail, Sandwell Mail, Midland Chronicle and Evening Dispatch.*

In early editions of some of these papers, the details of certain Albion goalscorers vary considerably, especially during the Victorian era of the late 19th century, but every last effort has been made to produce accurate statistics from what is an extremely complicated subject.

With reference to players' records, the total appearances and goals scored are for competitive games only, and the date given for debut is the year the player first appeared in Albion's senior team (not when he joined the club).

Attendances and transfer fees have been taken from the club's official records and not from newspapers or soccer magazines.

All the statistical information set out in this book is relevant to the end of the 1995-96 season.

With the help of Colin Mackenzie, I have covered in detail the complete history of West Bromwich Albion FC (1878 to 1996) and although it is not a story (as such) of the club's fortunes in chronological order, I believe that the contents which lie before you will certainly provide hours of interesting (and intriguing) reading, and open your eyes once more with regard to your own personal knowledge of a great football club – West Bromwich Albion.

I would like to stress that all the views expressed in this book are those of the author and not West Bromwich Albion FC.

Tony Matthews
May 1996

Fog caused the abandonment of the Forest-Albion FA Cup-tie at the City Ground in January 1973.

ABANDONED AND POSTPONED MATCHES

Nowadays it is unusual for a club to go through a complete season without having at least one match either abandoned or postponed due to adverse weather.

Abandoned Games

Albion have been fortunate that since 1888 they have had only 12 Football League matches halted before the scheduled 90 minutes had been completed.

Here is a list of those games with the score of the rearranged fixture alongside:

9 Mar 1895	Stoke 1	Albion 2	68 mins – rain	(1-1)
7 Dec 1895	Albion 0	Bury 0	15 mins – snow	(1-3)
18 Nov 1905	Grimsby T 1	Albion 0	65 mins – fog	(3-2)
19 Jan 1907	Albion 0	Barnsley 0	80 mins – light	(3-1)
6 Jan 1912	Albion 0	Tottenham H 0	52 mins – fog	(2-0)
13 Feb 1915	Oldham A 0	Albion 1	21 mins – snow	(1-1)
19 Sep 1925	Albion 0	Bury 2	51 mins – rain	(4-0)
22 Feb 1936	Albion 1	Aston Villa 0	26 mins – snow	(0-3)
19 Nov 1949	Albion 1	Blackpool 2	70 mins – fog	(1-0)
20 Dec 1958	Albion 1	Luton T 1	70 mins – rain	(2-0)
26 Dec 1962	Wolves 2	Albion 0	45 mins – snow	(7-0)
14 Dec 1965	Albion 0	Aston Villa 0	51 mins – rain	(2-2)

In the FA Cup, Albion have had only one tie abandoned, a third round replay at Nottingham Forest on 16 January 1973, when fog halted the action in the 79th minute with the scores level at 1-1. The replay also ended 0-0 before Albion eventually went through 3-1.

There have been a number of other games involving Albion which were forced into an early finish due to the weather.

Friendlies

10 Feb 1883	Albion 1	Notts Rangers 1	abandoned 60 mins
12 Nov 1883	Stoke 1	Albion 1	abandoned 80 mins
26 Jan 1884	Albion 2	Wednesbury OA 0	abandoned 15 mins
25 Apr 1885	Bolton W 1	Albion 0	abandoned 70 mins
28 Dec 1885	Albion 0	Bolton W 0	abandoned 75 mins

30 Mar 1889	Albion 4	Grimsby T 0	abandoned 60 mins
5 Dec 1892	Albion 1	Aston Villa 1	abandoned 35 mins
6 Jan 1940	Albion 0	Sheffield W 3	abandoned 47 mins

Staffordshire Cup

3 Dec 1883	Albion 1	Cocknage 0	abandoned 40 mins

Wartime Game

26 Dec 1944	Aston Villa 3	Albion 4	abandoned 81 mins•

This scoreline was allowed to stand.

NB: On 16 May 1970, the Lanerossi Vicenza-Albion Anglo-Italian Cup game in Italy was abandoned by the referee because of crowd and player disturbances (See CROWD DISTURBANCES, RIOTS).

Postponed Matches

There have been many instances where certain Albion matches have had to be postponed due to unforeseen circumstances which surrounded the fixture itself such as unfit pitches or sick players.

One fixture – a home fourth-round FA Cup-tie against Nottingham Forest in the 'arctic' winter of 1962-63 was called-off no fewer than 11 times before it was finally played 58 days late on 6 March 1963. This is the longest-delayed FA Cup-tie in Albion's history.

In the bitter winter of 1947, Albion did not play a single League or Cup game between 9 February and 14 March, and when similar conditions gripped England in 1962-63, Albion managed to fulfil only two fixtures (one in the League against Sheffield Wednesday and one in the FA Cup against Plymouth Argyle) between 16 December and 1 March.

ABERDARE ATHLETIC

Aberdare Athletic, members of the Football League (1921-27), have never played Albion at any level. The only connection between the clubs is that Harry Hadley, a player with Albion between 1897 and 1905, managed Aberdare in 1927-28.

ACCRINGTON

Albion's record against Accrington:

Football League

Venue	P	W	D	L	F	A	Pts
Home	5	4	1	0	18	5	9
Away	5	0	1	4	7	12	1
Totals	10	4	2	4	25	17	10

FA Cup

	P	W	D	L	F	A
Away	2	0	0	2	1	6

Albion and Accrington were founder members of the Football League, and all ten League games were played in the First Division over a five-year period between 1888 and 1893.

The first meeting was on Albion soil (at Stoney Lane) on 3 November 1888 and it ended in a 2-2 draw.

Albion's best win (of their four) over Accrington is 5-1 – achieved at home on 7 March 1891, while their heaviest defeat has been 5-4 (away) on 17 December 1892.

Tom Pearson scored seven goals in six League games against Accrington (1889-92). He also added one Cup goal to his tally.

Albion played their two FA Cup games against Accrington in January 1890. The first encounter at Moorhead ended in a 3-1 defeat, but Albion protested to the FA on the grounds that the pitch was unfit and asked that the tie be replayed. Albion's plea was upheld, but they were again well beaten, this time by 3-0, Entwhistle, Chippendale and Barbour scoring for the home side. The Accrington fans were incensed that Albion had found fault with their pitch and gave the Throstles a most hostile reception. One eye witness reported that the players were somewhat resentful, too, kicking the ball 'as far as possible with the wind' and making 'the Throstles go over several fields to fetch it back'. Remember, there were no ball boys in those days!

Albion League debutants v Accrington: Charlie Donnachie (1889), Sam Wheldon (1892), Ben Hadley (1892).

Players with both clubs: Sam Cox, Billy Harris, Fred Leedham, James Singleton, Sid Swinden.

ADAMS, Amos

West Bromwich-born full-back, who joined Albion from Springfields in 1897. Adams spent 13 seasons with the club, making 214 appearances and scoring three goals before retiring to become a sportsmaster at a local school. Later coached FC Amiens (France), becoming manager there in 1926. A strong tackler, he made his debut at centre-forward against Notts County in 1899 He won a Division Two championship medal in 1902 and formed a fine partnership with Jesse Pennington. He died in 1941, aged 60.

ADAMS, James

A hefty goalkeeper who weighed almost 15st at one stage in his career. Born in Norton Canes, Cannock, in 1908, Jimmy Adams played in 221 games for Albion from 1929 to 1945 when he retired. He joined the club from Cannock Town and took over from Harold Pearson. Adams died in August 1979.

ADAMS, William

A junior international full-back, born in Blackheath in 1892, Billy Adams played 98 first-team games for Albion between 1919 and 1928. He joined the club from Rowley Vics and left The Hawthorns for Barrow, later playing for Cradley Heath (1929). He retired in 1931 and became licensee in Smethwick. He died in 1945.

ADMISSION

Before the commencement of League football in September 1888, the general overall terrace charge for admission to an Albion home game varied from one old penny to 6d (3p) depending on the opposition and competition.

In fact, the 6d (3p) entry fee remained in force right from 1890 to 1919 when it was increased to one shilling (5p).

It stayed at that price until well into World War Two (1942) when it was increased to 1s 3d (8p).

From then on the minimum increases has been gradual, as the table below indicates:

Season	Terraces		Seats	
1951-52	1s 6d	(8p)	3s 6d	(18p)
1952-53	1s 9d	(9p)	4s 0d	(20p)
1955-56	2s 0d	(10p)	4s 6d	(23p)
1960-61	2s 6d	(13p)	5s 0d	(25p)
1963-64	3s 0d	(15p)	6s 0d	(30p)
1964-65	3s 6d	(18p)	7s 6d	(38p)
1965-66	4s 0d	(20p)	8s 6d	(43p)
1967-68	5s 0d	(25p)	10s 0d	(50p)
1970-71	7s 6d	(38p)	12s 6d	(63p)
1972-73	40p		75p	
1974-75	50p		£1.00	
1978-79	£1.00		£1.50	
1979-80	£1.30		£2.30	
1980-81	£1.50		£2.50	
1981-82	£2.00		£3.00	
1985-86	£3.00		£4/£6	
1990-91	£5.50/£6		£7/£8	
1992-93	£7.00		£11.00	
1995-96	£10/£15 (all seater)			

Season Tickets

It cost Albion supporters only three shillings (15p) to purchase a season ticket in 1883-84 – and in those days there were, on average, some 20 home games per season.

The price of the season tickets rose slowly and when League football arrived five years later, the average price for such a ticket, nationwide, had risen to five shillings (25p).

At the turn of the century (season 1900-01) which saw Albion move to The Hawthorns, the cost had risen to ten shillings (50p) and when Albion won the First Division championship in 1919-20, their fans were paying 15 shillings each (75p) for a season ticket (admitting them to 21 home League games) and this was for a seat in the grandstand (Halfords Lane).

By the mid-1920s, the price of a season ticket had risen to 30 shillings (£1.50) and in 1930-31 (when Albion won the 'double' – the FA Cup and promotion from Division Two) their fans were paying £2 for their season ticket.

In 1933-34 the outlay for the regular supporter had shot up to three guineas per season (63 shillings – £3.15) and immediately after World War Two, the charge had reached the £4 mark.

Ten years later it was £5, and in 1960-61 season tickets at The Hawthorns for Blocks 'F' and 'J' (centre stand, Halfords Lane side) were eight guineas each (£8.40) and for Blocks 'E' and 'H' (front of stand/paddock seats) they were five guineas each (£5.25).

Ground season tickets this season (1960-61) were £3 each – the price being the same as it was when these were first introduced to terrace fans for season 1958-59.

In 1979-80 season tickets at The Hawthorns ranged from £23 (terraces) to £65 (seats) before VAT. In 1988-89 the prices had risen to £90/£120 (seats) and £72 (terraces) and in 1992-93 it cost the fan £165/£200 for a seat and £80/£135 on the terraces.

The first time season tickets were issued for the all-seater Hawthorns stadium was in 1995-96 and the prices ranged from £133 to £285.

An Albion 'away' season ticket in 1995-96 cost £120 and a 'home' car park season ticket was £75.

Complimentary Tickets
For Football League matches, the visiting club can normally claim up to a total of 37 complimentary tickets – 25 for use by the players, manager, coach and 12 for the directors' Box. There is no limit on how many complimentaries the home club can issue.

All-Ticket Games
The first all-ticket game at The Hawthorns was for the England-Wales Victory International on 20 October 1945. For this game 56,000 ticket were printed and the official attendance was given as 54,611 (paying record receipts of £5,440). England lost 1-0.

The first time an Albion home game was made all-ticket was for the fifth-round FA Cup-tie against Chelsea on 12 February 1949. After consultation with the police, the club restricted the attendance to 62,000, but, in fact, the final attendance figure was 57,843.

The first League game to be made all-ticket at The Hawthorns was the Albion-Wolves local derby on 29 March 1958. Initially the crowd limit was placed at 60,000, but in the end fans were allowed to pay on the day (right up to kick-off) and the gate was given officially as 56,904. Wolves won 3-0.

Albion's home First Division game against Aston Villa on 10 November 1976 had a 44,000 all-ticket restriction placed on it – this being the first game when tickets were not sold on the day of the match (selling officially ended at 5pm on the Friday). The crowd in the end was officially given as 41,867, which generated record receipts of £41,037. The result was a 1-1 draw.

If a game is made all-ticket at The Hawthorns now (1996-97) with a set capacity of 26,296 (including the spaces on the terraces at the corner of the Rainbow Stand/Smethwick End) the tickets would be allocated (including box-holders etc.) as follows:

Birmingham Road End	8,286
Smethwick End	5,816
Halfords Lane Stand	5,110
Rainbow Stand	6,084
Corner terraces	1,000
Total capacity	26,296

Just the Ticket
Albion's ticket allocation for the 1931 FA Cup Final against Birmingham was 7,500, yet over 80,000 fans applied for them!

For their 1935 FA Cup Final showdown with Sheffield Wednesday, Albion's allocation was raised to 8,500; in 1954 (v Preston North End) they were given 12,500 tickets and for the 1968 Final against Everton, Albion received 16,000.

For their Football League Cup Finals of 1967 (v QPR) and 1970 (v Manchester City) Albion were given 30,000 and 32,000 tickets respectively, and when Port Vale were defeated 3-0 in the 1993 Second Division Play-off Final, 42,334 Albion supporters made the trip to Wembley. That was 79.2 per cent of the official attendance figure of 53,471 (receipts £856,000).

AGE
There have been instances in competitive football whereby players have appeared at the ages of 14 and 52 years. Albion have no one who has fallen into that category but over the years they have had footballers who have broken into the first team at the age of 16 and have also starred in League games well into their 30s.

Oldest players
The oldest player ever to don an Albion shirt in a League game is George Baddeley, who was 39 years, 345 days old when he lined up against Sheffield Wednesday at The Hawthorns, on 18 April, 1914. Baddeley was almost 38 when he played in the 1912 FA Cup Final.

Jesse Pennington holds the record for Albion's oldest FA Cup participant, being 38 years, 183 days old when he played against Notts County in February 1922.

Nigel Spink was Albion's oldest League debutant when he was well into his 37th year.

Goalkeeper Nigel Spink (born 8 August 1958) is Albion's oldest League debutant. He was 37 years, 179 days old when he lined up against Ipswich Town (away) on 3 February 1996 following his free transfer from Aston Villa.

Johnny Giles (born 6 January 1940) holds the record for the oldest debutant for Albion in the FA Cup, aged 35 years, 362 days against Carlisle United, in January 1976, and he is also the club's oldest League Cup player at 36 years, 260 days (v Brighton in September 1976).

The oldest player to wear an Albion shirt in any sort of game has been Ronnie Allen (born 15 January 1929) who came on as an 84th-minute substitute in the friendly at Cheltenham Town on 10 May 1995, at the age of 66 years, 115 days.

Youngest players
The youngest player to appear in a League game for Albion has been Charlie 'Tug' Wilson, who made his debut at Oldham Athletic on 1 October 1921, at the age of 16 years, 73 days.

Sid Bowser holds the record for Albion's youngest FA Cup debutant. He was only 16 years, 359 days old when he played against Bolton Wanderers (home) on 16 January 1909, a fortnight after his League bow against Grimsby Town.

Mickey Lewis (born 15 February 1965) was 16 years, 303 days old when he came on as a substitute for Albion in a League Cup-tie against Crystal Palace (away) on 15 December 1981.

Winger Frank Hodgetts (born 30 September 1924) is the youngest-ever Albion first-team player, lining up in a Regional wartime game against Notts County in October 1940 at the age of 16 years, 26 days.

Age Snippets

Billy Meredith of Manchester City was 48 years, 72 days old when he played against Albion in a League match in 1922.

Cameron Buchanan of Wolves was only 14 years of age when he played against Albion in a Regional wartime game at Molineux in September 1942.

Skipper Len Millard was 38 years, 226 days old when he played his last League game for Albion, against Leeds United in October 1957.

Millard was aged 35 when he skippered Albion to FA Cup glory in 1954, thus being the oldest player to win an FA Cup medal with the club. The youngest was Billy Bassett, aged 18 years two months, against Preston North End in 1888.

Tommy Magee (born 6 May 1899) is the youngest player to win a Football League championship medal with Albion. He was 21 when the Throstles won the prize in 1920.

Graham Lovett (born 5 August 1947) is Albion's youngest League Cup winner, being 18 years, eight months old when West Ham United were defeated in the 1966 Final.

Billy Bassett (aged 19) became Albion's youngest full international when he was capped by England against Ireland in 1888.

ALBION NEWS (matchday programme)

Albion's first in-depth matchday programme was published for season 1905-06. The first issue was for the home League game with Burnley on Saturday, 2 September 1905. It comprised eight pages and cost one old penny, and it is believed that 2,000 copies were printed. By 1907 the Albion News enjoyed a circulation of 5,000 copies per match and had readers as far afield as Canada, West Africa and Singapore.

The editor of the Albion programme for many years was Mr Harry Keys, who, even though a director of the club, chose to sit in the press box rather than with his fellow board members in their own box. Between 1915 and 1919 the Albion News was not published (owing to World War One) and from 1940 through to 1945 it was produced on a restricted scale because of a paper restriction.

Throughout the late 1940s and the 1950s

the programme was a basic two-colour publication, but once into the 1960s – after Peerless Press had taken over the printing of it from Joseph Wones Ltd (West Bromwich) – it gradually improved in both content and cover price.

At the start of the 1969-70 season, the Albion News became much more of a magazine than a programme and under the editorship of commercial manager, Les Thorley, it was voted top football programme in the country. Progress regarding content and design continued to be made and in 1974 a multi-coloured front cover was first seen for the first time. Ever since then, the much-collected (and circulated) Albion News has been printed in many different sizes, increasing from 24 to 48 pages as well as rising steadily in price: 30p, 40p, 50p, 60p (1985 – 32 pages), 70p, 80p, £1.00, £1.20 to £1.50 (the latter being the cover price in 1995-96 for 48 pages) and yet it has still been regarded as one of the best soccer programmes in the country, picking up several awards under a variety of editors, including Gordon Dimbleby, statistician Tony Matthews, Gordon Bennett and Tom Cardall, with excellent contributions and photographs coming in from various sources.

NB: Prior to 1905 most clubs (including Albion) used to issue one-page team-sheets rather than programmes.

ALBION STAFF

Albion's 1996 staff comprised the following-

Administration
Club secretary: Dr John Evans BA, PhD (Wales)
Office staff: Diane Aston, Alison Matthews, Kate Brown (reception)

Accounts Department
Financial Controller: Robert E.McGing
Accountant: John Reynolds
Staff: Deana Snipe, Lisa Cashmore

Commercial Department
Commercial Executive: Tom Cardall
Staff: Sonya Cox, Kate Evans

Club Shop
Manager: Derek Judge
Staff: Martin Harding, Ian Hebberts, Craig Sadler

Ticket Office
Manageress: Joanne Crowe
Staff: Craig Clayton, Joanne Kendrick

Football in the Community
Community Officer: Mark Ashton
Staff: Wendy Dellicott, Brett Bensley

Kit/Boot Room
Manager: Dave Matthews

Hawthorns Museum
Curator/Historian: Tony Matthews

Stadium Management
Manager: Andy Williamson
Ground Staff: Phil Kingston (chief), Rob Lane
Maintenance: Derek Edmund (foreman), Stan Beard, David Beard, Colin Hern

Club Laundry
Supervisor: Maureen Brookes

Social Club Steward
Steward: Alistair Brown

On a first-team matchday, there are 210 stewards on duty, plus some 40 extra helpers and assistants, all giving their support to the club.

ALDERSHOT

Albion have yet to play Aldershot at competitive level, but the clubs did meet in a testimonial match at the Recreation Ground in April 1981, when Albion won 2-0.

Players with both clubs: Fred Brown, Peter Hucker, Clive Jackman, Andy King, Tony Lange, Stewart Phillips, Brian Talbot.

Also associated with both clubs: Bobby Gould, Paul

Holsgrove, Wilf Vickers, Derek Finch and Pat Hilton. Gordon Clark managed both clubs – Aldershot 1949-55, Albion 1959-61 – and Wilf Dixon was trainer with both Aldershot and Albion (1960s). Albion's chief scout in 1995-96, Ronnie Mann, was an Aldershot player between 1956 and 1958.

ALLEN, Ronald

Supreme goalscorer for Albion between 1950 and 1961 when he left the club to become player-coach at Crystal Palace, Ronnie Allen was born in Fenton, Stoke-on-Trent, in 1929 and he played for several junior teams in the Potteries before signing for Port Vale in 1944. He was transferred to The Hawthorns for £20,000 after service in the RAF and went on to net 234 goals in 415 games for the Baggies (208 in the League, a tally bettered only by Tony Brown). Allen gained five England caps as well as playing for the 'B' team, the Football League and the FA XI. An FA Cup winner with Albion in 1954 (he scored twice in the Final against Preston), Allen scored 276 goals in 637 League matches in his career and in all games his record was 812 outings and 354 goals. He scored in each season from 1944 to 1965 inclusive and was the First Division's top marksman in 1954-55 with 27 goals. After retiring in 1965, Allen joined Wolverhampton Wanderers as coach and later became manager at Molineux. Thereafter he managed Athletic Bilbao (Spain) and Sporting Lisbon (Portugal), coached in Saudi Arabia, was manager of Walsall, returned to Albion in 1977, initially as scouting advisor, then manager later in the year, and after a spell in Greece as coach-manager of Panathinaikos he came back to The Hawthorns once more, again as manager in 1981-82, and as general manager until 1983. After becoming an Albion shareholder, he still helps with part-time coaching at the club and made a brief appearance as a substitute in a friendly at Cheltenham in 1995, aged 66. He is truly one of Albion's all-time greats.

AMATEURS

Bobby Hope is the only amateur to play for Albion's League side since World War Two, making his debut against Arsenal in a First Division match at The Hawthorns on 30 April 1960 when just 150 days short of his 17th birthday.

Over the years Albion have had several well-known amateur footballers on their books who appeared in their League side, among them Harold G.Bache (1914-16), Chris Charsley (1891), Ernie Fellows (1890s), Lester Finch (1939-45), Billy Folks (1904), Ernie Ford (1922-23), Bill Jackson (1912-17), Revd William C.Jordan (1904-09), John Rea (1894-95), Bethel Robinson (1889-91) and Norman Whitehead (1932-35). Forwards Bache, Finch and Jordan all won amateur international caps for England while goalkeeper Charsley was capped by England at senior level. Hope went on to become a full Scottish international.

ANGLO-ITALIAN CUP

Albion first entered the Anglo-Italian Cup competition in season 1969-70 and they have now played a total of 21 games, their full record being:

Venue	P	W	D	L	F	A
Home	10	3	3	4	16	13
Away	11	2*	4	5	7	13
Totals	21	5	7	9	23	26

*One of these two away wins was a 4-1 penalty shoot-out victory over Birmingham City in January 1995, but the goal statistics relate to actual outfield play only.

Ronnie Allen (9) wheels away after scoring Albion's opening goal in the 1954 FA Cup Final.

The Anglo-Italian Cup.

The Italian teams Albion have met in the competition are Brescia, Lanerossi Vicenza, AS Roma, Inter-Milan, Cagliari, Cosenza, Pescara, Fiorentina, Padova, Foggia, Salernitana and Reggiana, and in the away game against Lanerossi in 1970, crowd and player disturbances resulted in the referee, Kevin Howley, abandoning the tie 15 minutes from time (See CROWD DISTURBANCES, RIOTS).

Albion's best win in the Anglo-Italian Cup is 4-0 against AS Roma at home in May 1970, when Bobby Hope, Tony Brown (2) and John Talbot (with his only goal for the Baggies) scored in front of a near-12,000 crowd.

Albion's heaviest defeat is 4-3 at home to Padova in November 1993.

In front of a 9,000 plus crowd Albion beat rivals Birmingham City at a frost-bound St Andrew's in a penalty shoot-out to reach the English Final of 1995-96. The tie ended 2-2 after extra-time, but the Albion players kept their nerve and won the 'shoot-out' 4-1.

In the English Final, Albion played Staffordshire neighbours Port Vale and were beaten on aggregate over two legs. The first game ended 0-0 at The Hawthorns while the return, at Vale Park, resulted in a 3-1 defeat.

Serie 'B' side, Genoa, qualified from Italy and met Port Vale in the Wembley Final on 17 March 1996.

ANGLO-SCOTTISH CUP

Albion played six games in this short-lived competition.

In 1975 (group 2) they drew 1-1 with Mansfield Town at home, beat Hull City 2-1 away and lost 2-1 at Leicester.

The following year (based in Group 'B') Albion lost 1-0 at

Len Cantello's shot beats the Mansfield Town goalkeeper in the Anglo-Scottish Cup game at The Hawthorns in August 1975.

Bristol City and 3-2 at Nottingham Forest before defeating Notts County 3-1 at The Hawthorns.

They failed to progress in either competition, finishing second in their group in 1975 when a meagre aggregate of 17,017 fans saw their three matches, and third in their section in 1976 when a total of 18,895 fans attended the

three games. Joe Mayo scored three of Albion's five goals in the latter tournament.

APPEARANCES

Tony 'Bomber' Brown has appeared in more first-team games for Albion (1963-80) than anyone else. In fact, he is the only player to top 800 outings for the club.

Long-serving Tony Brown in action against West Midlands rivals Coventry City.

This is a breakdown on Brown's record:

Competition	Apps
Football League	561+13
FA Cup	53+1
League Cup	46+1
Fairs Cup	3
European Cup Winners Cup	6
UEFA Cup	7+1
FA Charity Shield	1
Watney Cup	3
Texaco Cup	9
Anglo-Italian Cup	8
Anglo-Scottish Cup	4
Tennent-Caledonian Cup	3
Friendlies etc	91+7
Totals	795+23

NB: Brown holds the record for most League, FA Cup and European Cup appearances for Albion. He also played in the abandoned FA Cup game against Nottingham Forest in 1972-73.

League appearances
Albion's Top Ten: Tony Brown 561+13, Ally Robertson 504+2, John Wile 499+1, Jesse Pennington 455, Tommy Glidden 445, Len Millard 436; Joe Smith 434, Ronnie Allen 415, Joe Carter 141, Ray Barlow 403.

FA Cup appearances
Albion's Top Ten: Tony Brown 53+1, Ray Barlow 47, Ronnie Allen 43, Len Millard 41, Billy Bassett 40, Jem Bayliss 39, Jesse Pennington 39, Charlie Perry 39, Joe Reader 39, Joe Carter 37.

League Cup appearances
Albion's Top Ten: Alistair Robertson 53, Tony Brown 46+1, John Wile 42, Derek Statham 34, John Kaye 31, Doug Fraser 29, Bobby Hope 29, Jeff Astle 28, Cyrille Regis 27+1, Ally Brown 27, Tony Godden 27.

European appearances
Albion's Top Ten: Tony Brown 16+1, Brendon Batson 12,

Tony Godden 12, Alistair Robertson 12, Bryan Robson 12, Derek Statham 12, John Wile 12, Jeff Astle 10, Alistair Brown 10, Doug Fraser 10, John Kaye 10, Cyrille Regis 10.

Top-Ten Appearance Makers

Player	League	FACup	Lge Cup	Others	Totals
Tony Brown	574	54	47	45	720
Len Millard	436	40	-	151	627
Ally Robertson	506	36	53	31	626
John Wile	500	42	42	35	619
Jesse Pennington	455	39	-	2	496
Ray Barlow	403	46	-	33	482
Tommy Glidden	445	33	-	1	479
Joe Smith	434	30	-	7	471
Ronnie Allen	415	42	-	1	458
Joe Carter	414	37	-	-	451

Other appearances include all wartime games etc (not friendlies).

Ever-presents
Centre-half and skipper John Wile was an ever-present in Albion's League side a record seven times: 1971-72, 1973-74, 1976-77, 1978-79, 1979-80, 1980-81 and 1981-82. Goalkeeper Joe Reader had five full seasons: 1890-91, 1892-93, 1894-95, 1897-98 and 1899-1900, and defenders George Shaw and Tom Perry each managed a full campaign four times.

Most games in a season
John Wile played in a club record 75 (out of 76) first-team games for Albion in season 1978-79. Brendon Batson and Alistair Brown each played in 73 matches that season, Bryan Robson in 72, Derek Statham 71 and Cyrille Regis 69.

Positional appearances
Players who have appeared in a single position most times for Albion at League level are:

(1)	Goal	Stuart Naylor	354+1
(2)	RB	Joe Smith	428
(3)	LB	Jesse Pennington	315
(4)	RH	Tommy Magee	323
(5)	CH	John Wile	449
(6)	LH	Alistair Robertson	478+2
(7)	OR	Tommy Glidden	389
(8)	IR	Joe Carter	400
(9)	CF	Ronnie Allen	306
(10)	IL	Bobby Hope	241+5
(11)	OL	Clive Clark	291+1

Consecutive appearances
From 20 August 1977 to 31 October 1981 inclusive, goalkeeper Tony Godden made a record 228 consecutive appearances for Albion (180 in the League). In the four-year period from 22 April 1978 to 20 May 1982 inclusive, defender John Wile played in 224 consecutive games for the club (172 in the League) while in the 1970s, Alistair Robertson had an unbroken run of 171 League outings for the Baggies.

Wing-half Jimmy Dudley played in 166 League games without a break between 1952-56; Don Howe in 141 also during the 1950s, and George Shaw appeared in 138 successive League matches between 1926-30.

Len Millard was absent from only 13 games out of a possible 420 in ten League seasons from 1946-47; George Shaw missed two out of 280 (1926-33) and Joe Smith appeared in all but six of 276 League matches (1919-25).

Most in Divisions
Tony Brown played in a record 459 First Division League games for Albion (1963-80); Ronnie Allen made all his 415 League appearances for the club in the First Division (1950-

61). Full-back Jesse Pennington made a record 214 appearances for the Baggies in Division Two (1904-11).

Appearance Snippets
Tony Brown also holds the club record for most Football League appearances at The Hawthorns – 282 – his first in October 1963 v Aston Villa, his last in December 1979 v Everton.

On 12 November 1977, Tony Brown became the first Albion player to make 500 League appearances v West Ham United (away).

Herbert Varney played in five League games for Albion (1906-07) and was on the winning side each time.

Len Cantello donned ten different numbered shirts for Albion's League side (1969-79); the only ones he didn't wear were those of No.1 (goalkeeper) and No.5 (centre-half). Bryan Robson wore nine (missing out with Nos.1, 4 and 9).

Over the last 50 years several players have appeared in all five forward positions (7-8-9-10-11) for Albion, including Ronnie Allen, Alistair Brown, Tony Brown, Len Cantello, Wilf Carter, Nicky Cross, Allan Glover, Alec Jackson, Steve Mackenzie, Gary Robson and David Shaw. Prior to 1946 only Tommy Glidden (1922-36) and Roddy McLeod (1891-97) had achieved this feat.

ARSENAL
Albion's record against Arsenal reads:

Football League

Venue	P	W	D	L	F	A	Pts.
Home	52	21	12	19	76	65	54
Away	52	9	13	30	63	112	32
Totals	104	30	25	49	139	177	86

FA Cup

Home	4	2	2	0	9	6
Away	4	2	0	2	3	5
Totals	8	4	2	2	12	11

Charity Shield

Neutral	1	0	0	1	0	1

Other Matches

Home	1	0	0	1	0	1
Away	6	3	1	2	7	10
Total	7	3	1	3	7	11

Freddie Morris scored four times in Albion's best League win of 7-0 over Arsenal at The Hawthorns in October 1922.

Albion's heaviest defeat in the League is 6-2, at Highbury in September 1970.

Arsenal also beat Albion 6-3 at Highbury in November 1951 when Cliff Holton hit a hat-trick for the Gunners.

Derek Kevan scored a hat-trick against Arsenal at Highbury in a 4-3 Albion defeat in October 1958.

Albion's 500th win in the First Division came at Arsenal's expense in April 1952 (3-1 at The Hawthorns).

By defeating Arsenal 2-1 at home on 12 April 1902, Albion clinched the Second Division championship.

Albion's 2-1 replay win at Highbury on 6 March 1957, put them into the FA Cup semi-finals. In this game Brian Whitehouse scored a controversial 'offside' goal for the Baggies and goalkeeper Jim Sanders saved Danny Clapton's penalty.

A crowd of 8,738 saw Albion draw 1-1 with Arsenal in a First Division game in April 1966 – one of the lowest attendances at Highbury since 1915.

Arsenal beat Albion 1-0 at neutral Villa Park to win the 1931 FA Charity Shield (See CHARITY SHIELD).

A record Hawthorns crowd of 64,815 saw Albion beat Arsenal 3-1 in a sixth-round FA Cup-tie in March 1937.

Albion have lost three FA Cup semi-finals on Arsenal's ground at Highbury: 1937 (v Preston North End), 1978 (v Ipswich Town) and 1982 (v Queen's Park Rangers).

Ronnie Allen scored 11 goals for Albion against Arsenal

Derek Kevan (on ground) scores one of his hat-trick goals against Arsenal in 1958.

(ten in the League); Freddie Morris hit eight, four in that 7-0 win in 1922.

Albion League debutants v Arsenal: Jimmy Varty (1912), Lewis Bedford (1921), Billy Ashurst (1926), Geoff Carter (1960), Bobby Hope (1960), Jim Cumbes (1969), Mickey Forsyth (1983), Garry Thompson (1983).

Players with both clubs: Kwame Ampadu, Paul Barron, Brendon Batson, Joseph Connor, David Cork, Freddie Cox, George Drury, Frank Dyer, Bobby Gould, Adam Haywood, Don Howe, Alan Miller, Brian Talbot, Steve Walford, Chris Whyte. Associated with both clubs: Vince Bartram.

Howe also managed both clubs, while George Wright was physio-therapist-trainer at Highbury and The Hawthorns. Brian Whitehouse was a player and coach with Albion and a coach with the Gunners; Archie Macaulay played for Arsenal and later managed Albion (1961-63); Gordon Clark was Albion's manager (1959-61) and chief scout at Arsenal (1966-77); Wilf Dixon was Albion's trainer in the 1960s and later assistant manager at Highbury (1976-77) and Colin Addison, Albion's assistant manager (1978-79 and 1987-88) was an Arsenal forward (1966-68).

ASTLE, Jeffrey
A splendid centre-forward, with great heading ability, Jeff Astle

scored 174 goals in 361 games for Albion between September 1964 and July 1974. He joined the club from Notts County for £25,000 and left for Hellenic (South Africa), later playing for Dunstable, Weymouth, Atherstone and Hillingdon Borough before retiring to run his own industrial cleaning business near Burton upon Trent. Born in Eastwood, Nottingham, in May 1942, Astle – who was groomed by Tommy Lawton at Meadow Lane – won five England caps and played in the 1970 World Cup finals in Mexico. He also represented his country's 'B' team and the Football League. A member of Albion's League Cup and FA Cup winning teams of 1966 and 1968 respectively, he scored in every round of the FA Cup in 1967-68 and was the first player to score in both the FA Cup and League Cup Finals at Wembley (1968 and 1970). Astle was voted Midlands Footballer of the Year in 1968.

ASTON VILLA
Albion's record against Villa reads:

Football League

Venue	P	W	D	L	F	A	Pts
Home	62	28	15	19	99	86	74
Away	62	15	8	39	74	118	38
Totals	124	43	23	58	173	204	112

FA Cup

Home	6	1	1	4	6	9	
Away	8	2	2	4	8	9	
Totals	14	3	3	8	14	18	

League Cup

Home	4	2	0	2	11	6	
Away	3	2	1	0	5	3	
Totals	7	4	1	2	16	9	

Other Matches

Home	54	28	8	18	115	78	
Away	77	21	16	40	129	198	
Totals*	131	49	24	58	244	278	

*Included are two matches played in July 1886 between

A goal for Dick Krzywicki in Albion's 2-1 win over Aston Villa in October 1966.

Villa and an Albion XI which were dubbed 'West Bromwich & District.'

Albion's record League win over Villa is 7-0 (away) in the First Division on 19 October 1935, when 'W.G.' Richardson scored four goals in front of a 38,000 plus crowd.

Villa beat Albion 7-1 at home, also in the First Division, on 24 April 1899, this being Billy Bassett's last game for Albion.

Villa won the first-ever League game 2-0 (h) in January 1889.

A record crowd of 66,094 saw Villa held at home 0-0 by Albion (the reigning champions) in a League game in November 1920.

Albion were relegated from the First Division in 1926-27, but they did have the pleasure of whipping fifth-placed Villa 6-2 at home in mid-March, five of their goals coming in the second half.

Villa beat Albion 6-1 at Villa Park in a crucial First Division game in April 1954 and this defeat ruined Albion's chances of taking the League championship which went to Wolves.

A late equaliser by Albion's Ronnie Allen sent Villa down into the Second Division when the teams met in the last vital League game of the 1958-59 season. Villa had to win, but were held 1-1.

Albion beat Villa 3-0 in the 1892 FA Cup Final, but lost in two more Finals, 2-0 in 1887 and 1-0 in 1895. (See FA CUP).

'Other' games, include testimonials for players Fred Turnbull, Ray Wilson, Brendon Batson and Gary Robson.

In May 1985, Villa drew 3-3 with Albion at Villa Park in the Bradford Fire Disaster Fund match.

In all Albion and Villa have now played against each other (at various levels) more than 270 times since December 1882, when they first met in a second-round Staffordshire Cup-tie which ended in a 3-3 draw at Perry Barr.

Almost 125,000 fans witnessed two third-round FA Cup matches between the teams in February 1925. A then record Hawthorns crowd of 64,612 saw Albion held to a 1-1 draw

and for the midweek replay, which Albion won 2-1, the turnout was 60,015.

Bobby Hope scored his only hat-trick for Albion in a 6-1 League Cup win over Villa at The Hawthorns in September 1966.

'W.G.' Richardson scored a total 12 League and Cup goals for Albion against Villa.

Five members of Aston Villa's European Cup-winning side of 1982 all later played for Albion: Nigel Spinks, Kenny Swain, Denis Mortimer, Ken McNaught and Tony Morley, albeit Mortimer only in friendly matches.

Albion League debutants v Villa: Joe Reader (1889), Oliver Norman (1893), Tom Higgins (1894), Albert Kelsey (1895), Sid Saunders (1895), Archie McKenzie (1897), Harry Clements (1903), Walter Boyes (1931), Ken Hodgkisson (1953), Gerry Howshall (1964), Ray Crawford (1965), Wayne Hughes (1977), Ken McNaught (1983).

England amateur international Harold Bache made his debut for Albion v Villa in a 1914 FA Cup-tie at Villa Park.

Players with both clubs: Albert Aldridge, Darren Bradley, Andy Comyn, Jim Cumbes, John Deehan, Jimmy Dugdale, Ugo Ehiogu Albert Evans, Graham Fenton, George Garratt, Bill Garraty, Andy Gray, Tommy Green (snr), Willie Groves, Harry Hadley, George Harris, Tom Haywood, Robert Hopkins, Steve Hunt, George Johnson, Phil King, Arthur Loach, Ken McNaught, Tony Morley, Tom Perry, Cyrille Regis, John Reynolds, Bob Roberts, Jimmy Spencer, Nigel Spink, Kenny Swain, Garry Thompson, Dave Walsh, Freddie Wheldon, Jimmy Williams and Charlie Wilson.

Other players associated with both clubs: Jack Crisp (Villa trialist), Keith Jones, Paul Kerr, Dennis Mortimer (Albion assistant manager and player, Villa player), Alf Newman, Tony Rees and Colin Withers. Jones gained Welsh international honours with Villa.

Ron Saunders (1970s and 1980s) and Ron Atkinson (also 1970s and '80s) managed both clubs; Brian Whitehouse was coach at both clubs; Phil Hunt was an Albion reserve (1930s) and later Villa's trainer; Fred Pedley was a physiotherapist at The Hawthorns and Villa Park; Ron

Wylie played for Villa and managed Albion; Stuart Williams played for Albion and was also trainer at both clubs; Paul Barron kept goal for Albion and later coached Villa (1995-96); Vic Crowe was an Albion amateur, who later played for and managed Villa as well as gaining full caps for Wales; Tom Cardall has been on the commercial staff at both clubs; Ray Fairfax was an Albion full-back and later Villa's ticket office clerk; Keith Smith played for Albion and later worked for Villa's lottery; Bob Brocklebank played for Villa and scouted for Albion; Bobby Downes was an Albion reserve and later became Villa's coach-assistant manager and Keith Leonard, a former Aston Villa striker and Albion trialist, was coach at The Hawthorns in the late 1980s.

ATTENDANCES

The record attendance for a senior game at The Hawthorns is 64,815 – for the sixth-round FA Cup-tie between Albion and Arsenal on 6 March 1937. This will never be bettered.

The top crowd for a League game is 60,945 Albion v Wolves in the First Division on 4 March 1950.

The best Football League Cup attendance on Albion soil is 41,188 v Walsall, second-round tie on 22 September 1965, and the highest 'European' attendance to date has been that of 35,118, Albion v Valencia, UEFA Cup fourth-round second-leg, on 6 December 1978.

The last 50,000 plus gate at The Hawthorns was 54,992, for the Albion v Tottenham fifth-round FA Cup-tie on 17 February 1962.

The lowest recorded League crowd at The Hawthorns – 1,050 – witnessed the Albion-Sheffield United, Second Division match on 30 April 1901.

Albion's lowest home FACup attendance – 5,230 – saw them play Leicester Fosse on 14 January 1905 in an intermediate round.

In the League Cup, the lowest crowd is that of 6,288 v Port Vale on 24 September 1985, and in a major European competition, Albion's lowest (at The Hawthorns) is 16,745 v Zurich Grasshoppers (UEFA Cup) on 30 September 1981.

Albion's best crowd for a home Second Division match is 52,415 v Charlton Athletic, 2 May 1931.

The lowest-ever League crowd for an Albion home game

The FA Cup is paraded before a crowd of 52,415 at The Hawthorns in May 1931 when Albion entertained Charlton in a League game as the unique double was achieved.

is 405 v Derby County at Stoney Lane on 29 November 1890.

There have been only four attendances of over 60,000 at The Hawthorns, the other two being 64,612 (Albion-Aston Villa FA Cup, 1925) and 61,088 (Albion-Newcastle United, FA Cup 1954).

Albion's best home wartime crowd was 38,077 for the visit of Wolverhampton Wanderers (League South) on 23 April 1946.

A crowd of 55,497 saw Albion play an International XI (Norman Heath's benefit match) on 15 April 1956.

Another packed terrace at The Hawthorns.

There was a record crowd of 22,372 at The Hawthorns to watch a Central League game between Albion Reserves and Aston Villa Reserves on 3 March 1934.

Attendance records were set at the following matches involving Albion: the 1886 FA Cup Final at The Oval – 15,156; the 1886 FA Cup Final replay at The County Ground (Derby) – 16,144; the 1887 FA Cup Final at The Oval – 15,534; the 1888 FA Cup Final at The Oval – 18,904; the 1892 FA Cup Final at The Oval – 32,710; the 1895 FA Cup Final at The Crystal Palace – 42,652; FA Cup-tie in 1912 v Sunderland at Roker Park – 43,383; First Division games at Villa Park (v Aston Villa) in September 1912 – 55,064; in November 1919 – 58,273; in November 1920 – 66,094; FA Cup-tie in 1925 v Sheffield United (at Bramall Lane) – 57,197; FA Cup semi-final at Old Trafford (v Everton) 1931 – 69,241; First Division game v Birmingham (at St Andrew's) on Boxing Day 1931 – 57,806; FA Cup semi-final replay 1935 v Bolton Wanderers (at Stoke) – 49,110; FA Cup tie 1937 v Coventry City (at Highfield Road) – 44,492; Division Two game v Southampton (at The Dell) 1949 – 30,856; First Division match v Nottingham Forest (at the City Ground) 1957 – 46,455; Friendly v Tiflis Dynamo (Russia) in 1957 – 35,000; Friendly v China in the National Stadium (Peking) 1978 – 89,400.

The largest attendance an Albion team has ever played in front of is that of 99,852 v Preston North End in the 1954 FA Cup Final at Wembley. There were 99,665 present for the 1968 FA Cup Final, 97,963 witnessed the 1970 League Cup Final between Albion and Manchester City and 97,952 fans saw Albion beaten by QPR in the 1967 League Cup Final. The largest crowd for a League game featuring Albion – 67,440 – assembled at Stamford Bridge to see the First Division match with Chelsea on 2 October 1954. Apart from the Final itself, the biggest FA Cup audience Albion have played to was that of 71,853 at White Hart Lane v Tottenham Hotspur in a fourth-round tie on 24 January 1948.

Albion's top European crowd has been 95,300 v Red Star Belgrade (away) for a UEFA Cup-tie in March 1979 and 62,556 fans saw the Second Division League game between Tottenham and Albion in London in January 1949.

A crowd of only 967 saw the Millwall-Albion Full Members' Cup-tie at The Den in 1986; there were a meagre 139 present for the Cosenza-Albion Anglo-Italian Cup-tie in Italy in December 1993 and 196 witnessed another Anglo-Italian Cup-tie v Brescia (away) in December 1995.

Albion's best average home League attendance for a season is 38,819 (aggregate 815,217 – 21 games) in 1949-50 (Division One).

Albion took 42,334 supporters with them to Wembley for the Second Division Play-off Final against Port Vale on 30

May 1993. This was a massive 79.2 per cent of the total attendance of 53,471

Albion's average home League crowd (1888-1996 inclusive) is 19,015 (aggregate 36,737,166 from 1,932 matches).

The average home League crowd at The Hawthorns (1900-96) is 20,302 (aggregate 35,772,681 from 1,762 matches).

AUTOGLASS TROPHY

Albion have played seven matches in this competition, their full record being:

Venue	P	W	D	L	F	A
Home	4	3	0	1	10	2
Away	3	2	0	1	4	3
Totals	7	5	0	2	14	5

In 1991-92 they beat Shrewsbury Town 4-0 (h) and Lincoln City 2-1 (a) before losing 1-0 to Exeter City at The Hawthorns. Then in 1992-93, they were ousted 2-1 at Stoke after accounting for Walsall 4-0 (h), Mansfield Town 1-0 (a) and Torquay United 2-1 (h) in earlier matches.

Striker James McCue made his Albion debut as a substitute at Mansfield.

AYLESBURY UNITED

Albion recorded their best-ever home FA Cup win when they defeated non-League side Aylesbury United 8-0 at The Hawthorns in a second-round tie on 14 November 1992. Kevin Donovan scored a hat-trick – his first 'treble' for Albion.

Former Albion midfielder Andy King had a brief association with Aylesbury United in 1988.

BACHE, Harold Godfrey

A brilliant England amateur international centre-forward, Harold Bache was tragically killed serving with the Lancashire Fusiliers in France in 1916. Born at Churchill, Kidderminster in 1889, he played for Cambridge University and the Corinthians before signing for Albion in 1914, scoring four goals in 14 games for the Baggies. He won seven amateur caps (1910-13) and in one game, against France, he hit seven goals in a 20-0 win. Bache also played for the Football League, and was a fine all-round sportsman, excelling at rugby, cricket and athletics as well as soccer.

BADDELEY, George

Strong in all aspects of half-back play, Baddeley, a former Stoke captain, spent six seasons with Albion (1908-14) appearing in 157 senior games, winning a Second Division championship medal in 1911 and an FA Cup runners-up medal a year later. Albion's oldest player, he retired in 1914 to become a publican in West Bromwich. He died in 1952, aged 78.

BALL BURST

It is not very often that the ball bursts during the course of a game, but here are a few instances when it did just that when Albion were in action: against Milton (away) in a friendly on 5 November 1881 when it took ten minutes to find a replacement; in an FA Cup-tie at Molineux in 1924 when Albion's Howard Gregory had a 'goal' disallowed as the bladder ended up in the Wolves net while the casing flew over the bar; and in the First Division game at The Hawthorns in November 1957, when Ronnie Allen scored from the penalty spot for Albion, bursting the ball in the process.

BANKS, Jack

An efficient left-half or left-winger who (1894-1901) played in 134 senior games for Albion, including the 1895 FA Cup Final. He left The Hawthorns for Newton Heath and later served with Plymouth Argyle, Leyton and Nottingham Forest, becoming coach and then manager of Exeter City (1908-11). He trained Barrow from 1913-38 and died in the Cumbrian town in 1947, aged 75.

BARLOW, Raymond John

One of the finest footballers ever to don an Albion shirt, Ray Barlow was mainly a left-half, but he also played at centre-half, centre-forward and inside-left. He served the club for 16 years (1944-60) appearing in 482 first-team games during and after World War Two, scoring 48 goals. He won an FA Cup winners' medal in 1954 and the same year gained his

only England cap, against Ireland. He also played for England 'B', the Football League, the FA XI and Swindon Town (as a wartime guest) and after leaving The Hawthorns he appeared briefly for Birmingham City and Stourbridge. On his retirement in 1962, he took over a tobacconist and confectionery shop in West Bromwich, later managing a post office/newsagent's business in Stourbridge. Born in Swindon in 1926, he now lives in Pedmore.

BARNES, Peter Simon

A fast-raiding winger who had a fine career which started in 1972 with Manchester City, thereafter Peter Barnes played for Albion (1979- 81, moving to The Hawthorns for a record fee of £748,000), Leeds United (transferred for a record fee of £930,000), Real Betis (Spain), Leeds (again), West Ham, Coventry, Manchester United, Manchester City (for a second spell), Bolton, Hull, Sporting Farense (Portugal), Bolton (again), Sunderland, Droghedra, Wrexham, Stockport, Hamrun Spartans, Mossley, and Northwich Victoria. In 1994 he was coach at Maine Road and in 1995 was appointed manager of Runcorn. Barnes hit 25 goals in 92 games for Albion, including a hat-trick against Bolton in 1980. A former Schoolboy and Youth international, he won 22 full caps for England, one at 'B' and nine at Under-21 levels. He helped Manchester City win the 1976 League Cup, scoring in the Final against Newcastle United.

BARNET

Albion have yet to play Barnet in either League or Cup competition, but they did play two friendlies against them at the Underwood Stadium in 1980, winning both: 2-1 in March and 5-0 in December.

George Reilly played with both clubs at first-team level, while goalkeeper Gary Phillips was an Albion reserve and later played for and managed Barnet. Dave Barnett also played for Albion Reserves and Barnet's League side. The England amateur international left-winger Lester Finch who played for Barnet, guested for Albion during World War Two. He died in 1995, aged 86.

BARNSLEY

Albion's record against Barnsley reads:

Football League

Venue	P	W	D	L	F	A	Pts
Home	23	12	8	3	60	34	35
Away	23	6	9	8	28	32	21
Totals	46	18	17	11	88	66	56

FA Cup

Home	1	0	0	1	0	1
Away	3	0	1	2	0	2
Totals	4	0	1	3	0	3

Other Matches

Home	1	0	1	0	0	0
Away	1	1	0	0	1	0
Totals	2	1	1	0	1	0

The first League meetings took place in 1901-02 (Division Two) when Albion won 3-1 at home and 2-0 away.

Albion's best League win over Barnsley is 7-0 (home) in November 1989 (Martyn Bennett's last game for the Baggies), while Barnsley's best is 3-0, at Oakwell in April 1906.

General view of the Albion-Barnsley FA Cup Final at The Crystal Palace in 1912.

Barnsley beat Albion 1-0 after a replay and extra-time in the 1912 FA Cup Final (See FA CUP).

In a Zenith Data Systems Cup-tie at The Hawthorns in season 1990-91, Barnsley beat Albion 5-3, former Baggies' midfielder Ian Banks scoring a second-half hat-trick in 12 minutes for the Tykes.

Albion League debutants against Barnsley: Jack Dawes (1904), Bill Garraty (1908), Gilbert Price (1910), Jimmy Hibbert (1910), Enos Bromage (1928), Eddie Wilcox (1948), Graham Harbey (1989), Kieran O'Regan (1993), Simon Garner (1993).

Players with both clubs: Ian Banks, Dick Bourne, Joe Brooks, John Chadburn, Stan Davies, John Deehan, Tony Rees, Fred Richardson, Alf Ridyard, Mark Robinson, David Speedie,.

Associated with both clubs: Colin Brookes, Bobby Downes, Frank Warrilow. John Jarman (Albion's trainer-coach 1954-65) also served with Barnsley.

BARROW

Albion have yet to play Barrow (a Football League club 1921-72) in a competitive game.

Two players have been associated with both clubs: Billy Adams and David Bradford, while Norman Bodell managed Barrow (1967-70) and was later Albion's chief scout and former Albion player Jack Banks was trainer of Barrow (1913-38).

BASS CHARITY CUP

Although this competition is extant as the Bass Charity Vase with League clubs playing their reserve sides, Albion, along with several other clubs, fielded teams of near first-team strength when competing for this trophy in the 1890s.

In 1892-93 Albion and Stoke shared the Cup after 3-3 and 1-1 draws at Stoney Lane and in the Potteries respectively, while in 1893-94, Albion lost to Aston Villa 5-2 in the semi-final after beating Burton Swifts 4-1 in the first round.

BASSETT, William Isaiah

One of Albion's all-time greats, Billy Bassett was born in West Bromwich in 1869 and played for several junior teams before signing for Albion as a profes-sional in 1886. Over the next 13 years he starred in Albion's forward-line, firstly at inside-right and then on the right wing. He was quick, possessed

Billy Bassett, one of Albion's all-time great players who went on to serve the Baggies as chairman and altogether gave the club over half a century of service.

superb ball-control and could score goals as well as make them, hitting 77 in 311 matches for Albion. He won two FA Cup winners' medals (1888 and 1892) and also played in the 1895 losing Final. Bassett gained 16 England international caps (eight against Scotland) and he also represented the Football League and FA sides. After retiring in 1899, he went into the licensing trade and later had interests in the cinema. He became a director at The Hawthorns in 1905 and was elected chairman in 1908. Between 1905 and 1932, he rarely missed a board meeting and his influence at Albion was incalculable. At the club's annual meeting in 1936 he was presented with a silver casket and an 'illuminated' scroll on the occasion of his completing 50 years' service with the Albion (as player, coach, shareholder, director and chairman). From 1930 to 1937 he was a member of the Football League management committee, being on the international selection panel in 1936-37. Bassett, who became a JP in 1935, died shortly before Albion's FA Cup semi-final with Preston in 1937 – and on the announcement of his death, the *Albion News* described him as 'guide, philosopher and friend' to the Albion club and Football League secretary, Fred Howarth, declared him to be 'the most popular man in the game'.

BASSETT, Idris Charles

No relation to Billy, Idris Bassett was a tough-tackling, never-say-die full-back who played in 100 first-team games for Albion, mostly during World War Two. He joined the club from Sutton Town in 1936 and was registered with Albion for seven years, retiring through injury in 1943. He was born in Sutton Coldfield in 1915 and died in Birmingham in 1979.

BATSON, Brendon Martin

Brendon Batson was a highly-efficient right-back and manager Ron Atkin-son's first signing for Albion, costing £30,000 from Cambridge United in 1978. He appeared in 220 games during a six-year stay at The Hawthorns to 1984, when he retired through injury. Born in Grenada, West Indies, in 1953, Batson started his career with Arsenal, making his League debut against Albion in 1971. He won an FA Youth Cup winners' medal that same year. After being capped by England 'B' in 1980, Bat-son's career came to an end at the age of 31 and he immediately joined the Professional Footballers' Association' full-time staff and progressed to deputy chief executive, a position he still held in 1996.

BAYLISS ('Jem') Edward James Matthias

'Jem' Bayliss was both Albion player and director in 1891-92, taking the latter position when the club became a limited liability company in August 1891. He remained on the board until 1905 when he was replaced by Bassett. Born in Tipton in 1863, Bayliss joined Albion from Wednesbury Old Athletic at the age of 21 and in eight years as a centre-

Johnny Giles (front) with his testimonial XI in 1975. The other players are (left to right): Mulligan, Wile, Wilson, Osborne, Dougan, Charlton, Hurst, Stiles, Johnston and Cantello.

forward, scored 36 goals in senior 95 games (claiming over 150 in all matches). He appeared in three successive FA Cup Finals: 1886-87-88, gaining a winners' medal in the latter. A footballing gentleman whose nickname came from the initials of his christian names, Bayliss was capped once by England as a wing-half in 1891. Six years later he actually read his own obituary in a local paper after returning from holiday in Gibraltar. It was rumoured that whilst abroad he had died of typhoid, but Bayliss was as fit as ever and lived for another 36 years!

BENEFIT and TESTIMONIAL MATCHES

Albion have played in more than 150 testimonial and benefit games since participating in their first in March 1883 when they beat Wellington 4-0 at home, the proceeds of which went to the West Bromwich Hospital Fund. Most of these games have involved clubs from the Football League and many have been for the benefit of current or former players.

Before 1900, 14 Albion players each had a benefit: Jim Stanton, Bob Roberts, George Timmins, Charlie Perry, George Woodhall, Billy Bassett, Tom Pearson, Sam Nicholls, Roddy McLeod, Jack Horton, Joe Reader, Billy Williams, Tom Perry and Jack Banks.

From 1900 to 1914 many more Albion players received benefits including Amos Adams, Arthur Randle, Harry Hadley, Billy Richards, Jesse Pennington (who was granted two), Jack Manners, Charlie Simmons, Fred Buck, Hubert

Pearson and George Baddeley.

Very few benefit games were played between 1919 and 1964 but then they started up again and over the last 30 years or so, they have become more frequent with Jeff Astle, Tony Brown, Brendon Batson, Martyn Bennett, Len Cantello, Bobby Cram, Johnny Giles, Tony Godden, Bobby Hope, Stuart Naylor, John Osborne, Alistair Robertson, John Wile, Graham Williams and Ray Wilson all having testimonial matches at The Hawthorns.

Both Tony Brown and Ally Robertson had second testimonials (after leaving Albion).

It is said that John Osborne banked £30,000 from his 1978 testimonial and John Wile collected £32,000 in April 1982.

Billy Bassett's benefit match was, in fact, a League game: Albion against Sheffield Wednesday in November 1893.

Sam Nicholls' benefit in 1894 earned him a mere £10; Joe Reader's in 1897 realised £110.

The first Albion player to have a benefit match at The Hawthorns was Billy Richards against Wolves in October 1900 when 5,000 fans witnessed a 3-3 draw.

Almost 55,000 spectators saw Albion draw 5-5 with an International XI in Norman Heath's testimonial match at The Hawthorns in April 1956.

Len Cantello's testimonial match in May 1979, was between an Albion XI and Cyrille Regis' 'All Black' team. The latter won 3-2 before 7,023 fans at The Hawthorns. Cantello left Albion soon afterwards, joining Bolton Wanderers for £350,000.

The all-black line-up for Len Cantello's testimonial game at The Hawthorns in 1979.

BENNETT, Martyn

Excellent central defender who also played at right-back and in midfield, Bennett's Albion career was halted in 1990 through injury. Born in Birmingham in 1961, he graduated through Albion's junior ranks to make his League debut against Everton in 1979 – the first of 218 senior appearances for the club. After leaving The Hawthorns, he became player-manager of Worcester City and finally announced his retirement from football in 1992.

BENTLEY, Alfred

An 'eager-beaver' utility forward, who scored 47 goals in 106 games for Albion:1913-22, helping the Baggies win the League championship in 1920 when he teamed up with Fred Morris. Born in Alfreton, Derbyshire, in 1887, Alf Bentley – nicknamed 'Snobby' – played for Derby and Bolton before Albion and after leaving The Hawthorns he served with Burton Town and Alfreton Town, retiring in 1926. He scored four times on his Albion debut, against Burnley in 1913, and scored 99 goals in 151 League games for Derby. He died in 1940 after a short illness.

Alf 'Snobby' Bentley, helped Albion to the League championship in 1920.

BETTELEY, Richard Harold

Bilston-born full-back of some calibre, Dick Betteley appeared in 89 games for Albion over a period of six years (1906-12). Signed from Wolverhampton Wanderers for whom he played in 123 matches, Betteley won a Second Division championship medal with Albion as partner to Jesse Pennington, and after leaving the club he played for Bilston United, retiring in May 1914. He died in Wolverhampton in 1942, aged 62.

BIRMINGHAM CHARITY CUP (Lord Mayor's)

From 1884 to 1933 Albion played a total of 41 games in this competition, winning 13, drawing five and losing 23. They scored 66 goals for and conceded 98.

In all, Albion appeared in 16 Finals, winning the trophy five times – in 1899 (1-0 v Walsall); in 1913 (1-0 v Aston Villa); 1914 (3-2 v Aston Villa); 1922 (2-0 v Birmingham) and 1925 (3-1 v Birmingham). They shared the trophy with Birmingham in 1921 (2-2 draw).

Aston Villa beat Albion 5-1 in the 1912 Final and 4-0 in the 1933 Final – both games being staged at The Hawthorns.

Albion's first-ever tie in the competition resulted in a 4-1 defeat at the hands of Aston Villa in April 1884.

Albion's first win did not arrive until September 1897 when they beat Small Heath (Birmingham) 7-4.

From 1910 onwards an appearance in the Lord Mayor's Charity Cup Final was by invitation only. In May 1926, Albion were due to play Villa at St Andrew's in the Final, but the game was postponed because of the General Strike.

BIRMINGHAM CITY (Small Heath)

Albion's record against Blues reads:

Football League

Venue	P	W	D	L	F	A	Pts
Home	47	21	15	11	66	47	62
Away	47	20	13	14	66	52	58
Totals	94	41	28	25	132	99	120

FA Cup

	P	W	D	L	F	A
Home	2	0	1	1	1	2
Away	6	6	0	0	15	5
Totals	8	6	1	1	16	7

League Cup

	P	W	D	L	F	A
Home	1	1	0	0	3	1
Away	1	0	1	0	0	0
Totals	2	1	1	0	3	1

Anglo-Italian Cup

	P	W	D	L	F	A
Away*	1	0	1	0	2	2

*Albion won this game 4-1 on penalties

Texaco Cup

	P	W	D	L	F	A
Home	1	0	1	0	0	0

Other matches

	P	W	D	L	F	A
Home	33	22	3	8	87	49
Away	42	15	8	19	71	101
Totals	75	37	11	27	177	150

Albion have encountered Blues under four different guises: Small Heath Alliance (1883-88), Small Heath (1888-1905), Birmingham (1905-43) and Birmingham City (1943 to date). Albion beat Blues 5-3, 6-0 and 7-1 at St Andrew's in successive First Division games (1957-60) with Ronnie Allen and Derek Kevan scoring hat-tricks in that 7-1 Easter win in 1960, Albion's best-ever League victory over Blues. Blues' best League win over Albion is 4-0 at St Andrew's in a Second Division match on 29 March 1948.

In April 1931, Albion won the FA Cup by beating Blues 2-1 at Wembley with 'W.G.' Richardson scoring both goals. In fact, Richardson hit a record 11 goals for Albion in games against Blues (League and Cup).

The two League Cup matches were played in season 1984-85.

The Texaco Cup-tie was played in August 1974.

Albion's 4-1 penalty shoot-out win over Blues at a frost-

Birmingham's Harry Hibbs saves from Albion's Joe Carter during a League game at The Hawthorns on Christmas Day 1931.

bound St Andrew's in the Anglo-Italian Cup in January 1996 saw them through to the English two-legged Final against Port Vale.

Albion and Blues have met in two friendlies on the Channel Island of Guernsey – in February 1979 they drew 1-1 and in January 1982, Blues won 2-1.

The first-ever Albion-Blues game was a friendly at Muntz Street (Birmingham's former ground) on 5 May 1883. Albion won 5-1.

Albion League debutants v Blues: Tommy Green (1895), John Richards (1895), Fred Cook (1903), Frank Fenton (1903), Sammy Short (1926), Sid Swinden (1936), Harry Baldwin (1938), Glyn Hood (1946), Cliff Edwards (1946), Peter Billingham (1960), Stan Jones (1960), Eddie Readfern (1963), Doug Fraser (1963), Brendon Batson (1978) and Colin West (1989).

Bethel Robinson (1899) and Hubert Pearson (1908) both made their Albion debuts in FA Cup ties v Blues.

Players with both clubs: Ray Barlow, Bill Bowser, Dennis Clarke, Chris Charsley, Gary Childs, Jack Crisp, Dicky Dale, Stan Davies, Ronnie Fenton, Tony Godden, Tommy Green (snr), Phil Hawker, Paul Holmes, Bobby Hope, Robert Hopkins, Alec Jackson, Willie Johnston, Steve Lynex, Paul Mardon, Alan Miller, Tony Morley, John Paskin, Garry Pendrey, Sid Oliver, Tony Rees, Darren Rogers, Andrew Smith, Billy Smith, David Smith, Joe Smith, David Speedie, Kevin Summerfield, John Trewick, Ike Webb, Fred Wheldon, Norman Whitehead, Chris Whyte, Harry Wilcox.

Other players associated with both clubs: Dave Barnett, Ted Duckhouse, Dennis Jennings, Albert Lindon, Jim Southam, George Tranter, Colin Withers.

Peter Latchford (left) of Albion and his brother Bob (Birmingham City) in action in 1972.

Paskin is the only player to represent Albion, Blues and Wolves at first-team level.

Also associated with both clubs: Ron Saunders managed Blues (1982-86) and Albion (1986-87). Tony Brown was a player with Albion and also coached at both clubs; Ron Wylie played for Blues and later managed Albion (1982-84); Garry Pendrey (after retiring) managed Blues (1987-89); Alan Buckley played for Blues (1978-79) and later managed Albion (1994-96); Dennis Mortimer, Albion's assistant manager of the 1990s, was a Blues midfielder in 1986-87; Mike Kelly played in goal for Blues and later coached at Albion; Keith Leonard was a coach with Albion and Blues; John MacGowan and Graham Doig were both physiotherapists at Blues and Albion; Norman Bodell was a scout with both Blues and Albion; John Westmancoat was secretary at both clubs; Tommy Jones was trainer at St Andrew's and The Hawthorns; Keith Smith played for Albion and was later with Blues' lottery team; Bob Brocklebank was a scout for Blues and Albion.

Tom Hedges kept goal for Small Heath against Albion in the 1886 FA Cup semi-final. In 1904 he became an Albion director.

BIRMINGHAM CUP

Albion's first Birmingham Cup-tie saw them beat Calthorpe 3-2 (away) on November 12th 1881. All told Albion went on to play a further 79 games in the competition (at senior level), the last being against Aston Villa (home) in September 1905 which they lost 5-1.
In 1906, the Birmingham FA decreed that all local clubs should field their reserve sides in the competition.
Albion's full record in the Birmingham Cup was:

Venue	P	W	D	L	F	A
Home	34	26	3	5	141	33
Away	46	22	9	15	99	76
Totals	80	48	12	20	240	109

Albion played in the Final nine times between 1886 and 1905, winning the trophy outright twice – in 1886 (1-0 v Walsall Swifts after a 1-1 draw) and in 1895 (1-0 v Aston Villa after a 0-0 draw). They shared the prize with Wolverhampton Wanderers in 1894 (after a 3-3 draw).
Albion lost 7-2 to Birmingham (Small Heath) in the 1905 Final and were defeated 5-2 by Wolves in the Final of 1892.
Albion's best win in their history is 26-0 – achieved in a first-round Birmingham Cup-tie against Coseley at home on 11 November 1882. Albion led 17-0 at half-time in this game.
Wolves inflicted upon Albion their heaviest defeat in the Birmingham Cup, winning 7-0 at Stoney Lane in January 1899.
During recent times Albion Reserves have competed in the renamed Birmingham Senior Cup. In 1988 they won it for the first time since 1895 when beating Bedworth United 3-1, and three years later they defeated Nuneaton Borough 2-0 to take the trophy again.

BIRMINGHAM & DISTRICT LEAGUE

Albion first fielded a reserve team in 1882, playing against local opposition. For the next ten years the second XI fulfilled a number of fixtures and they also entered (and won) several local cup competitions before joining the Birmingham & District League for season 1889-90. They finished runners-up in 1894-95 and their first championship came in 1901-02 when they won 26 of their 34 matches, totalling 54 points (out of 68) to finish eight ahead of Stourbridge. Their best wins were against Druids 10-0 and Kidderminster Harriers 10-1 and championship medals were awarded to John Chadburn, Platt Gollings, Oliver Taylor, Arthur Randle, Fred Buck, Andrew Smith, Ted Smith, Billy Walker, Sam Edwards, Bill Poynton, Fred Hobson, Billy Harper, George Williams, Ben Appleby and Tom Jones.

Three third places and two fourths were gained before Albion collected their second Birmingham & District League title in 1912-13, amassing 47 points (out of 68) after 21 wins and five draws.
Worcester City were beaten 6-0 and Kidderminster 6-1 and the following players received medals: Matt Wood, Amos Lloyd, Charlie Deacey, Walter Hackett, Jack Mann, Howard Gregory, Bill Jackson, Arthur Cook, Wallace Fletcher, Jimmy Varty and Fred Morris.
Albion's third (and last) title win in this competition (before they entered the Central League) coincided with the seniors taking the Football League championship in 1919-20. This time Albion's second string accumulated 45 points (out of 68); they registered 18 victories and nine draws, scored 61 goals and conceded 45, beating Coventry City 5-0 for their best triumph.
Most appearances were made by Arthur Cook, Roland James, George Ashmore, Tommy Newall (top scorer with 27 goals), Sam Hatton, Billy Adams, Tommy Magee, Fred Reed, Ernie Edwards, Matt Wood, Bill Hobbs and Arthur Lea and it is believed that all received championship medals.
Albion's best-ever win in the Birmingham & District League was 13-2 against Oldbury Town (h) in January 1892.
Their heaviest defeats were those of 11-1 at Wolverhampton Wanderers in March 1898 and 11-2 at Coventry in April 1908.

BLACKBURN ROVERS

Albion's record against Blackburn Rovers:

Football League

Venue	P	W	D	L	F	A	Pts
Home	48	25	13	10	95	58	65
Away	48	11	7	30	54	104	32
Totals	96	36	20	40	149	162	97

FA Cup

Home	4	2	0	2	8	8	
Away	7	2	2	3	5	7	
Totals	10	3	2	5	10	13	

Other matches

Home	6	3	0	3	11	14	
Away	3	0	0	3	7	10	
Totals	9	3	0	6	18	24	

Albion and Blackburn were founder members of the Football League in 1888.
Albion's best League win is 8-1 at The Hawthorns in January 1936. 'W.G.' Richardson and Jack Mahon both scored hat-tricks.

Rovers' best League over Albion is 6-2 at home in September 1888 (the first-ever League meeting between the clubs and it was also Albion's first defeat in the competition).
Blackburn beat Albion 4-1 at home on 25 April 1912 to clinch their first ever Football League championship.
During Albion's League championship-winning campaign of 1919-20 they beat Blackburn 5-2 at The Hawthorns and 5-1 at Ewood Park in the space of eight days.
Albion (4-1 down after 70 minutes) fought back to earn a point from a 4-4 League draw

George Ashmore made his Albion debut against Blackburn Rovers in 1920.

Ronnie Allen scores in the 2-1 FA Cup win over Blackpool at The Hawthorns in February 1957.

at Blackburn in September 1932. Albion lost the 1886 FA Cup Final to Blackburn 2-0 (after a replay. (See FA CUP).

Blackburn also defeated Albion 3-2 in the FA Cup semi-final at Stoke in February 1891 before a record crowd of 21,774.

Albion gained revenge by ousting Rovers 1-0 after extra-time in the FA Cup semi-final at Sheffield after a 0-0 draw at Liverpool.

Albion's lost their 200th FA Cup game 1-0 to Blackburn at Ewood Park in February 1952, Bill Eckersley's 86th-minute penalty ruining Johnny Nicholls' debut for Albion.

England international Freddie Morris scored a record ten goals for Albion in senior games against Rovers.

Of the 'other matches' played between the clubs, the most exciting contest was in October 1887 when Rovers beat Albion 7-6 after trailing 5-0 at one stage

Albion League debutants v Blackburn: George Haynes (1888), John Reynolds (1891), Jack Banks (1894), George Cave (1896), Bill Ford (1896), Ben Garfield (1896), Tom Evans (1896), Peter McManus (1896), Albert Flewitt (1896), Archie Dunn (1898), Andrew Smith (1900), Archie Smith (1903), Ben Clark (1920), George Ashmore (1920), Billy Long (1920), Ted Crowe (1934), Keith Smith (1960), Stan Steele (1961), Gary Bannister (1990) and Graham Roberts (1990). Joe Matthews (1885), Charlie Perry (1886) and Johnny Nicholls (1952) made their Albion debuts in FA Cup games v Rovers.

Players with both clubs: Paul Bradshaw, Jack Byers, Jack Crisp, Graham Fenton, Simon Garner, Mark Grew, Archie Heywood, Andy Marriott, Nicky Reid, David Speedie.

David Bradford played for Rovers (1971-74) and was an Albion reserve (1976-78); another Albion reserve, Pat Hilton, played for Blackburn in 1974-75; Asa Hartford was a player with Albion and later became coach at Blackburn (1993); John Reynolds played for Blackburn reserves (1884-85) and Albion's first team (1891-93); Ossie Ardiles played

for Blackburn (1988) and managed Albion (1992-93); Norman Bodell was a coach and scout with Rovers and Albion and Jesse Carver was a Blackburn player and later became manager-coach of Albion (1952).

BLACK LAKE VICTORIA

Albion's first-ever recorded victory (as West Bromwich Strollers) was against Black Lake Victoria, whom they beat 1-0 at home (Dartmouth Park) in a friendly on 13 December 1879. It is believed that Harry Aston scored the winning goal and about 500 spectators were in attendance.

BLACKPOOL

Albion's record against Blackpool reads:

Football League

Venue	P	W	D	L	F	A	Pts
Home	37	21	6	10	86	46	49
Away	37	12	6	19	43	60	30
Totals	74	33	12	29	129	106	79

FA Cup

Venue	P	W	D	L	F	A
Home	5	4	1	0	18	5
Away	4	1	2	1	2	3
Totals	9	5	3	1	20	8

Other matches

Venue	P	W	D	L	F	A
Home	1	0	0	1	1	2
Away	1	1	0	0	3	2
Totals	2	1	0	1	4	4

Derek Kevan scored four goals in Albion's record 7-1 League win over Blackpool at The Hawthorns in April 1962.

Albion also won 7-2 in a home Second Division game in February 1902, when 'Chippy' Simmons hit a hat-trick.

Blackpool's best League victory over Albion is 5-1 at Bloomfield Road in March 1956.

Albion were leading Blackpool 2-0 at Bloomfield Road in a Second Division game in November 1908 when Charlie Hewitt's 'goal' was disallowed by the referee who said that the ball had not crossed the line. In fact, it rebounded into play off the stanchion holding up the net! This 'no goal' decision cost Albion promotion to the First Division at the end of the season, the Baggies missing out by ¹/₅₆th of a goal.

Jimmy Cookson set an individual scoring record when he scored all six goals in Albion's 6-2 home win over Blackpool in a Second Division game at The Hawthorns on 19 September 1927.

One of Albion's biggest FA Cup wins is 8-0 against Blackpool (then known as South Shore) in January 1899. Billy Bassett scored a rare hat-trick and Albion led 7-0 at half-time.

Albion League debutants v Blackpool: Arthur Davies (1904), Llewellyn Davies (1904), Sammy Timmins (1906), Albert Evans (1907), Billy Young (1907), Harry Burton (1909), Jimmy Murphy (1930), Bert Trentham (1930), Graham Williams (1955), Eric Robinson (1958), Brian Macready (1960), Glen Johnson (1970), John Wile (1970), Simon Garner (1992), Ian Hamilton (1992) and Steve Lilwall (1992).

Players with both clubs: Scott Darton, George Elmore, Jabez Foster, Henry Hancock, Carl Heggs, Joe Mayo, Andy McCall, Craig Madden, Micky Mellon, Len Moorwood, Ebenezer Owers, Bob Ward.

Goalkeeper Barry Siddall had spells on loan with Blackpool (1983) and Albion (1990) and played regularly for the Seasiders' first team, between 1986 and 1989; another goalkeeper, Vince Bartram had spells at Blackpool (1989) and Albion (1991); Bert Baverstock, an Albion reserve full-back in the early 1900s, played for Blackpool from 1921-23; Sam Allardyce was a player-coach with Albion and became Blackpool's manager in 1995; Wilf Dixon was trainer at both clubs; Wilf Smith and Bobby Downes played in Albion Reserves and for Blackpool's League side, and goalkeeper Vince Bartram was on loan to Blackpool and Albion from Wolves and Bournemouth respectively.

BLOOD, Robert

Bobby Blood was an all-action, courageous centre-forward, who despite having one leg shorter than the other, found goalscoring easy! Unfortunately World War One interrupted his career yet he still managed to score over 70 goals in under 150 League games for Port Vale, Albion and

Stockport, and at all levels of football (1909-31) he hit 408 goals, 100 in two seasons immediately prior to entering the Football League with Port Vale. Born at Harpur Hill, Buxton, in 1894, Blood played for Buxton Lime Firms and Leek Alexandra before joining Vale. He was transferred to Albion in 1921, and hit 26 goals in 53 games for the Baggies before leaving The Hawthorns for Edgeley Park in 1924. He later played for Winsford United, Mossley and Ashton National, retiring in 1931. He died in Buxton in 1988, aged 94.

BOLTON WANDERERS

Albion's record against the Wanderers reads:

Football League

Venue	P	W	D	L	F	A	Pts
Home	57	26	18	13	108	79	72
Away	57	14	15	28	61	107	44
Totals	114	40	33	41	169	186	116

FA Cup

Home	4	4	0	0	13	1	
Away	4	1	1	2	3	4	
Totals	8	5	1	2	16	5	

Other matches

Home	4	2	1	1	9	2	
Away	6	0	2	4	5	10	
Totals	10	2	3	5	14	12	

Albion and Bolton were founder members of the Football League.

Albion's best League win is 7-2, at The Hawthorns in a First Division match on 8 December 1900.

Albion also won a home First Division match by 6-2 in February 1962 and later that year (22 September) Albion won a nine-goal thriller at home by 5-4 when both Derek Kevan (Albion) and Francis Lee (Bolton) hit hat-tricks.

Bolton registered their best League win over Albion on 7 December 1889, beating them 7-0 at Pike's Lane.

The first League meeting resulted in a 5-1 win for Albion at Stoney Lane on 5 November 1888. Near the end of this game, Bill Hendry (Albion) and Teddy Siddons (Bolton) came to blows. Neither was sent-off, but later both players were suspended for a month by the Football League commission for violent conduct.

Albion pipped Bolton for a First Division place after a titanic struggle during the last three months of the 1975-76 season.

Ronnie Allen scored 14 goals v Bolton; Derek Kevan scored 11.

Albion beat Bolton 2-0 in a FA Cup semi-final replay at Stoke in 1935 (after a 1-1 draw at Leeds) and they also won a Hawthorns replay by 4-0 in January 1975.

Bolton's lone Cup triumph over Albion came at frost-bound Burnden Park in January 1966 by 3-0.

On 6 November 1993 Bolton's Aidan Davison became the first goalkeeper to be sent-off in a League game at The Hawthorns.

Albion League debutants v Bolton: Willie Johnstone (1889), Tom Roberts (1890), Archie Bastock (1892), Abe Jones (1897), Ralph Brett (1898), Freddie Buck (1900), John Cole (1903), Fred Shinton (1905), Arthur Richards (1910), Joe Smith (1910), Harry Taylor (1920), Jonathan Blagden (1921), George Savage (1921), George James (1921), Joe Carter (1922), Tom Sproson (1925), Bill Brockhurst (1936), Jimmy Dugdale (1952), Chuck Drury (1958), Jock Wallace (1959), Bobby Cram (1959),

Players with both clubs: Sam Allardyce, Peter Barnes, Laurie Bell, Alf Bentley, Harry Boston, Len Cantello, Barry Cowdrill, David Cross, Julian Darby, Andy Dibble, Frank Dyer, Michael Gallagher, Asa Hartford, Nelson Howarth, Tony Kelly, Harry Kinsell, Bethel Robinson, Fred Shinton, Richard Sneekes, John Thomas, Gavin Ward.

Also associated with both clubs: goalkeeper Barry Siddall was on loan to Albion in 1990 after playing for Bolton

Bolton goalkeeper Eddie Hopkinson watches Bobby Hope's shot enter the net at The Hawthorns in February 1961.

David Cross had two spells with Albion and also played for Bolton.

between 1972 and 1976; Bert Baverstock started his career with Albion in the early 1900s and later played 366 League games for Bolton, and Frank Costello and Bill Chambers were Albion reserves before joining Bolton. Mick Brown, Albion's assistant manager (1979-81) was a coach at Bolton (1989-92).

(AFC) BOURNEMOUTH

Albion's record against AFC Bournemouth reads:

Football League

Venue	P	W	D	L	F	A	Pts
Home	5	3	2	0	11	3	11
Away	5	1	1	3	6	8	5
Totals	10	4	3	3	17	11	16

FA Cup

	P	W	D	L	F	A
Away	1	1	0	0	1	0

Other matches

	P	W	D	L	F	A
Home	2	1	0	1	3	2
Away	2	2	0	0	3	1
Totals	4	3	0	1	6	3

The first League meeting between the clubs was on 19 September 1987 when Albion won a home Second Division game 3-0.

On 11 January 1992, Albion recorded their best League win over Bournemouth, beating them 4-0 at The Hawthorn in Division Three.

The only FA Cup-tie took place at Dean Court on 8 January 1955, when Albion, the holders, won 1-0 with a goal by Welsh international Stuart Williams in front of a near 19,500 crowd.

Two of the four 'other' games were the two-legged Wartime League Cup-tie in 1939-40 ,which Albion won 5-2 on aggregate.

Albion League debutant v Bournemouth: Vetle Andersen (1989).

Players with both clubs: Luther Blissett, Meynell Burgin, Reg Cutler, Billy Elliott, Wayne Fereday, Billy Gripton, Carl Heggs, Billy Lunn, Andrew Smith, David Smith.

Also associated with both clubs: Winger Freddie Cox played for Albion in the 1950s and was manager of Bournemouth from 1965 to 1970; Vince Bartram played for Bournemouth (1991-94) and was on loan to Albion (1991). John Turner, Jack Lewis, Jack Thomas and Ken Allen were all players associated with Albion and Bournemouth at one level or another.

Luther Blissett, one of ten players to have appeared for both Albion and Bournemouth.

BOWSER, Sidney

The tenacious, resilient and hard-working Sid Bowser had two excellent spells with Albion: 1908-13 and 1914-24. He divided his immense talents between two completely different roles – those of inside-forward and centre-half – and he excelled in both. A goalscorer in his first spell at The Hawthorns, having earlier played for Astbury Richmond, Willenhall and Birmingham (trial). He scored over 50 goals in some 130 appearances, helping the Baggies win the Second Division title and reach the 1912 FA Cup Final. When he returned, after eight months with Belfast Distillery, he was converted into a defender, and was a key figure as Albion won the First Division title in 1920. Bowser gained his only England cap against Ireland in 1919, having

earlier represented the Irish League whilst a Distillery player. In 1919 he scored a hat-trick of penalties when Albion beat Bradford City 3-1 on their way to the League title. He left Albion, second time round, for Walsall, retiring in 1927 to become a licensee in Dudley, a job he held for 25 years. Bowser was born a stone's throw from The Hawthorns in Handsworth in 1892 and died in Birmingham in 1961.

BOYES, Walter Edward

Standing 5ft 4ins, Wally Boyes was a diminutive but strongly-built footballer who occupied three positions for Albion – outside-left, inside-left and left-half, always giving 100 per cent. Born at Killamarsh, Sheffield in 1913, he joined Albion in 1931 after representing Sheffield Boys and Woodhouse Mills United. His Albion debut was in front of 60,000 fans against Aston Villa nine months after signing, this the first of 165 games for the Baggies. He scored 38 goals, including one in the 1935 FA Cup Final defeat against Sheffield Wednesday. Boyes left Albion for Everton in 1938 and at the end of his first full season at Goodison Park won a League championship medal. He gained four England caps (two with Albion, two with Everton) and during the war he guested for Aldershot, Brentford, Clapton Orient, Leeds, Manchester United, Middlesbrough, Millwall, Newcastle, Preston and Sunderland. In 1949, Boyes became player-coach of Notts County. A year later he was appointed player-trainer at Scunthorpe and managed Retford Town and Hyde United before becoming Swansea's trainer in 1959. He retired through illness in 1960 and died soon afterwards.

BRADFORD CITY

Albion's record against Bradford City reads:

Football League

Venue	P	W	D	L	F	A	Pts
Home	19	11	6	2	37	15	30
Away	19	3	7	9	18	39	14
Totals	38	14	13	11	55	54	44

FA Cup

Home	1	0	0	1	1	2

League Cup

Home	2	1	0	1	5	3
Away	1	1	0	0	5	3
Totals	3	2	0	1	10	6

Other Matches

Away	2	2	0	0	2	0

Albion's best League win is 6-1, achieved in a home Second Division match in November 1905. Fred Shinton scored a hat-trick and City finished the game with nine men.

City's best League win over Albion is 5-0 at Valley Parade in a First Division game December 1914. The only FA Cup was in February 1909.

Albion beat City 3-1 in a League game at the Odsal Rugby League ground in December 1986, when Robert Hopkins scored a brilliant goal for the Baggies.

Albion beat City 4-0 at home on their way to the 1970 League Cup Final, and in 1989-90 they came back to win a two-legged second-round tie on the away goals rule after a tremendous 5-3 victory at Bradford, having lost the first leg 3-1 at The Hawthorns. Albion's John Thomas scored hat-trick in that eight-goal thriller at Valley Parade – his first (and only) treble for Albion.

Sid Bowser was the first Albion defender to score a hat-trick in a competitive game when he scored three times (two penalties) in a 4-1 League win over Bradford City (h) in September 1919.

Albion League debutants v City: Tom Haywood (1905), Jimmy Williams (1905), John Durnin (1988) Kevin Bartlett (1989), Wayne Fereday (1991), Frank Sinclair (1991), Andy Hunt (1993).

Goalkeeper Gavin Ward made his only appearance for Albion in a Littlewoods League Cup match against Bradford City in 1989.

Players with both clubs: Ian Banks, Lewis Bookman, Geoff Carter, Tony Ford, Don Goodman, Jack Hallows, Gary Robson, Martin Singleton, Gavin Ward.

Stuart Pearson was coach of Albion and later assistant manager-coach at Valley Parade; Irish international David Campbell was an Albion reserve trialist and City striker; Jack Hallows played for Albion's second string before joining City; Bob Brocklebank was City's manager (1961-64) and later Albion scout and Geoff Hudson played for City (1957-59) and was later Albion's coach (1970-72); former Albion reserve 'keeper Jonathan Gould joined Bradford City in 1996.

Kevin Bartlett, one of seven Albion players to have made their debut against Bradford City.

BRADFORD PARK AVENUE

Albion's record against Bradford reads:

Football League

Venue	P	W	D	L	F	A	Pts
Home	13	8	2	3	30	9	18
Away	13	4	3	6	27	30	11
Totals	26	12	5	9	57	39	29

FA Cup

Home	2	1	1	0	7	1
Away	2	0	1	1	1	3
Totals	4	1	2	1	8	4

Albion ran up a 7-1 League win over Bradford at The Hawthorns in April 1949 when Dave Walsh scored four goals as promotion to the First Division beckoned for the Baggies.

Bradford's best League win over Albion is 5-1 at Park Avenue in January 1930.

George Drury (far right) scores for Albion against Brentford in a Second Division game at The Hawthorns in September 1947.

By defeating Bradford 3-1 at The Hawthorns on 4 April 1920, Albion clinched their first and only League championship win.

When Albion beat Bradford 6-0 at home in a fifth-round tie in February 1929, Jimmy Cookson scored four times.

Cookson hit a total of eight goals in games against Bradford.

The other three Cup games took place in 1935-36, Bradford going through to the fifth round after two replays.

Albion League debuts v Bradford: Bob Pailor (1909), Herbert Webster (1929) and George Drury (1946).

Players with both clubs: Harry Brown, Danny Campbell, Tom Dilly, Chuck Drury, Jack Haines, Derek Kevan and Fred Leedham.

England international Haines was transferred from Albion to Bradford for a record fee of £20,000 in 1949.

Also associated with both clubs: Vic Buckingham managed at Park Avenue before taking over at The Hawthorns in 1953 when he brought Derek Kevan to Albion as well as reserve full-back Harry Haddington. Goalkeeper Geoff Hickman was also associated with both clubs while Geoff Hudson played for Bradford (1949-57) and later coached at Albion. Ernie Shepherd was a winger with Albion (1948-49) and later became Bradford's trainer.

BRADLEY, Darren Michael
Albion's manager Alan Buckley released Darren Bradley on a free transfer at the end of the 1994-95 season after the Birmingham-born defender/midfielder had hit 13 goals in 288 appearances in a nine-year spell at The Hawthorns. Albion's skipper at Wembley in 1993 when promotion was achieved to the First Division, Bradley often played with vision and tact, although occasionally his temper got the better of him with suspensions blighting his progress from time to time. Bradley captained both the Aston Villa and the England Youth teams as a teenager before transferring to Albion in 1986 in a deal which took Steve Hunt to Villa Park. He was born in 1965.

BRENTFORD
Albion's record against Brentford reads:

Football League

Venue	P	W	D	L	F	A	Pts
Home	6	6	0	0	13	5	13
Away	6	2	2	2	7	6	7
Totals	12	8	2	2	20	11	20

FA Cup

Home	1	1	0	0	2	0	

Other matches

Home	1	0	0	1	3	4	
Away	1	0	0	1	0	2	
Totals	2	0	0	2	3	6	

Albion's best League win over the Bees' is 4-3 at home in April 1938. Their heaviest defeat is 2-1 at Griffin Park in November 1936.

Darren Bradley came to Albion as part of the deal that took Steve Hunt to Aston Villa in 1986.

Derek Kevan scored both goals in Albion's 2-0 FA Cup win over Brentford 2-0 in February 1959 when the crowd was over 41,000.

One of Brentford's earliest professional signings (in 1900) was Roddy McLeod the former Albion inside-forward.

Albion League debutants v Brentford: Sammy Heaselgrave (1937), Bob Taylor (1992).

Played with both clubs: Laurie Bell, Ian Benjamin, Joseph Connor, Alan Dickens, Ronnie Fenton, Allan Glover, Roland James, Eric Jones, Peter McKennan, Roddy McLeod, Hugh Reed, Fred Rouse.

Archie Macaulay played for Brentford and later managed Albion (1961-63) and Ken Lawrence was a reserve with Albion and a Brentford first-teamer (1974-76). Goalkeeper Gary Phillips, an Albion reserve, was Brentford's senior goalkeeper (1984-88).

Cyrille Regis heads a spectacular goal against Brighton in August 1980.

BRIBERY

In 1913, a few days prior to a First Division game at The Hawthorns between Albion and Everton, scheduled for 29 November, Albion's skipper Jesse Pennington was offered £55 by a man who wanted him to 'fix' the result of the match so that Everton would not lose! Pennington duly informed the Albion officials, who in turn contacted the police. A trap was set and the culprit – Pascoe Bioletti (alias Samuel Johnson and Frederick Pater) was arrested near The Hawthorns. He was found guilty at Stafford Assize Court and was sentenced to five months imprisonment by Lord Justice Lush. The game finished 1-1 and the £55 was evenly divided between to West Bromwich Charities.

On 20 September 1964, the *People* newspaper alleged that a group of Everton players had got together and raised money in an attempt to bribe certain Albion players to lose a vital League game at The Hawthorns on 7 May 1963, the winning of which would ensure that Everton became League champions. The *People* stated: "We have no evidence that the bribe was accepted by any of the West Brom players, but the fact is that Everton won the match by a wide margin of 4-0."

During the game Albion lost defender Ron Bradley with a broken arm, Graham Williams put through his own-goal and Everton were awarded a penalty, but separate enquiries by both clubs failed to establish whether or not any one player had been bribed or had been offered a bribe.

BRIGHTON & HOVE ALBION

Albion's record against Brighton reads:

Football League

Venue	P	W	D	L	F	A	Pts
Home	9	5	4	0	17	4	18
Away	9	3	3	3	9	10	11
Totals	18	8	7	3	26	14	29

League Cup

Home	1	0	0	1	1	3

Full Members' Cup

Away	1	1	0	0	2	1

Other Matches

Home	1	0	0	1	0	2
Away	1	0	0	1	2	3
Totals	2	0	0	2	2	5

Albion's best League win is 5-0 at The Hawthorns on 1 September 1982 when Ally Brown scored twice before 11,546 fans.

Brighton's best League win over Albion is 2-0 at Hove on 20 September 1986.

When Brighton won 3-1 in a third-round League Cup at The Hawthorns on 22 September 1976, Albion had Willie Johnston sent-off for kicking out at Worcester referee Derek Lloyd.

The Full Members' Cup Group game at Hove was in 1985-86 when goalkeeper Paul Bradshaw made his Albion debut and Garth Crooks scored both goals in a 2-1 win.

On 25 February 1970, Brighton beat Walsall 3-0 in a Third Division League game at The Hawthorns. The fixture had been transferred from Walsall's Fellows Park ground which had been waterlogged for several weeks.

Albion League debutants v Brighton: Alan Webb (1982), Darren Rogers (1991), Scott Darton (1993).

Players with both clubs: Gerry Armstrong, Harry Baldwin, Mark Barham, Harry Chamberlain, George Chapman, Eddie Connelly, Harry Dutton, Ben Garfield, Tony Grealish, Dennis Gordon, Kieran O'Regan, Geoff Spencer, Mickey Thomas.

Archie Macaulay was manager at The Hawthorns from 1961 to 1963 and was then in charge at Brighton from 1963 to 1968.

Dennis Mortimer, Albion's assistant manager of the 1990s, and was a Brighton player (1985-86). Three Albion reserves, Pat Hilton, Ernie King and Wilf Vickers, all played for Brighton.

Brighton goalkeeper Perry Digweed (1981-93) was on loan with Albion in October 1993. In the early part of 1988-89 he was seriously injured playing for Brighton against Albion and missed the rest of the season.

BRISTOL CITY

Albion's record against City reads:

Football League

Venue	P	W	D	L	F	A	Pts
Home	17	8	6	3	24	14	24
Away	17	5	4	8	16	20	14
Totals	34	13	10	11	40	34	38

FA Cup

Home	2	2	0	0	8	3
Away	1	0	1	0	1	1
Totals	3	2	1	0	9	4

League Cup

Home	1	0	1	0	2	2
Away	1	0	0	1	0	1
Totals	2	0	1	1	2	3

Anglo-Scottish Cup

Away	1	0	0	1	0	1

Other matches

Home	1	0	1	0	3	3
Away	7	2	2	3	11	12
Totals	8	2	3	3	14	15

Albion's best League win has been 3-0 at home on 30 August 1930, while City's best win is 3-1 at Ashton Gate on 19 February 1906. Both these games were in Division Two.

Albion scored six 'goals' in their home League game against Bristol City in February 1906. However, only one counted and they lost 3-1!

Albion beat City 4-1 at home in a third-round FA Cup tie in January 1926 before a crowd of over 33,000.

The two League Cup games were played in season 1990-91.

Albion also went down 1-0 away at City in an Anglo-Scottish Cup-tie in August 1976.

In a Wartime League Cup game in March 1945, City's Don Clark scored a hat-trick as Albion went down 5-2.

Albion League debutants v City: Sam Edwards (1904), Charlie Bradley (1905), Bruce Rankin (1906), Trevor Thompson (1974), John Trewick (1974).

Trevor Thompson made his Albion debut against Bristol City in 1974, one of only five Baggies players to have made their bow against the Ashton Gate side.

Players with both clubs: Tommy Broad, Davey Burnside, Joseph Connor, Alf Dean, Chuck Drury, Cliff Edwards, Fred Fenton, Alf Geddes, Bobby Gould, Joe Johnson, Paul Mardon, Micky Mellon, Ebenezer Owers, Alonzo Poulton, Nicky Reid, Ben Shearman, Bob Taylor, Clive Whitehead, Cyril Williams.

Gould also managed both clubs; Tony Rance was secretary of both clubs and Albion reserves Mike Gibson, Kevin Slabber and John Turner all played for City.

BRISTOL ROVERS

Albion's record against Rovers:

Football League

Venue	P	W	D	L	F	A	Pts
Home	3	2	1	0	8	3	6
Away	3	0	2	1	3	4	2
Totals	6	2	3	1	11	7	8

League Cup

Home	1	0	1	0	0	0
Away	1	1	0	0	4	1
Totals	2	1	1	0	4	1

Other Matches

Away	1	1	0	0	3	2

Albion's best League is 3-0 at The Hawthorns in February 1976. City's best is 2-1 at their Eastville Stadium in October 1974.

The League Cup games were played in 1992-93.

Albion had to beat Rovers at Twerton Park, Bath, in the last League game of season 1991-92 to save themselves from relegation. They drew 1-1 and went down to Division Three.

Dave Rushbury played for both Albion and Bristol Rovers.

Albion beat Rovers 3-2 at the Eastville Stadium in Dick Sheppard's testimonial game in May 1979.

Lee Ashcroft's Albion's debut was against Rovers, League Cup (1993).

Players with both clubs: Ben Appleby, Paul Bradshaw, George Elmore, Alf Geddes, Bobby Gould, Carl Heggs, Walter Jack, Jack Kifford, Jimmy McLean, Jack Nevin, Garry Pendrey, David Pritchard, Dave Rushbury, Dick Sheppard, Andy Smith, Kenny Stephens, David Walker.

Also associated with both clubs: Gould managed both clubs; Don Howe was a player and manager with Albion and coach with Rovers; Gordon Bennett was associated with both clubs on the administration side; and Albion reserves Jack Smith, John McIlvenney, Alan Scarrott and Jack Pitt all later played for Rovers.

BROADCASTS (Radio and TV & Video)

The first time a live radio broadcast of an Albion home match was heard on the radio was of the second half of their sixth-round FA Cup-tie against Wolverhampton Wanderers on 28 February 1931 (1-1 draw).

The first League game broadcast live' from The Hawthorns was the Albion v Sheffield United Second Division match on 10 September 1938 when the second half was covered.

The first live television pictures transmitted from The Hawthorns came from Albion's floodlit friendly with CDSA (Moscow) on Wednesday, 29 October 1957 when a crowd of 52,805 braved pouring rain to see Albion win 6-5.

In the BBC archives, albeit from pre-television days, there is black and white film footage of Albion in action at Blackburn in the 1898 (showing goalkeeper Joe Reader) and also a nine-minute clip of the 1912 FA Cup Final draw between Albion and Barnsley at the Crystal Palace.

Since the introduction of video recorders and video cameras, several companies have produced cassettes of Albion matches (past and present) along with seasonal reviews, and an official club history (on video) was produced in 1993.

In the early 1930s, one of the main radio broadcasters was the former Albion player (and later club director) Alan Claude Jephcott.

The whole of the Albion v Bristol City League game at The Hawthorns on New Year's Day, 1979, was broadcast live on BBC Radio 2 – this being the first time an English fixture, other than an international match or Cup Final, had been covered from start to finish. The commentators who covered the game were Peter Jones and Alan Parry.

During the 1978-79 season, two League games were transmitted live from The Hawthorns for Scandinavian television, the first being Albion against Leeds United on 24 February.

Albion (like most other clubs) nowadays video every first-team game which is played at The Hawthorns.

BROWN, Alistair

A key figure in Albion's attack during the 1970s and early 1980s, Ally Brown played alongside some fine marksmen, including Jeff Astle, his namesake Tony and Cyrille Regis, and he scored his fair share of goals, netting 85 in 359 senior outings for the Baggies between 1972 and 1983. Born in

Musselburgh in 1951, Brown played for Edinburgh & District Schools before joining Leicester for whom he top-scored in 1970-71 when the Foxes won the Second Division title. He was transferred to Albion for the unusual fee of £61,111 in March 1972 and scored on his debut, against Crystal Palace. He had a couple of lean seasons under Don Howe's management (1973-75), but was a vital cog in Albion's attack under Johnny Giles, Ronnie Allen and Ron Atkinson. After 11 years with Albion (and a spell in the NASL with Portland Timbers), Brown went on to play (and score) for Crystal Palace, Walsall and Port Vale, retiring in 1986 to become a licensee. In 1995 he was appointed steward of The Halfords Lane Throstle club, opposite The Hawthorns..

BROWN, Anthony

One of the greatest footballers in the club's history, Tony 'Bomber' Brown scored more goals (312) and appeared in more first-team games (818) than any other Albion player during his more than 20 years at The Hawthorns (1961-81). In fact, he played more senior matches at The Hawthorns than any other player: 361, including 282 in the Football League. His League record for the club was 218 goals in 574 appearances. Oldham-born (in October 1945) Brown, a penalty-expert, had two excellent years as an apprentice, and joined Albion's professional ranks on his 18th birthday after making a scoring League debut in a 2-1 win at Ipswich in September 1963. He quickly established himself in the first team and was a regular from 1964-79, helping Albion win both the League Cup (1966) and FA Cup (1968), also playing in two losing League Cup Finals of 1967 and 1970. Capped by England at Youth level, he played in one full international against Wales at Wembley in 1971, and represented the Football League. He was voted Midlands Footballer of the Year in 1969, 1971 and 1979, and also topped the First Division scoring charts in 1970-71 with 28 goals. After spells in the NASL with the New England Teamen and Jacksonville Teamen, Brown left Albion for Torquay United in 1981, later playing for Stafford Rangers and the Albion All Stars (in charity matches). He returned to The Hawthorns in 1984 as coach (under Giles) and took a similar position with Birmingham (under Garry Pendrey) in 1987, quitting football in 1989. Brown, who has had two hip replacements, lives with his wife Irene and family in

Tony Brown, scored more goals and appeared in more first-team games than any other player in Albion's history. Here he is pictured in action against Liverpool.

Walsall and is a regular visitor to Albion's home matches as well as being a columnist in a local sports paper.

BUCK, Frederick Richard

The smallest centre-half ever to don an Albion shirt and indeed, to play in an FA Cup Final, Freddie Buck at 5ft. 4ins. tall, was a real 'tough-nut' who gave Albion tremendous service during the second

of two spells with the club. Born at Newcastle-under-Lyme, in 1879, he played his early football with Stafford Wesleyans and Stafford Rangers, joining Albion in 1900. He stayed at The Hawthorns until 1903, when he moved to Liverpool, switching to Plymouth soon after, only to return to Albion in 1906. His second spell at The Hawthorns lasted until 1914, during which time he took his club record to an impressive 319 games and 94 goals, mostly scored as an inside-forward before he moved to centre-half from where he skippered the team. Buck represented the Football League in 1910-11, the same season Albion won the Second Division title, and the following year he gained a runners-up medal when Barnsley beat the Baggies in the Cup Final replay. After leaving Albion (for a second time) Buck had a spell with Swansea, retiring in 1917 and later becoming a licensee in Stafford. He died in 1952.

BUNN'S FIELD (The Birches)

Albion's first enclosed ground, situated in Walsall Street (now Alfred Street) West Bromwich where they played for one season (August 1881 to May 1882) after agreeing on a nine-month lease. Albion players equipped the ground themselves, levelling and rolling flat the pitch then erecting two sets of goal posts with a tape acting as the crossbar at each end. The 'main' entrance was opposite Christ Church School, attended by several early Albion players, while the changing rooms were at first based inside the White Hart public house, at the junction of Herbert Street, Bull Street and Walsall Street, and later in the Roebuck Inn which was situated on the corner of New Street and Walsall Street.

Having an enclosed ground the club was now able to charge admission prices for the first time and the opening game on Bunn's Field saw Albion beat Oldbury 5-1 on 10 September 1881 before 600 spectators. Albion, wearing yellow and white quartered jerseys at first and then chocolate and blue halves with the Staffordshire Knot embroidered on the front, were practically unbeatable on their new ground and among their many victories were those of 12-0 v Milton, 10-0 v St Luke's, 9-1 v Nechells, 6-1 v West Bromwich Rangers and 5-0 v Fallings Heath Rovers. Albion also reached the semi-final of the Birmingham Cup whilst at Bunn's Field before taking a new ground, the Four Acres, home of West Bromwich Dartmouth Cricket Club.

BURGESS, Daryl

A first-team regular in Albion's defence since making his debut in 1989 at Port Vale, Burgess started off as a right-back, but has since played in the middle of the back-four and as sweeper. A strong-tackling

Daryl Burgess, a regular in Albion's defence since making his debut for the Baggies in 1989.

player, born in Birmingham in 1971, he joined Albion as an apprentice in 1987, turning professional two years later. Burgess passed the milestone of 200 League appearances for Albion during the second half of the 1995-96 season.

BURNLEY

Albion's record against Burnley reads:

Football League

Venue	P	W	D	L	F	A	Pts
Home	56	29	11	16	113	65	71
Away	56	18	12	26	70	101	48
Totals	112	47	23	42	183	166	119

FA Cup

Venue	P	W	D	L	F	A
Home	1	1	0	0	5	1

Other Matches

Venue	P	W	D	L	F	A
Home	2	1	0	1	3	3
Away	1	1	0	0	1	0
Totals	3	2	0	1	4	3

Albion and Burnley were founder members of the Football League in 1888.

Albion's best League win is 8-1 in a First Division game at The Hawthorns on 11 November 1967.

Burnley's best League win over Albion is 6-1, also in Division One, at Turf Moor on 8 September 1951, when Billy Morris scored four times for the Clarets.

The one FA Cup-tie was played in February 1889 when Albion also had three 'goals' disallowed.

Albion League debutants v Burnley: Walter Perry (1888), Charlie Shaw (1888), Luther Walker (1888), Sid Oliver (1888), Jack Pittaway (1889), Jack Riley (1890), Henry Boyd (1893), Franklin Roberts (1893), Archie Heywood (1896), 'Chippy' Simmons (1898), Jimmy Chadburn (1900), Laurie Bell (1904), Freddie Haycock (1904), Walter Jack (1904), Albert Lewis (1904), Jack Manners (1904), Eli Bradley (1905), Edward Perkins (1905), Adam Haywood (1905), George Young (1905), Dick Betteley (1906), Ross Fielding (1908), Alf Bentley (1913), Herbert Nicholls (1913), Jack Byers (1924), Geoff Spencer (1938), Doug Witcomb (1938), Mick Gallagher (1953), Ian Collard (1964).

Players with both clubs: Colin Anderson, Henry Boyd, Ronnie Fenton, Andrew Marriott, Len Moorwood, Tony Morley, Mike Phelan, John Talbut, Winston White.

Irish international David Campbell had trials with Albion and played League

Colin Anderson played for both Albion and Burnley.

football for Burnley, while Bill Chambers was an Albion reserve before moving to Turf Moor. Stuart Robertson, an Albion trialist in 1982, had been a first-team player with Burnley (1979-82) and Bob Brocklebank played 128 games for Burnley (1935-39) and was a 1950s scout for Albion.

Alan Stevenson was Burnley's senior goalkeeper between 1972 and 1983 and was Albion's commercial manager for five years, from 1987 until 1992.

BURNSIDE, David Gort

Highly skillful inside-forward, Davey Burnside was associated with Bristol City as a schoolboy and later had a long career playing League football for Albion (who signed him as an amateur in 1955, taking him on professional forms in 1957), Southampton (transferred from The Hawthorns for £17,000 in 1962 with Welsh international Stuart Williams), Crystal Palace, Wolverhampton Wanderers, Plymouth Argyle, Bristol City and Colchester, becoming player-manager of Bath City in 1972. He was then assistant manager at Walsall, playing next for Cadbury Heath, Bridgwater Town and Taunton Town before retiring in 1980 as a qualified FA coach, later managing the England Youth team. He was still on the England coaching staff in 1996.

Born in Bristol in 1939, Burnside amassed a total of 403 League appearances and scored 88 goals. His Albion record was 42 goals in 235 senior games and whilst at The Hawthorns he represented England Youth, the Under-23 XI (two caps) and the FA XI. He was also a member of Wolves' Second Division promotion-winning side of 1966-67. He was a fine ball juggler who used to come out on to the pitch at half-time in some of Albion's early televised friendly games against foreign opposition and entertain the crowd.

BURTON SWIFTS/UNITED

Burton United were members of League Division Two from 1892 to 1907 when they failed top gain re-election. Burton Swifts were in existence from the early 1880s, but a name change occurred in 1901 when, after finishing bottom of Division Two, the Swifts amalgamated with Burton Wanderers (also an early League side) to form Burton United. The statistics relate to those League games played between Albion and Burton Swifts and Burton United, and the last match was played on 27 April 1907.

Football League

Venue	P	W	D	L	F	A	Pts
Home	4	4	0	0	14	2	8
Away	4	2	1	1	11	5	5
Totals	8	6	1	1	25	7	13

Other Matches

Venue	P	W	D	L	F	A
Home	3	2	1	0	12	3
Away	6	3	1	2	10	9
Totals	9	5	2	2	22	12

Albion's best League win is 6-0 (away) on 21 April 1905, while their only defeat (2-0) was also suffered at Burton on 27 April 1907.

Albion League debutants v Swifts/United: Billy Poynton (1902), Jimmy Millar (1904).

Players with both clubs: Bob Crone, Ernie Peers, Walter Perry, Seth Powell.

BURTON WANDERERS

Albion's record against Burton Wanderers:

FA Cup

Venue	P	W	D	L	F	A
Home	1	1	0	0	6	0

Other Matches

Venue	P	W	D	L	F	A
Home	1	1	0	0	23	0

Away	3	2	1	0	16	3	
Totals	4	3	1	0	39	3	

The FA Cup first-round tie was played on 30 October 1886.

When Albion beat Wanderers 23-0 at home in a Staffordshire Cup-tie on 1 February 1890, five different players scored hat-tricks, Billy Bassett claiming a six-timer. Albion also beat the Wanderers 12-2 (away) in another Staffordshire Cup-tie in October 1887.

Players with both clubs: Ben Appleby, Ben Garfield, Adam Haywood.

BURY

Albion's record against Bury reads:

Football League

Venue	P	W	D	L	F	A	Pts
Home	19	10	4	5	41	21	24
Away	19	3	4	12	22	48	10
Totals	38	13	8	17	63	69	34

FA Cup

Home	1	1	0	0	2	1
Away	1	0	0	1	0	1
Totals	2	1	0	1	2	2

League Cup

Away	1	0	0	1	0	1

Other Matches

Home	2	0	1	1	0	2
Away	1	1	0	0	2	1
Totals	3	1	1	1	2	3

Albion's best League win is 6-0 (home) on 11 March 1939 when England international Joe Johnson scored four times.

Bury's best League win is 7-3 at Gigg Lane on 11 September 1926. They led 7-1 after 58 minutes, having scored three goals in four minutes just before half-time. Bury also defeated Albion 6-1 at home in a First Division game in October 1900.

Arthur Gale played for both Albion and Bury.

Bury whipped Albion 5-1 at home in a first-round FA Cup-tie in January 1902 with Sagar hitting a second-half hat-trick in treacherous conditions. This remained as Albion's heaviest FA Cup defeat until 1967.

First Division Albion were ousted from the League Cup by Third Division Bury at a fog-bound Gigg Lane in November 1977.

Albion League debutants v Bury: Dick Roberts (1899), George Dudley (1938), Peter McKennan (1947), Carl Hoggs (1992).

Players with both clubs: Luther Blissett, Peter Butler, Len Cantello, Geoff Carter, Eddie Colquhoun, David Cross, Harry Dutton, Paul Edwards, Arthur Gale, Tony Godden, Willie Hendry, Craig Madden, John Paskin, Winston White.

Former Albion reserve Gary Leonard played for Bury in 1988-89 and Jesse Carver starred for Bury in the 1930s and was appointed manager-coach of Albion in 1952.

BYERS, John Edwin

An outstandingly quick winger, who scored 12 goals in 111 games for Albion between 1924-28. Born in Selby in 1897, Jack Byers played his early football for Knaresborough before joining Huddersfield Town in 1921, switching to Blackburn Rovers two years later. He cost Albion £1,750 from Ewood

Arthur Byers, cost Albion £1,750 from Blackburn Rovers in 1924.

Park and he left The Hawthorns for Worcester City, later serving with Torquay United (1929) and Kidderminster Harriers, retiring in 1931. He died in Worcester later the same year.

CAMBRIDGE UNITED

Albion have yet to play Cambridge United in a competitive game. They have, however, met in a testimonial match at the Abbey Stadium, in April 1980 when Albion won 2-1.

Players with both clubs: Jack Bannister, Kevin Bartlett, Brendon Batson, Ian Benjamin, Peter Butler, Wayne Ebanks, Ian Hamilton, Joe Mayo, George Reilly, Dave Rushbury, Graham Smith.

Ron Atkinson, managed both Albion and Cambridge United.

Other players associated with both clubs: Russell Allen, David Campbell, Derek Finch, Brian Hart.

Also associated with both clubs: Ron Atkinson managed Cambridge United (1974-78) before taking over at Albion in 1978; Mick Brown, Albion's assistant manager (under Atkinson: 1979-81) was a player and coach with Cambridge United and Geoff Hudson was coach at Cambridge in 1967-68 and at Albion 1970-72.

CANTELLO, Leonard

Scorer of 21 goals in 369 games for Albion between 1967 and 1979, Len Cantello also donned ten different shirts at first-team level for the Baggies. Playing with style, artistry and commitment, Cantello was mainly a midfielder, but also

Bobby Robson skippered Albion in 1960-61.

Ray Barlow leads out Albion in 1957.

filled in at left-back and occasionally as a forward. He won six Schoolboy, four Youth and eight Under-23 caps for England and played for Albion in the 1970 League Cup Final at the age of 18. Six years later he helped the Baggies win promotion from the Second Division and in December 1978, he scored ATV's Goal of the Season against Manchester United at Old Trafford when Albion won 5-3. After leaving Albion, immediately following his testimonial match, Cantello played for Bolton Wanderers (signed for a then record £350,000), Eastern Athletic (Hong Kong), Burnley (trial), Altrincham, Stafford Rangers (two spells), Hereford United and Bury (as a non-contract player), SC Cambuur (Holland) as player-coach, Peterborough United (trial) and Northwich Victoria. He was then with Stockport County (as assistant manager to Asa Hartford), manager of Radcliffe Borough and the scouted for both Peterborough United and Wigan Athletic. In the summer of 1978 he also assisted Dallas Tornados (NASL).

CAPTAINS

Billy Bisseker was Albion's first-team captain, appointed in 1879. Since then several different players have skippered the side as the official club captain, among them:

1880	Jimmy Stanton
1881	George Bell
1882	John While
1883	Jimmy Stanton/Harry Aston
1884	Ezra Horton
1886	'Jem' Bayliss
1891	Charlie Perry
1894	Tom Perry
1895	Tom Higgins
1896	Billy Bassett
1899	Tom Perry
1900	Fred Wheldon
1901	Dan Nurse
1904	Harry Hadley
1905	Amos Adams
1906	Ted Pheasant
1908	Albert Evans/Bill Garraty
1910	Freddie Buck
1911	Jesse Pennington
1922	Sid Bowser
1924	Fred Reed
1926	Tommy Magee
1927	Bill Ashurst/George Shaw
1928	George Shaw/Harry Chambers
1929	Tommy Glidden
1936	Teddy Sandford
1938	'Sandy' McNab
1939	Cecil Shaw
1945	Harry Kinsell
1946	Billy Elliott
1948	Jack Vernon/Elliott
1952	Joe Kennedy
1953	Len Millard/Stan Rickaby
1953	Len Millard
1957	Ray Barlow

Chris Whyte was one of three players to skipper Albion in 1989.

Graham Williams leads out Albion at White Hart Lane in 1965.

John Wile, who captained Albion from 1977 to 1983.

1960	Bobby Robson
1962	Don Howe
1965	Graham Williams
1969	Doug Fraser
1970	Jeff Astle
1971	John Kaye
1972	John Wile
1975	Johnny Giles
1977	John Wile
1983	Ally Robertson/Clive Whitehead/Ken McNaught
1984	Ally Robertson/Martyn Bennett
1985	Clive Whitehead
1986	Paul Dyson
1987	Brian Talbot
1989	Brian Talbot/Steve Parkin/Chris Whyte
1990	Darren Bradley/Craig Shakespeare/Graham Roberts
1991	Darren Bradley/Graham Roberts
1992	Darren Bradley
1995	Mike Phelan/Paul Mardon
1996	Bob Taylor

In 1994-95, 11 different players captained Albion's first team at least once during the duration of the season with Mardon the main club skipper.

In their 1948-49 Second Division promotion-winning season, Albion had two captains – centre-half Jack Vernon looked after the defence and winger Billy Elliott was in charge of the forwards.

Albion's five FA Cup winning teams were skippered by 'Jem' Bayliss (1888), Charlie Perry (1892), Tommy Glidden (1931), Len Millard (1954) and Graham Williams (1968). Williams also skippered Albion to victory in the 1966 League Cup Final and was the first Albion captain to lead the club into a major European competition (Fairs Cup in 1966-67).

Freddie Buck captained Albion to the 1910-11 Second Division championship, and Jesse Pennington was skipper when Albion reached the 1912 FA Cup Final (v Barnsley) and won the Football League title in 1919-20.

Jimmy Millar captained Albion in his only League game for the club against Burton United (home) on 8 October 1904.

Ally Robertson, at the age of 20 years, 2 months, is the youngest player ever to captain Albion's League side (at Norwich City on 18 November 1972).

CARDIFF CITY
Albion's record against Cardiff is:
Football League

Venue	P	W	D	L	F	A	Pts
Home	19	11	3	5	40	23	25
Away	19	7	4	8	32	32	18
Totals	38	18	7	13	72	55	43

FA Cup

	P	W	D	L	F	A	
Home	2	1	0	1	4	1	
Away	2	0	2	0	3	3	
Totals	4	1	2	1	7	4	

Other matches

	P	W	D	L	F	A	
Home	2	2	0	0	9	5	
Away	5	2	3	0	11	9	
Totals	7	4	3	0	20	14	

Ronnie Allen scored four goals when Albion registered their best League win over Cardiff, beating them 6-1 in a First Division match at The Hawthorns on 21 November 1953.

Albion also won 6-3 at Cardiff early in their double-winning season of 1930-31. Jimmy Cookson hit four of the Baggies' goals.

Albion's best League win at Cardiff is 5-0 in a Second Division fixture on 24 April 1948.

Outside-left Derek Hogg skippered Cardiff against his former club, Albion, at The Hawthorns on 3 March 1962 and ended up on the wrong end of a 5-1 defeat.

Cardiff's best win over Albion is 4-2 at The Haw-- thorns on 10 November 1923 (Division One). Len Davies scored all four City goals that day.

In a wartime game in August 1941, Harry Jones scored four times as Albion beat Cardiff City in a Regional League game at The Hawthorns.

Albion League debutants v Cardiff: Harry Dutton (1922), Jimmy Spencer (1922), Harry Smith (1923), Elfed Evans (1952), Roy Horobin (1956).

Walter Robbins played for both Albion and Cardiff and was a prolific scorer for the Ninian Park club.

Players with both clubs: Kevin Bartlett, Stan Davies, Andy Dibble, Elfed Evans, Wayne Fereday, Mark Grew, Derek Hogg, Wayne Hughes, Steve Lynex, Mick Martin, Johnny Nicholls, Mel Rees, Walter Robbins, Kevin Summerfield, Garry Thompson, Gavin Ward.

Other players associated with both clubs: Gary Bell, Phil Griffiths, Eli Postin and Ronnie Stockin. Ronnie Rees played for Albion (1960s) and later worked in the Ninian Park offices.

Walter Robbins was a prolific scorer from outside-left for Cardiff when they were relegated from Division Two in 1930-31. He was top marksman with 12 goals, including a hat-trick against Millwall in early December. He then scored 21 goals in the Third Division South in 1931-32 and from 6-22 February 1932 he created a club record for the Welsh side by scoring 11 times in four matches, including a five-timer against Thames in the League (three goals coming in the space of five minutes: 20-25) and a treble against Llanelli in the Welsh Cup. Robbins also scored three times earlier in the season against Reading.

CARLISLE UNITED
Albion record against United is:
Football League

Venue	P	W	D	L	F	A	Pts.
Home	2	1	1	0	4	1	3
Away	2	1	1	0	2	1	3
Totals	4	2	2	0	6	2	6

FA Cup

	P	W	D	L	F	A	
Home	1	1	0	0	3	1	
Away	1	0	0	1	2	3	
Totals	2	1	0	1	5	4	

League Cup

	P	W	D	L	F	A	
Home	1	1	0	0	4	1	
Away	1	0	0	1	0	1	
Totals	2	1	0	1	4	2	

Other match

	P	W	D	L	F	A	
Away	1	1	0	0	1	0	

Albion's best League win is 3-1 at home on 3 April 1976, on their way to winning promotion from Division Two.

Albion's home FA Cup win came in January 1976, 12 months after losing 3-2 in the same competition at Brunton Park.

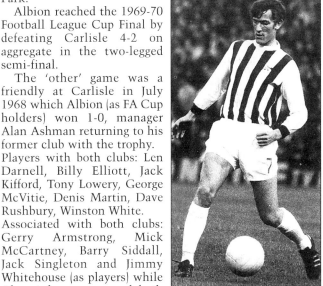

George McVitie, one of eight men to have appeared in both Albion's and Carlisle's colours.

Albion reached the 1969-70 Football League Cup Final by defeating Carlisle 4-2 on aggregate in the two-legged semi-final.

The 'other' game was a friendly at Carlisle in July 1968 which Albion (as FA Cup holders) won 1-0, manager Alan Ashman returning to his former club with the trophy. Players with both clubs: Len Darnell, Billy Elliott, Jack Kifford, Tony Lowery, George McVitie, Denis Martin, Dave Rushbury, Winston White. Associated with both clubs: Gerry Armstrong, Mick McCartney, Barry Siddall, Jack Singleton and Jimmy Whitehouse (as players) while Alan Ashman managed both clubs, taking Albion to the 1968 FA and 1970 League Cup Finals.

CARTER, Joseph Henry
Joe Carter gave Albion 15 years' loyal service as a quality inside-right, appearing in 451 games and scoring 151 goals.

As partner to his captain, Glidden, he helped Albion achieve the unique Cup and promotion double in 1930-31, played in the 1935 FA Cup Final and won three England caps. He left Albion for Sheffield Wednesday in 1936, but returned to The Hawthorns after only six days after failing a medical examination. He then transferred to Tranmere Rovers but quickly joined Walsall. He retired in 1940 after a spell as player-manager of Vono Sports (Tipton). Born in Aston, Birmingham in 1901, Carter died of dehydration in Handsworth in 1977 aged 75.

CASUALTIES

Deaths

The following Albion players lost their lives during World War One: Frank Costello, the former Albion, Southampton, West Ham United and Bolton centre-forward died in action in December 1914. Fourteen months later, on 15 February 1916, 2nd Lieut Harold G.Bache of the Lancashire Fusiliers was shot dead on a Flanders battlefield. Sapper Billy Vale, formerly of Langley St Michael's, Albion and Wednesbury Old Athletic, was killed in November 1916 while serving in the trenches. In May 1917, 2nd Lieut William H.Jackson of the West Yorkshire Regiment, an amateur centre-forward from Oldbury Secondary School who had played for Leamington St Mary's, Langley Old Church and Albion, was killed while serving in the Armed Forces.

Those Albion players who died during World War Two were: Walter Wheatley of Exhall Old Boys – an Albion trialist – was killed while serving with the Royal Warwickshire Regiment in July 1940.

Lance-Corporal George Handley, the former Albion, Crystal Palace, Brierley Hill Alliance and Darlaston junior international centre-forward, was killed while on Army duty in Sicily on 9 July 1943.

William A.Darby, a reserve centre-forward with Albion, also lost his life in February 1944 on service in Italy with the Coldstream Guards..

Peacetime fatalities

Albion's star centre-forward of the 1930s, 'W.G.' Richardson, collapsed and died when playing in a local charity match in Birmingham in 1959.

Ted 'Cock' Pheasant, the 'tough-guy' centre-half with Albion and Wolves in the early 1900s, died of peritonitis two weeks after leaving The Hawthorns for Leicester Fosse in July 1910.

Jack Beynon, a former Albion reserve outside-right, also died of peritonitis when on Aberdeen's close-season tour of South Africa in April 1937.

Defender Matt Wood, who was with Albion from 1911-22, died shortly after an appendix operation in December 1923, aged 33.

Jack Taggart, Albion's left-half in the 1895 FA Cup Final, died of cancer in may 1927, aged 53.

Arthur Randle, who played alongside Pheasant for Albion, died of cancer in 1913 at the age of 32.

Former Albion defender, Jim Stevenson, was tragically killed at Leven Shipyard in March 1925, aged 49.

Albion's 1912 FA Cup Final full-back, Arthur Cook, died when he fell out of a bedroom window while sleep-walking at his licensed premises in Stafford in February 1930.

One of Albion's earliest captains, John While, was killed in a traffic accident in Victoria, Australia, in July 1944 only a few weeks before he was to visit England.

Johnny Nicholls, star of Albion's forward-line in the 1950s, died of a heart attack on his way home after watching the League game with Middlesbrough at The Hawthorns on 1 April 1995.

Albion's dashing winger of the 1970s, Laurie Cunningham, lost his life in a road accident on the outskirts of Madrid in July 1989.

Zambian international goalkeeper David Chabala, who played for Albion reserves in September 1990, was subsequently killed in a plane crash in 1992.

Hughie Reed and Jim Holton, two of Albion's reserves of the 1970s, both died of heart attacks in 1992, and in 1993 goalkeeper Mel Rees died of a bowel tumour at the age of 26, while another Baggies' goalkeeper, Bill Harris, died of cancer in 1996.

Albion vice-chairman, Tom Silk, was killed with his wife, Ruth, when the aircraft he was piloting to Albion's mid-week League Cup-tie with Everton at Goodison Park, crashed in France on 24 September 1980.

Hughie Reed, one of two Albion reserves of the 1970s, who both died of heart attacks in 1992.

Clive Jackman, whose career was ended after an injury sustained in a minor representative match for the FA against the RAF in 1958.

Cyril Williams, an Albion forward in the 1940s, died in a car crash in 1980.

Mick Brown, assistant commercial manager at Albion, was killed in a road crash in November 1987 while commuting between his home in Hartlepool and The Hawthorns.

Serious Injuries

During World War Two, RAF pilot Jimmy Sanders was seriously injured when his aircraft was shot down by enemy fire over Europe. At the time (1942) it was feared that Sanders (then a Charlton goalkeeper) would never play again but he defied the doubters and went on to play in more than 360 games for Albion (1945-58), gaining an FA Cup winners medal in 1954.

Also during World War Two, several junior players registered with Albion were seriously injured: goalkeepers George Dale and Cliff Wright both lost a leg, Dick Pike was wounded in France and Tom Griffiths was seriously injured in 1945. Another goalkeeper, Bill Harris, was wounded in Normandy.

Graham Lovett was involved in two serious car crashes in the late 1960s – and the injuries suffered in the second one eventually forced him to quit top-class football in June 1972. At Birmingham Crown Court, on 29 January 1973, Lovett was awarded £14,000 damages against the West Midlands Transport Executive whose bus driver was found to be responsible for the second accident which occurred in Quinton, Birmingham. Lovett's first crash was on the M1 motorway.

Former Albion player David Mills was involved in a road accident in North Yorkshire in January 1988 and as a result his playing career was terminated. His father, who was a passenger in his car, suffered fatal injuries.

Welsh wartime international Alun 'Bungo' Evans lost the sight of his right eye while playing for Albion against Doncaster Rovers in a Second Division game at The Hawthorns on 3 April 1948. He never played top-class football again.

Several Albion players saw their respective careers ended abruptly through injury suffered on the pitch, among them: forward Jimmy Spooner (1895), centre-half Tom Higgins (1897), England full-back Billy Williams (1900), inside-forward Ernie Edwards (1914), right winger Claude Jephcott (1922), left-half Nelson Howarth (1928), goalscorer Harry 'Popeye' Jones (1943), goalkeeper Lew Twigg (1946 – fractured skull), right-back Jim Pemberton (1951), goalkeepers Norman Heath (1954) and Clive Jackman (1958 – back injury playing for an FA XI v RAF), left-back Ray Wilson (1975) and right-back Brendon Batson (1984) although the latter did continue to play in friendly matches for another year.

Former Albion goalkeeper Dick Sheppard fractured his skull playing for Bristol Rovers in 1973 and he quit the game soon afterwards. Ike Webb, Albion's goalkeeper, 1901-04, played, unknown to him at the time, with a fractured skull towards the end of his career, while Joe Reader, who was Albion's goalkeeper before Webb, played one game with his arm in a sling.

Albion's skipper John While (aged 22), broke his leg playing in the Wednesbury Cup Final v Nottingham Forest in May 1883. He never played again.

Bryan Robson fractured his left leg three times during the 1976-77 season - once playing for the Reserves and twice whilst on duty with the first team.

Full-back Albert Evans broke his leg on four separate occasions during a lengthy career – three times with Aston Villa (1901, 1903 and 1906) and once with Albion (1908).

Jack Sankey, Albion's wing-half, fractured his right leg playing at Charlton on 11 March 1937. In fact, the injury was not confirmed as a 'break' until a month later after he had complained to his own doctor about 'a tedious pain'.

Sunderland's Len Duns, guesting for Albion in the war, broke his leg playing against Nottingham Forest on 4 March 1944.

Outside-left Bobby Barker suffered two broken arms, a broken leg, a bruised collar-bone and concussion in 1948-49.

George Timmins (1889), Alec Jackson (1958), Frank Griffin (1958) and Ken Foggo (1965) all fractured a leg playing for Albion, and all recovered to continue their careers in the Football League, although Timmins and Griffin were never the same again.

Bob Pailor (1915) and Lyndon Hughes (1966) both had kidney operations during their careers which left them each with only one functional kidney.

Joe Carter was transferred from Albion to Sheffield Wednesday on 6 February 1936, but the deal collapsed six days later when a doctor diagnosed that Carter had a cartilage problem.

Albion's Asa Hartford 'signed' for Leeds United for £175,000 in November 1971, but the transfers was called-off within 48 hours after doctors revealed that the Scottish international had a heart normality. Hartford went on to play until 1989.

Six Albion players, Wally Boyes, Tommy Glidden, Tommy Green, Norman Male, Walter Robbins and Teddy Sandford all underwent cartilage operations over an 18-month period in 1935-36.

In season 1900-01 Albion were so severely plagued by injury and illness that they had to play with ten men for the greater proportion of nine of their 38 League and Cup matches, while in another two they finished with only nine men on the field.

Asa Hartford, seen in action here against Liverpool's Ray Kennedy (whose own career was curtailed by Parkinson's Disease), saw his move to Leeds called off after a routine medical inspection revealed a potential heart problem. Hartford, though, went on to enjoy a long and successful career.

CAVE, George Henry

A Black Country-born full-back, George Cave played 83 games for Albion around the turn of the century Short and stocky, he had good positional sense and was a keen tackler. He joined the club from Great Bridge Unity in 1895 and retired through injury and illness in 1901. He died in Dudley in 1904, aged 30.

Centenary Match Result

WEST BROMWICH ALBION....1
P. Barnes

AJAX 0

West Bromwich Albion F.C.
The Hawthorns
West Bromwich

CENTENARY MATCH

Although it was later discovered that Albion may have been founded in 1878 (as West Bromwich Strollers) the club celebrated its Centenary on 11 August 1979 with a friendly at The Hawthorns against one of Europe's leading sides, Ajax of Amsterdam. Albion won the game 1-0, Peter Barnes scoring in front of a crowd of 13,334. Albion's team was: Katalinic; Batson, Statham; Trewick(Mills), Wile, Robertson; Robson, A. Brown, T. Brown, Owen, Barnes. The Dutch international Ruud Krol captained Ajax.

CENTRAL and PONTIN'S LEAGUE (Reserves)

Albion's second team first entered the Central League in 1921-22 – ten years after the competition was introduced – and at the end of that initial season they finished 14th in the table with 42 points from their 42 games

The following season Albion were crowned champions after a superb run of 25 games without defeat from 22 November to 28 April. Their best win (of the 26 recorded) was 10-0 v Blackburn Rovers (h) in late December. Albion used 28 players during the campaign, the regulars being captain Fred Reed, goalkeeper George Ashmore, defenders Arthur Perry, Sammy Richardson, Harry Dutton and Ted Rooke and forwards Bobby Blood, Tommy Glidden, Charlie Wilson, Jonathan Blagden, Joe Carter and Arthur Fitton.

Albion retained the title in 1923-24, collecting 25 wins for a total of 62 points, one fewer than the previous year, pipping Huddersfield Town on goal-average after a terrific contest.

Albion's best wins this time were 6-1 v Birmingham and 6-4 over Bury (both at home) and among the regulars in the side were goalkeeper Hubert Pearson, defenders Billy Adams, Reed (again skipper), Perry, Harold Chamberlain, Richardson and Dutton, and forwards Carter, Ivor Jones, Wilson, Blood, George James and Fitton.

Harry Raw, a regular in the side which lifted the Central League title in 1932-33, the first of a hat-trick of such successes.

Albion's next title success came in 1926-27 when they ran up 27 wins and totalled 59 points. They clinched the championship with a last-match 3-0 win over Burnley. Their best victories were 7-4 over Derby County and six-goal drubbings of Burnley and Oldham, all at home. The Baggies also succumbed 7-0 at runners-up Manchester

Albion's Central League championship-winning team of 1922-23. Back row (left to right): J.Spencer, W.Lammus, E.Rooke, W.Guest (trainer), J.Carter, A.Perry, A.Fitton. Middle row: G.James, L.Nurse (director), W.Bassett (chairman), F.Everiss (secretary), G.Ashmore, D.Nurse (director), H.Keys (director), H.Chamberlain. Front row: J.Blagden, S.Richardson, T.Glidden, F.Reed, H.Dutton, R.Blood, C.Wilson.

United and lost 6-5 at home to Aston Villa, Manchester City were also 5-1 winners at the Hawthorns. Sammy Short top-scored in 1926-27 with 27 goals (out of 114) including a five-timer in that win over Bury.

Curiously their seniors were relegated from the First Division of the Football League.

Tom Sproson, Dicky Baugh, Bob Finch, Joe Evans, Francis Corbett, Jimmy Edwards, Len Darnell, Harry Dutton, Sammy Short, Sammy Richardson, George James, Horace Smith, Charlie Wilson, Ernie Fryer, Ernest Pattinson and Arthur Fitton all gained championship medals this season.

After a break of five seasons, Albion won their fourth Central League title in 1932-33 – this being the first leg of a hat-trick of successes – Albion also being the first club to achieve this feat.

Albion beat neighbours Aston Villa 1-0 at Villa Park on 30 April to clinch the championship – and victory also brought the Baggies the double over their arch rivals. Albion's best two wins (of 26 registered) were those of 7-1 over both Birmingham and Leeds United – and when Sheffield United Reserves visited The Hawthorns in early March, a record Central League crowd of 11,343 turned up.

The most frequent members of the side this season were Stan Horrocks, Ted Crowe, Bob Finch, Hugh Foulkes, Wally Boyes, 'Bos' Trevis, Walter Robbins, Arthur Gale, Harry Raw, Jimmy Cookson, Jack Sankey, Tommy Magee, Jack Rix and Alf Ridyard. Cookson top-scored with 29 goals (out of 106) and along with Magee was coming to the end of his Baggies' career.

Albion's second championship win of their treble came in 1933-34, when they totalled 28 wins, scored 101 goals and amassed 64 points. Most of the players who had formed the basis of the team the previous season were still in the second team this time round, along with newcomers Phil Griffiths (a Welsh international winger), Lol Coen, Harry 'Popeye' Jones, Tommy Green and Sid Swinden. Full-back Bob Finch skippered the side.

Albion beat both Sheffield United and Newcastle 8-0 at home with top marksman Arthur Gale scoring five against the Blades. He hit 39 all told. And there was a record crowd of 22,372 for the 2-2 home draw with Aston Villa reserves on 3 March – 6,000 more than the first team attracted for the home League game against Huddersfield the following week.

Albion's third successive Central League title was obtained in 1934-35 when Harry Raw was captain. Albion's success was mainly down to a terrific forward-line which rattled in 121 goals, Gale again leading the rush, this time with 41 (in only 22 appearances). He netted two five-timers – in an 8-1 win against his former club Bury and in the 7-1 success over Burnley. Fifteen players received championship medals: Foulkes, Raw, Crowe, Finch, Stan Wood, Norman Whitehead, Trevis, Lol Coen, Gale, Green, Rix, Ridyard, Jack Screen, Harry Jones and Robbins.

During their great treble-winning era Albion amassed a staggering 184 points out of a possible 252. They won 82 of their 126 matches, scored 328 goals for and conceded 168.

After those triumphs of the 1920s and 1930s, Albion's

Bob Finch with the Central League trophy in 1934.

reserve side then went almost 50 years before winning their next Central League title. This came in season 1982-83 when they clinched the championship with a 2-0 home win over Sheffield Wednesday in their final home game in front of 4,150 fans on 18 May. Among their best wins were those of 5-0 at Stoke and 5-2 at Bury while the full Wolves' first team were held to a 0-0 draw at Molineux.

Defenders Wayne Ebanks and John Smith, midfielders Gary Childs. Mickey Lewis and Mark Jones, utility player Noel Luke and skipper Barry Cowdrill all made over 20 appearances, while Kevin Kent top-scored with ten goals.

At the end of the 1985-86 season both Albion's senior side and reserve team suffered relegation from their respective First Divisions, the Reserves going down for the first

Arthur Fitton, appeared in a record 261 Central League games for West Bromwich Albion.

time despite fielding several experienced players including Garth Crooks, Tony Grealish, Ally Robertson and Imre Varadi.

Albion regained their First Division status in season 1987-88 by finishing fourth with 61 points from 34 games.

In 1990-91 Albion were Pontin's League Division Two champions with 76 points from 34 games, but relegation followed a season later with Albion second from bottom of Division One.

In 1992-93 Albion missed out on promotion on goal-difference, but a season later they were promoted as runners-up to Tranmere Rovers.

1995-96 was the Reserves' worst-ever season and relegation was inevitable after two-thirds of the campaign had gone.

Facts and Figures

First Central League match: v Manchester United (a) 27 August 1921 (lost 1-0).

Record victory: 12-2 v Derby County (h) 2 November 1929 Albion's top post-World War Two Central League victory is 9-0 v Stoke City (h) on 1 January 1949. They also weighed in with 8-0 scorelines over Manchester City (h) and Barnsley (a) in 1963-64 and Bury (h) in 1964-65; 8-1 victories came against Sheffield United (h) in 1959-60 and both Blackburn Rovers (h) and Chesterfield (h) in 1960-61 and in 1963-64 Blackburn Rovers were defeated 8-3 at Ewood Park.

Heaviest defeat: 10-2 v Huddersfield (a) 20 February 1932.

Albion's biggest post-World War Two defeat is 8-3 at Wolverhampton on 1 May 1963.

Record away win: 9-1 v Burnley, 22 March 1930.

Plaque presented by the Central League to mark Albion's hat-trick of championships.

Most goals in a match: 7 by Jimmy Cookson v Liverpool (h) won 10-1 on 14 November 1931.

Most goals (by player) in a season: 50 by 'W.G.' Richardson in 1929-30. Jimmy Cookson scored 43 in 1931-32.

Record Central League home attendance: 22,372 v Aston Villa, 3 March 1934.

Albion scored over 100 goals in a Central League season nine times, the best tally of 128 coming in 1929-30.

Arthur Gale scored a record 146 Central League goals for Albion; Sammy Short hit 103, Cookson 95 and George James 87.

Arthur Fitton appeared in a record 261 Central League games for Albion (1922-32); Bob Finch amassed 231, Hugh Foulkes 229, Graham Williams 228, Roger Minton 208 and Bobby Cram 206.

Albion utilised 59 players in their 40 Central League matches in 1945-46 – a club record.

Between 17 September 1932 and 11 September 1935, Albion reserves did not lose a single Central League game at The Hawthorns.

After being treated for an injury, Albion's goalkeeper Jimmy Sanders scored direct from a left-wing against Derby County reserves at The Hawthorns in December 1946.

Among the Albion players who have been sent-off in Central League/Pontin's League games are: goalkeeper Fred Brown v Wolves (a) in February 1956; Ernie Pattinson and Jimmy Poxton v Sheffield Wednesday (a) in October 1927; Paul Raven and Colin West in the same match at Rotherham; goalkeeper Mel Rees v Blackpool and Blackburn, Gary Strodder against Sheffield United and Steve Parkin v Bolton.

Albion's 1,000th victory in the Central League was over Preston North End (3-1) at Deepdale on 30 April 1979.

CHAIRMEN

Albion first appointed a chairman in 1885, six years before the club became a limited liability company.

The full list of chairmen who have been in office is:

1885-88	Henry Jackson
1888-90	Edward W.Heelis
1891	Henry Jackson
1891-95	George Salter
1895-99	T.Harris Spencer
1899-1903	Harry Keys
1903-05	A.J.M. 'Jem' Bayliss
1905-08	Harry Keys
1908-37	William I.Bassett
1937-47	L.J. 'Lou' Nurse
1947-63	Major H.Wilson Keys
1963-74	'Jim' W.Gaunt
1974-83	F.A. 'Bert' Millichip
1983-88	J. 'Sid' Lucas
1988-92	John G.Silk
1992-94	Trevor J.Summers
1994-	'Tony' B.Hale

Harry Keys was a blunt, outspoken man, who called a spade a spade and sometimes a sanguinary shovel. He was nicknamed 'John Bull' by the players and resigned as chairman after a disagreement with his fellow directors in 1903. He returned as chairman two years later and was immediately elected on to the Football League management committee, becoming its vice president in 1910, a position he held until his death in 1929. He was also an FA Councillor and member of the international selection committee. Two of his brothers were also closely associated with Albion, W. Hall Keys as a director and Clement Keys as secretary and auditor. Major H. Wilson Keys, son of Harry, joined the Albion board shortly after his father's death.

George Salter, educated at Malvern College, was a goalkeeper with West Bromwich FC (1881-82) and a West

George Salter, Albion chairman from 1891 to 1895.

Harry Keys, chairman 1899-1903 and 1905-08.

Major H.Wilson Keys, in the chair from 1947 to 1963.

'Jim' W.Gaunt, who succeeded to the chairmanship in 1963 and held the position for eleven years.

Bert Millichip, Albion chairman 1974-83 and also chairman of the Football Association.

Sid Lucas, Albion chairman 1983-88.

Bromwich Dartmouth cricketer, who was forced to retire from soccer through injury. An avid Albion supporter, he was, like so many Albion directors, a prominent freemason, and in 1891-92 and again in 1895-97 he was sworn in as Lord Mayor of West Bromwich. He was also Albion's first president in August 1882. 'Jem' Bayliss was the first former Albion player to join the board of directors. Bayliss was, in fact, the first former player to become chairman of the Club, having earlier served on the selection committee (from 1886). He resigned as chairman in 1905 when financial troubles within the club were coming to a head.

Louis Nurse was the brother of Dan Nurse, who played in Albion's 1901-02 Second Division championship winning side. Lou had been an Albion scout for many years before his election to the board in 1922. He became an FA Councillor in 1941.

H. Wilson Keys spent ten years as Albion's vice chairman before taking over as chairman in 1947. A very influential figure at The Hawthorns, like his father before him, he was also a leading light in FA circles, eventually becoming FA vice president in 1969. No-one has yet served on the Albion board of directors longer than the Major – 35 years: 1930-65.

Jim Gaunt, 11 years Albion's chairman, was elected president of the club on his retirement in 1974. He died in April 1989.

Sir 'Bert' Millichip, was a partner in Sharp and Millichip, High St, West Bromwich, for many years solicitors to the Albion club. He became a director at The Hawthorns in 1964, replacing W. H. Thursfield. and in 1969 was elected to the FA Council. A year later he was made Albion's vice chairman, moving up to chairman in 1974. He resigned in 1983 because of the pressures from his FA commitments. When he left the Albion board in 1984, he was elected club president and in 1991 was knighted for his services to football. Sir 'Bert' retired as chairman of the FA in the summer of 1996 shortly before his 82nd birthday.

Sid Lucas became an Albion director in 1975, moving into the vacancy caused by the untimely death of former player, Tommy Glidden. A local businessman, and one-time terrace supporter on the Birmingham Road End, he was chairman for five years (from 1983) and then stayed on as a director for another three years before being elected vice president in 1991. He died a year later.

John Silk was elected a director in August 1984. A local solicitor, also with business interests in West Bromwich and Brierley

John Silk, chairman 1988-92.

Hill, Mr Silk was born in West Bromwich. He has been an Albion shareholder since 1948.

Trevor Summers – Born and educated in West Bromwich. A former chairman of West Bromwich Dartmouth CC, he had interests in the timber business. Elected a director in August 1984, he became chairman in 1992.

Tony Hale was elected to the board in August 1988 to fulfil a lifetime ambition. Moseley-born, he built up a business concern involving car component spares and became Albion chairman in 1994. Thereafter was a major shareholder who was closely involved in the restructuring of the club's shares in 1995 and 1996.

CHAMBERS, Henry

Nicknamed 'Smiler', Harry Chambers, with his distinctive bow-legs, was a player of ice-cool temperament with a brilliant footballing brain. He played at inside-left for most of his career but during his spell with Albion he occupied

the centre-half berth. Born at Willington Quay, (now in Tyne and Wear), in 1896, he played his earlier football with Willington United Methodists and North Shields Athletic before signing for Liverpool in 1915. During the War he guested for Distillery and Glentoran and played in the Irish Cup Final of 1919 with the latter. After the hostilities he helped Liverpool twice win the League title and he went on to score 151 goals for the Merseysiders in 338 appearances – a fine record. Predominantly left-footed, Chambers top-scored for Liverpool in each of the first five post-war seasons and was capped eight times by England as well as representing the Football League on five occasions. He moved to Albion for £2,375 in March 1928 and left for Oakengates Town (as player-manager) in June 1929. He retired in 1948 after playing his last game at the age of 51 and he died in Shrewsbury a year later.

CHAMPIONSHIP OF THE WORLD

On 19 May 1888, Albion, the English FA Cup winners, met their counterparts from Scotland, Renton, in a match billed as the 'Championship of the World'. The game was played at Hampden Park in atrocious conditions, heavy rain making the pitch very soggy, and there was thunder and lightning as well.

Just 6,000 hardy souls braved the wet weather to see Renton win 4-1, Tom Pearson scoring for Albion, who fielded this team:

Roberts; Charlie Mason (guesting from Wolves), Harry Green; Ezra Horton, Charlie Perry, George Timmins; George Woodhall, Billy Bassett, 'Jem' Bayliss, Pearson and Joe Wilson.

CHARITY SHIELD (FA)

Albion have played in this annual fixture four times.

In May 1920, as League champions, they defeated the FA Cup holders Tottenham Hotspur 2-0 at White Hart Lane, Andy Smith scoring both goals before a 38,168 crowd.

In October 1931, as FA Cup winners, Albion succumbed to Arsenal, the League champions, 1-0 at Villa Park, England's Cliff Bastin scoring the winner four minutes from time in front of a crowd of 21,276.

In September 1954, again as

Andy Smith, scored both goals when Albion beat Spurs 2-0 in their first appearance in a Charity Shield game.

FA Cup winners, Albion shared the trophy after a thrilling 4-4 draw with neighbours and First Division champions Wolverhampton Wanderers at Molineux in front of a 45,035 crowd. Ronnie Allen scored a hat-trick for Albion that night

And, finally, in August 1968 when once again as FA Cup holders, the Baggies crashed 6-1 to League champions Manchester City at Maine Road when the attendance was 35,510.

CHARLTON ATHLETIC

Albion's record against Charlton Athletic:

Football League

Venue	P	W	D	L	F	A	Pts
Home	17	8	6	3	27	18	25
Away	17	5	4	8	27	34	14
Totals	34	13	10	11	54	52	39

FA Cup

Home	4	1	1	2	6	8	
Away	3	1	1	1	4	3	
Totals	7	2	2	3	10	11	

League Cup

Home	1	1	0	0	3	1

Others

Home	1	0	0	1	2	5
Away	2	0	1	1	1	6
Totals	3	0	1	2	3	11

The first League meeting took place at The Hawthorns on 7 December 1929 when a crowd of almost 11,000 witnessed a 1-1 draw in Division Two.

Albion's best win is 4-0 in a Second Division match at The Valley on 1 September 1930. The return fixture that season was a crucial one which was played on the very last day of the campaign. Albion had to win to gain a place in the First Division and at the same time also complete that unique FA Cup and promotion double. A crowd of 52,415 attended The Hawthorns on 2 May 1931 to cheer Albion on to a 3-2 victory, 'W.G.' Richardson hitting the winning goal in the 68th minute of a tension-packed game.

Charlton's best win over Albion is 5-1 – at The Valley in a First Division match on 11 February 1956.

Albion League debutants v Charlton: Lol Coen (1937), Ike Clarke (1937), George Lee (1949), Allan Crowshaw (1954), Alec Jackson (1954), Eric Perkins (1955), Kwame Ampadu (1991), Winston White (1991), Paul A.Williams (1991), Shaun Cunnington (1995), Dave Gilbert (1995).

Players with both clubs: Ray Crawford, Garth Crooks, Simeon Hodson, Tony Lange, Steve Mackenzie, Jimmy Sanders, Maurice Setters, Ray Treacy, Brian Whitehouse, Chris Whyte.

Associated with both clubs: Bobby Gould and Geoff Hurst

Ex-England international and football commentator Garth Crooks is one of ten players to have been with both Albion and Charlton.

(both coaches at Charlton and players with Albion), Peter Burridge, David Campbell and Brian Ord were reserves with Albion and first-teamers with Charlton and Ron Saunders was a 1960s centre-forward with Charlton and manager of Albion (1986-87).

CHELSEA

Albion's record v Chelsea:

Football League

Venue	P	W	D	L	F	A	Pts
Home	50	21	13	16	89	56	55
Away	50	14	14	22	72	98	42
Totals	100	35	27	38	161	154	97

FA Cup

Home	4	2	1	1	4	1
Away	6	1	2	3	9	10
Totals	10	3	3	4	13	11

League Cup

Home	1	0	1	0	1	1
Away	2	1	0	1	2	2
Totals	3	1	1	1	3	3

Full Members' Cup

Home*	1	0	1	0	2	2

*Albion lost 5-4 on penalties

Other Matches

Home	3	2	0	1	11	4
Away	1	0	0	1	4	7
Totals	4	2	0	2	15	11

Albion were the first team to play Chelsea at Stamford Bridge on a Saturday, losing 1-0 in Division Two on 23 September 1905.

Albion's best League win over Chelsea is 5-2 – achieved twice – at Stamford Bridge on 17 April 1929 (Division Two) and at home on 24 October 1953 (Division One) when Ronnie Allen scored a hat-trick.

Chelsea's best League win over Albion is 7-1 at home on 3 December 1960 (Division One) when Jimmy Greaves scored five. Chelsea also won 5-0 in London in the return fixture of 1953-54, a defeat which severely dented Albion's championship ambitions.

A crowd of 67,440 witnessed the 3-3 draw between Chelsea and Albion in the First Division in October 1954. Albion came back from 3-1 down with 15 minutes left, and levelled in the dying minutes through full-back Len Millard – his first League goal for six years. Earlier in the game, Roy Bentley scored his 100th goal for Chelsea.

In March 1969 Albion beat Chelsea 2-1 at Stamford Bridge to reach the FA Cup semi-finals for the second year running.

Tony Brown equalled Ronnie Allen's total of 208 League goals for Albion by scoring in a 3-1 win at Chelsea in September 1978.

Dave Walsh netted a hat-trick in Albion's 3-0 FA

W.G.Richardson scores the winning goal for Albion in their 3-2 success against Charlton in May 1931.

Jimmy Millar, trainer at both Stamford Bridge and The Hawthorns.

Cup win over Chelsea in a fifth-round tie in February 1949.

Albion and Chelsea met four times in the 1952-53 FA Cup competition, the Londoners finally going through 4-0 at Highbury after draws of 1-1 (at Stamford Bridge), 0-0 (at The Hawthorns) and 1-1 (at Villa Park). The tie lasted some 420 minutes.

Ronnie Allen scored 14 goals in all games v Chelsea.

Albion League debutants v Chelsea: Walter Robbins (1932), Sid Rawlings (1935), Andy McCall (1951), Graham Lovett (1964), Ray Wilson (1965), Johnny Giles (1975), Geoff Hurst (1975).

Jack Sankey (1934) and David Mountford (1953) both made their Albion debuts in FA Cup ties v Chelsea.

Players with both clubs: Alan Dickens, Tony Godden, Derek Kevan, Paddy Mulligan, Fred Richardson, Graham Roberts, Fred Rouse, Frank Sinclair, David Speedie, Kenny Swain, Mickey Thomas.

Albion's first team manager Jack Smith played for Chelsea before World War Two and was a guest for Albion during the hostilities; Geoff Hurst managed Chelsea (1979-81) and Don Howe (a player with Albion) was later coach with Chelsea. Gordon Dimbleby was secretary/commercial manager at Albion and Chief Executive at Chelsea; Bobby Robson played for Albion and was later scout at Chelsea; Jimmy Millar was a trainer at both clubs and Bob Ward, former Albion goalkeeper, became physiotherapist at Stamford Bridge (1988).

CHESTER (CITY)
Albion's record v Chester:
Football League

Venue	P	W	D	L	F	A	Pts
Home	2	1	1	0	3	1	4
Away	2	2	0	0	5	2	6
Totals	4	3	1	0	8	3	10

Other Match

Away	1	1	0	0	2	0

Albion doubled up over Chester in their promotion-winning season of 1992-93, winning 2-0 at home and 3-0 away.

The 'other' match was played in October 1939 when Harry Jones scored both goals in a 2-0 win at Sealand Road.

Players with both clubs: Arthur Albiston, Ian Benjamin, Tony Brien, Frank Cresswell, Ian Edwards, Arthur Gale, Gary Hackett, Jack Haines, Tony Kelly, Joe Kennedy, Neil Parsley,

Welsh international Ian Edwards, joined Chester from Albion for £20,000 in 1976.

Cyrille Regis, Fred Richardson, John Thomas, 'Bos' Trevis.

Welsh international Edwards was transferred from Albion to Chester for a record £20,000 in 1976.

Associated with both clubs: Bill Chambers, an Albion 1920s reserve and Chester forward (1936-38); goalkeepers Gary Leake and Barry Siddall both played for Albion's reserve side and in Chester's League team; John Turner was an Albion reserve, then Chester League player, and Charlie Hewitt was an Albion player (1908-10) and Chester manager (1930-36).

CHESTERFIELD
Albion's record v Chesterfield:
Football League

Venue	P	W	D	L	F	A	Pts
Home	10	7	2	1	23	8	16
Away	10	3	4	3	14	10	10
Totals	20	10	6	4	37	18	26

Other matches

Venue	P	W	D	L	F	A
Home	1	0	0	1	2	3
Away	1	0	1	0	3	3
Totals	2	0	1	1	5	6

Albion's best win over Chesterfield is 5-2 at The Hawthorns in a Second Division match on 24 November 1906.

Chesterfield's best win is 3-1 (h) on 18 February 1939 (Division Two).

Arthur Albiston, played for Albion and Chesterfield.

In a Wartime League Cup game in March 1943, 'W.G.' Richardson scored a hat-trick for Albion in a 3-3 draw at Chesterfield.

Albion League debutants v Chesterfield: Olly Taylor (1901), Billy Lee (1901), Edward Burton (1905), Tom Picken (1906), Billy Lunn (1947), Reg Ryan (1947), Alun Evans (1947), Danny Smith (1947), Cyril Williams (1948).

Played with both clubs: Arthur Albiston, Gerry Armstrong, George Ashmore, Tony Brien, Tommy Broad, Jimmy Cookson, Billy Lee, John Osborne, Ebenezer Owers, David Rushbury, Charlie Simmons, Danny Smith, Winston White.

Two former Albion players who served Chesterfield well in a managerial capacity were Harry Hadley (1920s) and Harry Parkes (secretary-manager: 1922-27). Bob Brocklebank was Chesterfield's manager (1945-49) and later an Albion scout.

Former Albion commercial manager Alan Stevenson was a Chesterfield goalkeeper between 1969 and 1972.

CHINA
In May 1978, Albion became the first British professional

The Chinese national team who faced Albion at The Hawthorns in 1979.

club to tour the People's Republic of China and Hong Kong, winning all five games.

Four of the victories came in China: 3-1 against a Peking XI, 2-0 over China, 2-0 versus Shanghai and 6-0 v Kwangtung Province. The other triumph (3-0) was achieved against a Hong Kong Select XI on the homeward journey.

Cyrille Regis scored in all five tour games (six goals in total).

In August 1979, China came over to England to play Albion at The Hawthorns in a return friendly match. A crowd of 11,382 saw Albion win 4-0 with Regis again figuring on the scoresheet.

CHRIST CHURCH SCHOOL

Many early day players of the Albion club were educated at Christ Church School, West Bromwich, which stood at the junction of New Street and Walsall Street. Among them were: Billy Bassett, Billy Bisseker, Fred Bunn, Harry Green, Tom Pearson, the Perry brothers (Tom, Charlie and Walter), Bob Roberts, Jimmy Stanton and George 'Darkie' Timmins. These 'lads' were encouraged to play soccer by the school's sports-minded headmaster, 'gaffer' Tom Phillips, himself a staunch football supporter – hence the strong association with Christ Church School and the Albion club.

There is record of an Albion v Christ Church match, played in West Bromwich on 1 May 1880; however, it is not clear whether this was the same school team.

CLARK, Clive

Dashing outside-left who could score goals as well as make them. Nicknamed 'Chippy', he joined Albion from Queens

Park Rangers in 1961 for £20,000 and became an instant success at The Hawthorns. In the next eight-and-half years he netted 98 goals in 353 League and Cup games for the Baggies, figuring in both the 1966 League Cup and 1968 FA Cup winning teams. He also played in the 1967 losing League Cup Final, scoring twice against his old club QPR. Born in Leeds in 1940, Clark had trials with Huddersfield before joining Leeds United as a professional in 1957, moving to QPR later that same year. Capped by England at Under-23 level whilst with Albion, he left The Hawthorns for his former club, QPR in 1969 and later played for Preston, Southport, Telford United, Washington Diplomats, Dallas Tornado and Philadelphia Fury (NASL) and Skegness Town, retiring in 1977.

CLARKE, Isaac

Fearless inside or centre-forward with boundless energy, solid frame and terrific goalscoring technique. Born in  Tipton in 1915, Clarke joined Albion from Toll End Wesley in 1937 and spent over ten years at The Hawthorns before transferring to Portsmouth for £5,000 in 1947. He netted 98 goals in 213 games for Albion (including a war record of 55 goals in 96 outings). He also guested for Nottingham Forest and Walsall during the hostilities. He helped Pompey twice win the First Division championship (1949 and 1950) and also represented the FA in five tour games against Australia in 1951. After retiring two years later, he managed Sittingbourne, Yeovil Town, Canterbury City, Ashford Town, finally quitting football in 1973. He now lives at Herne Bay, Kent.

COACHES

Albion's first officially appointed club coach (in 1910) was former left-back Albert Evans whose career was ended prematurely by a broken leg.

Since then several other former players have been coaches  at The Hawthorns, including Jesse Pennington (1922-23), Tommy Glidden (1936-39), Teddy Sandford and Jack Sankey (in wartime), 'W.G.' Richardson (1946-59, who also acted as assistant-trainer until his death), Harold Pearson (1948-52), Frank Hodgetts (1958-62), George Lee (1959-63), Graham Williams (1970-72), Brian Whitehouse (1971-75), Tony Brown (1984-86), John Trewick (1993-96) and Ronnie Allen (1990s).

Albert Evans, Albion's first officially appointed coach in 1910.

COLCHESTER UNITED
Albion's record v Colchester:
FA Cup

Venue	P	W	D	L	F	A
Home	1	1	0	0	4	0
Away	1	0	1	0	1	1
Totals	2	1	1	0	5	1

Watney Cup

Home*	1	0	1	0	4	4

*Colchester won 4-3 on penalties to win the trophy.

Other Matches

Away   2   0   0   2   0   4

Albion's 1967-68 FA Cup winning campaign began with a 'lucky' 1-1 draw at Colchester in the third round, Tony Brown netting with a late penalty after which United had a 'goal' disallowed 40 seconds from time.

Colchester were in Division Four when they beat Albion in the 1971 Watney Cup Final (See WATNEY CUP).

The 'other' matches were a friendly at Layer Road in 1973 (Albion lost 3-0) and a testimonial at the same venue in 1979.

Players with both clubs: Davey Burnside, Bobby Cram, Ray Crawford, Tony Godden, Robert Hopkins, Tony Kelly, Billy Light, Andrew Marriott, Graham Smith, Winston White.

Dick Graham, managed Colchester and was a trainer at West Brom.

Associated with both clubs: Albion reserves Dave Barnett, Phil Bloss and Brian Wood all played for Colchester; Dick Graham was Albion's trainer (1956-60) and Colchester manager (1968-72) and Jock Wallace, Albion's goalkeeper (1959-62) later managed Colchester.

COLLARD, Ian

Footballing inside-forward or wing-half who also played at left-back, Collard helped Albion win the 1968 FA Cup and

all told scored eight goals in 97 games for the Baggies between 1964 and 1969, when he left The Hawthorns in exchange for the Ipswich Town player, Danny Hegan, plus £55,000. Born in County Durham in 1947, Collard also played in the 1967 League Cup Final and served with Portsmouth (on loan from Ipswich) before retiring to coach in Kuwait (1978-79).

COLOURS

During their near 120 years' existence Albion have experienced quite a number of colour variations and shirt changes as the following indicates:

1878-80 white jerseys; 1880-81 cardinal red and blue quarters and also maroon jerseys; 1881-82 yellow and white quarters, also chocolate and blue halves; 1882-83 chocolate and blue halves, also red and white hoops; 1883-84 chocolate and white jerseys; 1884-85 cardinal red and blue halves; 1885-89 blue and white stripes; 1889 scarlet and blue broad stripes; 1889-1919 blue and white stripes; 1919-41 navy blue and white stripes; 1941-47 royal blue shirts; 1947-61 navy blue and white stripes; 1961-72 navy blue and white stripes with white sleeves; 1972-83 navy blue and white broad stripes; 1983-96 variation of navy blue and white stripes, thin, broad, pin-striped.

Albion first adopted their now traditional blue and white stripes at a committee meeting on 15 September 1885 and the navy blue stripes were officially introduced for the first full season after World War One (1919-20).

Albion reverted back to wearing their normal blue and white shirts after World War Two for the home FA Cup-tie against Leeds United on 11 January 1947.

In the late 1940s the *Albion News* continually advertised for supporters to donate clothing coupons so that they could purchase material to manufacture new sets of blue and white striped shirts.

Since 1885 Albion players have sported white shorts but during the 1970s and eighties they did often wore navy blue shorts as a change to the set pattern.

As for the socks (stockings) Albion started off wearing plain navy blue, then came the traditional navy blue and white hoops (in various designs) which were followed by plain white and occasionally all navy blue.

Change Colours

The 'change' colours of the Albion club (from their early days through to the mid-1950s) were normally white shirts (jerseys) and black (or navy blue) shorts. But in the 1935 FA Cup Final v Sheffield Wednesday they wore royal blue shirts and white shorts.

Towards the end of the 1950s Albion's change strip was all-red and they wore this in that disastrous 1967 League Cup Final defeat by QPR. The following season Albion switched to wearing all-white. Into the 1970s, occasionally they donned the 'Brazilian' strip of yellow shirts and light blue shorts; then (under Johnny Giles' management) it was yellow and green stripes and green shorts, followed in 1991-92 and 19922-93 by red and yellow striped shirts and red or yellow shorts, and into the mid-1990s it was a case of wearing light blue and yellow shirts, with blue or yellow shorts.

From time to time throughout the last 25 years or so, Albion have worn an odd kit, once taking Queens Park Rangers' black and red hooped jerseys with them for a game at Plymouth.

COOKSON, James

Jimmy Cookson was a magnificent marksman – a real poaching centre-forward who netted 110 goals in 131 games for Albion between 1927 and 1933. Manchester-born, he had been a prolific scorer with Clayton FC, Manchester North End and Manchester City before joining Chesterfield for whom he struck 85 League goals in three years. Three months after joining Albion he hit a double hat-trick in a 6-2 home win over Blackpool in a Second Division match and four years later helped the Baggies win promotion to the First Division. After Albion, he scored well for Plymouth Argyle and Swindon before retiring in 1938 to become a publican, turning out in charity matches until 1952. In 15 years as a professional, Cookson hit 255 League goals. He was leading scorer in Division Three North in 1925-26 and Division Two in 1927-28,

and his 100th League goal came up in his only his 89th match – a record for the quickest-ever century of goals. He died in 1970, aged 66.

COOPER'S HILL

West Bromwich Strollers (later Albion) had their earliest kickabouts on open land at Cooper's Hill between Walsall Street and Beeches Road which is now the site of St Phillip's Church. Initially players' coats and hats were used as 'goal-posts' but later four wooden uprights were assembled with a piece of string tied across each pair to form the crossbar. A local cricket team also played here, so to preserve the grass, the Strollers occasionally used a pitch in Dartmouth Park, taking the goal-posts with them.

CORNER-KICKS

The corner-kick was introduced in 1872 and for some 20 years all such kicks were usually taken by the wing-halves, with Ezra Horton excelling for Albion in the 1880s. Thereafter the respective right and left wingers took over.

Goalkeeper Jim Sanders, scored direct from a corner against Derby County reserves in 1946.

For 52 years, a goal could not be scored direct from a corner-kick but when the law was changed (in 1924) players all over the country became adept at swinging the ball into the goal and sometimes straight into the net. Tommy Glidden was the first Albion player to perfect the corner-kick, usually moving over from the right-wing to the opposite flank to get a good curve on the ball.

Goalkeeper Jimmy Sanders scored direct from a corner-kick when playing for Albion's reserves versus Derby County in a Central League game at The Hawthorns on 7 December 1946.

He had been injured and after treatment ran along the touchline to take a left-wing corner. The ball ended up in the net and Albion went on to win the match 4-3.

Four of Albion's League goals in season 1925-26 were obtained direct from corner-kicks, with inside-left Charlie 'Tug' Wilson scoring two.

CORONATION CUP

To celebrate HRH Queen Elizabeth II's ascendancy to the throne, on 4 May 1953 Albion met rivals Wolverhampton Wanderers at The Hawthorns in a game billed 'The Coronation Cup' and a crowd of 5,802 saw the visitors win 3-1, George Lee scoring for Albion.

COVENTRY CHARITY CUP

Albion have competed for this trophy once – on 28 April 1930 – when they beat Coventry City 2-1 at Highfield Road with goals from Jimmy Edwards and Jimmy Cookson. The attendance was 8,000. This was the first-ever meeting between Albion and City.

COVENTRY CITY

Albion's record against Coventry is:

Football League

Venue	P	W	D	L	F	A	Pts
Home	20	10	7	3	41	18	29
Away	20	7	4	9	25	30	21
Totals	40	17	11	12	66	48	50

FA Cup

Home	4	2	0	2	8	4	
Away	3	1	2	0	6	5	
Totals	7	3	2	2	14	9	

League Cup

Home	3	3	0	0	12	5	
Away	2	0	2	0	1	1	
Totals	5	3	2	0	13	6	

Other matches

Home	14	9	3	2	39	20	
Away	14	4	4	6	21	33	
Totals	28	13	7	8	60	53	

Albion's biggest win over Coventry City (League or Cup) is 7-1 in a home First Division match on 21 October 1978 when the visitors wore a chocolate-coloured strip. Len Cantello scored a great goal in this game and both Laurie Cunningham and Cyrille Regis netted twice.

Coventry's best win over Albion is 4-2 – achieved twice, both at Highfield Road in First Division matches, on 23 September 1967 and 27 August 1968.

A then record crowd at Highfield Road of 44,492 saw Albion beat Coventry City 3-2 in a fifth-round FA Cup-tie on 20 February 1937.

Jeff Astle scored a hat-trick in Albion's emphatic 6-1 fourth-round League Cup replay win over Coventry at The Hawthorns on 10 November 1965.

Albion hit 16 goals against Coventry in 1978-79, ten in two First Division matches and six in two FA Cup games.

In a 3-1 League win at Highfield Road in 1979, Albion's most expensive signing at that time, David Mills, scored his first goal for the club.

In a Wartime Regional League game on 29 October 1939, Coventry humbled Albion 6-3, and on Christmas Day 1943, centre-

A young David Burrows, started his career with Albion and is presently with Coventry City.

forward Tommy Crawley scored five times in City's 8-0 thumping of Albion in a Wartime League Cup game.

Albion League debutants v Coventry: Arthur Rowley

(1947), Gordon Nisbet (1969), Mickey Lewis (1981), Mickey Thomas (1985).

Players with both clubs: Sam Allardyce, Gilbert Alsop, Gary Bannister, Peter Barnes, Eli Bradley, Albert Brown, David Burrows, George Bytheway, Laurie Coen, Francis Corbett, Jack Crisp, David Cross, Julian Darby, Paul Dyson, Paul Edwards, Arthur Fitton, Bobby Gould, Tommy Green, George Harris, Steve Hunt, Maarten Jol, Jack Kifford, Sammy Legge, Albert Lewis, Fred Morris, Billy Newall, Bobby Newsome, Harry Parkes, Cyrille Regis, Reg Ryan, Ronnie Rees, Jimmy Sanders, Maurice Setters, Oliver Taylor, Martin Singleton, Billy Smith, David Smith, David Speedie, Garry Thompson, Chris Whyte, Paul A.Williams, Paul R.Williams, Charlie Wilson.

Associated with both clubs: Sid Bowser, Howard Gregory, Jesse Pennington and Frank Waterhouse all guested for Coventry (from Albion) during World War One; Jonathan Gould, Jim Holton, Eric Perry, Frank White and Jimmy Whitehouse were Albion reserves who later played for Coventry; Welsh international Don Nardiello was on Coventry's books (1974-80) and had a brief spell with Albion (1981-82); Former Albion full-back Albert Evans managed Coventry City from 1902 to 1924; Bobby Gould was a manager of both clubs as well as a player; Ron Atkinson also managed both clubs; Jesse Carver was manager-coach at Albion (1952) and later assistant manager at Coventry; Bill Asprey was coach at both clubs; Garry Pendrey, a player with Albion, became a coach at Coventry in 1995; Stewart Bowen and Jim Cumbes played for Albion and were later connected with Coventry; Mick Brown was assistant manager at both clubs; Dennis Mortimer was a Coventry player and coach at Albion; Ron Wylie managed Albion and coached at Coventry; Danny Thomas was a player with Coventry and later became Albion's physiotherapist (1990s) and Mike McGinnity has been a director at both clubs.

COWDRILL, Barry

Born in Birmingham in 1957, Cowdrill was signed as a outside-left from Sutton Coldfield Town in 1979, and was successfully converted into a competent left-back by Albion. He went on to appear in 149 first-team games for the club (scoring one goal v Grimsby Town in an FA Cup-tie) before transferring to Bolton Wanderers in 1988 after a loan spell with Rotherham United. He later played for Rochdale and returned to Sutton in 1994.

CRAM, Robert

Hard-tackling defender and Albion's penalty-expert, Bobby Cram became the second full-back to score a hat-trick in a First Division League game, doing so for Albion against Stoke City in 1964. Stan Lynn of Aston Villa had earlier netted three goals v Sunderland in 1958. Born in Hetton-le-Hole, Co. Durham in 1939, Cram joined Albion as a youngster in 1955 and remained at The Hawthorns until 1967 when he transferred to Bromsgrove Rovers. Later he played for Vancouver Royals, Vancouver All Stars, Colchester United, Royal Canada FC and Bath City, returning to Canada in 1974 to run a coaching school. He

Bobby Cram, only the second full-back ever to score a hat-trick of penalties in the top flight.

Paul Dyson, played for Albion and Crewe Alexandra.

scored 26 goals in 163 games for Albion, making his last appearance in the 1967 League Cup Final.

CREWE ALEXANDRA

Albion's record against Crewe:

FA Cup

Venue	P	W	D	L	F	A
Away	1	0	0	1	3	4

Other Matches

Away	3	3	0	0	9	2

Albion's first-ever game against the Alex was a friendly at Gresty Road on 2 August 1976, which they won 6-2 before a crowd of 1,089. Ally Brown scored twice.

The first competitive match was a third- round FA Cup-tie, also at Crewe, on 6 January 1996, which the 'Alex' won 4-3 in front of an all-ticket crowd of 5,750.

Players with both clubs: Paul Dyson, Graham Easter, Paul Edwards, Stewart Evans, George Garratt, Freddie Haycock, Tom Haywood, Fred Hobson, Eric Jones, Tony Lange, Michael Lee, David Mountford, Stuart Naylor, Sammy Peters, Hughie Reed, Mel Rees, Arthur Smith, Danny Smith, Kenny Swain.

Kenny Swain was also assistant manager at Crewe; Geoff Hudson played for Crewe (1962-63) and later coached at Albion (1970-72), and three Albion reserves Ron Floyd, Dick Jones and Ray Russell all played for 'Alex'; former Albion chief scout Norman Bodell played for Crewe (1963-66).

CRICKETING FOOTBALLERS

Over the years Albion have had several footballers who were also quality cricketers, some of them playing at county and even Test Match levels.

Here is a list of cricketer footballers, with the county cricket club he played for alongside their name. The asterisk (*) indicates that he played League football with Albion:

Harold G. Bache*	(Worcestershire)
Jimmy Burns*	(Essex)
Bob Clarke	(Northamptonshire)
James Cumbes*	(Surrey, Lancashire, Worcestershire, Warwickshire)
Tom Dollery	(Warwickshire)
Jack Flavell	(Worcestershire)
Brian Gomm	(Somerset)
George Hickman	(Warwickshire)
Geoff Hurst*	(Essex)
Don Kenyon	(Worcestershire)
Albert Lewis*	(Somerset)

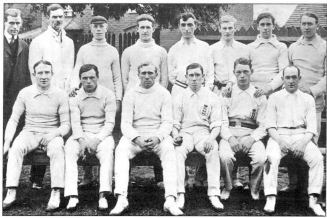

Albion's cricket team which met Aston Villa in 1914. Back row (left to right): R.Pailor, J.Reader, C.Jephcott, B.Millward, F.Everiss, T.Fletcher, M.Wood, H.Pearson. Front row: J.Manners, J.Smith, J.Pennington, R.McNeal, F.Morris, A.Lloyd.

John Major	(Warwickshire)
Jack Shilton	(Warwickshire)
Cyril Washbrook	(Lancashire)
Fred Wheldon*	(Worcestershire)

Dollery (4 Tests), Flavell (4 Tests), Kenyon (8 Tests) and Washbrook (37 Tests) all represented England at international cricket, while Hurst (49 caps) and Wheldon (4 caps) played football for England, the former scoring a hat-trick in the 1966 World Cup Final win over West Germany.

Andy Goram was an Albion reserve goalkeeper who went on to represent Scotland at both international football and cricket.

Two other former Albion goalkeepers who later became associated with county cricket clubs were John Osborne, who was appointed commercial manager of Worcestershire in 1985 and Jim Cumbes, who was commercial manager of Warwickshire (1984-88) before moving in the same capacity to Lancashire CCC.

Albion reserve goalkeeper Andy Goram went on to represent Scotland at both cricket and football.

West Bromwich Dartmouth Cricket Club

Situated only 400 yards from The Hawthorns, on the main A41 Birmingham Road near the M5 motorway, West Bromwich Dartmouth Cricket Club has been associated with Albion for well over 100 years. The Dartmouth club, founded in 1834, played on the Four Acres for many years and it was here that Albion also played their football for three seasons in the early 1880s with Dartmouth as their landlords. (See THE FOUR ACRES).

The Dartmouth club had a football section at this time, but Albion's meteoric rise to fame eventually put the footballers out of business.

The Cricket Club flourished, however, and down the years a number of Albion players and officials have been associated with the club, among them Ronnie Allen, George Baddeley, Harold Bache, Ray Barlow, Billy Bassett, Billy Brookes, Sid Corfield, Fred Everiss, Arthur Fitton (wicketkeeper), Jim Gaunt, Walter Hackett, Frank Heaven, 'Swin' Jackson, Clive James, Graham Lovett, Tony Matthews, 'Bert' Millichip, Jesse Pennington, Eric Perry, Bobby Robson, George Salter, Ephraim Smith, Gerry Summers, Trevor Summers, Horace Thursfield and Ray Wilson.

'Bert' Millichip skippered West Bromwich Dartmouth to the Birmingham League championship.

Other Albion footballers who also played minor cricket include Gary Hackett (for Belbroughton CC), Peter Latchford, Bobby McNeal, Jack Mahon, Bob Pailor, Hubert Pearson, David Shaw and Nigel Spink, and former Albion commercial manager/secretary Gordon Dimbleby and secretary Tony Rance also performed well in village cricket.

CRISP, John

Birmingham-born winger Jack Crisp was a key figure in Albion's attack during their 1919-20 League championship-winning side, appearing in 38 games and scoring eight goals while making at least another dozen. A spirited forward, with good pace and strong shot, he played for Walsall, Aston Villa (trial), Leicester Fosse and Ordnance FC before joining Albion in 1914, and after leaving The Hawthorns (in 1923) he served with Blackburn Rovers, Coventry City, Bromsgrove Rovers, Birmingham and Cheltenham Town, retiring in 1935. He died four years later, aged 44.

CROSS, David George

A fine goalscorer on his day, David Cross had two spells with Albion – 1976-77 and 1984-85 – both under Johnny

Giles' management, netting 23 goals in 62 appearances. Born in Heywood, Lancashire in 1950, Cross played for Rochdale, Norwich and Coventry City before 1976; for West Ham, Manchester City, Vancouver Whitecaps (two stints) and Oldham Athletic between his years with Albion; and for Bolton and Bury after leaving The Hawthorns second time round. He hit over 200 goals in more than 600 League and Cup games as a professional.

Nicky Cross, 40 of his 119 senior games for Albion were as a substitute.

CROSS, Nicholas Jeremy Rowland

Utility forward Nicky Cross scored 19 goals in 119 competitive games during his eight years with Albion (1977-85). Forty of his outings were as 'sub' and he donned six different numbered shirts whilst on first-team duty for the Baggies. Born in Birmingham in 1961 he made his debut for

the club at Old Trafford and left The Hawthorns for Walsall, later playing for Leicester City, Port Vale and Hereford United.

CROWD DISTURBANCES

Albion, 2-0 down with 15 minutes left, bounced back to defeat Nottingham Forest 3-2 in a First Division League game at Trent Bridge on 30 September 1893. At the final whistle, about 100 irate Forest supporters broke through the barriers and headed towards the referee who had to be protected by Albion players. It was noted that no Forest player came to the aid of the official, who had added several minutes on to normal playing time following an injury to Albion's full-back Bob Crone.

On 16 May 1970, the Anglo-Italian Cup-tie between Lanerossi Vicenza and Albion in Italy was abandoned in the 75th minute by English referee Kevin Howley after a tackle by Asa Hartford on Vicenza's Petri had sparked off a free-for-all involving several players from both sides. Four Italian players chased Hartford to the touchline and when other Albion players came to their colleague's rescue, fighting broke out. Armed police moved in as the hostile crowd hurled bottles and stones on to the pitch. The official had no alternative but to abandon the contest with the scores level at 1-1. As a result, both sides had a point deducted from their final totals.

In the 69th minute of a vital First Division match between Albion and Leeds United at Elland Road on 17 April 1971, Jeff Astle stunned the home side by putting Albion 2-0 ahead with a tap-in goal that looked suspiciously offside following Tony Brown's break from the halfway line. Initially Leeds' players appealed to Boston referee Ray Tinkler that Colin Suggett was offside when Brown first collected the ball, but he waved play on, indicating that Suggett was not interfering with play. The goal was allowed

Crowd disturbance at Elland Road in 1971 after Boston referee Ray Tinkler had allowed Jeff Astle's goal.

to stand and immediately scores of angry Leeds fans forced their way on to the pitch. Fighting broke out and the Police moved in. Thankfully, everything was sorted out after ten minutes and Albion went on to win the game 2-1 – their first away victory for almost 18 months – and at the same time ruined Leeds' chances of winning the championship.

Two months later, on 10 June 1971, The Football Association announced that Elland Road would be closed for four matches from 18 August to 4 September 1971 as a result of what had happened during that Leeds-Albion game.

During the pre-match build-up to the Red Star v Albion UEFA Cup match in the giant Maracana Stadium in Belgrade on 7 March 1979, rival fans from the two local teams in the Yugoslavian capital – Red Star and Partizan – battled with each other on the open terraces and, sadly, a Partizan youth was killed after being beaten about the head and body with sticks and other weapons. During the game, a firework was tossed into the packed crowd of over 95,000 which exploded in the face of a home supporter. He also died from his injuries. Albion lost the match 1-0.

Other games involving Albion when crowd disturbances have marred the proceedings:

Albion v Bolton Wanderers, original Football League, 5 November 1888 (players and spectators fighting).

Albion v Small Heath, FA Cup semi-final, 6 March 1888 (rival fans fighting)

RFC Brugge v Albion, European Cup Winners Cup, 18 September 1968 (players, officials, and spectators seen to scuffle).

Albion v Liverpool, Division One, 27 September, 1969 (referee attacked at end of game after adding eight minutes on to the normal playing time during which Liverpool equalised at 2-2).

Visiting supporters caused disturbances inside (and outside) The Hawthorns during Albion's second- round second- leg League Cup game with Millwall on 25 October 1983. Albion lost the first leg 3-0, but came back to win the return leg 5-1.

Leeds United supporters caused thousands of pounds worth of damage as they knocked down the perimeter wall at the Smethwick End of The Hawthorns during a vital relegation match on 18 May 1982. Albion won the game 2-0 and Leeds were relegated to the Second Division.

CRYSTAL PALACE

Albion's record against Palace:

Football League

Venue	P	W	D	L	F	A	Pts
Home	12	6	2	4	19	19	16
Away	12	4	2	6	12	15	10
Totals	24	10	4	10	31	34	26

League Cup

	P	W	D	L	F	A
Away	1	1	0	0	3	1

Full Members' Cup

	P	W	D	L	F	A
Home	1	1	0	0	2	1

Other Match

	P	W	D	L	F	A
Away	1	1	0	0	2	1

Albion first met Palace in a friendly match at Selhurst Park on 25 January 1930, winning 2-1.

Albion's best League win over Palace is 3-1 (away) on 20 September 1969, while Palace's best over Albion is 4-0 at The Hawthorns on 10 February 1973. At the end of the season both Albion and Palace were relegated to the Second Division.

Jeff Astle scored a hat-trick in Albion's 3-2 win over Palace in the First Division at The Hawthorns on 10 January 1970.

When Palace beat Albion 3-2 in Division One game at The Hawthorns on 23 December 1995, their full-back Dean Gordon scored a hat-trick. This is believed to be the only instance of a visiting defender scoring three times in a

match at The Hawthorns.

Albion League debutants v Palace: Ally Brown (1972), Remi Moses (1980).

Mickey Lewis played his first game for Albion in the League Cup-tie at Palace on 15 December 1981 at the age of 16 years 303 days.

Mickey Lewis, made his debut against Palace when he was still only 16.

Players with both clubs: Ronnie Allen, Jack Bannister, Paul Barron, Jeroen Boere, Ally Brown, Davey Burnside, Bill Davies, George Garratt, Adam Haywood, Charlie Hewitt, Roy Horobin, Derek Kevan, Tommy Magee, Tony Millington, Paddy Mulligan, Ray Potter, Dick Roberts, Keith Smith, Arthur Swift, Garry Thompson, Brian Whitehouse, Chris Whyte.

Other players associated with both clubs: Billy Birch, Peter Burridge, George Handley, Jack Lewis, Steve Mackenzie, Pat Mulcahy, Darren Patterson, Alec Ross, Jack Thomas, Geoff Turton, Brian Wood.

Also associated with both clubs: Charlie Hewitt played for Albion (1908-10) and managed Palace (1910-14); Tommy Magee was also coach at Palace (1930s); Dick Graham was Palace manager (1963-66) having earlier been Albion's trainer; Arthur Rowe managed Palace (1960-63) and later scouted for Albion; George Irwin was an Albion reserve goalkeeper before serving Palace as player, trainer, coach and manager (1939-47); Mike Kelly held coaching positions at Palace and Albion in the 1980s.

CUMBES, James

Tall, commanding goalkeeper and good shop-stopper, who played 79 times for Albion during a two-year stay at The

Hawthorns (1969-71). Signed from Tranmere Rovers by manager Alan Ashman for £33,350, Cumbes was a friend of another Albion 'keeper, John Osborne, and between them they worked on local radio and went into the sports trade business as partners. Both players later became commercial managers of County cricket clubs, Cumbes with Warwickshire and Lancashire, Osborne with Worcestershire. After leaving Albion, Cumbes played for Aston Villa, Portland Timbers, Coventry City, Runcorn (an earlier club), Southport, Worcester City and Kidderminster Harriers, winning a League Cup winners tankard with Villa in 1975. He played in more than 400 League and Cup games and also achieved much as a fast bowler on the cricket square with Surrey, Warwickshire, Worcestershire and Lancashire.

CUNNINGHAM, Laurence Peter

Laurie Cunningham was tragically killed in a road accident on the outskirts of Madrid during the early hours of 8 July 1989 at the age of 33. He was a brilliant footballer with pace, loads of skill, shooting power and charisma. Known as the 'Black Pearl' and 'Black Beauty' he joined Albion from Leyton Orient in 1977 for £110,000 and stayed two years at The Hawthorns, scoring 30 goals in 114 games, helping Albion reach the FA Cup semi-final and the UEFA Cup quarter-finals in successive seasons. He became the first

coloured footballer to don an England jersey in a major international, lining up for the Under-21 side against Scotland at Bramall Lane soon after joining Albion. He added another five Under-21 and six senior caps to his collection, as well as playing for his country at 'B' team level. Born in Archway, London in 1956, Cunningham left Albion for Real Madrid in a record £995,000 deal, helping them win the Spanish League and Cup double in his first season there (1979-80). He later played for Olympique Marseille, Manchester United, Sporting Gijon, Leicester City, RSC Charleroi (Belgium), Wimbledon, with whom he gained an FA Cup winners medal in 1988, Real Betis and Rayo Vallecano (two spells). He was associated with the latter Spanish club when he sadly lost his life.

DARLINGTON

Albion's record against Darlington:

Football League

Venue	P	W	D	L	F	A
Home	1	1	0	0	3	1
Away	1	1	0	0	1	0
Totals	2	2	0	0	3	1

FA Cup

Venue	P	W	D	L	F	A
Home	1	1	0	0	3	2

The two League games were played in season 1991-92, with Don Goodman scoring at The Feethams and on-loan Frank Sinclair netting his only goal for Albion in the return fixture at The Hawthorns.

The FA Cup-tie at The Hawthorns on 30 January 1937, was a fourth-round encounter and 'W.G.' Richardson was Albion's hero with a hat-trick before a 15,917 crowd in wintry conditions.

Albion League debutant v Darlington: Gary Piggott (1991)

Players with both clubs: Ian Banks, Gary Bannister, David Cork, Paul Dyson, Hugh Foulkes, Tom Hutchinson, David Mills, Ebenezer Owers, Keith Smith, David Speedie.

Harry Ashley, an Albion reserve and wartime player, was with Darlington in the 1930s; Billy Jordan, ex-Albion centre-forward, became a director of Darlington in 1936; Albion's reserve goalkeeper of the 1920s, George Irwin, was Darlington's manager from 1950 to 1952.

DARTMOUTH PARK

During the three years before Albion moved to their first enclosed ground (Bunn's Field) in 1881, they utilised both

Left: **David Cork, played for Albion and Darlington.** *Far left:* **Laurie Cunningham, known as the 'Black Pearl'.**

Cooper's Hill and Dartmouth Park (See BLACK LAKE VICTORIA) playing in Dartmouth Park regularly in season 1880-81 under skipper Jimmy Stanton. The pitch used was near to the main entrance to the park (at the end of New Street) although occasionally (owing to bad weather) they occupied a 'stretch of grass' at the Herbert Street end, changing in the nearby Globe Inn in Reform Street.

Even after Albion moved to Bunn's Field, and then to The Four Acres, the occasional pre-season friendly was staged at Dartmouth Park, usually against Wednesbury Old Athletic to officially open the annual West Bromwich Flower Show. In September 1979, a crowd of 10,000 saw a mixed team of current and former Albion players take on and beat a Celebrity Press XI at Dartmouth Park to celebrate the club's centenary.

DARWEN
Albion's record against Darwen:
Football League

Venue	P	W	D	L	F	A	Pts
Home	2	1	1	0	14	2	3
Away	2	0	1	1	2	3	1
Totals	4	1	2	1	16	5	4

Other Match

Home	1	1	0	0	4	0

Albion set a First Division scoring record (later equalled in 1909 by Leicester Fosse) by beating Darwen 12-0 at home on 4 April 1892. Unfortunately only 1,109 loyal fans turned up to see the goal-feast which included a four-timer from Tom Pearson and a hat-trick for Billy Bassett.

Darwen spent only six years in the Football League (1893-99).

DAVIES, Stanley Charles
Versatile footballer who occupied six different positions for Wales, winning a total of 19 caps and skippering his country.

Big and strong Stan Davies was born in Chirk in 1898 and played for Rochdale, Preston and Everton before joining Albion as a centre-forward in 1921 for £3,300. He scored 83 goals in 159 games during a six-year stay at The Hawthorns, transferring to Birmingham for £1,500 in 1927. Afterwards he was associated with Cardiff City, Rotherham (player-manager), Barnsley, Manchester Central, Dudley Town and Chelmsford City (trainer), retiring to become a publican in West Bromwich in 1938. He died in Birmingham in 1972, aged 71.

DEBUTS
(For youngest and oldest see AGE; for scoring debuts see GOALS)

Gordon Nisbet's first game for Albion was in goal (1969). Two years later he was converted into a right-back and won England Under-23 honours.

Amos Adams was introduced to League football by Albion as a centre-forward in 1899. Within a year he was a star full-back.

A total of 23 players made their Football League debuts for Albion in season 1946-47 – eight of them in the opening game v Swansea Town on 31 August at Vetch Field: Jimmy Sanders, Jim Pemberton, Harry Kinsell, George Tranter, Len Millard, Dave Walsh, Jimmy Duggan and Frank Hodgetts. Two other goalkeepers (with Sanders) made their League bows this term – John Tighe and Tom Grimley.

Twenty players made their Football League debuts for Albion in the first-ever League season of 1888-89 and 19 made the breakthrough in 1904-05. Albion's team of debutants for their

Jimmy Duggan, one of eight Albion debutants in the first League game after World War Two.

first-ever Football League game v Stoke (away) on 8 September 1888 was: Bob Roberts; Jack Horton, Harry Green; Ezra Horton, Charlie Perry, George Timmins; Billy Bassett, George Woodhall, Bill Hendry, Tom Pearson, Joe Wilson.

The players who made their FA Cup debuts for Albion v Wednesbury Town (home) on 10 November 1883, were: Bob Roberts; Harry Bell, Jim Stanton; Ezra Horton, Fred Bunn, Jack Swallow; Jack Whitehouse, Harry Aston, Billy Bisseker, George Timmins, George Bell.

Albion's first League Cup-tie was against Walsall (home) on 22 September 1965 and these players made their debuts for the club in this competition: Ray Potter; Bobby Cram, Ray Fairfax; Graham Lovett, Stan Jones, Doug Fraser; Tony Brown, Jeff Astle, John Kaye, Bobby Hope, Clive Clark.

Albion's 'debut' in European football was in the Fairs Cup v DOS Utrecht (in Holland) on 2 November 1966 when this team earned a 1-1 draw: Ray Potter; Campbell Crawford, Ian Collard; Graham Lovett, Stan Jones, Doug Fraser; Graham Williams, Jeff Astle, John Kaye, Bobby Hope, Clive Clark.

Jesse Pennington made his League debut for Albion at Liverpool on 26 September 1903. His last League game – 19 years later – was also against Liverpool (home) on 6 May 1922.

Cyrille Regis set a club record by scoring on his League,

Cyrille Regis, enjoyed the distinction of scoring for Albion on each of his debuts in five different competitions.

League Cup, FA Cup, Tennent-Caledonian Cup and Central League debuts for Albion in 1977-78.

Goalkeepers George Ashmore (v Blackburn Rovers in October 1920) and Bill Harris (v Everton in April 1938) both conceded five goals on their League debuts for Albion.

Goalkeeper Billy Walker (Wolves) broke his leg while making his League debut against Albion in December 1929 and never played again at senior level.

Derek Statham is the only full-back to score on his League debut for Albion v Stoke City, away, December 1976.

Ronnie Rees made his debut for Albion against Everton in a home First Division game in March 1968 and was on the losing side: 2-6.

Andy Hunt scored a hat-trick on his home League debut for Albion v Brighton in April 1993.

DERBY COUNTY

Albion's record against Derby County:

Football League

Venue	P	W	D	L	F	A	Pts
Home	47	25	13	9	82	48	65
Away	47	6	13	28	58	110	25
Totals	94	31	26	37	140	158	90

FA Cup

Home	3	1	0	2	3	4	
Away	5	1	1	3	5	8	
Totals	8	2	1	5	8	12	

League Cup

Home	1	0	0	1	0	1	
Away	2	0	0	2	1	6	
Totals	3	0	0	3	1	7	

Zenith Data Systems Cup

Home	1	0	0	1	0	5	

Other Matches

Home	6	3	1	2	20	13	
Away	9	1	2	6	12	18	
Totals	15	4	3	8	32	31	

Albion's best League win over Derby is 5-0 at home on 6 October 1888.

Derby's biggest win over Albion is 9-3 at the Baseball Ground on 8 December 1934, Reg Stockhill and Sammy Crooks both scoring hat-tricks. All Derby's goals came between the 12th and 75th minutes.

Albion have not won at Derby in the League since 20 December 1919 (4-0). Their last major victory at the Baseball Ground was 3-2 in a fifth-round FA Cup-tie in February 1978. They also won a Football League (North) game on Derby soil by 5-1 in September 1943, 'W.G.' Richardson scoring four of the goals.

Richardson also scored four goals (including a hat-trick in six minutes) when Albion beat Derby 5-1 at home on 30 September 1933 (Division One). Richardson, in fact, netted 12 goals for Albion in all games v Derby.

Steve Bloomer scored a hat-trick in Derby's 8-1 League win over Albion on Christmas Day 1896. During his long career with Derby, Bloomer (who was born on Albion's doorstep in Cradley Heath) scored 17 League goals against Albion, including the first-ever goal at The Hawthorns when Derby were the first visitors for a Division One League game on 3 September 1900 (1-1).

Albion denied Derby promotion to the First Division by holding them to a 0-0 draw at The Hawthorns on 30 April 1910. County needed to win to go up.

Albion on the offensive at the Baseball Ground in 1911.

Dean Saunders scored three of Derby's five goals in their emphatic Zenith Data Systems Cup win over Albion at The Hawthorns in November 1989.

Bob Taylor scored his 100th goal for Albion in a 3-2 win over Premiership-bound Derby at The Hawthorns on 5 May 1996.

Albion League debutants v Derby: George Evans (1889), Jack Taggart (1893), Billy Neale (1893), Abraham Law (1897),

Allan Crowshaw played for Albion and Derby and was at the Baseball Ground at the same time as Reg Ryan, another former WBA player.

Joe Lowe (1900), Jack Brittain (1903), George Farrington (1903), Harry Aston (1904), Ebenezer Owers (1904), Billy Adams (1920), Roly James (1920), Alf Ridyard (1933), 'Sandy' McNab (1938), Reg Cutler (1952), Kevin Summerfield (1979), Peter Barnes (1979), Gary Owen (1979), Kevin Steggles (1987).

Players with both clubs: Alf Bentley, Enos Bromage, Andy Comyn, Allan Crowshaw, Tom Dilly, Mickey Forsyth, Graham Harbey, Jack Kifford, Mickey Lewis, Shane Nicholson, Reg Ryan, Mickey Thomas, Herbert Varney, Frank Waterhouse.

Players also associated with both clubs: Brett Angell; Harry Ashley and Mark Grew; Colin Addison was manager at Derby and assistant manager at Albion; Gerry Summers played for Albion and later became Youth Development Officer with Derby; Alan Ashman was Albion's manager (1967-71) and later scout at Derby; Jimmy Hagan played for Derby and managed Albion (1963-67); Jimmy Dunn was also a player with County and later trainer to Albion; John Jarman was coach at Albion and later Community Officer for Derby and Ken Hodgkisson was an Albion inside-forward (1950s) and later Derby chief scout.

DEVELOPMENT ASSOCIATION (COMMERCIAL)

Albion first formed their Development Association in August 1961 with a number of fund-raising schemes including a 3d on the ball competition and a daily draw.

In November 1961, the Albion Pool was formed and registered with the FA and this was run exclusively by the Albion club.

A full-time organiser, former player Reg Ryan, was appointed and over 300 agents were engaged in a relatively short time.

Out of every shilling (5p) paid in, 10d (4p) was paid out in prize-money, with 2d (1p) retained by the Development Association.

By 1964, the Pool's top prize was £850 and in 1966-67, a lucky winner received £1,500. Come 1969 – under new organiser Les Thorley – there were over 1,000 agents operating for West Bromwich Albion, in what had mushroomed into the largest football club pool in the Midlands.

Since then things have grown considerably and when Albion celebrated their centenary in 1979, there was also a lottery in operation with £1,000 as its bumper prize each month. Albion 'Bingo' tickets were also being sold with

Albion line up in 1985, sporting the 'No Smoking' logo of Sandwell Council.

instant cash pay-outs to numerous winners.

Throughout the 1980s, many assorted scratch-cards were introduced and these were still being sold in 1996. Various other promotional activities were started up within the club, including 'Golden Goal' tickets, lucky matchday draw tickets, etc. etc. And in the early 1990s Ladbrokes, one of the country's leading bookmakers, opened matchday 'betting counters' inside The Hawthorns, allowing supporters to bet on the result of the game, time of the first goal, the first goalscorer, and much more – all beneficial to the club in the long run.

Tom Cardall, steering the commercial department at The Hawthorns in 1996.

Les Thorley was the first commercial manager appointed by West Bromwich Albion FC. He has been followed, in turn, by Gordon Dimbleby (1973), former Burnley goalkeeper Alan Stevenson and Tom Cardall, who was given the title Commercial Executive in 1993 soon after returning to the club for a second spell following a sojourn with rivals Aston Villa.

The commercial department (including the lottery/pools) at The Hawthorns in 1996 was supervised by director Barry Hurst and Tom Cardall.

In 1995, a splendid new club shop was opened within the "Tom Silk complex" adjoining the Hawthorns Throstle Club in Halfords Lane down from the ground (the old shop was part of the Halfords Lane stand, and was built in 1961). The newly-designed club offices for the commercial department, team manager, secretary, accountancy staff, the administration staff and Football in the Community. There is also an extensively equipped ticket office next to the main office reception area.

Sponsorship

Sponsorship is a crucial factor in football these days and there are a variety of options available for local and national businesses and supporters (young and old, male or female) at Albion, including the leasing/renting of Executive Boxes; membership to the Executive Club and/or The Albion Sporting Club; advertising around the ground as well as in the matchday programme and club newspaper; match, match ball and programme sponsorship; kit sponsorship for a year; end-of-season shirt sponsorship and guided tours of the ground and the Hawthorns museum, which was officially opened in August 1995.

Club Sponsors

West Bromwich Albion Football Club shirts first carried sponsorship in season 1981-82 when the 'BSR' logo was displayed

In 1982-83 and 1983-84 the 'Swan; logo appeared, advertising Swan electrical goods.

From 1984 to 1986 a 'No Smoking' insignia was adopted on the shirt fronts, reflecting Sandwell Council's 'no smoking' sponsorship.

In 1987 Apollo 2000 took over as official club sponsors (until 1989), and they were followed by Sandwell Council again.

In 1993, the 'Coucher and Shaw' (solicitors) logo appeared on the club's jerseys, succeeded by Guest Motors, the club's sponsors (1994-96). Albion also have an efficient PA system which can be used for advertising.

DIRECTORS

West Bromwich Albion Football Club became a Limited Liability Company in June 1891. The first board of directors (under chairman George Salter) took office in September 1891. Prior to this the club itself was run by a committee, and it is interesting to know that from 1878 to 1986 there was an ex-Albion player on the club's committee/board of directors. This sequence (unique in football) was broken when Cliff Edwards left the board in 1986.

From 1891 to 1986, seven former players held Albion directorship, these being: 'Jem' Bayliss, Charlie Perry, Billy Bassett, Dan Nurse, Claude Jephcott, Tommy Glidden and Cliff Edwards.

Claude Jephcott, one of seven former Albion players to become a director of the club.

From the club's earliest days (until 1891) Albion's fortunes were guided by a committee which in 1882 comprised six first-team players: Fred Bunn, George Bell, Harry Bell, James Stanton, Billy Bisseker and John Stokes, and five non-playing members of the club (mainly local businessmen but ardent supporters).

Meetings were held at the club's head quarters – the Plough and Harrow pub – when the team was selected by the committee.

A number of other players also served on the Albion committee during the 1880s, among them 'Jem' Bayliss, Ezra Horton, Bob Roberts and George 'Darkie' Timmins while the leading lights on the non-playing side were such local worthies as Dr Herbert Manley, Thomas Cotterill, James J.Raybould, John Bowen, D.Robert Rees, James Couse, William Mould, Dr Isaac Pitt, John Homer and Dr William Lawson.

Two other gentlemen, not named above, but worthy of a mention are Henry S.Jackson and Edward W.W.Heelis.

The former was the chairman of the committee when the move was made to Albion's former ground Stoney Lane in 1885. He was the Clerk to the local magistrates at the time and was rewarded for all the hard work he put in when Albion won the FA Cup for the first time in 1888.

Mr Heelis was the Mayor of West Bromwich when he was opted on to the committee in 1887. He was elected chairman of the said committee in 1888 (in succession to Mr Jackson) but resigned in December 1890. He eventually came off the committee in April 1891, but in the following August joined the board of directors.

Albion's first board of directors, elected at a shareholders' meeting at the Plough and Harrow on 1 September 1891 comprised: William Bache, James 'Jem' Bayliss, James Couse, Edward Heelis, Henry Jackson, James Lavender, John Phillips, Dr Robert Rees and George Salter (chairman).

Albion Directors elected between 1891 and 1910: William Bache (1891-92), James 'Jem' Bayliss (1891-1905); James Couse (1891-92 and 1895-96); Edward W.W.Heelis (1891-95); Henry S.Jackson (1891-93); James Lavender (1891-92); John Phillips (1891-93); Dr Robert Rees (1891-95); George Salter (1891-95); Louis Ford (1892-96); Harry Roberts (1892-97); Enoch Wood (1892-95); Dr Isaac Pitt (1893-1904); J.A.Fellows (1896-99); T.Harris Spencer (1895-1902 and 1905-07); W.Hall Keys (1896-97); Harry Keys (1896-1903, 1905-08 and 1919-29); Charles Perry (1896-1902); Harry Powell (1896-1904); Thomas Brennand (1897-1900); Joseph Lones (1900); George W.East (1901-05); George Mason (1902-05); Joseph S.Round (1903-05 and 1927-40); Thomas Hedges

Tommy Glidden, another former player who joined the board.

(1904-05); Richard Mason (1904-05); J.W.B.Stephens (1904-05); William I.Bassett (1905-37); Charles Couse (1905-10); James V.Webster (1907-08); Major (later Lt. Col.) Harold Ely (1909-27); Daniel Nurse (1910-27); Albert Seymour (1910-22).

All these gentleman faced a common problem: Albion's chronic lack of funds.

Things became so bad in March 1905 that the entire board (under pressure from the Bank and several creditors) resigned and only the intervention of Harry Keys, Billy Bassett, Tom Harris Spencer and Charles Couse, who offered to stand in their places, saved the day.

Albion Directors elected after World War One: Louis J.Nurse (1922-48); Walter W.Hackett (1927-37); Major H.Wilson Keys (1930-65); James Everiss (1930-32); Alan Claude Jephcott (1934-50); W.Horace Thursfield (1937-64); Norman W.Bassett (1937-52); W.Ellery Jephcott (1941-53); Frederick Everiss (1948-51); Thomas W.Glidden (1951-74); James W.Gaunt (1951-76); Samuel R.Shepherd (1952-63); Leonard Pritchards (1953-71); Clive H.James (1963-70); Frederick A.'Bert' Millichip (1964-79); Thomas H.Silk (1965-80); E.John Gordon (1970-79); Clifford I.Edwards (1971-86); J.Sidney Lucas (1975-91); D.Brian Boundy (1976-88); Alan E.Everiss (1981-86); John G.Silk (1984-92); Trevor J.Summers (1984-96); Joseph W.Brandrick (1986-96), Michael McGinnity (1986-92); Anthony B.Hale (1988-96); Clive M.Stapleton (1991-96); Terry K.Guy (1992-96); Barry Hurst (1992-96); Paul Thompson (1996).

Finances
Since World War One, generally the club's finances have been much more stable than they were in earlier days, and the club's directors have rarely had to face the financial pressures which almost brought about the end of West Bromwich Albion FC on two separate occasions in 1905 and 1910. However, the board did have to battle through a difficult period in the 1970s when Albion were in the 'old' Second Division. In fact, in their relegation season of 1972-73 Albion showed a loss of £104,000 – and there followed two further campaigns which produced big losses: £126,000 and £139,000 respectively. Despite these results the board remained resolute and their reward for maintaining a First Division set-up at The Hawthorns came at the conclusion of the 1975-76 season when the Baggies climbed back into the top flight.

During the period 1976 to 1982 Albion did well both on and off the field, but then during the mid to late eighties and during the early 1990s the financial state of the club was very worrying at times.

In 1986-87 Albion had their worst-ever operating loss: £583,692. And there were more heavy operating losses to come – £509,803 in 1987-88; £304,868 in 1990-91 and

Cliff Edwards, played for Albion and then became a director.

£722,508 in 1991-92. (By 1991 Albion had an overdraft of £1,129,849.) For the first time in three seasons, Albion announced an operating profit of £93,824 for 1992-93 (following promotion). But transfer fees turned this profit into an overall loss of £254,882.

In 1993-94 there was another loss for the club, this time of £476,268 – and then, at the commencement of the 1994-95 season, Albion declared that the club had a £1.6 million overdraft.

At the end of that campaign Albion confirmed an overall loss of £488,604 – and for season 1995-96, the club's financial statement told the shareholders that another small trading loss had been made.

Paul Thompson, chairman of the Sanderson Electronics Company, joined the Albion board in 1996 after agreeing to put £2.5 million into the club.

DONCASTER ROVERS
Albion's record against Rovers:
Football League

Venue	P	W	D	L	F	A	Pts
Home	3	1	1	1	9	6	3
Away	3	1	0	2	2	4	2
Totals	6	2	1	3	11	10	5

FA Cup

Home	1	1	0	0	2	0	
Away	1	0	1	0	1	1	
Totals	2	1	1	0	3	1	

Other Matches

Away	3	2	1	0	13	6

The first meeting between the clubs was a friendly at Doncaster's Intake ground on 31 March 1894. Albion won 7-1.

Albion also won the first League encounter by 6-1 at The Hawthorns in a Second Division game on 24 September 1904. Albion scored five times in the second half of this match.

Doncaster's best League win over Albion is 3-1 at The Hawthorns on 3 April 1948 (Division Two).

Doncaster were the only team Albion did not beat when winning the Second Division championship in 1901-02.

The two FA Cup games took place in 1956-57, Ronnie Allen scoring both Albion's goals in their 2-0 third-round replay win.

Simeon Hodson, played for Albion and Doncaster Rovers.

Kevin Donovan, scored Albion's third goal at Wembley in 1993.

Albion League debutants v Doncaster: James Bowden (1904).

Players with both clubs: Simeon Hodson, Paul Holmes, Billy Law, Jack Mahon, Paul Mardon, Neil Parsley, Paul Raven, Paul Reece, Ronnie Robinson, David Rushbury, George Shaw, Winston White, Paul A.Williams, Stewart Woolgar.

Other players associated with both clubs: Jack Beynon, Steve Burke, Scott Colcombe, Sid Glidden, Ernie Pattinson and Stuart Robertson, none of whom appeared in Albion's senior side.

DONOVAN, Kevin
Right-sided midfield player, nicknamed Jason, who joined Albion from Huddersfield Town for £70,000 in October 1992, having been on loan to Halifax Town eight months earlier. Born in Halifax in 1971, he helped Albion win promotion via the Wembley play-off Final in 1993, scoring his side's third goal. A skillful footballer, with a strong shot, he passed the milestone of 150 appearances for Albion in 1996.

DORSETT BROTHERS (George and Joseph)
Both men were born in Brownhills – George in 1881, Joe in 1888 – and both were left wingers who later played together for Manchester City. George joined the Baggies from Brownhills Albion in 1901 having been an amateur with Shrewsbury Town and a Small Heath trialist before that. He scored 22 goals in exactly 100 games for Albion, helping them win the Second Division title in 1902 before transferring to Manchester City two years later for a record fee for a winger of £450. He collected another Second Division championship medal with City, and before

George Dorsett, the more successful of the brothers to play for Albion.

The West Brom party arrive at Paddington Station a few days before the 1931 FA Cup Final.

Happy Albion with the Cup after beating West Midlands rivals Birmingham.

announcing his retirement in 1912 (through injury) he represented the Football League. He died in 1943. Like his brother, Joe also left Brownhills Albion for The Hawthorns (in 1905), and departed for Manchester City in 1910, after scoring three goals in 18 outings. He went on to appear in almost 150 games for City before switching to Colne in 1920, later playing for Southend United. He retired in 1923 and died in 1951.

DOUBLE WINNERS

In 1930-31 Albion achieved what is universally described as the 'unique' double – that of winning the FA Cup and promotion from the Second Division in the same season. They beat neighbours Birmingham 2-1 in the Cup Final with 'W.G.' Richardson netting both of their goals and then clinched promotion soon afterwards with a last League match win at home over Charlton Athletic by 3-2,

Richardson again netting the vital winning goal before a 52,415 crowd.

Albion's full League record for the season was:

Venue	P	W	D	L	F	A	Pts
Home	21	14	3	4	40	16	31
Away	21	8	7	6	43	33	23
Totals	42	22	10	10	83	49	54

Albion finished seven points behind champions Everton and three ahead of third-placed Tottenham Hotspur.

Three players were ever-presents in the League side: goalkeeper Harold Pearson, full-back George Shaw and centre-half Bill Richardson. 'W.G.' Richardson top-scored with 18 goals; skipper Tommy Glidden netted 15, outside-left Stan Wood 13 and inside-forward Jimmy Cookson 11.

Albion's best wins were both away from home – 6-1 over Nottingham Forest and 6-3 at Cardiff City – while Barnsley were beaten 5-0 at home. Plymouth Argyle inflicted upon Albion their heaviest defeat, 5-1 at Home Park.

Albion's average home League attendance this season was 21,722.

In the FA Cup, Albion knocked out Charlton Athletic (at the third attempt), Tottenham Hotspur, Portsmouth, neighbours Wolves (after a replay) and Everton, before accounting for Blues at Wembley in front of 90,368 rain-soaked fans. 'W.G.' Richardson was leading scorer in the Cup with six goals.

DRURY, Charles Edward

Chuck Drury, 160 League and Cup games for Albion.

Rugged. determined, hard-tackling wing-half, who scored once in 160 League and Cup games for Albion during ten years with the club (1954-64). 'Chuck' was born in Darlaston in 1937 and joined Albion from F.H.Lloyd's FC, leaving The Hawthorns for Bristol City for £7,500. He later played for Bradford Park Avenue, Tamworth, Warley and Bromsgrove Rovers, retiring in 1974. His only goal was a cracker against Wolves at Molineux in 1962 (won 5-1).

DUDLEY BROTHERS (George and James)

Both men were born in the village of Gartcosh near Glasgow – George in 1916, Jimmy in 1928. Both were able to play at inside-forward or wing-half, Jimmy settling into the latter berth superbly for Albion during the 1950s. George was an a strong, forceful player, who scored five goals in 25 first-team games for Albion over a period of nine years: 1937-46. He joined the club from Vono Sports and went on to serve Banbury Spencer, Dudley Town, Netherton and Cradley Heath before retiring in 1953. He died in 1979, aged 63. Jimmy, after starting off at inside-forward in 1949, became Albion's regular right-half two years later, and he occupied that berth until 1959. He went on to appear in 320 first-team matches for Albion,

George Dudley, played for Albion from 1937 to 1946. Thus his career was badly affected by World War Two.

scoring 11 goals, including a vital equaliser against Port vale in the 1954 F.A,. Cup semi-final. Part of a terrific middle-line at The Hawthorns – Dudley, Kennedy, Barlow – over a period of four years (1952-56) Jimmy appeared in 166 consecutive League games for Albion, a record beaten later by Ally Robertson. An FA Cup winner in 1954, Dudley junior was capped by Scotland 'B' that same year and after

Jimmy Dudley, 12 years younger than his brother he played for Albion from 1949 and made 320 first-team appearances.

leaving The Hawthorns, he went on to play in 175 games for Walsall, helping the Saddlers win both the Fourth and Third Division championships in successive seasons (1961 and 1962). He left Fellows Park for Stourbridge in 1964 and later played for Guest Motors FC, his work's team, until retiring in 1990.

DUGDALE, James Robert

Excellent centre-half who shared the No.5 shirt at Albion with Joe Kennedy during the early 1950s before moving to neighbours Aston Villa. A Liverpudlian, born in 1932, Dugdale arrived at The Hawthorns in 1950 from Harrowby FC and in the next six years appeared in 75 League and Cup games for Albion, winning an FA Cup medal in 1954,

Jimmy Dugdale foils George Robb of Spurs at White Hart Lane in January 1954.

Albion's team which met the Third Lanark Rifle Volunteers in 1885.

gaining three England 'B' caps and representing the Football League. With Kennedy taking priority at the heart of defence, Dugdale was sold to Villa for £25,000 in 1956 and the following year won his second FA Cup winners medal. He then helped Villa win the Second Division title in 1960 and the Football League Cup 12 months later before seeing out his career with Queens Park Rangers, retiring in 1963 to become a publican. Sadly he had a leg amputated in 1993.

DUNN, Archibald

'Soldier' Dunn was a useful full-back or wing-half, awkward to get past, who played 81 games for Albion over a period of three years: 1898-1901. Born in Glasgow in 1878, he joined the Baggies straight from the Queen's Gordon Highlanders and left The Hawthorns for Grimsby Town, Millwall Athletic and Motherwell, retiring during World War One. He died in 1943.

EARLY YEARS (1878-1888)

West Bromwich Strollers (Albion's former name) played their first recorded match against Hudson's on 23 November 1878.

There is no newspaper mention of any other game being played in 1878-79, and throughout the following two seasons the Strollers (Albion) seemed to have remained unbeaten. In fact, their first recorded defeat was suffered on 1 October 1881, when they lost 3-2 away to The Grove (Handsworth) before 1,000 spectators.

By this time the club was known as West Bromwich Albion, the name change having occurred in March 1880.

In the early days of original football (in England) scorelines were often exceptionally high, as the opposition proved far too weak, and Albion went to town on a number of occasions, some of their biggest wins being: 14-0 v Oakfield and 8-0 v West Bromwich Rovers in 1880-81; 12-0 v Milton, 10-0 v St Luke's and 9-1 v Nechells in 1881-82; a club record 26-0 v Coseley (in a Birmingham Cup match), 11-0 v St John's United, 10-0 v Stourbridge Standard and 10-1 v Birmingham Junior Association in 1882-83, and 8-0 v Sheffield Heeley and 7-0 v West Bromwich Sandwell in 1883-84. In season 1882-83, Albion played 39 games of

which 27 were won and seven drawn. They scored 177 goals and conceded 59. They also won their first trophy – the Staffordshire Cup – by beating Stoke 3-2 away in the Final. But in another Final (of the Wednesbury Cup v Nottingham Forest) Albion were beaten 5-3 and they also lost the services of skipper John While with a broken leg. He never played again.

Albion entered the FA Cup for the first time in 1883-84, losing their opening tie to Wednesbury Town at home 2-0. Albion progressed to the quarter-finals of the FA Cup in 1884-85 and reached the semi-finals of the Staffordshire Cup.

In a Birmingham Cup-tie in November 1884 Albion whipped Bloxwich Strollers 15-0 with 'Jem' Bayliss scoring six times.

Albion started the 1885-86 season by playing on new home territory – Stoney Lane – and they celebrated with a 4-1 'friendly' win over Third Lanark Rifle Volunteers before 2,122 spectators.

Albion became the first Midland club to reach the FA Cup Final this season, but they couldn't beat red-hot favourites Blackburn Rovers who took the prize after a replay. Albion gained some consolation, however, by winning both the Staffordshire and Birmingham Senior Cup Finals.

In 1886-87 Albion again reached the FA Cup Final – and again they lost, beaten this time by arch rivals Aston Villa 2-0. Albion also lost in the Final of the Birmingham Cup.

A notable debutant in season 1886-87 was William Isaiah Bassett.

At the third attempt, Albion finally won the coveted FA Cup in season 1887-88 when they beat 'Proud' Preston North End 2-1 at The Oval. Albion also won the West Bromwich Charity Cup and they reached two other local Finals, losing to Wolverhampton Wanderers in the Staffordshire Cup and to Aston Villa in the Birmingham Cup.

A total of 58 games were played this season of which 42 ended in victories, one being a 12-2 hammering of Burton Wanderers in the Staffordshire Cup. Albion averaged around four goals a game, hitting 195 in total, with Bayliss registered 50, including ten in the FA Cup.

EDWARDS, Clifford Ivor

A short, thick-set half-back, strong in the tackle and very reliable, Cliff Edwards scored three goals in 102 games for Albion during a ten-year association with the club (1938-48). Born in Chase Terrace, Cannock, in 1921, he joined The Hawthorns staff from Cannock Town and left Albion for Bristol City in a player-exchange deal involving Cyril Williams. He later played for Gravesend and Northfleet, returning to The Hawthorns as a director in August 1971, retiring in 1986 through ill-health. He died three years later.

Cliff Edwards, played in 102 games for Albion and it would have been many more but for the fact that he missed seven seasons due to World War Two.

During World War Two, Edwards guested for Bath City, Blackpool and Carlisle United. When he left the board in 1986, Edwards broke a sequence that had been running since 1891, that of an ex-player always being on the club's board of directors.

EDWARDS, James

Known affectionately as 'Iron' Edwards, this Tipton-born, tough-tackling defender, gave Albion tremendous service at

all levels for 11 years (1926-37) during which time he accumulated a record of 202 appearances, scoring nine goals. He joined the club from Stourbridge and after making his League debut in 1928 (initially as an inside-forward) he reverted to left-half and was a key figure during Albion's double-winning season of 1930-31 and in 1934-35 when the Baggies again reached the FA Cup Final. He also represented the Football League XI. Edwards left The Hawthorns for Norwich City and retired in 1944 after serving with Bilston, Kingswinford and Dudley Town. He died in 1982, aged 76.

ELLIOTT, William Bethwaite

Brilliant outside-right, fast and clever with incredible close ball control and powerful shot, Billy Elliott was rejected by Wolverhampton Wanderers as a 16 year-old and went to play for Bournemouth, transferring to Albion for £4,000 in 1938. He stayed at The Hawthorns for 13 years, appearing in 303 games and scoring 157 goals (in all competitions). During the 1939-45 hostilities, he was quite superb, netting 117 goals in just 148 games – and he also played for England twice v Wales and Scotland, in Wartime and Victory internationals respectively. If it hadn't been for a certain Stanley Matthews, then Elliott would have surely gained full England recognition. He helped Albion win promotion from the Second Division in 1948-49 and was in tip-top form when he suffered an Achilles tendon injury in 1951 which ended his League career. He left Albion to become player-manager of Bilston United in 1951, retiring in 1954 to

take over the Farcroft Hotel in Handsworth, Birmingham. Elliott died whilst holidaying in the Canary Islands in 1966, aged 47.

EUROPEAN CUP-WINNERS' CUP

Albion have played once in this competition – in 1968-69 – having qualified after winning the FA Cup the previous season.

Albion were eliminated in the quarter-finals after playing six games:

Rd 1 (1)	RFC Brugge	(a)	1-3 (Hartford)	28,000
Rd 1 (2)	RFC Brugge	(h)	2-0 (T. Brown, Hartford)	33,747

*Albion went through on the away goal rule

Rd 2 (1)	Dinamo Bucharest	(a)	1-1 (Hartford)	15,000
Rd 2 (2)	Dinamo Bucharest	(h)	4-0 (T.Brown 2 (1pen), Astle, Lovett)	33,059
Rd 3 (1)	Dunfermline Ath	(a)	0-0	22,073
Rd 3 (2)	Dunfermline Ath	(h)	0-1	32,373

There was trouble between players, officials and spectators in Belgium during the game v Brugge; Albion's Ronnie Rees was sent-off in the game v Dinamo Bucharest in Romania and the temperature at The Hawthorns for the second-leg clash with Dunfermline was five degrees below freezing.

EVANS, Charles James

World War Two interrupted Charlie Evans' playing career with Albion. Nevertheless, this West Bromwich-born utility forward gave the club tremendous service, scoring 31 goals in 130 first-team games. He joined the club at the age of 14 in 1937 from Cordley Vics and progressed through the

John Talbot in action against Dinamo Bucharest in the 1968-69 European Cup-winners' Cup.

'Nig Nog' League to make his debut in 1941. He left Albion for Stafford Rangers in 1950. Later he served with Nuneaton Borough and Dudley Town and became trainer-coach of Stourbridge in 1962, retiring two years later to work for the Eclipsol Oil Company.

EVERISS FAMILY

There has been a member of the Everiss family associated with West Bromwich Albion Football Club for 100 years.

Fred Everiss, born in Spon Lane, West Bromwich in May 1882, joined the Albion staff as an office boy in September 1896. He was put in charge of compiling the team-sheets as well as doing general duties. He acquitted himself so well that the directors had no hesitation in appointing him secretary at the age of 20 in 1902, a tremendous responsibility for one so young, which he shouldered magnificently. He became a much-admired and loved figure in the game and with the assistance of Billy Bassett and Harry Keys in particular, he brought great respectability to the Albion club. In 1926 an unusual tribute was paid to Fred Everiss by past and present Albion players who presented

Fred Everiss (left) with Jack Smith (centre) and 'Eph' Smith in 1948.

him with an illuminated address as a tangible token of the high regard in which he was held. From 1927 he was secretary of the Football League Secretaries' and Managers' Association and later he became its chairman.

During World War Two he had to combine the jobs, at The Hawthorns, of secretary-manager, typist, telephonist, office-clerk, part-time groundsman and ARP night watchman.

In October 1946, he was presented with a silver casket and a second illuminated address, this time on the occasion of his completing 50 years service with Albion. For the last three years of his life Fred Everiss *JP*, was on the board of directors and when he passed away in 1951 he had served the club for over 54 years. Undoubtedly one of the greatest names in the history of West Bromwich Albion Football Club.

Fred Everiss's son, Alan, was introduced to office work at The Hawthorns in August 1933, earning £1 a week as a 14 year-old junior. He, like his father, made rapid progress and duly carried on the family name and tradition of long service magnificently.

After serving his apprenticeship in the 'office', he was made assistant secretary in 1948 to Ephraim Smith (who was his brother-in-law incidentally), and when Smith retired in May 1960, Alan was upgraded to secretary, a position he held for 20 years, until 1980, when Tony Rance took over.

Alan Everiss *JP*, continued the proud family tradition of service to West Bromwich Albion.

He compiled most of the text for the Albion programme throughout the 1960s and was a great help to me when I first started my research in readiness for the publication of the first 'A-Z of Albion' and then the 'Complete Record'.

Like his father, Alan was also a Justice of the Peace (in West Bromwich) in 1968 and he, too, was chairman of the Football League Secretaries', Managers' and Coaches' Association. After retiring he was made a director of the club (1981-86), also becoming a Life Member of West Bromwich Albion in August 1980.

EVERTON

Albion's record against fellow founder members of the Football League, Everton:

Football League

Venue	P	W	D	L	F	A	Pts
Home	66	35	17	14	137	79	88
Away	66	14	14	38	84	145	42
Totals	132	49	31	52	221	224	130

FA Cup

Venue	P	W	D	L	F	A
Home	2	1	1	0	2	1
Away	7	2	1	4	5	10
Totals	9	3	2	4	7	11

League Cup

Venue	P	W	D	L	F	A
Away	1	1	0	0	2	1

Other Matches

Venue	P	W	D	L	F	A
Home	6	3	1	2	8	7
Away	9	2	0	7	11	34
Totals	15	5	1	9	19	41

No other club has played more League games against Albion than Everton.

Albion recorded their first away League win against Everton, beating them 1-0 at Anfield Road on 23 February 1889.

Alec Jackson scores against Everton at The Hawthorns in March 1961.

John Kaye heads clear from Everton's John Hurst in the 1968 FA Cup Final.

Albion's biggest League win over the Merseysiders is 6-1 at home on 7 December 1935 (Division One).

Derek Kevan scored five goals in Albion's 6-2 First Division win over Everton at The Hawthorns on 19 March 1960 and totalled 15 in all appearances against Everton.

Albion's heaviest League defeat is 7-1, at Everton, on 30 December 1893 when the home centre-forward Jack Southworth scored six goals.

By defeating Albion 4-0 at The Hawthorns on 7 May 1963, Everton became First Division champions.

Alan Ball scored four goals when Everton beat Albion 6-2 at The Hawthorns in a First Division match on 16 March 1968 – less than two months before the teams met in the FA Cup Final.

Albion beat the then reigning League champions Everton 4-0 at home on the opening day of the 1891-92 season.

Albion fielded only ten men (for the first and only time in the club's history) during the away League game at Everton on 29 September 1894. Billy Richards was the absentee and Albion lost 4-1.

Everton condemned Albion to the Second Division in 1900-01, beating them 2-1 at The Hawthorns on 22 April and the Merseysiders sent Albion down again when winning 4-0 in Liverpool on 16 April 1904.

'Dixie' Dean scored the last of his record-breaking 37 League hat-tricks for Everton in their 4-2 win over Albion on 7 November 1936.

Everton beat Albion 2-1 in the 1906-07 FA Cup semi-final. Albion then defeated Everton 1-0 (with a Tommy Glidden goal) in the 1930-31 FA Cup semi-final, and at the end of the season both teams were promoted to Division One, Everton as champions.

A Jeff Astle goal in extra-time gave Albion a 1-0 FA Cup Final victory over Everton at Wembley in May 1968.

Albion's first-ever Sunday match was a 0-0 draw in a fourth-round FA Cup-tie at Everton on 27 January 1974 before 53,509 fans.

Albion League debutants v Everton: Fred Crabtree (1889), Sammy Nicholls (1890), Frank Dyer (1890), Robert Roberts (1890), Magnus Nicholson (1891), Alf Geddes (1891), Harry Wood (1892), Harry Brown (1903), Matt Wood (1912), Howard Gregory (1912), Jack Crisp (1914), Tommy Glidden (1922), Arthur Perry (1923), Bill Harris (1938), Don Howe (1955), Derek Kevan (1955), Ronnie Rees (1968), Ron Potter (1968), Martyn Bennett (1979), Andy King (1981), Gary Childs (1982), Kevin Kent (1984), Colin Anderson (1985), George Reilly (1985).

Peter Eastoe played for both Albion and Everton.

Players with both clubs: Brett Angell, Laurie Bell, Wally Boyes, David Burrows, John Cameron, Stan Davies, Tommy Dilly, Peter Eastoe, Albert Flewitt, Andy Gray, Asa Hartford, Paul Holmes, Willie Jordan, Andy King, Ken McNaught, Bruce Rankin, Sid Rawlings, Fred Rouse, Mickey Thomas, Imre Varadi.

Also associated with both clubs: players Phil Griffiths, Andrew Hannah, Kevin Steggles and John Thomas. Wilf Dixon was trainer at The Hawthorns and Goodison Park.

EXETER CITY

Albion's record against Exeter reads:

Football League

Venue	P	W	D	L	F	A	Pts
Home	2	2	0	0	8	3	6
Away	2	1	1	0	4	3	4
Totals	4	3	1	0	12	6	10

Willie Johnston scoring his first Albion goal against Exeter City in a League Cup game at The Hawthorns in October 1973.

League Cup

Home	1	0	0	1	1	3

Autoglass Trophy

Home	1	0	0	1	0	1

Other Match

Away	1	0	1	0	2	2

Campbell Crawford played for Albion and Exeter City.

Albion's first-ever game in the 'old' Third Division was against Exeter City at The Hawthorns on the opening day of the 1991-92 season. Albion won 6-3 with goals by Shakespeare (2, both penalties), Goodman (2), Foster and Williams.

Willie Johnston scored his first goal for Albion in that 3-1 League Cup defeat against then Fourth Division Exeter City at The Hawthorns on 31 October 1973. Defender Frank Sinclair was the first Albion 'loan' player to be sent-off while playing against Exeter City (away) on 28 December 1991.

Albion League debutant v Exeter: Alan Miller (1991).

Players with both clubs: Colin Anderson, Jack Banks, Dickie Baugh, Ian Benjamin, Wilf Carter, Campbell Crawford, Adrian Foster, Mickey Fudge, Phil King, Johnny Nicholls, Gordon Nisbet, Neil Parsley, Ronnie Robinson, Maurice Setters, Kevin Summerfield, Clive Whitehead.

Geoff Hudson played for Exeter in 1961-62 and later became Albion's coach (1970-72).

FAIRFAX, Raymond

Stern-tackling full-back, who scored once in 92 games for Albion during the 1960s. Born in Smethwick in 1941, Fairfax was a Staffordshire County FA player before joining Albion in 1959. He had to wait four years for his debut (at Liverpool) and then helped Albion win the League Cup in 1966. His only goal was a terrific effort in the Fairs Cup clash v Bologna at The Hawthorns in March 1967. Fairfax left Albion for Northampton Town in 1968 and later played for Wellingborough and Olney Town. He retired in 1974 when he returned to The Hawthorns to work in the commercial department, becoming assistant secretary in 1975. Between 1985 and 1987 he was secretary of Port Vale and is now working in the ticket office at Villa Park.

FAMILY LINKS

Brothers

Since 1888, a total of 14 sets of brothers have played for Albion in the Football League:

Ezra and Jack Horton played together many times in the late 1880s and early '90s, and were present in Albion's first League game against Stoke on 8 September 1888.

The Perrys – Charlie, Tom and Walter – all played in Division One between 1888 and 1901, and their total number of appearances in the Football League was in excess of 400.

Charlie and Tom each played in an FA Cup Final for Albion and they both represented England.

The Paddocks – William and John – were first-team left wingers for Albion: William (1886-88) and John (1894-96 and 1899-1900).

Arthur, Ted and Billy Smith, were Albion forwards for a short while together either side of 1900.

Forwards Billy and David Walker turned out for Albion in seasons 1898-99 and 1907-08 respectively.

Also in 1898-99 Sam and Ralph Brett occupied positions in Albion's forward-line.

Left wingers George and Joe Dorsett were at The Hawthorns during the early 1900s and both left for Manchester City.

Outside-right Arthur and full-back Llewellyn Davies, the Welsh brothers, were members of Albion's League side in 1904-05, Llewellyn being the only player ever to displace Jesse Pennington in the first team.

Ben Hadley (1892-96) and his brother Harry Hadley (1897-1905) were both Albion wing-halves, the latter playing 173 games more than Ben.

Bill and England star Sid Bowser were together at The Hawthorns during the first decade of the 20th century, Bill making only one League appearance to Sid's 341.

Right-back Joe Smith and outside-left Horace Smith played together twice in Albion's League side in 1923-24. Joe won England honours and made 471 appearances for the Baggies.

Centre-forward Ernie Edwards (1913-14) and his brother Jimmy 'Iron' Edwards (1926-37) from Tipton played for Albion's first team in the years indicated.

There was a Richardson brother in Albion's half-back line for over 20 years. Right-half Sammy started off in 1915 and centre-half Billy continued until 1937. Between them they amassed more than 560 senior appearances for the Baggies.

George and Jimmy Dudley, the Scots from Gartcosh near Glasgow, were League players with Albion ten years apart. George was in the side in 1938-39 and Jimmy, an FA Cup winner in 1954, made the first of his 320 appearances for the Baggies in 1949.

Other Family Links

The Bunn family was strongly represented at Albion in the mid 1880s with Abraham, Thomas (known as 'Fred' or 'Little Bunny') and Walter all being top-line players.

Cousins Harry and George Bell, both founder-members of the Albion club, turned out together regularly before League football commenced in 1888.

The son of Albion's 1880s inside-forward Tommy Green, who was also named Tommy, was in the Baggies' first team during the 1930s.

Brothers Herbert and John Cole were reserve-team players with Albion in the early 1900s. The former fractured his left leg in a reserve game in September 1902 and never played again.

Hubert Pearson was Albion's goalkeeper from 1906-26 and he was followed between the posts by his son, Harold, who kept goal for the Baggies until 1937. Both players' careers overlapped at The Hawthorns and both appeared in FA Cup Finals for Albion with Harold a winner in 1931 and also an England international in 1932. They accumulated over 650 appearances between them for Albion.

Tommy Green, an Albion player in the 1930s; his father of the same name played for the Baggies in the 1880s.

Billy Bassett, who was associated with Albion for 51 years (1886-1937) as a player, director and chairman, was followed on to to the board of directors at the club in 1937 by his son, Norman, who was a Albion reserve for two years: 1919-21. Billy's brother, Harry, had one season in Albion's second team (1892-93).

Manager Alan Buckley recruited his two sons – Adam and Simon – from Grimsby Town to join him at The Hawthorns in 1995-96.

Besides the three Perry brothers (mentioned earlier), a further four members of the family have all figured in Albion's playing ranks at some sort of level. Arthur was a League player in the 1920s, while William, Edward and Eric all assisted the club by performing adequately in the reserve and various intermediate teams.

Teddy Sandford, Albion's star of the 1930s, was the nephew of former Albion centre-half 'Abe' Jones (1896-1901).

Sid Glidden, brother of Albion's 1931 FA Cup Final winning skipper, Tommy, was an Albion reserve: 1925-28.

1950s star Jimmy Dudley was the cousin of 1930s wing-half Jimmy 'Iron' Edwards.

Russell Allen, the son of Ronnie, Albion's utility forward of the 1950s and later manager, was a Central League player at The Hawthorns in the early 1970s.

The Everiss family have been associated with Albion for 100 years (See EVERISS FAMILY).

Harry 'John Bull' Keys, was a director and chairman of Albion between 1896 and 1919. After him came his son, Major H.Wilson Keys. The Keys family was associated with Albion for 78 years (to 1974). Harry's brothers – W.Hall Keys and Clement Keys – were also closely associated with Albion, the former as a director, the latter as secretary and auditor.

The Nurse family, too, has been well represented at the Albion. Dan Nurse was a player (1901-04), then shareholder and director (1910-27); Lou Nurse was a director (1922-48) and relative David Nurse is now a shareholder and supporter.

Alan Claude Jephcott, a player and director of Albion between 1911-50; William Jephcott, a journalist who covered most of Albion's matches (starting in 1892); and W.Ellery

Ronnie Allen's son Russell was an Albion reserve in the early 1970s.

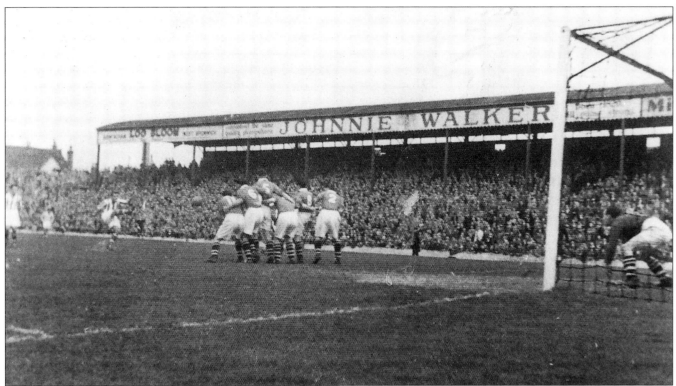

Albion's defensive 'wall' holds firm against a Floriana free-kick at The Hawthorns in a Festival of Britain match in 1951.

Jephcott, the editor of the *Albion News* for many years during the 1920s and later director (1941-53) provided the Jephcott family with a considerable say in Albion affairs for more than 60 years.

In 1984-85 Albion manager Johnny Giles had his son Michael with him at The Hawthorns and likewise in 1992, when boss Bobby Gould's son, Jonathan, was Albion's reserve goalkeeper. In fact, Bobby and his son played for Albion in a friendly match in Gibraltar on 17 March 1992.

The only other instances of a father and son playing in Albion's first team are: Ronnie Allen (1950-61) and son Russell (1972), Tommy Green senior and Tommy Green junior, Hubert Pearson and son Harold and Charlie Perry and his son Arthur.

FESTIVAL OF BRITAIN

To celebrate the Festival of Britain in 1951, Albion played two friendly matches at The Hawthorns against foreign opposition, the details being:
12 May
v SC Wacker (Austria), lost 3-4. Scorers: Allen (2), Barlow.
Attendance: 16,074
15 May
v FC Floriana (Malta), won 2-0.
Scorers: Smith, Barlow.
Attendance: 15,133
Former Albion full-back George Shaw was coach of the Floriana team.

FINCH, Abel Robert

Redoubtable full-back who spent 14 years at The Hawthorns (1925-39) during which time he played in 234 League and Cup games for the

Abel Finch, made 234 senior appearances during a 14-year career with Albion.

Baggies. Quick-witted, zealous, alert and confident in his kicking, Finch had to compete for a first-team place with so many other fine players and missed out on Albion's two FA Cup Final appearances in the 1930s. He did, however, skipper the Central League side to three successive championship triumphs and played in two England international trials. He left Albion for Swansea Town and later played for Hednesford Town (the club he was with prior to joining Albion) and Tamworth (as a guest in the War). From 1942 to 1956 Finch served in the Police Force, based at Hednesford, where he was born in 1908. He was Albion's oldest surviving ex-player in 1996, aged 88.

FIRSTS

Albion were the first British professional football team to win a match in Soviet Russia (3-0 v Dynamo Tbilisi on 7 June 1957) and China (3-1 v Peking XI on 17 May 1978).

Albion were the first club to top the Football League – going to the head of the table after beating Stoke 2-0 away in their initial game in the competition on 8 September 1888.

Tommy Glidden was the first outside-right to skipper an FA Cup winning team (Albion v Birmingham in 1931).

Jeff Astle became the first player to score in both an FA Cup Final and League Cup Final at Wembley – for Albion against Everton (1968) and Manchester City (1970) respectively.

Albion champion marksman Tony Brown was the first player to score in every round of the League Cup, doing so in 1965-66. And Albion's outside-left Clive Clark was the first player to score in every game of a League Cup competition, achieving the feat in 1966-67.

Albion were the first Midlands club to play in three FA Cup Finals, 1886, 1887 and 1888, and the first team to play in three League Cup Finals, 1966, 1967 and 1970.

When Albion won the FA Cup for the first time in 1888 they also became the first team to lift the trophy with an all-English XI.

Full-back Dennis Clarke was the first substitute to be used in an FA Cup Final, replacing John Kaye after 90

Far left: **Clive Clark, the first player to score in every game of a League Cup campaign.**
Bottom: **Tommy Glidden, with the trophy, leads Albion down the steps from the Royal Box at Wembley after the Baggies beat Birmingham in the 1931 FA Cup Final to become the first club to win the Cup and promotion in the same season.**

minutes of Albion's 1-0 extra-time win over Everton in 1968.

In 1930-31 Albion became the first (and so far only) team to win the FA, Cup and gain promotion from the Second Division in the same season.

Albion were the first team to score over 100 goals in a full Division One season: 104 in 1919-20.

Johnny Giles was the first player-manager of Albion, appointed in May 1975.

Ex-player Ronnie Allen was the first manager to return for a second term of office with Albion: 1977 and again in 1981-82.

Albion were relegated to the Third Division for the first time at the end of the 1990-91 season – and their first-ever League game in

Dennis Clarke, the first substitute to be used in an FA Cup Final.

Division Three saw them beat Exeter City 6-3 at The Hawthorns.

FITTON, Arthur

'Mother' Fitton was a penetrative outside-left, who gave Albion distinguished service both on and off the field for a total of 18 years – as a player from 1922-32 and then as assistant-trainer-coach and first-team trainer 1948-56. Born at Melton Mowbray in 1902 and educated in Kinver, he played his early football with Kinver Swifts, Cookley St Peter's and Kidderminster Harriers, joining Albion for £400 in 1922. In his ten years service as a player, besides his senior games, he also appeared in a record 261 reserve-team matches (56 goals) helping Albion win the Central League championship on three occasions: 1923, 1924 and 1927. After leaving Albion in 1932, he played for Manchester United, Preston North End and Coventry City, retiring in 1937 to become third-team trainer at Highfield Road, a position he held until returning to The Hawthorns three years after the war. On leaving Albion (second time round) he became chief warden of the Kinver National Park. Fitton died at Worcester in 1984, aged 82.

FLOODLIGHTS

Floodlights were first installed at The Hawthorns in September 1957 at a cost of £18,000. The first game played under the lights was the Albion v Chelsea League Division One match on the 18th of that month which ended in a 1-1 draw before a 36,835 crowd.

The game officially opened the floodlights saw Albion beat the Moscow team, CDKA (the Centralniy Dom Krasnoy Armiy – Central Home of the Red Army) 6-5 in a thrilling contest in front of the BBC cameras and 52,805 rain-soaked spectators. Davey Burnside did his ball-juggling act during the half-time interval.

In 1970 the lighting itself was updated considerably following the arrival of colour TV, and on the introduction of live match broadcasts during the 1980s, the floodlighting was again extensively revamped. And when The Hawthorns was redeveloped in 1995, a new set of floodlights along with pylons were erected at a cost of £88,000.

Rays of Light

On 24 September 1888, some 7,000 spectators saw Albion draw 2-2 away with Walsall Town Swifts in a friendly under 'electric lighting'. The game was curtailed to 30 minutes each way.

On 20 March 1896, Albion beat Thames Ironworks (now West Ham United) 4-2 away in a friendly under 'lights'. The crowd was given as 1,500.

Albion's first post-war floodlit match was on 24 March 1953 when they played Wolverhampton Wanderers in a game to commemorate the switching on of the new floodlighting system at Hednesford United's ground. Wolves won 4-2 before a crowd of 3,500.

The 1954 FA Charity Shield game between Wolves and Albion at Molineux was played partly under floodlights. The result was a 4-4 draw (SEE CHARITY SHIELD).

Albion played the Hungarian side, Honved, under floodlights at the Heysel Stadium, Brussels, on 6 October 1954. when 55,000 fans saw Albion lose 5-3 (SEE HONVED).

On Wednesday 24 September 1958, Albion played Port Vale in a game arranged to officially switch on the floodlights at Vale Park. Albion were defeated 5-3 before 18,795 spectators.

FOGGO, Kenneth Taylor

Impish right winger, born in Perth in 1943, Ken Foggo came down to The Hawthorns with three other Scots, Campbell Crawford, Bobby Hope and Bobby Murray, in 1959. He did well and he went on to score 29 goals in 136 appearances for

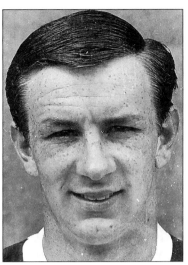

Ken Foggo, scored 29 goals in 137 games for Albion.

Albion after taking over the no.7 shirt from Alec Jackson. He left the club in 1967 to join Norwich City for £15,000, and afterwards served, in turn, with Portsmouth, Brentford (loan), Southend United, Chelmsford City, and Brereton Social, retiring in 1982 to go into the laundry and dry-cleaning business in London.

FA CUP

Albion first entered the FA Cup (then known as the English Cup) in season 1883-84 and they lost their opening tie, beaten 2-0 at home by neighbours Wednesbury Town.

Since then Albion have accumulated one of the best records in the competition, playing in ten Finals (12 with replays). They have won the trophy five times (1888, 1892, 1931, 1954 and 1968) and finished runners-up in 1886, 1887, 1895, 1912 and 1935.

Albion have appeared in 19 semi-finals (23 if you include replays), and their nine defeats were suffered in 1889, 1891, 1901, 1907, 1937, 1957, 1969, 1978 and 1982.

Jem Bayliss heads towards the Aston Villa goal in the 1887 FA Cup Final.

Albion's full FA Cup record (1883 to 1996 inclusive) reads;

Venue	P	W	D	L	F	A
Home	161	100	30	31	355	155
Away	180	70	41	69	251	242
Totals	341	170	71	100	606	397

Biggest wins: 10-1 v Chatham (away) 2 March 1889; 8-0 v Aylesbury United (home) 14 November 1992; 8-0 v South Shore (Blackpool) (home) 28 January 1899; 7-1 v Sheffield United (home) 26 January 1935; 7-1 v Spennymoor United (home) 16 January 1937.

Heaviest defeats: 0-5 v Leeds United (away) 18 February 1967; 0-4 v Tottenham Hotspur (semi-final at Villa Park) 8 April 1901; 0-4 v Chelsea (third replay at Highbury) 11 February 1953; 2-5 v Leicester Fosse (home) 14 January 1905.

Top home attendance: 61,088 v Newcastle United, 20 February 1954

Lowest home attendance: 2,484 v Wednesbury Old Athletic, 15 October 1887

Top away attendance (other than Final): 69,241 v Everton (semi-final at Old Trafford) 14 March 1931.

FA Cup winners in 1892. Left to right: Bassett, Nicholson, Reynolds, McLeod, Reader, Nicholls, Perry, Pearson, Groves, McCulloch, Geddes.

Lowest away attendance: 2,100 v Derby Junction, 20 November 1886.

Most goals by Albion player in FA Cup game: 4 – 'Jem' Bayliss v Stoke, 7 January 1888 (won 4-1).

Most goals by opponent in FA Cup game: 4 – 'Sandy' Brown for Tottenham Hotspur (semi-final, Villa Park), 8 April 1901 (0-4).

Cup Final Line-ups

Here are details of Albion's ten FA Cup Final appearances:

3 April 1886 v Blackburn Rovers (at The Oval) Drew 0-0
Attendance: 15,156
Team: R.Roberts; H.Bell, H.Green; E.Horton, C.Perry, G.Timmins; G.Woodhall, T.Green, J.Bayliss, A.Loach, G.Bell.

10 April 1886 v Blackburn Rovers replay (at Derby) Lost 0-2
Attendance: 10,144
Team: unchanged.

2 April 1887 v Aston Villa (at The Oval) Lost 0-2
Attendance: 15,534
Team: R.Roberts; A.Aldridge, H.Green; E.Horton, C.Perry, G.Timmins; G.Woodhall, T.Green, J.Bayliss, T.Pearson, W.Paddock.

24 March 1888 v Preston North End (at The Oval) Won 2-1
Scorers: Woodhall, Bayliss
Attendance: 18,904
Team: R.Roberts; A.Aldridge, H.Green; E.Horton, C.Perry, G.Timmins; G.Woodhall, W.Bassett, J.Bayliss, T.Pearson, J.Wilson.

19 March 1892 v Aston Villa (at The Oval) Won 3-0
Scorers: Geddes, Nicholls, Reynolds.
Attendance: 32,710
Team: J.Reader; M.Nicholson, T.McCulloch; J.Reynolds, C.Perry, W.Groves; W.Bassett, R.McLeod, S.Nicholls, T.Pearson, A.Geddes.

20 April 1895 v Aston Villa (at The Crystal Palace) Lost 0-1
Attendance: 42,652
Team: J.Reader; W.Williams, J.Horton; T.Perry, T.Higgins, J.Taggart; W.Bassett, R.McLeod, W.Richards, T.Hutchinson, J.Banks.

20 April 1912 v Barnsley (at The Crystal Palace) Drew 0-0 aet
Attendance: 55,213
Team: H.Pearson; A.Cook, J.Pennington; G.Baddeley, F.Buck, R.McNeal; C.Jephcott, H.Wright, R.Pailor, S.Bowser, B.Shearman.

24 April 1912 v Barnsley replay (at Sheffield) Lost 0-1 aet
Attendance: 38,555
Team: unchanged.

25 April 1931 v Birmingham (at Wembley) Won 2-1
Scorer: W.G.Richardson 2
Attendance: 90,368
Team: H.Pearson; G.Shaw, H.Trentham; T.Magee, W.Richardson, J.Edwards; T.Glidden, J.Carter, W.G.Richardson, E.Sandford, S.Wood.

27 April 1935 v Sheffield Wednesday (at Wembley) Lost 2-4
Scorers: Boyes, Sandford

Albion's 1912 FA Cup Final side. Back row (left to right, players only): Baddeley, Pearson, Bowser, Pailor. Middle row: Cook, Pennington, McNeal, Buck. Front row: Jephcott, Shearman, Wright.

The 1931 Cup-winning side and Second Division runners-up. Back row (left to right): Mr F.Everiss (secretary), W.Richardson, Carter, Pearson, Trentham, Sandford, F.Reed (trainer). Front row: Shaw, Magee, W.G.Richardson, Mr W.I.Bassett (chairman), Edwards, Wood, Glidden.

Attendance: 93,204
Team: H.Pearson, G.Shaw, H.Trentham; J.Murphy, W.Richardson, J.Edwards, T.Glidden, J.Carter, W.G.Richardson, E.Sandford, W.Boyes.
1 May 1954 v Preston North End (at Wembley) Won 3-2
Scorers: Allen 2 (1 pen.), Griffin
Attendance: 99,852
Team: J.Sanders; J.Kennedy, L.Millard; J.Dudley, J.Dugdale, R.Barlow; F.Griffin, R.Ryan, R.Allen, J.Nicholls, G.Lee.
18 May 1968 v Everton (at Wembley) Won 1-0 aet
Scorer: Astle
Attendance: 99,665
Team: J.Osborne; D.Fraser, G.Williams; T.Brown, J.Talbut, J.Kaye; G.Lovett, I.Collard, J.Astle, R.Hope, C.Clark. Sub: D.Clarke (for Kaye).

FA Cup Miscellany

Tony Brown played in more FA Cup games than any other Albion player (54) and he scored a record 27 goals in the process.

Right-half Ezra Horton played in each of Albion's first 36 FA Cup matches (1883-90).

The 1912 FA Cup Final between Albion and Barnsley at The Crystal Palace was the first to go into extra-time. The replay at Sheffield also went into extra-time.

When Albion met Newcastle United in a League game on 4 March 1933, no fewer than 18 of the participating players were in possession of FA Cup winning medals (ten from Albion).

Albion led South Shore (Blackpool) by a record score of 7-0 at half-time in their Cup meeting in January 1899.

Jeff Astle scored in every round of the 1967-68 FA Cup competition – the only Albion player to achieve this feat.

Albion's first FA Cup goal was scored by George Bell after 30 seconds in their first-ever victory in the competition v

Derby Street Junction, on 25 October 1884.

Albion's first FA Cup-tie at The Hawthorns saw them beat Manchester City 1-0 on 26 January 1901, Ben Garfield the scorer before a crowd of 10,026.

From 15 October 1887 to 2 March 1889 inclusive Albion won ten FA Cup-ties on the trot.

Albion have twice lost two FA Cup matches in the same season. They were beaten 3-1 at Accrington in a first-round tie in 1889-90, but protested over the state of the pitch and played again, losing the second game 3-0. And they were also defeated 1-0 at home and 3-1 away by Derby County in the two-legged competition of 1945-46.

In a Cup-tie against Druids (Wales) on 24 January 1885, Albion took the field and scored without their opponents being present to defend their goal. The referee insisted that the Druids 'come out of the dressing hut' and when they did, Albion 'scored' again to officially win the contest 1-0.

Albion were drawn at home in rounds 3, 4, 5 and 6 of the 1953-54 FA Cup competition, and played the semi-final four miles away at Villa Park.

Because of a misunderstanding, right-half Tom Perry missed the train taking the Albion players to Luton for an FA Cup-tie in January 1897. Perry was a vital member of the team and so club director Harry Keys authorised that a special train, bearing a single carriage, should be ordered to take Perry (along with the Albion secretary Frank Heaven) south. Albion won the game 1-0.

The first time the gates were shut at a football match in England was at the 1888 FA Cup Final between Albion and Preston North End. A record crowd of 18,904 attended.

Preston had asked if they could have their photograph taken with the Cup before the game – so confident were they of beating Albion. But the referee, Major Marindin, who was also the president of the FA, stepped in and said, bluntly: "No – hadn't you better win it first."

Above: **The Albion-Port Vale FA Cup semi-final at Villa Park in 1954.**

A record crowd of 32,710 saw the last FA Cup Final at The Oval when Albion defeated Aston Villa 3-0 in 1892.

Albion appeared in six FA Cup semi-finals in seven seasons between 1885-86 and 1891-92.

The replay of the 1886 Final between Albion and Blackburn Rovers at the County Cricket Ground, Derby, was the first FA Cup Final to be staged outside London.

Albion's longest FA Cup-tie spanned four matches and lasted 420 minutes. It was the fourth-round tie v Chelsea in 1953 which Albion eventually lost 4-0 after 0-0, 1-1 and 1-1 draws.

After playing in all the previous rounds, goalkeeper Norman Heath and right-back Stan Rickaby were forced to miss the 1954 FA Cup Final win over Preston North End through injury – but both players were later presented with winners' medals.

In their 1968-69 FA Cup run, Albion ousted three London clubs on their way to the semi-finals – Fulham, Arsenal and Chelsea.

Albion's line-up for their first-ever FA Cup-tie v Wednesbury Town in 1883 was: R.Roberts; H.Bell, J.Stanton; E.Horton, A.Bunn, J.Swallow; J.Whitehouse, H.Aston, W.Bisseker, G.Timmins, G.Bell – all local-born players.

Wally Boyes' goal for Albion in the 1935 FA Cup Final against Sheffield Wednesday.

Albion's first FA Cup substitute was Graham Lovett who came on during the third-round tie at Layer Road against Colchester United on 27 January 1968.

Cup Debutants

The following players all made their first major appearances for Albion in the FA Cup: Harry Aston (1883), George Bell (1883), Harry Bell (1883), Billy Bisseker (1883), 'Fred' Bunn (1883), Ezra Horton (1883), Bob Roberts (1883), Jimmy

Jeff Astle's semi-final goal against Birmingham City at Villa Park in 1968.

Stanton (1883), John Swallow (1883), George Timmins (1883), Jack Whitehouse (1883), 'Jem' Bayliss (1884), Harry Green (1884), Jack Horton (1884), Arthur Loach (1884), George Woodhall (1884), George Bushell (1885), Tommy Green (1885), Joe Matthews (1885), Albert Aldridge (1886), George Holden (1886), Billy Paddock (1886), Charlie Perry (1886), Luther Walker (1886), George Askin (1887), Billy Bassett (1887), Tom Pearson (1887), Joe Wilson (1887), Bethel Robinson (1889), Roddy McLeod (1891), George Johnson (1896), George Elmore (1903), Harry Parkes (1907),

Hubert Pearson (1908), Alf Taylor (1928), Jack Sankey (1933), Graham Wilkes (1939), Lew Twigg (1946), Dennis Gordon (1948), Johnny Nicholls (1952), Dave Mountford (1953) and Nicky Reid (1992).

Ousted by the Minnows
Listed here are the instances whereby Albion were knocked out of the FA Cup by teams from a lower Division or from outside the Football League:

1899-1900 – Southampton (Southern League); 1900-01 – Tottenham Hotspur (Southern League); 1902-03 – Tottenham Hotspur (Southern League); 1907-08 – Southampton (Southern League); 1911-12 – Barnsley (Division Two); 1912-13 – West Ham United (Southern League); 1914-15 – Hull City (Division Two); 1919-20 – Barnsley (Division Two); 1921-22 – Notts County (Division Two); 1922-23 – Charlton Athletic (Division Three South); 1926-27 – Hull City (Division Two); 1929-30 – Wrexham (Division Three North); 1932-33 – West Ham United (Division Two); 1935-36 – Bradford Park Avenue (Division Two); 1937-38 – York City (Division Three North); 1949-50 – Cardiff City (Division Two); 1951-52 – Blackburn Rovers (Division Two); 1960-61 – Lincoln City (Division Three); 1965-66 – Bolton Wanderers (Division Two); 1979-80 – West Ham United (Division Two); 1981-82 – Queens Park Rangers (Division Two); 1983-84 – Plymouth Argyle (Division Three); 1984-85 – Orient (Division Three); 1986-

Clark and Williams shoulder high as Albion celebrate their Wembley triumph of 1968.

87 – Swansea City (Division Four); 1990-91 – Woking (Vauxhall League); 1992-93 – Halifax Town (GM Vauxhall Conference); 1995-96 – Crewe Alexandra (Division Two).

The 4-2 defeat by Woking in the third round of the competition on 5 January 1991, was the first time Albion had lost at The Hawthorns to non-League opposition for 90 years – not since Tottenham Hotspur of the Southern League won a first-round replay 2-0 in February 1903.

FOOTBALL LEAGUE (1888 to 1996)

Along with 11 other clubs, West Bromwich Albion were founder members of the Football League in 1888. Their full record in the competition (to the end of the 1995-96 season) is:

Venue	P	W	D	L	F	A	Pts
Home	1,932	1,007	463	462	3,731	2,259	2,622
Away	1,932	503	471	958	2,372	3,509	1,547
Totals	3,864	1,510	934	1,420	6,103	5,758	4,169

First League game: Stoke (a), on Saturday 8 September 1888 (kick-off 3.30pm). Albion won 2-0 with goals from Joe Wilson and George Woodhall. The team was: Bob Roberts; Jack Horton, Harry Green; Ezra Horton, Charlie Perry, 'Jem' Bayliss; Billy Bassett, George Woodhall, Willie Hendry, Tom Pearson, Joe Wilson. The attendance was 4,524.

League Champions

Albion have won the League championship once, in 1919-20, the first season after World War One and the first time 22 teams were in the top flight.

In winning the greatest prize in English football Albion created three new records in the competition – they amassed 60 points, gained 28 wins and scored 104 goals.

They finished nine points clear of runners-up Burnley and clinched the title with four games left to play, on Saturday, 10 April, after beating Bradford Park Avenue 3-1 at home.

Albion's home record went a long way in seeing them through to the championship. They won 17 and drew one of their 21 games, whilst on their travels they registered 11 victories, a club record which was not equalled until 1978-79.

Albion's best win (of the 28) was 8-0 at home to Notts County on 25 October when Fred Morris scored five times. In both games against Blackburn Rovers, Albion netted five goals and they put four past Aston Villa, Bradford City, Bradford PA, Bolton Wanderers, Burnley, Chelsea, Derby County, Everton, Middlesbrough, Preston North End and Sunderland.

Morris headed the scoring charts with a new club record of 37 goals. Alf Bentley, Howard Gregory and centre-half Sid Bowser gave him good support with 15, 12 and ten goals respectively.

Bobby McNeal was the only ever-present; Bowser missed one game, Sammy Richardson and Joe Smith two, Morris and goalkeeper Hubert Pearson three and winger Jack Crisp four.

Albion's average home League attendance was 30,532; their best turnout being that of 43,579 for the Sunderland game on Boxing Day (won 4-0).

The following personnel received League championship medals: players – Alf Bentley, Sid Bowser, Arthur Cook, Jack Crisp, Howard Gregory, Claude Jephcott, Tommy Magee (in his first season as a professional), Bobby McNeal, Fred Morris, Hubert Pearson, skipper Jesse Pennington, Sammy Richardson, Andy Smith and Joe Smith; secretary-manager Fred Everiss and trainers Bill Barber and Bill Gopsill also received medals.

Division Two Champions

Albion have twice won the Second Division championship – in 1901-02 and 1910-11.

When winning the title in 1901-02, it was their first season in the Second Division and they had four points to spare over Middlesbrough at the finish (55-51).

An unbeaten run of 17 League games (from November to mid-March) paved the way for promotion and 25 victories were recorded out of 34 games played (14 at home, 11 away).

Charlie Simmons top-scored with 23 goals (out of 82) while Dan Nurse, Jim Stevenson and Tom Worton were ever-presents.

Albion's best win was 7-0 at home to Gainsborough Trinity and the average League attendance at The Hawthorns was 7,822.

Championship medals were awarded to 12 players – Amos Adams, George Dorsett, Harry Hadley, Jack Kifford, Billy Lee, Jimmy McLean, Dan Nurse, Charlie Simmons, Andrew Smith, Jimmy Stevenson, Ike Webb and Tom Worton.

Club secretary Frank Heaven, his assistant Fred Everiss, trainer Bill Brierley and Mr Alf Green also received medals.

Albion clinched the championship in 1910-11 after a last-match victory over Huddersfield Town at The Hawthorns. Before the game Albion required just a point, but a 15th-minute penalty by Freddie Buck gave them a 1-0 win and with it a place in the First Division. Albion finished on 53 points, two ahead of Bolton Wanderers.

A crowd of 30,135 – the best of the season – saw that win over Huddersfield and it pushed Albion's average home attendance for the season to a creditable 15,601.

Albion's best win was a 5-1 home triumph over Leicester Fosse on 5 November.

Sid Bowser finished up as top-scorer with 22 goals, and he and defender Frank Waterhouse were the only ever-presents.

The following all received championship medals this season: players – George Baddeley, Sid Bowser, Freddie Buck, Amos Lloyd, Bobby McNeal, Bob Pailor, Hubert Pearson, Jesse Pennington, Joe Smith, Frank Waterhouse, Billy Wollaston and Harry Wright. secretary-manager Fred Everiss and trainer Bill Barber received medals as well.

Promotion and Relegation

Automatic promotion and relegation was introduced to League football in 1898-99. Before then Test Matches (similar to the current Play-offs) were contested by clubs seeking to win a place in a higher Division or fighting to avoid demotion.

Albion have suffered relegation from the 'top' (the old First) Division six times: in 1900-01 (their first season at The Hawthorns), 1903-04, 1926-27, 1972-73 and 1985-86. They lost their Second Division status in 1990-91.

In 1895-96 they narrowly avoided demotion from Division One by virtue of winning two and drawing one of four vital end-of-season Test Matches (See the section on TEST MATCHES on page 79).

Albion also held on to their Second Division status in 1989-90 by the skin of their teeth after being sucked into the danger zone during the last month. They only won one of their remaining eight matches and only saved themselves with a 2-2 draw at Barnsley on the penultimate Saturday of the campaign.

When they were relegated to the Third Division for the first time in the club's history at the end of the 1990-91 season, Albion amazingly drew seven of their last eight League matches (six of them 1-1). They needed to win at Twerton Park, Bath, against Bristol Rovers on the final day to stay up. They could only draw.

Two more tense battles against relegation occurred at the end of the 1993-94 and 1994-95 seasons. In the former, Albion had to win at Portsmouth on the last Sunday to save themselves from the drop – and they did just that with a Lee Ashcroft goal. Then the following season they had to battle right to the death before saving themselves with two games remaining.

Promotion, apart from when they were Second Division

Albion's 1901-02 Second Division championship team. Players only (left to right), back row: J.Stevenson, A.Adams, I.Webb, J.Kifford, H.Hadley, Front: A.Smith, W.Lee, D.Nurse, C.Simmons, T.Worton,. On ground: J.McLean, G.Dorsett.

champions, has been achieved in 1930-31 (See DOUBLE WINNERS) and 1948-49 (each time as runners-up), in 1975-76 (when they took third place) and in 1992-93 via the play-offs.

After an excellent season, Albion – with six wins in the last nine games – clinched promotion from the Second Division in 1948-49 with a 3-0 victory at Leicester in the 41st match. Inspired by Irish internationals Jack Vernon at centre-half and Dave Walsh at centre-forward, Albion played some superb football and deservedly regained their top-League status after an absence of 11 years.

It was nail-biting stuff in 1975-76 when Albion, under the player-managership of another Irishman, Johnny Giles, had to win their final League game of the season at Oldham to take third place ahead of Bolton Wanderers and so return to the First Division after a break of four years. Over 15,000 supporters made the trip to Boundary Park to cheer Albion on to a 1-0 win, Tony Brown scoring the all-important goal early in the second-half.

The last time promotion was achieved was from the 'old' Third Division (now the present Second) in 1992-93 – and this time Albion, with the Argentinian Ossie Ardiles at the helm, did the honours at Wembley with more than 42,300 of their supporters present. After qualifying for the Play-offs, Albion defeated Swansea City on aggregate in the semi-final and then beat Port Vale 3-0 before a crowd of 53,471 at the Empire Stadium with Andy Hunt, Nicky Reid and Kevin Donovan on target after Vale's defender Peter Swan had been sent-off for a professional foul on Bob Taylor in the 58th minute.

In 1908-09 Albion missed promotion to the First Division by 1/56th of a goal. Tottenham Hotspur went up instead, on goal-average (See under BLACKPOOL).

At the Football League's Annual General Meeting on 29 May 1908, Albion secretary Fred Everiss seconded a proposal by Mr T. C.Newbold of Derby County that three clubs each season should be relegated from the First to the Second Division and that three should be promoted. This resolution was narrowly defeated by 19 votes to 17. It was not until 65 years later that this scheme was finally introduced.

Runners-Up

Albion finished runners-up in the First Division in 1924-25 (to Huddersfield Town) and 1953-54 (to neighbours Wolverhampton Wanderers).

Huddersfield took the title by two points (58-56) after Albion, who had been in touch throughout the campaign, stuttered at the end of the season, winning only one of their last four matches.

There was a terrific battle between Albion and Wolves throughout the 1953-54 season, and in the end the League honours went to the Molineux club while Albion settled for the FA Cup.

Albion were right on course for the double this season and there is no doubt that injuries ruined their chances at a vital stage in the campaign. Albion led the table going into the last month, but out of the six games played in April they won only one, and lost a crucial home match against their

Albion players, directors and staff pictured with the Football League championship trophy and the FA Charity Shield in 1920. Back row (left to right): W.Barber (trainer), Pearson, W.Gopsill (assistant trainer), E.Smith (assistant secretary). Second row: F.Everiss (secretary), D.Nurse (director), Cook, W.I.Bassett (chairman), H.Keys (vice-chairman), Jephcott, Mr Seymour (director), Lieut-Col Ely (director). Front row: Crisp, A.Smith, McNeal, Pennington, Bowser, Morris, Gregory. On ground: J.Smith, Magee, Bentley, Richardson.

rivals Wolves, which no doubt gave the Molineux men a terrific boost. They went on to lift the crown for the first time, finishing four points clear of Albion (57-53).

Test Matches
By finishing in the bottom two places in the First Division in 1895-96, Albion and neighbours Small Heath (now Birmingham City) were required, along with Manchester City and Liverpool from Division Two, to contest Test Matches to see who would be playing in which Division the following season. Both clubs from the First Division had to play the two from the Second at home and away. Albion, along with Liverpool, gained five points from their four games and thus remained in the top flight, while Manchester City and Small Heath (three points apiece) were forced to play in Division Two.
The details of Albion's four crucial Test matches played in 1896:
18 April v Manchester City (a) 1-1
Scorer: T.Perry
Attendance: 8,000
20 April v Manchester City (h) 6-1
Scorers: Flewitt 2, J.Richards, Johnson, Higgins, Williams
Attendance: 8,000
25 April v Liverpool (a) 0-2
Attendance: 20,100
27 April v Liverpool (h) 2-0
Scorers: Williams (pen), W.Richards
Attendance: 15,000

Clubs Never Met
Of the other 91 clubs currently in the Premiership and Endsleigh League, Albion have yet to engage the following in League action:
Barnet, Cambridge United, Colchester United, Crewe Alexandra, Gillingham, Hereford United, Rochdale, Scarborough, Scunthorpe United, Wimbledon, Wycombe Wanderers and Wrexham.
However, Albion have met all but Rochdale and Scarborough in certain Cup tournaments and/or friendly matches.

Ten Men
On Saturday, 29 September 1894, Albion played Everton away in a First Division game fielding only ten men for the entire 90 minutes, centre-forward Billy Richards being the missing player.
The Albion directors, at a special meeting arranged 24 hours later to discuss Richards's absence (he failed to meet the train on the morning of the match), suspended the player for three months, until 1 January 1895.
Twenty-four hours after receiving his punishment, Richards sent a letter of apology to the Albion secretary, Mr H.S.Jackson, stating why he was not at the station to board the train. This was seen by each member of the board and the next morning Richards was called into the secretary's office to be told that his sentence had been cut and instead he was to pay a fine of one guinea (£1.05) – this being the amount the Football League had imposed on the Albion club for fielding a player short at Everton. The money was deducted from Richards' wages. For the record, Albion lost the game 4-1.

Worst Start to a Season and Worst Ever League Season
Albion's worst start to a League season came at the

The 1948-49 promotion-winning side. Back row (left to right) F.Reed (trainer), E.Wilcox, J.Kennedy, H.Kinsell, R.Barlow, R.Barker, G.Hood, J.Haines, R.Ryan, W.G.Richardson (coach). Front row: L.Millard, W.Elliott, C.Williams, D.Walsh, J.Vernon, J.Sanders, J.Pemberton, A.Smith, J.Boyd.

commencement of the 1985-86 campaign when they lost nine of their opening ten matches and won only one of 21 starts up to mid-December. In fact, this was to be Albion's worst-ever season. They won only four games all told (out of 42) and collected a mere 24 points (out of 126), finishing bottom of the table and being relegated.

Their full record in 1985-86 was:

Venue	P	W	D	L	F	A	Pts	Pos
Home	21	3	8	10	21	36	17	
Away	21	1	4	16	14	53	7	
Totals	42	4	12	26	35	89	24	22nd

After starting badly, Albion's performances gradually deteriorated and subsequently they suffered relegation for the sixth time in the club's history.

In the course of the campaign Albion set several 'unwanted' records and had the statistically-minded supporters thumbing frantically through the record books as well as making additional entries. These are the facts of that disastrous campaign with the previous record totals alongside:

Fewest League wins	4	(9)
Record number of defeats	26	(23)
Most home defeats	10	(equalling record)
Least number of away wins	1	(equalling record)
Fewest number of home wins	3	(6)
Least number of home points	17	(22)
Fewest number of home goals	21	(22)
Lowest points tally (42 games)	24	(28)
Most consecutive games lost	9	(8)
Most players used	33	(equalling record)

Albion also conceded more goals at home (36) and away (53) than any other club in the First Division in 1985-86; they used five different goalkeepers in League and Cup competitions; 18 players were given their Albion debuts during the campaign; Albion dropped to the bottom of the Division after the third game, and stayed there – and to cap it all, the Reserves were relegated from the First Division of the Central League.

Some supporters never saw Albion win a match in 1985-86.

League Doubles

The most League doubles recorded by Albion in a season is nine – in 1901-02 and 1919-20. They completed seven in 1978-79, and six in 1924-25 and 1953-54 when they finished runners-up in the First Division.

Albion went through the whole of the 1980-81 season for the first time ever without having a League double recorded against them.

Half-time Scores

The highest half-time score in an Albion League match occurred at Maine Road on 5 September 1936 in a First Division game. At the 45 minute mark hosts Manchester City were leading Albion 6-2, which was, in fact, the final result.

Albion's best half-time lead has been by five goals: 6-1 v Blackpool (home) on 22 February 1902 (Division Two) and 5-0, achieved three times (all in Division One) v Wolverhampton Wanderers (away) on Boxing Day December 1893, v Darwen

The 1975-76 promotion squad. Back row (left to right): George Wright (physiotherapist), Willie Johnston, Ian Edwards, Bryan Robson, Len Cantello, John Osborne, Peter Latchford, Tony Brown, Ray Wilson, John Trewick, Allan Glover, Brian Whitehouse (coach). Front row: Alistair Robertson, Mick Martin, David Rushbury, John Wile, Johnny Giles (player-manager), Joe Mayo, Gordon Nisbet, Alistair Brown, Paddy Mulligan.

(home) on 4 April 1892 and against Burnley at The Hawthorns on 11 November 1967. All these games were in the First Division.

Sunday League Games
Albion's first Sunday League game was against Portsmouth at Fratton Park on 3 February 1974 when they drew 1-1 in the Second Division before a near 20,000 crowd – Pompey's biggest for six years. Albion's first Sunday home League game was against Watford at The Hawthorns on 22 December 1985 which they won 3-1 in front of 11,092 spectators.

Void 1939-40 League Games
World War Two broke out on 3 September 1939 and on this day League football in England was suspended, as it turned out until August 1946. Prior to the announcement, most clubs (Albion included) had already fulfilled three League games at the start of the ill-fated 1939-40 season. These were automatically declared null and void.
Albion's three fixtures in Division Two went as follows:
26 August v Swansea Town (away) 2-1
Scorer: H.Jones 2. Attendance: 15,034
28 August v Coventry City (away) 3-3
Scorers: E.Jones, Banks, Connelly. Attendance: 26,182
2 September v Tottenham Hotspur (home) 3-4
Scorer: E.Jones 3. Attendance: 17,008

First and Last Christmas Day League Games
The Albion played their initial Christmas Day League game in 1896 when they lost 8-1 away to Derby County in the First Division.
Albion's first Christmas Day League encounter at The Hawthorns saw them draw 1-1 with Clapton Orient in 1905 before an 18,000 crowd.
Their last Christmas Day League match came in 1956 when they defeated Newcastle United 1-0 at The

Hawthorns in a First Division fixture in front of 13,780 fans. Ray Barlow scored the winning goal.
In all Albion played 28 League matches on 25 December – 12 were won, four drawn and 12 lost.
Jack Vernon scored his only League goal for Albion in a 1-0 Christmas Day victory over Sheffield Wednesday at The Hawthorns in 1950.

Duration of Season
The 1946-47 League season spanned nine months – starting on 31 August and ending on 31 May – the longest in Albion's history. This was due to the Arctic weather conditions which gripped Great Britain early in 1947.

Longest League Runs
Undefeated matches: 17 (23 December 1901 to 29 March 1902 and 7 September to 7 December 1957).
Undefeated home matches: 19 (2 September 1901 to 11 October 1902 and 7 September 1908 to 6 September 1909).
Without a win: 14 (28 October 1995 to 3 February 1996).
Successive wins: 11 (5 April 1930 to 8 September 1930).
Successive defeats: 11 (28 October 1995 to 26 December 1995).
Home matches without a win: 9 (2 May 1921 to 26 November 1921 and 21 August 1971 to 11 December 1971).
Undefeated away matches: 11 (23 April 1957 to 14 December 1957 and 26 January 1980 to 13 September 1980).
Without an away win: 27 (27 December 1969 to 12 April 1971).
Successive home wins: 11 (20 October 1906 to 1 April 1907).
Successive away wins: 7 (22 April 1953 to 31 October 1953).

Points Deducted
Albion have never had League points deducted from their total for any wrong-doing since entering the competition as

Nicky Reid's goal in the 3-0 Play-off win over Port Vale at Wembley in May 1993.

John Wile, whose 20-second own-goal against Spurs was a record he could probably have done without.

founder members in 1888. However, Sunderland are one of the few clubs who have – and the game in question was against Albion at Stoney Lane on 20 September 1890. They beat Albion 4-0 that day to record their first away win of the season, but afterwards an inquiry revealed that Sunderland had fielded an illegible player – goalkeeper Ted Doig – who had not been registered in time to play in the First Division match. The two 'win' points were therefore deducted from Sunderland's total and the club was also fined £50 for infringing the rules. Albion were not awarded the points.

Goals For and Against

The least number of goals conceded by Albion in a full 42 match League season is 33 in 1975-76. In 1908-09 they gave away 27 goals in 38 matches and conceded 29 in 34 games in 1901-02.

The most goals Albion have conceded in a season is 98 in 42 First Division matches in 1936-37. In this same season they also had a record 66 goals put past them in 21 away matches.

The following season four Albion goalkeepers – Jimmy Adams, Harry Baldwin, Bill Harris and Billy Light – had 91 League goals swept past them.

The least number of goals conceded in 21 home League games is ten in 1922-23, while the fewest number of League goals conceded in 21 away games has been 17 in 1924-25.

The lowest number of goals scored by Albion in a season of 21 home League games is 21 in 1985-85. And in this same season Albion netted a record low of 12 goals in their 21 away matches.

Over a period of five seasons, 1925-26 to 1929-30 inclusive, Albion's defence conceded a staggering 384 goals in 210 League games. In seven full seasons from 1932-33 to 1938-39 (294 games) they gave away 572 goals.

On the debit side, in nine League games between 25 December 1914 and 6 March 1915, and again between 20 October and 9 December 1973, Albion gave away just three goals in each sequence. Albion's defence kept a clean-sheet in each of the last six First Division matches in season 1949-50.

John Wile's 20-second own-goal v Tottenham Hotspur (away) in the First Division match on 4 December 1982 was the fastest-ever by an Albion player in any major competition.

Clean Sheets

Goalkeeper John Osborne, an ever-present during Albion's promotion-winning side of 1975-76, kept a club record 22 clean sheets in 42 Second Division matches. In all 'Ossie' conceded just 33 goals – another record.

League Defeats

Albion's heaviest defeat in the Football League is 10-3 – at The Victoria Ground against Stoke City in a First Division game on 4 February 1937 (See STOKE CITY).

The most defeats suffered in a 42 match League season is 26 in 1985-86 (Division One).

The fewest defeats in a full season of 42 games is seven in 1978-79 (Division One). And the fewest away defeats in a season is four, also in 1978-79.

During the first-half of the 1995-96 season (late October to late December) Albion suffered a record 11 successive League defeats. Albion's most common League defeat is 2-1.

Albion 5 Grimsby Town 6 has been Albion's closest League defeat (30 April 1932).

Albion's heaviest home League defeat is 6-1 – suffered twice, at the hands of Sunderland on 23 October 1937 and Nottingham Forest on 20 October 1900 – both games in Division One.

Most home defeats suffered by Albion in a single season is ten in 1950-51 and 1985-86 (each time in Division One).

League Victories

Albion's best League win is 12-0 at home to Darwen on 4 April 1892 (See DARWEN).

Away from home Albion's best League victory is 8-0 at Molineux against Wolverhampton Wanderers on 27 December 1892 (also in Division One).

The fewest League victories gained by Albion in a season is four in 1985-86 – the most is 28 when they won the First Division championship in 1919-20.

In 1901-02 season Albion recorded a record ten successive home League wins, starting on 7 December and finishing on 18 January.

Albion's most common win is 2-1.

Albion did not register a single away win in their First Division season of 1891-92 – the only time this has happened.

Undefeated

During the course of winning the Second Division title in 1901-02, Albion created a club record of 17 League games without defeat (7 December to 29 March). This record was equalled in 1957-58 when Albion again went 17 games without defeat (7 September to 7 December).

Also in the 1957-58 season, Albion went a record 11 away games without defeat, the run coming to an abrupt end when they crashed 5-1 at Luton in early December. This record was equalled between 26 January and 13 September 1980.

Away Form

Albion failed to win any of their 27 First Division away games between 27 December 1969 and 12 April 1971 – a club record.

The longest time Albion have gone without registering an away League win is almost two years – from 25 October 1890 to 8 October 1892.

Albion recorded seven successive away League wins from 22 April 1953 to 17 October 1953 inclusive.

League Draws

Not one of Albion's 19 away League games in 1909-10 ended in a draw.

Only one draw was recorded at home in seasons 1919-20, 1929-30, 1932-33, 1962-63 and 1966-67.

Ten draws were achieved from 21 away League games in 1957-58.

The most draws accumulated by Albion in a League season is 19 (eight at home, 11 away) in season 1979-80. (Ten of these were goalless – also a club record).

Albion drew five successive League games in 1914-15, 1961-62 and 1990-91. They were relegated from Division Two at the end of the latter campaign after drawing their last five games by a scoreline of 1-1.

Between 24 March and 13 November 1982 Albion played 29 League games without recording a single draw.

4-4 has been Albion's highest-scoring League draw to date.

100 League Games Against One Club

Albion have played 100 (or more) League games against 14 different clubs: Arsenal (104), Aston Villa (124), Bolton Wanderers (114), Burnley (112), Chelsea (100), Everton (132), Liverpool (108), Manchester City (110), Manchester United (100), Nottingham Forest (102), Stoke City (110), Sunderland (124), Tottenham Hotspur (106) and Wolverhampton Wanderers (126).

The first century of League encounters was achieved against Burnley on 31 December 1966 and three weeks later Albion met Everton for the 100th time in the competition. Albion have now met Everton more times (132) than they have any other club in Football League competition.

League Miscellany

On 30 September 1961, Albion's 18 year-old goalkeeper Tony Millington made his League debut v Manchester City, whose 'keeper was the 38-year-old German, Bert Trautmann. Millington's first five League outings for Albion all ended in draws.

Tony Millington – his first five League games all ended in draws.

Of 47 League games played by Albion between September 1957 and October 1958, not one ended in a 2-1 scoreline.

There was not one foul awarded against Albion during their home League game v West Ham United on 25 October 1947.

Albion's total of 50 goals in season 1975-76 was the second lowest total ever recorded by a team winning promotion to the First Division. In 1922-23 Notts County scored 46.

The Hawthorns crowd had to wait 494 minutes to see Albion score a League goal in season 1921-22. They were goalless in their opening five matches, finally breaking their duck in a 2-2 draw with Cardiff City in late October.

Albion had the privilege of playing the first League game at Elland Road – against Leeds City on 9 September 1905. Albion won 2-0 before a 6,800 crowd.

Albion played their 1,000th Football League game against Tottenham Hotspur at White Hart Lane on 30 January 1922 (lost 2-0). Their 2,000th (which was also their 1,000 League game at home) was against Manchester United at The Hawthorns on 29 November 1952 (won 3-1). Albion's 3,000th League match saw them again beat Manchester United, this time by 4-0 at home on 16 October 1976 before a 36,615 crowd.

On 6 November 1897, left-back Billy Williams declined the offer to play for the Football League v the Irish League at Manchester, choosing to line-up for Albion against Everton in a First Division game instead. He was later awarded a medal for his loyalty.

One of the fastest League goals ever scored came from the foot of former Albion centre-forward Keith Smith, who found the net after six seconds play for Crystal Palace against Derby County on 12 December 1964.

South African-born striker John Paskin is the only player ever to appear for Albion, Birmingham City and Wolverhampton Wanderers in Football League matches.

FOOTBALL LEAGUE CUP

The Football League Cup competition was introduced for season 1960-61, but Albion, along with a handful of other First Division clubs, did not enter immediately. In fact, Albion did not participate during the opening five seasons and when they did take part for the first time, in 1965-66, they went on to win the trophy, beating West Ham United in the last of the two-legged Finals.

Over the last 15 years the 'League' Cup has been sponsored thus: the Milk Cup 1982-86, the Littlewoods Challenge Cup 1986-90; the Rumbelows Cup 1990-92 and the Coca-Cola Cup 1992-96. And Albion's full League Cup record (1965-96) is as follows:

Albion and QPR take the field before the 1967 League Cup Final.

Venue	P	W	D	L	F	A
Home	55	30	14	11	104	59
Away	61	19	17	25	74	91
Totals	116	49	31	36	178	150

Three Finals

Albion have played in three Football League Cup Finals, winning in 1965-66 and losing in both 1966-67 and 1969-70. On their way to beating West Ham in the 1966 Final, Albion ousted, in turn, Walsall (h) 3-1, Leeds United (a) 4-2, Coventry City (h) 6-1 (after a 1-1 draw), Aston Villa (h) 3-1

and Peterborough United in the two-legged semi-final 2-1 (h) and 4-2 (a). The first leg of the Final went West Ham's way by 2-1 but Albion won the return leg at The Hawthorns 4-1 to take the trophy 5-3 on aggregate.

For the first leg of the Final at Upton Park on 9 February 1966, Albion fielded: Ray Potter; Bobby Cram, Ray Fairfax; Doug Fraser, Danny Campbell, Graham Williams; Tony Brown, Jeff Astle, John Kaye, Graham Lovett, Clive Clark. Astle scored the goal and the attendance was 28,588.

For the second leg at The Hawthorns a fortnight later (23 February) Albion had Bobby Hope in place of Lovett, and they overpowered the Hammers with Kaye, Brown, Clark and Williams on target in front of a 32,013 crowd. Skipper Graham Williams duly collected the trophy, Albion's first in 12 years.

A year later – on 4 March 1967 – Albion were in the Final again – this first at Wembley. They met Third Division outsiders Queens Park Rangers and were favourites to retain the Cup, but after leading 2-0 at half-time thanks to two fine goals from former Rangers player Clive Clark, Albion slipped up after the break and the Londoners charged in for a 3-2 victory before a then record 97,952 crowd.

Albion's team was: Dick Sheppard; Bobby Cram, Graham Williams; Ian Collard, Dennis Clarke, Doug Fraser; Tony Brown, Jeff Astle, John Kaye, Bobby Hope, Clive Clark. Sub: Ken Foggo.

Albion's third League Cup Final appearance took place on 7 March 1970, again at Wembley, when their opponents this time were Manchester City. On a pudding of a pitch Albion scored early on through Astle, but City equalised before full-

Disappointment after losing to Manchester City in the 1970 League Cup Final.

time and then stole the winning goal (via Glen Pardoe) in extra-time to take the trophy to Maine Road. The attendance was 97,963 and Albion fielded: John Osborne; Doug Fraser, Ray Wilson; Tony Brown, John Talbut, John Kaye; Len Cantello, Colin Suggett, Jeff Astle, Asa Hartford, Bobby Hope. Sub: Dick Krzywicki (for Hartford).

Arthur Mann played for City in the 1970 Final and 25 years later he became Albion's assistant manager.

League Cup Snippets

Tony Brown scored in every round of the 1965-66 League Cup competition, including a hat-trick in the away leg of the semi-final v Peterborough, and Clive Clark scored in every game of the 1966-67 tournament.

Clark was also the first player to score a League Cup goal at Wembley, doing so in the seventh minute of that 1967 Final.

When Astle headed Albion's goal in the 1970 Final v Manchester City, he became the first player to score in both the FA Cup and League Cup Final at Wembley.

On reaching Wembley in 1970, Albion became the first Midlands club to play in three Football League Cup Finals.

Albion lost in the 1981-82 League Cup semi-final to Tottenham Hotspur, 1-0 on aggregate.

Albion scored in each of their first 23 League Cup games. And they won their first 13 at The Hawthorns, which included two record 6-1 victories over Coventry City (1965-66) and Aston Villa (1966-67).

Nottingham Forest have inflicted upon Albion their heaviest League Cup defeat, winning 6-1 at The City Ground in 1982-83.

Tony Brown had the distinction of scoring Albion's first League Cup goal, in the club's first-ever game in the competition v Walsall at The Hawthorns on 22 September 1965 when a record crowd of 41,188 turned out.

Jeff Astle has scored most League Cup goals for Albion – 19.

Ally Robertson made a record 53 League Cup appearances for Albion following an unfortunate debut in the competition v Charlton Athletic in September 1970 when he broke a leg.

On 7 November 1979 Albion flew to a match in the UK for the first time – to Norwich for a League Cup-tie (lost 3-0).

Three League Cup-ties have taken three games to decide, each tie lasting 300 minutes – Albion v Leeds United in 1978-79, Albion v Preston North End in 1980-81 and Albion v West Ham United in 1981-82.

Albion were 3-0 down from the first leg of an away League Cup-tie at Millwall in October 1983, but they turned things round and won the return fixture 5-1 at The Hawthorns.

Albion were beaten 3-1 at home by Bradford City in the first leg of a League Cup-tie in September 1989, but thanks to a hat-trick by John Thomas in the return leg at Valley Parade, which went Albion's way 5-3, the Baggies won through on the away goals rule.

The following players all made their Albion debuts in League Cup matches: Danny Campbell (West Ham United, 1966 Final, first leg); Kenny Stephens (v Manchester City, 1966), Hugh MacLean (v Tottenham Hotspur, 1971), Paddy Mulligan (v Fulham, 1975), Cyrille Regis (v Rotherham United, 1977), Mickey Lewis (v Crystal Palace, 1981), John Smith (v Millwall, 1983), Graham Easter (v Peterborough United, 1988), Chris Whyte (Peterborough United 1988), Gavin Ward (v Bradford City, 1989), Mark Barham (v Bradford City, 1989), Adrian Foster (v Bradford City, 1989), Stacy Coldicott (v Plymouth Argyle 1992).

Both Stephens and Regis scored on their debuts.

FOOTBALL LEAGUE JUBILEE FUND

Albion played neighbours Aston Villa in two League Jubilee Fund matches at Villa Park in the late 1930s. On 20 August 1938, a crowd of 26,640 witnessed a 1-1 draw with Harry Jones scoring for Albion, and 12 months later, on 19 August 1939, an attendance of 16,007 witnessed another 1-1 draw, when 'W.G.' Richardson netted for Albion.

FOOTBALLER/PLAYER OF THE YEAR AWARDS

Six different Albion players have won the annual 'Midland Footballer of the Year' award organised by the *Birmingham Evening Mail*.

1962	Don Howe
1966	John Kaye
1968	Jeff Astle
1969	Tony Brown
1970	John Kaye
1971	Tony Brown
1978	John Wile
1979	Tony Brown
1980	Bryan Robson

Brown is the only player to have won the coveted prize three times. He received his 'hat-trick' award from Sir Matt Busby prior to the Albion v Manchester United League game at The Hawthorns on 5 May 1979.

In 1977-78 Albion's left-back Derek Statham was voted 'Young Footballer of the Year' by the Midland Sportswriters.

Albion's player-manager Johnny Giles was named runner-up (to Emlyn Hughes of Liverpool) in the annual FWA 'Footballer of the Year' awards in 1976-77.

Albion's Cyrille Regis was voted 'Young Player of the

Bryan Robson with his Midlands Footballer of the Year award in 1980.

Year' by PFA members in 1978-79; Laurie Cunningham was runner-up and Derek Statham was placed fourth.

Bryan Robson was the Sportsco/Sports Argus 'Footballer of the Year' in 1979 and also the Midland Sportswriters' 'Footballer of the Year' in 1980, and Ally Brown and Tony Brown shared the honour of being voted 'Footballer of the Year' in 1978-79 by Midland Sportswriters. In 1982 Cyrille Regis was voted Midland Sportswriters' 'Footballer of the Season' and was also runner-up in the PFA 'Footballer of the Year' awards that same year.

Centre-half Jack Vernon, an Albion player from 1947-52, was voted 'Irish Footballer of the Year' in 1951.

Albion's flying winger of the 1880s and 1890s, Billy Bassett, was presented with a silver cup in 1894 after being voted 'Player of the Season' by readers of the 'Answers' journal.

FORMATION OF THE CLUB

It is now thought likely that the formation of the Albion club first took shape in 1878 when a friendly match was arranged by a West Bromwich Strollers team against a team called Hudson's in West Bromwich on 23 November that year. The result was a 0-0 draw.

Several players who took part in this initial match were employees at the George Salter Spring works in West Bromwich and during the summer months they played a lot of cricket. Obviously wanting something to occupy their minds in the winter months, and with no one really interested in rugby, these players stayed together and the following year adopted the name of West Bromwich Strollers to start playing football in earnest.

Their first recorded victory was 1-0 v Black Lake Victoria in mid-December 1979, and they went from strength to strength thereafter, changing their name from Strollers to Albion in March 1880.

Among the early Albion stalwarts (all local men working at George Salter's) were George Bell, Robert Biddulph, Billy Bisseker, Joey Law, Denny Smith, Tom Smith, John Stokes, Luther Walker and John While.

On 2 May 1960, Albion's League side played George Salter's Works team in a friendly to commemorate the West Bromwich firm's Bicentennial. A crowd of 2,000 at Salter's Springfields Sports Ground saw Albion win 13-2 with Alec Jackson (5), Davey Burnside (3) and Graham Williams (2) the leading scorers. Albion, whose goalkeeper Jock Wallace played at centre-forward in the second-half, led 7-0 at the interval.

FOUR ACRES

In September 1882, Albion moved from their primitive ground in Walsall Street to more comfortable accommodation at The Four Acres, home of West Bromwich Dartmouth Cricket Club, who had been playing there since 1834. The Four Acres – taken initially on a one-year agreement – was a well-known local centre where athletics meetings were staged at festivals and on public holidays. It was originally dedicated by William, fourth Earl of Dartmouth, to the recreation of local inhabitants.

There was a clause in the agreement, however, whereby Albion could only play football matches there two days a week – on a Saturday and Monday.

Season tickets were issued at a cost of 2s 6d (13p), and the opening fixture saw Albion beat Stourbridge Standard 10-0 in a friendly on 7 October 1882, Billy Bisseker scoring six goals.

Improvements were made to the ground gradually and by the summer of 1883 the playing area had been enclosed by a form of tubing instead of by ropes, and wooden racks were laid on the ground around the reserved portion for the comfort of the spectators.

At Albion's AGM in July 1883 it was disclosed that the cricket club had agreed to let The Four Acres for a further two years at a rental of £15 per annum and that Albion would have to cover the costs of building a new ticket office and pavilion.

The biggest match ever staged at The Four Acres was an FA Cup-tie between Albion and Blackburn Rovers on 21 February 1885. A record crowd of 16,393 packed in to see Rovers win 2-0 despite a battling performance from Albion.

All told Albion played 61 first-team games at The Four Acres (22 of them Cup-ties). They won 48 and lost only seven, scoring 268 goals 'for' and conceding just 56.

Albion's best win on the ground was 26-0 v Coseley in a Birmingham Cup-tie on 11 November 1882 and their heaviest defeat was a 5-1 whipping by Stoke in a friendly fixture in October 1882.

The last game at The Four Acres (now Park Crescent in Seager Street) was played on 6 April 1885 when Albion beat Wednesbury Old Athletic 3-2 in a friendly wearing cardinal and blue halved shirts and white shorts.

FRASER, Douglas Michael

A craggy Scot, born in Busby, Lanarkshire in 1941, Doug Fraser joined Albion from Aberdeen for £23,000 in 1963 and immediately established himself in the English First Division. A stern-tackling wing-half, who eventually switched to full-back, Fraser helped Albion win the League Cup and FA Cup in 1966 and 1968 respectively, and he skippered the side in the 1970 League Cup Final defeat against Manchester City, having earlier played in the 1967 losing Final v QPR. He made 325 appearances for Albion (12 goals) in eight years with the club, up to 1971, when he was

transferred to Nottingham Forest. He later joined Walsall and became manager at Fellows Park in 1975. He quit soccer in 1977 to join the Nottingham prison service. Fraser, capped twice by Scotland, had unsuccessful trials with Celtic and Leeds before going on to play 70 times for Aberdeen (1960-63).

FRIENDLY MATCHES

The total number of friendly matches played by Albion since 1878 is in the region of 800. Before League Football started in 1888, all major clubs, including Albion, used to arrange friendlies on a weekly basis, sometimes playing over 30 a season.

But once the League and FA Cup competitions became firmly established, so the number of friendly matches dropped, and they have been reduced even more dramatically following the introduction of other tournaments over the years. Nowadays a team averages about five friendlies per season.

Albion's best friendly win is 23-2 v Studley & District XI (away) on 17 September 1888.

The closest defeat is 7-6 away to Blackburn Rovers on 22 October 1887.

Albion played a record number of 35 friendlies in 1887-88, winning 24 and losing six. In 1885-86 they fulfilled 31.

The biggest crowd to watch a friendly match involving Albion is 89,400 which assembled in the national stadium in Peking on 19 May 1978 to watch Albion beat China 2-0.

The best crowd for a friendly at The Hawthorns has been 55,497 for Norman Heath's Testimonial match on 25 April 1956, when Albion drew 5-5 with an International XI.

Ronnie Allen became the oldest player ever to appear for Albion's first team when he came on as substitute in a friendly match at Cheltenham in May 1995 at the age of 66 (See AGE).

FULHAM

Albion's record against Fulham:

Football League

Venue	P	W	D	L	F	A	Pts
Home	26	17	3	6	70	32	38
Away	26	11	6	9	26	33	28
Totals	52	28	9	15	96	65	66

FA Cup

Venue	P	W	D	L	F	A
Home	2	2	0	0	7	1
Away	1	1	0	0	2	1
Totals	3	3	0	0	9	2

League Cup

Venue	P	W	D	L	F	A
Home	2	0	2	0	2	2
Away	2	1	0	1	1	1
Totals	4	1	2	1	3	3

Other Matches

Venue	P	W	D	L	F	A
Home	1	1	0	0	3	1
Away	1	1	0	0	4	1
Totals	2	2	0	0	7	2

Albion have twice beaten Fulham 6-1 in home League games – on 23 November 1946 (Division Two) and 8 September 1962 (Division One). Derek Kevan scored four goals in that last victory.

Fulham's best League win over Albion is 4-0 at Craven Cottage on 30 August 1975 (Division Two) and they have twice defeated Albion 4-2 at The Hawthorns – on 10 October 1959 and on 27 August 1960, each time in the First Division.

Albion and Fulham were promoted together to the First Division at the end of the 1948-49 season, Fulham going up as champions.

Albion League debutants v Fulham: Charlie Hewitt (1908), Willie Thompson (1908), Fred Brown (1908), George Harris (1909), Harry Chambers (1928), Tom Grimley (1946), Wilf Carter (1951), Archie Styles (1959), Kenny Foggo (1962), Dick Krzywicki (1964). Micky Mellon (1993).

Players with both clubs: Harry Brown, Joseph Connor, Mark Grew, Tony Lange, Stacey North, Bobby Robson, Arthur Rowley, Ernie Shepherd, Kevin Steggles, Brian Talbot.

Other connections: Martin Pike, an Albion reserve, later played over 200 games for Fulham (1990-94); Vic Buckingham managed both Albion (1953-59) and Fulham (1965-68); Archie Macaulay played for Fulham (1950s) and managed Albion (1961-63) while Gordon Clark was Albion's manager (1959-61) and later assistant manager at Fulham (1977). Ernie Shepherd played League games for both Albion and Fulham in that promotion-winning season of 1948-49. Bobby Robson had two spells with Fulham as a player (before and after serving with Albion) and later became manager at Craven Cottage (1968). And goalkeeper Perry Digweed was with Fulham (1977-81) and on loan with Albion (1983).

FULL MEMBERS' CUP

Albion played in this competition for two seasons (1985-86 and 1986-87) and their full record is:

Venue	P	W	D	L	F	A
Home	2	1	1	0	4	3
Away	2	1	0	1	2	3
Totals	4	2	1	1	6	6

Albion drew 2-2 at home with Chelsea in the Southern

Sean Hayward, made his only Albion appearance in the Full Members' Cup when a crowd of only 967 saw the Baggies lose at The Den.

Area semi-final on 13 November 1985, but then lost 5-4 in a penalty shoot-out in front of 4,070 spectators.

Just 967 fans saw Albion lose 2-0 at Millwall on 21 October 1986 when Sean Hayward made his one and only first-team appearance in the Baggies' defence.

Garth Crooks scored both goals in Albion's 2-1 away win at Brighton on 2 October 1985 – their first game in the competition.

Steve Bull made his Albion debut as a substitute in the Full Members' Cup-tie v Crystal Palace (h) on 23 October 1985.

GAINSBOROUGH TRINITY

Albion's record against Trinity:

Football League

Venue	P	W	D	L	F	A	Pts
Home	8	7	0	1	29	5	14
Away	8	2	2	4	12	16	6
Totals	16	9	2	5	41	21	20

Trevor Thompson, an Albion defender in the 1970s, went on to play for Gainsborough Trinity.

Albion's best win of their nine is 7-0 at home in a Second Division match on 5 October 1901 – this was also the first meeting between the clubs.

Trinity were defeated 5-0 at The Hawthorns on 16 February 1907 when England amateur international centre-forward Billy Jordan scored a hat-trick on his Albion debut.

Trinity's best win over Albion is 4-2 at home on 1 October 1904 (also in Division Two).

Albion League debutants v Trinity: Dick Bourne (1907), Billy Jordan (1907), George Simpson (1909), Jack Nevin (1910).

Players with both clubs: Fred Fenton, Fred Hobson, Ben Shearman and Stewart Evans. Trevor Thompson, an Albion left-back of the 1970s, played non-League football with Trinity in 1982-83.

Albion's reserve goalkeeper Tom Daley (1956-60) was player-manager of Gainsborough in the early 1960s.

GARFIELD, Benjamin Walter John

A rare bundle of energy on Albion's left-wing, Ben Garfield was always involved in the action and he gave Albion six years excellent service. Born in Burton-on-Trent in 1872, he joined Albion from Burton Wanderers in 1896 and went on to score 38 goals in 117 appearances for the club before transferring to Brighton & Hove Albion in 1902. Capped once by England in 1898, Garfield guested for Aston Villa in 1900 and later helped Brighton win the Second Division championship before retiring in 1905. He died in 1942.

GATE RECEIPTS

Top ten attendance receipts for games involving Albion at The Hawthorns:

£244,501	v Coventry C	FA Cup Rd 3	18 January 1995
£218,536	v Wolves	Division One	20 January 1996
£215,516	v Derby Co	Division One	5 May 1996
£184,668	v Wolves	Division One	5 September 1993
£182,293	v Stoke C	Division One	23 January 1993
£162,705	v West Ham U	FA Cup Rd 3	2 January 1993
£161,790	v Bristol C	Division One	26 December 1994
£161,632	v Aston Villa	FA Cup Rd 5	17 February 1990
£153,127	v Wolves	Division One	15 March 1995
£152,799	v Swansea C	Play-off SF, second leg	19 May 1993

Money Talk

The record takings for a League Cup game at the Hawthorns are £79,494 v Tottenham Hotspur in the semi-final, first leg on 3 February 1982.

Top European game receipts at The Hawthorns: £74,594 v Red Star Belgrade, UEFA Cup, 21 March 1979.

Receipts of £427,900 (57 million pesetas) were taken at the Valencia-Albion UEFA Cup game in Spain on 22 November 1978.

A meagre £5,400 was banked from an 89,400 capacity crowd in the national stadium, Peking, for the China-Albion friendly on 19 May 1978. (Admission charges ranged from 3p to 9p a time.)

The 17,000 crowd for the Chatham-Albion FA Cup-tie on 16 March 1889 generated just £4 in gate money, collected during the half-time break. No entry charge was made to spectators who wanted to see the game which was staged in a Kent public park.

A crowd of almost 51,000 paid £131,286 to watch the 1978 FA Cup semi-final between Albion and Ipswich at Highbury.

Albion's share of the £60,605 gate receipts from the 1967 League Cup Final v QPR amounted to £8,689, and their cut of the £122,900 'gate' from the 1970 League Cup Final v Manchester City was £18,023.

Albion played ten games when winning the FA Cup in 1968, and the combined gate receipts from those matches amounted to £236,739. The Final v Everton realised £109,649 and from the semi-final clash with Birmingham City, the takings were £37,028.

When Albion reached the 1969 FA Cup semi-final at Hillsborough, the gate receipts from the four previous ties totalled £107,725. Nine years later over £150,000 was taken from Albion's FA Cup semi-final clash with Ipswich Town at Highbury, and in 1982, the Albion v QPR FA Cup semi-final, also played at Highbury, yielded gate receipts of over £190,000.

At Stoney Lane, Albion's record takings for a senior game were £822 from the FA Cup-tie with Liverpool on 25 February 1899.

At their Four Acres ground, Albion's best take in terms of cash through the turnstiles was £602 from their FA Cup encounter with Blackburn Rovers on 21 February 1885.

A total of £1,576 was accumulated by Albion from their 11 home games in the first League season of 1888-89. Surprisingly this was a drop of some £200 on the previous season's figures for a similar number of matches.

Nowadays clubs keep all of their own gate receipts from home League matches, paying out only the necessary and required expenses. Prior to 1982 home clubs took two/thirds of the gate receipts, with the other third split two ways, with the visiting club and the Football League each receiving one-sixth.

GATESHEAD (South Shields)

Albion's record against Gateshead:

Football League

Venue	P	W	D	L	F	A	Pts
Home	1	1	0	0	3	0	2
Away	1	1	0	0	3	2	2
Totals	2	2	0	0	6	2	4

FA Cup

	P	W	D	L	F	A	
Away	2	2	0	0	5	1	

Albion's best win over Gateshead (formerly South Shields) is 3-0, and it came in the first meeting between the clubs in a Second Division game at The Hawthorns on 17 December 1927.

By scoring the winning goal (3-2) in the 65th minute of the return match at South Shields that season (28 April 1928) Jimmy Cookson broke Albion's individual League scoring record in his first season with the club. It was his 38th goal. In February 1952 Albion beat Gateshead 2-0 in a fourth-round FA Cup-tie at St James's Park, Newcastle, Ronnie Allen scoring both goals before a near 39,000 crowd.

Albion League debutant v South Shields: Harold Pearson (1927).

Players with both clubs: Albert Lewis, Billy Thompson. Albion reserves Pat Hewson, Jimmy Ord and Tommy Watson all later played for Gateshead, while Tony Lowery, Gary Robson and John Trewick (all Albion first-team players) later served with Gateshead in non-League football in the 1990s.

GEDDES, Alfred John

'Jasper' Geddes was a mercurial outside-left, fast, energetic with a powerful shot. He was also a temperamental player, a little greedy at times, but nevertheless an outstanding footballer. Born in West Bromwich in 1871, he joined the club from Causeway Green Villa in 1889. Three years later he scored a vital goal to help Albion win the FA Cup and in 1894 was transferred to Clapham Rovers, later playing for Millwall Athletic. He returned to Albion for a second spell in 1895, helping them stave off relegation, but went back to Millwall within a month, going on to play for Bedminster

and Bristol City prior to his retirement in 1908. He was Millwall's first professional footballer, and skippered them to two Southern League championships in the mid 1890s. Geddes, who scored 38 goals in 93 games for Albion, represented the Southern League v the London FA in 1897 and he died in 1927.

GILES, John Michael

Johnny Giles was Albion's first player-manager. Signed from Leeds United for £48,000 in 1975 (to replace Don Howe) he

Johnny Giles tangles with his former Leeds United teammate Allan Clarke.

Philadelphia Fury in 1978 and coached Vancouver Whitecaps (1980-83) whilst still retaining his position with Shamrock. He returned to Albion for a second time as manager in 1984, but on this occasion he couldn't work a miracle and left after 18 months. He dropped out of football but did play in several local charity matches when free from his duties as a soccer columnist in the *Daily Express*. One of the finest midfield players ever to pull on an Albion shirt, Giles scored five goals in 88 appearances for the Baggies and in his playing career (1959-77) he netted 99 goals in 554 League games. In all competitions (club and country) he notched 125 goals in 863 outings – a fine set of statistics for an exceptionally fine footballer. His son Michael was with him during his second spell at The Hawthorns.

GILLINGHAM

Albion's record v Gillingham:

FA Cup

Venue	P	W	D	L	F	A
Away	1	1	0	0	1	0

Other Match

Away	1	1	0	0	3	2

The first game between the clubs was a friendly at New Brompton (Gillingham's former name) in March 1902.

Full-back Derek Statham hit a late winner to give Albion that fourth-round FA Cup victory over the Gills before a 16,038 crowd at the Priestfield Stadium on 23 January 1982.

Players with both clubs: Enos Bromage, Joseph Connor, Adrian Foster, Adam Haywood, Billy Lee, Jimmy Poxton, David Rushbury, George Shaw, Terry Simpson, Steve Walford, Bill Williams. The latter became commercial manager of Gillingham (1991-95).

Terry Simpson, played for both Gillingham and Albion.

Three former Albion players became manager of Gillingham: Harry Hadley (1929-30), Freddie Cox (1962-65) and Gerry Summers (1975-81).

Also associated with both clubs: Irish international Gerry Armstrong had trials with Gillingham (1989) after playing for Albion; Geoff Hudson (Gillingham player 1963-65, Albion trainer 1970-72). Three Albion reserves, Geoff Turton (1930s), goalkeeper Mike Gibson (1950s) and Pat Hilton (1970s) all later played for Gillingham. Gillingham's centre-forward in 1957-58 was Ron Saunders who later became Albion's manager (1986-87).

Keith Burkinshaw, Albion's manager (1993-94) was briefly in charge of Gillingham (1988-89). Mel Eves, an ex-Gillingham forward, was a non-contract player with Albion in 1988 and defender Steve Walford was on loan to both clubs in 1988-89.

succeeded in getting Albion out of the Second Division in his first season in charge and then took them to the brink of European football before he left The Hawthorns to become player-manager of Shamrock Rovers in the summer of 1977, much to the dismay of the supporters.

Born in Dublin in 1940, Giles had earlier starred as a right winger for Home Farm and Manchester United, gaining an FA Cup winners medal with the latter in 1963. He then moved to Leeds for £35,000 and whilst at Elland Road was converted into a splendid scheming midfielder under Don Revie. He collected medals galore with Leeds, including winners prizes for both the First and Second Division championships, the FA Cup, League Cup, and Fairs Cup as well as becoming an established member of the Republic of Ireland national team, for whom he won a total of 60 full caps before becoming national team manager (1973-80). He played in 11 FA Cup semi-final matches and five FA Cup Finals (six if you count the 1970 replay). He guested for

Tommy Glidden, a fine skipper and a goalscoring outside-right, seen here with the FA Cup.

participate in an England trial in 1925. He died from a heart attack in 1974.

NB: Tommy's brother, Sid, was an Albion reserve, 1925-28.

GLOSSOP (North End)

Albion's record against Glossop:

Football League

Venue	P	W	D	L	F	A	Pts
Home	9	5	3	1	20	7	13
Away	9	4	2	3	15	11	10
Totals	18	9	5	4	35	18	23

The first meeting was at Stoney Lane on 14 October 1899 when 5,629 fans witnessed an exciting 3-3 draw in Division One.

Albion's biggest win is 6-0, at The Hawthorns (Division Two) on 24 February 1906 when Ted Pheasant ripped a hole in the net from the penalty spot!

Glossop were the first-ever visitors to The Hawthorns for a Second Division game and they caused a major shock, beating champions-to-be Albion 1-0 on 2 September 1901.

Fred Shinton hit four goals in Albion's 5-1 defeat of Glossop at The Hawthorns on 3 November 1906.

Albion League debutants v Glossop: Ben Appleby (1901), Jack Kifford (1901), Jimmy McLean (1901), Dan Nurse (1901), Ike Webb (1901), Tom Worton (1901), Ted Smith (1902), Arthur Bamford (1905), Dick Corbett (1910).

Players with both clubs: George Elmore, Adam Haywood, Billy Law.

GOALS & GOALSCORERS

Since League football started in 1888 Albion have scored over 6,000 goals in more than 3,850 matches (See FOOTBALL LEAGUE).

The three most prolific goalscorers in the club's history have been Tony Brown, Ronnie Allen and 'W.G.' Richardson, who between them netted almost 950 goals in competitive first-team matches for the club (wartime included in Richardson's case) and 628 have come in the Football League alone.

Richardson is Albion's champion marksman with a total of 328 goals to his name; Brown claimed 279 and Allen 234. Taking into consideration friendlies and other matches, Richardson's tally is in excess of 350, Brown's haul amounts to 312 and Allen netted 258.

GLIDDEN, Thomas William

A fine captain and terrific goalscoring outside-right, who served the club admirably for more than 50 years, first as a player (1922-36), then as a coach (to the reserves), next as an influential shareholder and finally as a director (1951-74). Born in Newcastle-upon-Tyne in 1902, Tommy Glidden joined Albion from Sunderland West End and retired after 14 splendid years at The Hawthorns, during which time he scored 140 goals in 479 first-team appearances, leading the Baggies to the coveted FA Cup and promotion double in 1930-31 and to the Cup Final again in 1935. After taking over from Jack Crisp, he formed a fine partnership on the right flank with Joe Carter and was perhaps unfortunate not to win international recognition, although he did

Players who have scored 100 or more goals for Albion

Player	League	FA Cup	League Cup	Others*	Totals
'W.G.' Richardson	202	26		100	328
Tony Brown	218	27	17	17	279
Ronnie Allen	208	23		3	234
Jeff Astle	137	14	19	4	174
Derek Kevan	157	16			173
Joe Carter	145	10			155
Tommy Glidden	135	5			140
Fred Morris	112	4		2	118
Cyrille Regis	82	10	16	4	112
Jimmy Cookson	103	7			110
Bob Taylor	84	3	5	8	100
Dave Walsh	94	6			100

Tony Brown scoring against Liverpool in 1965.

'Others' include local and domestic competitions, European games, FA Charity Shield, Anglo-Italian & Anglo-Scottish matches, wartime games etc. Friendlies/testimonials/tours are not included.

Divisional Goals
Ronnie Allen scored all his 208 League goals in the First Division while Jimmy Cookson netted all of his 103 in the Second Division.

Disallowed Goals
Albion had five 'goals' disallowed during their 3-1 League defeat by Bristol City at The Hawthorns on 10 February 1906.

Four Albion 'goals' were ruled out in their away League game v Burslem Port Vale on 23 December 1905. Albion still won 1-0.

Charlie Hewitt had a goal disallowed at Blackpool on 28 November 1908 – and in the end it cost Albion promotion (on goal-average) from the Second Division! (See Goal Average).

Outside-left Howard Gregory had a 'goal' disallowed while playing for Albion against Wolves at Molineux in 1924. He struck the ball so hard that it burst – the bladder went into the net but the casing flew over the bar!

Colchester United had a 'goal' disallowed in the last minute of a third-round FA Cup-tie against Albion at Layer Road on 27 January 1968. The game ended 1-1; Albion took the replay 4-0 – and they went on to win the trophy at Wembley.

Most Goals in a Match (for Albion)
Six
George Bell v St Luke's (Friendly) 4 March 1882
Billy Bisseker v Stourbridge Standard (Friendly) 7 October 1882
Harry Aston v Birmingham Junior Association (Friendly) 19 February 1883
'Jem' Bayliss v Bloxwich (Birmingham Cup) 22 November 1884
Billy Bassett v Burton Wanderers (Staffordshire Cup) 1 February 1890
Bill Garraty v Gefle (Sweden) (tour game) 21 May 1909
Jimmy Cookson v Blackpool (League Division Two) 17 September 1927
'W.G.' Richardson v RAF (Friendly) 24 May 1941
'W.G.' Richardson v Luton Town (Regional League) 22 November 1941

Bobby Robson v Alberta All Stars (tour game) 27 May 1959
Five
Billy Bisseker v Milton (Friendly) 8 October 1881
Harry Aston v Coseley (Birmingham Cup) 11 November 1882
Billy Bassett v Studley & District XI (Friendly) 17 September 1888
Billy Richards v Aberystwyth (Friendly) 28 January 1895
Fred Morris v Notts County (League Division One) 25 October 1919
George James v Lampard Vachell's XI (Friendly) 4 May 1925
'W.G.' Richardson v Swansea Town (Regional League) 18 October 1941
'W.G.' Richardson v Aston Villa (Regional League) 1 May 1943
Derek Kevan v Everton (League Division One) 19 March 1960
Alec Jackson v George Salter's Works XI (Friendly) 2 May 1960
'Jem' Bayliss holds the record for most goals in an FA Cup-tie for Albion – scoring four v Stoke on 7 January 1888.

Against Albion
Six
John Southworth of Everton (League Division One) 30 December 1893
Five
Arthur Chandler of Leicester City (League Division One) 25 December 1926
Freddie Steele of Stoke City (League Division One) 4 February 1937
Tommy Crawley of Coventry City (Regional League) 25 December 1943
Jimmy Greaves of Chelsea (League Division One) 3 December 1960
Brian Dear of West Ham United (League Division One) 16 April 1965
Hugo Sanchez of Real Madrid (San Jose Cup) 18 May 1990

No Goals
From 2 May to 8 October 1921 Albion played six home First Division League games without scoring a goal.

Albion failed to score in 16 of their 21 away League matches in 1923-24 (a club record). They also failed to score in ten consecutive away fixtures between 1 September & 25 December.

Albion's defence did not conceded a goal in the last six League games of the 1949-50 season (8-29 April inclusive).

Between 28 August and 11 September 1971 Albion played four First Division matches and a League Cup-tie and failed to score a goal. This sequence was repeated in November/December 1977.

Goal Average

Albion missed promotion by 1/56th of a goal in season 1908-09 as a result of a disallowed 'goal' in the away game at Bloomfield Road against Blackpool. (See BLACKPOOL). Tottenham Hotspur went up into the First Division with a slightly better goal-average of 67-32 to Albion's 56-27.

Long Distance Goals

Billy Williams, Albion's left-back, scored a goal from fully 60 yards in a home FA Cup-tie against Nottingham Forest on 26 February 1898. The papers reported it as '...a tremendous punt upfield.'

England international right-back Bill Ashurst scored a goal for Albion against Blackburn Rovers in a Second Division game at The Hawthorns on 18 April 1927 from 55 yards, and left-back Len Millard netted from the halfway line in Albion's home First Division game against Cardiff City on 27 December 1954.

The Blackburn Rovers defender Walter Crook found the back of the Albion net from some 80 yards in a First Division game at Ewood Park on 1 April 1939. Albion's goalkeeper, Jimmy Adams, slipped just as he was about to gather Crook's long clearance and the ball bounced over his hands and into the unguarded net. Albion lost 3-0.

Former Albion goalkeeper Tony Godden, fly-kicking the ball downfield, scored a 90-yard goal while playing for Peterborough United reserves against Northampton Town in 1989-90.

Scoring in Successive Games

During World War Two, Harry Jones scored in 11 successive Midland Regional League games for Albion (October-December 1939) – a club record.

Fred Morris scored in ten successive First Division games for Albion: 29 November 1919 to 24 January 1920 (15 goals in all).

England's Ronnie Allen scored in ten successive first-team games for Albion (nine League, one Charity Shield) between August and October 1954 (total 14).

Centre-forward 'W.G.' Richardson netted in nine successive League games between February and April 1933 and winger Billy Elliott hit the net in nine successive Football League South games between September-December 1941.

Dave Walsh netted in each of his first six Football League games for Albion at the start of the 1946-47 season.

Jeff Astle heading one of his hat-trick goals in a 4-2 win over Sheffield Wednesday in 1965.

100 Goals in a Season

Albion have scored a century of League goals in a season twice – in 1919-20 (104 in Division One) and 1929-30 (105 in Division Two).

In the 1945-46 transitional season (after the war) Albion netted 104 goals in the Football League (South).

Albion's first team scored a total of 195 goals in season 1887-88; a total of 113 were netted in 1893-94; in 1934-35 they hit 103; registered 102 in 1953-54 and 119 in 1957-58.

In 1958-59, Albion scored 160 goals in all games – 88 in the League, five in the FA Cup and 66 in friendlies (a modern-day record). In 1965-66 and 1978-79 they amassed 133 – and the last time Albion accumulated a century of goals (at first-team level) was in their promotion-winning season of 1992-93 when they notched 130.

During World War Two, the 100 goal barrier was breached three times – in 1939-40 (107), 1941-42 (115) and 1945-46 (110 including six FA Cup goals).

Fast Goals

George James recorded the fastest League goal by an Albion player when he netted after just five seconds of the home First Division game against Nottingham Forest on 13 December 1924.

Ronnie Allen scored after 12 seconds in Albion's away League game with Manchester United on 15 December 1951 and Ally Brown was on target 22 seconds after kick-off in Albion's home First Division clash with Ipswich Town on 19 August 1978.

Before joining Albion Brown had scored a record-breaking goal for Leicester City against Huddersfield Town after only 19 seconds in August 1971.

Alf McMichael, the Newcastle United full-back, conceded a 12-second own-goal in the League game against Albion at The Hawthorns on 5 September 1951.

John Wile netted an own-goal after just 20 seconds in the away First Division game at Tottenham Hotspur on 4 December 1982.

It is believed that the earliest own-goal scored by an Albion player at The Hawthorns came in the fifth minute – from the boot of Gary Robson against Newcastle United on 1 November 1989.

Rapid Scoring

Fred Morris scored two goals inside the first minute of Albion's home League game against Manchester City on 13 December 1919.

'W.G.' Richardson equalled a League record by scoring four goals in five minutes for Albion at West Ham in a First Division game on 7 November 1931. His strikes came in the fifth, seventh, eighth and ninth minutes of a match Albion won 5-1.

Andy Hunt hit nine goals in his first 10 League games for Albion (March to May 1993) and ended the season with 11 in 13 outings.

Five goals were scored in 11 minutes (77th-88th) during the Albion-Lincoln City Second Division game on 21 December 1907.

Albion scored five goals in 12 minutes in the home League fixture against Barnsley on 11 November 1989. Albion won 7-0.

Albion hit five goals in 13 minutes of their home League game against Arsenal on 14 October 1922. Albion won 7-0.

Ten goals – four by Albion, six by Grimsby – were netted in 55 minutes of a Division One game at The Hawthorns on 30 April 1932.

Eight goals (four by each side) were scored in 46 minutes of the Aston Villa-Albion League match on 28 April 1934.

The Derby County-Albion League game on 3 October 1993 was goalless at half-time. The result in the end was County 5 Albion 3 – all eight goals coming in the space of 26 minutes.

Dave Walsh scoring one of his 100 goals for Albion, against Brentford at The Hawthorns in September 1947.

The Albion-Huddersfield League match on 6 October 1923, produced five goals in an eight-minute spell. Albion lost 4-2.

Five goals were also scored in a 12-minute spell during the Albion-Leeds United Division One game on 6 October 1934.

All 13 goals in the Stoke City 10 Albion 3 First Division game at The Victoria Ground on 4 February 1937 came in the space of 71 minutes.

Eight goals were netted in 36 first-half minutes of the Manchester City v Albion League game at Maine Road on 5 September 1936. City won 6-2.

Ten goals – six to Albion, four to Sunderland – were recorded in 57 minutes of a Division One match at The Hawthorns on 27 February 1937.

The last half-hour of the Albion v Notts County League clash on 25 October 1919 produced six goals. Albion won 8-0.

Albion scored five goals between the seventh and 20th minutes of their home League game with Blackburn Rovers on 18 January 1936. Albion won 8-1.

Five of Jimmy Cookson's six goals against Blackpool at The Hawthorns in a Second Division game on 17 September 1927, were scored in the space of 24 minutes (47th-70th).

Brian Dear of West Ham scored five goals in 20 first-half minutes of a League game against Albion on 16 April 1965.

Derby County scored four goals in five second half minutes of their Zenith Data Systems Cup win at The Hawthorns on 29 November 1989.

When Albion beat Alberta All Stars 15-0 in a friendly in Canada on 27 May 1959, ten of their goals came in the second half, six of them scored by Bobby Robson.

Port Vale scored eight times in 55 minutes during their 8-1 League win over Albion in the Potteries on 9 March 1929.

Steady Scoring

Albion scored 59 goals in nine games when touring Canada and USA in May/June 1959. That was an average of 6.5 goals per game.

In October 1887 Albion scored 47 goals in eight first-team games. 'Jem' Bayliss claimed 14 of them.

Albion scored in every recorded first-team game they played between 1879 and 1883.

Albion scored 32 goals in a run of seven home League games in season 1925-26. In 12 consecutive games in that same season they scored a total of 44.

In their 21 home League matches in 1929-30, Albion scored a club record 73 goals.

Dutchman Richard Sneekes scored nine goals in his first 10 League games for Albion, 12 March to 20 April 1996.

High-scoring Games

Here is a list of instances when 15 or more goals have been scored in a game involving Albion:

26 Albion 26 Coseley 0 (Birmingham Cup) 11 November 1882

25 Studley & District 2 Albion 23 (friendly) 17 September 1888

23 Albion 23 Burton Wanderers 0 (Staffordshire Cup) 1 February 1890

17 Albion 11 Kaffirs 6 (friendly) 22 November 1899

15 Albion 15 Bloxwich 0 (Birmingham Cup) 22 November 1884

15 Albion 6 Football League XI 9 (King George V Trust) 8 May 1935

15 Hereford United 10 Albion 5 (testimonial) 1 November 1954

15 Alberta All Stars 0 Albion 15 (tour game) 27 May 1959

15 George Salter's Works XI 2 Albion 13 (friendly) 2 May 1960

15* Albion 7 Colchester United 8 (Watney Cup) 7 August 1971

* This game ended 4-4, but Colchester won 4-3 in a penalty shoot-out.

NB: The highest scoring game involving any Albion team is believed to be the 36-0 victory over Bearwood Juniors in a Handsworth League game on 8 September 1951. Kenny Knight, an amateur, scored 15 of those goals.

Goalscoring Debuts

Cyrille Regis created a unique record by scoring on his debut for Albion in five different competitions (1977-78):

v Sheffield Wednesday (h), Central League, 27 August 1977
v Rotherham United (h), League Cup, 31 August 1977
v Middlesbrough (h), League Division One, 1 September 1977
v Blackpool (h), FA Cup, 7 January 1978
v Southampton (at Ibrox Park) Tennent-Caledonian Cup, 5 August 1978.

Alf Bentley scored all four Albion goals on his League debut v Burnley at The Hawthorns on 6 September 1913.

Two other players who scored hat-tricks on their League debuts for Albion were England amateur international Billy Jordan against Gainsborough Trinity in a home match on 16 February 1907 and Albert Lewis in the away clash with Burnley at Turf Moor on 3 September 1904, both in the Second Division.

Peter McKennan hit three goals when making his Albion debut in a wartime fixture against Northampton Town at The Hawthorns on 6 December 1941.

Andy Hunt netted three goals on his home debut for Albion against Brighton in a Second Division match in April 1993.

Several players have celebrated their Albion debuts by scoring twice, among them Derek Kevan v Everton (League) in August 1955 and Colin Suggett v Southampton (League) in August 1969.

Ray Treacy had two separate spells with Albion (10 years apart) and he scored on his 'debut' each time – first at Sunderland in October 1966 and then at Derby County in September 1976, netting twice in the latter game.

Goal Shots

Playing for Albion against South Shields in a home Second Division match on 17 December 1927, Jimmy Cookson scored his 100th League goal of his career in only his 89th match – the quickest century of goals ever recorded in the competition.

Ten different players figured on the scoresheet when Albion beat Coseley 26-0 in a Birmingham Cup-tie in 1882 – Aston (5), Bisseker (4), Timmins (4), G.Bell (3), Whitehouse (2), While (2), Horton (2), Bunn (2) H.Bell and Stanton. Goalkeeper Roberts was the odd-man out.

Nine different players scored in Albion's 23-0 Staffordshire Cup win over Burton Wanderers in 1890 and likewise when Studley & District were defeated 23-2 in a friendly in 1888.

Centre-half Bill Richardson and outside-right Jimmy Frew scored their first and only goals for Albion in a 2-1 League win over Wolverhampton Wanderers at The Hawthorns on 17 October 1936.

Full-back Jesse Pennington never scored a goal in 496 senior games for Albion (1903-22). Fellow full-back Joe Smith was goalless in 471 outings.

Arthur Rowley holds the record for most League goals in a career, 434, the first four of which were scored in 1948 when he was playing for Albion.

When Albion drew 1-1 with Leicester City at The Hawthorns on 9 April 1988, both goals were scored by forwards playing against their former clubs: Nicky Cross (ex-Albion) netted first and Steve Lynex (ex-City) equalised.

Albion scored 18 goals in three successive away First Division games against Birmingham City – winning 5-3 in 1957-58, 6-0 the following season and 7-1 in 1959-60.

Ronnie Allen scored in every season from 1944-45 to 1964-65 inclusive, for Port Vale (up to 1950), for Albion (up to 1961) and then for Crystal Palace.

Tony Brown scored in every season for Albion from 1963-64 to 1979-80 inclusive and 'W.G. Richardson netted in every campaign from 1929-30 to 1944-45.

Tony Brown shares the Football League record for a goalscoring half-back, netting 15 in season 1968-69, thus equalling the record by former Albion player Jack Lewis (Reading) set in 1951-52.

The following Albion players topped the First Division scoring charts in the season given: Fred Morris (1919-20) with 37 goals; Ronnie Allen (1954-55) 27; Derek Kevan (1961-62) 33*; Jeff Astle (1969-70) 25 and Tony Brown (1970-71) with 28. (* Shared with Ipswich Town's Ray Crawford, later to play for Albion.)

Albion's Jimmy Cookson (38 goals) was leading scorer in Division Two in season 1927-28.

GODDEN, Anthony Leonard

In October, 1981, Albion's goalkeeper Tony Godden set a record which will take some beating – he appeared in his 228th consecutive first-team match and in doing so eclipsed Ally Robertson's previous total of successive outings by a considerable margin. Four-and-a-half years earlier, the Gillingham-born Godden, then aged 21, made his Albion debut in a 2-0 away win at Tottenham, and the media

immediately described him as '...a 'keeper with a big future.' How right they were, for Godden went from strength to strength, and in the next nine years amassed 329 appearances for the Baggies, and he was granted a testimonial to celebrate ten years at The Hawthorns, having joined Albion from Ashford Town in 1975 following unsuccessful trials with Wolves. During his time with Albion he was loaned out to Preston North End, Luton Town,. Walsall (twice) and Chelsea, and after leaving The Hawthorns (in May 1986) he played for Chelsea (again), Birmingham City, Sheffield Wednesday and Peterborough United. He then took over as manager of Wivenhoe Town (1990), and was a non-contract player with Colchester United before managing Warboys Town (1991-92). In 1992 he was a non-contract player with Torquay United, then subsequently manager of Kings Lynn (1994-95), Bury Town (1996) and a coach at Northampton Town.

GOODMAN, Donald Ralph

Exciting striker, fast, aggressive, with good ability and strong shot, Don Goodman was born in Leeds a month before England won the World Cup in 1966. He joined

Albion from Bradford City for £50,000 in 1987, soon after that horrific fire disaster at Valley Parade and became a huge hit with the Baggies' fans, scoring 63 goals in 181 appearances before leaving The Hawthorns for Sunderland in a £900,000 deal in 1991. He spent three years at Roker Park (netting over 40 goals) and in 1994 moved back to the Midlands to sign for Wolverhampton Wanderers for £1.1 million, teaming up with ex-Baggie Steve Bull at Molineux. He was Wolves' top-scorer in 1995-96 when he also fractured his skull.

GREEN, Harry

Excellent full-back, meaningful, sure-footed and one of the best of his era, Green, who was born in West Bromwich in 1860, played 65 games in Albion's senior side, making three

successive FA Cup Final appearances: 1886-87-88, gaining a winners' medal in the latter against Preston North End. He joined Albion in 1881 and left for Old Hill Wanderers ten years later. He died in 1900.

GREGORY, Howard

'Known as the 'Express man' and 'Greg', ginger-haired Howard Gregory was a fine outside-left, quick-witted, fast and plucky who teamed up exceedingly well with Fred Morris immediately after World War One. Born in Birmingham in 1893, he joined Albion from Birchfield Trinity in 1911 and in the next 15 years scored 45 goals in 181 appearances for the Baggies, helping them win the League in 1920. Gregory retired through injury in 1926 and became 'mine host' of the Woodman Inn (next to The Hawthorns), remaining in the licensed trade until 1933. He died in 1954.

GRIFFIN, Frank Albert

Scorer of Albion's FA Cup winning goal in the 1954 Final, Manchester-born Frank Griffin was a fine outside-right with good pace, excellent skills and fine shot. He cost the club £9,500 when signed from Shrewsbury Town in 1951 and spent eight years at The Hawthorns, notching 52 goals in 275 first-team games. He broke his leg playing against Sheffield United in an FA Cup match in 1958 and never really regained full fitness. He left Albion for Northampton Town in 1959

Frank Griffin drinks from the FA Cup after Albion's 1954 triumph over Preston North End.

and later played for Wellington Town and GKN Sankey's before managing Worthen United. Griffin quit football in 1966 at the age of 38. He now lives in Shrewsbury.

GRIMSBY TOWN

Albion's record against the Mariners:

Football League

Venue	P	W	D	L	F	A	Pts
Home	19	14	2	3	55	26	22
Away	19	5	4	10	30	36	15
Totals	38	19	6	13	85	62	37

FA Cup

Venue	P	W	D	L	F	A
Home	4	4	0	0	10	0
Away	2	0	2	0	2	2
Totals	6	4	2	0	12	2

Other Matches

Venue	P	W	D	L	F	A
Home	1	1	0	0	4	0
Away	4	1	0	3	5	13
Totals	5	2	0	3	9	13

The first meeting was a friendly, played at Stoney Lane on 30 March 1889, which Albion won 4-0. The second encounter was a return friendly later that year, on 7 September, when Albion were invited to open Grimsby's new headquarters at Abbey Park. A crowd of 4,000 saw Grimsby win 6-1.

Albion's best League win is 7-0 at home on 2 January 1909.

Albion had earlier won 6-1 at The Hawthorns on Christmas Day 1906, Fred Shinton scoring four goals. Another big Albion win was 6-0 at Blundell Park on 7 January 1928. Jimmy Cookson hit a four-timer this time.

Grimsby's best victory over Albion at League level was achieved at The Hawthorns on 30 April 1932 when they won an 11-goal thriller by 6-5 in front of just 7,796 fans. Holmes and Dyson both scored hat-tricks for the Mariners who were relegated at the end of the season.

Barry Cowdrill scored his only goal for Albion in a 3-0 FA Cup win at The Hawthorns in January 1981.

Craig Shakespeare, played for both Grimsby and Albion.

Albion League debutants v Town: Bill Davies (1908), George Baddeley (1908), Sid Bowser (1909), Reg Fryer (1927), Jimmy Frew (1936), Norman Male (1937), Robert Hopkins (1986).

George Johnson made his FA Cup debut v Grimsby in 1896.

Players with both clubs: Paul Agnew, James Bowden, Peter Butler, John Chadburn, Gary Childs, Shaun Cunnington, Charlie Deacey, Alf Dean, Archie Dunn, Tony Ford, Dave Gilbert, Chris Hargreaves, Paul Reece, Tony Rees, Brian Rice, Fred Rouse, Craig Shakespeare, Charlie Wilson.

Other players associated with both clubs: goalkeeper Tom Daley, Dennis Jennings, Jimmy McStay and brothers Adam and Simon Buckley. Kenny Swain, who was on loan with Albion in 1988, became Grimsby's assistant manager in 1994.

Also associated with both clubs: Alan Buckley managed Grimsby Town for six years before becoming Albion's boss in 1994 (See MANAGERS). Arthur Mann and Richard O'Kelly were Buckley's assistant and youth team coach

respectively at Blundell Park before moving to The Hawthorns; and both Paul Mitchell (physiotherapist) and Ronnie Mann (chief scout) followed Buckley from Grimsby to The Hawthorns.

In season 1995-96 there were 14 former Grimsby Town personnel at The Hawthorns – manager Buckley, his four off-field assistants and nine players.

GRIPTON, William Ernest

A hard but scrupulously fair centre-half, Billy Gripton gave Albion excellent service for 13 years, playing for the club before, during and after World War Two. He accumulated 208 appearances and scored three goals, and took over the pivotal role late in the 1938-39 season. Born in Tipton in 1920, he moved to The Hawthorns from Brownhills Albion in 1935 and left the club for Luton in 1948 for £3,000. He later served with Bournemouth and Worcester City, retiring in 1956 to take over as groundsman at the Dudley Sports Centre, Tipton and adviser to Vono FC. He died in 1981.

GROVES, William

Enthusiastic, hard-working, highly-skilful centre-forward or half-back, who scored ten goals in 69 games for Albion over

a period of three years: 1890-93. A Scotsman, born in Leith in 1869, Willie Groves served with Hibernian and Celtic before joining the Baggies. He won an FA Cup winners' medal in 1892 (v Villa) and after leaving the club for Aston Villa, he helped Albion's arch rivals win the 1894 League championship. He left Villa Park to return to Hibernian and after a second spell with Celtic (1896-98) he rounded off his career with Rushden, retiring in 1902. Capped three times by his country (scoring a hat-trick against Ireland in his second international) Groves played for Hibernian and Celtic in three Scottish Cup Finals and represented the Football League XI. He was the first player in Football League history to command a £100 transfer fee. He died in February 1908 after a short illness.

HADLEY, Henry

'Harry' Hadley was a cool, calculating, easy-going wing-half who scored twice in 181 appearances for Albion between 1897 and 1905. Born in Barrow-in-Furness in 1878, he was brought up in Cradley Heath and joined Albion from Halesowen. He left The Hawthorns for Aston Villa after helping Albion win the Second Division title in 1902 and gaining an England cap. After Villa, he played in turn for Nottingham Forest, Southampton and Croydon Common, returning to Halesowen in 1910. Thereafter he managed Merthyr Town on three separate occasions between 1919-31 and was also in charge at Chesterfield, Aberdare (1927-28), Gillingham and Bangor City. He retired from football in 1936 and died in West Bromwich six years later.

HAINES, John Thomas William

A short, aggressive inside-forward who scored 23 goals in 62 games for Albion in the late 1940s. Born in Wickhamford near Evesham in 1920, Jackie Haines had trials for Liverpool before joining Swansea in 1939. He moved to Leicester City in 1947 and signed for Albion in 1948 in a deal which took Peter McKennan to Filbert Street. Haines helped Albion win promotion from the Second Division in his first full season at The Hawthorns and also scored twice on his debut for England v Switzerland that same year. After leaving Albion in 1949, he served with Bradford Park Avenue, Rochdale, Chester, Wellington, Kidderminster Harriers, Evesham and Bretforton Village, retiring in 1961. He died in 1987.

HALIFAX TOWN

Albion's record against Halifax:

FA Cup

Venue	P	W	D	L	F	A
Away	1	0	0	1	1	2

Watney Cup

Away	1	1	0	0	2	0

Colin Suggett scored both Albion goals in that Watney Cup semi-final victory at The Shay in 1971.

Halifax were a non-League side, playing in the GM Vauxhall Conference, when they knocked Albion out of the FA Cup in a first-round tie at The Shay in season 1993-94.

Players with both clubs: Kevin Donovan, Ernie Hoyland, Andy McCall, Kieran O'Regan, John Thomas, Stan Wood.

Also associated with both clubs: Alf Brookes and Sid Glidden (Albion reserves, Halifax players), Geoff Hudson (Halifax player 1959-61, Albion trainer 1970-72) and Norman Bodell (Halifax player 1966-67, Albion chief scout 1986-94).

HARTFORD, Richard Asa

Hartford was a tremendous midfielder, who amassed well over 900 League and Cup appearances in the space of 24 years, playing for Albion (1966-74), Manchester City, Nottingham Forest, Everton, Manchester City (again), Fort

Lauderdale Sun, Norwich City, Bolton Wanderers, Stockport County (player-manager) and Oldham Athletic. In 1989 he was appointed coach at Shrewsbury Town, later taking over as manager at Gay Meadow. Thereafter he played briefly for WBA All Stars and Boston United before joining Blackburn Rovers in 1992 as coach under Kenny Dalglish. From Ewood Park he joined Stoke City as assistant to Lou Macari and in 1995 went back to his old club, Manchester City as assistant manager. He also had trials with Wolves (1984) and 13 years earlier Hartford actually left Albion for Leeds United in a £170,000 deal, but returned to The Hawthorns 24 hours later after doctors diagnosed a heart problem! He was eventually sold to Manchester City for a then record fee of £225,000. Capped by Scotland 50 times, Hartford also represented his county at youth, Under-21 and Under-23 levels and he played in the 1970 League Cup Final for

Albion and then in two more for Manchester City (1976) and Norwich City (1985), collecting winners' medals in the last two. In 1986 he again visited Wembley, this time in the Freight Rover Trophy Final with Bolton. His last League appearance was at the age of 40, for Shrewsbury Town at Brentford on New Year's Day 1991. Hartford, born in Clydebank in 1950, was christened Asa after the great American singing star, Al Jolson.

HARTLEPOOL UNITED

Albion's record against Hartlepool:

Football League

Venue	P	W	D	L	F	A	Pts
Home	2	1	0	1	4	3	3
Away	2	0	2	0	2	2	2
Totals	4	1	2	1	6	5	5

Albion first played Hartlepool in a Division Two match at the Victoria Ground on Bonfire Night 1991 when 500 of their supporters in a 2,810 crowd saw a 0-0 draw in Arctic conditions.

When 'Pool beat Albion at The Hawthorns in the return fixture that season, the turnout was 10,307.

Luther Blissett scored his only goal for Albion in a 3-1 home League win over 'Pool in November 1992 – and it took an 88th minute equaliser by Paul Raven to earn Albion a point in the 2-2 draw at Hartlepool in March 1993.

Players with both clubs: Fred Richardson, 'W.G.' Richardson, John Thomas, John Trewick, Paul A. Williams.

Former bus driver 'W.G.' Richardson was transferred to Albion in 1929 from Hartlepool and two years later he scored twice in the FA Cup Final!

John Trewick, played for both Albion and Hartlepool.

Also associated with both clubs: Albion reserves Ken Allen, Bill Chatterton and John Honour, along with Bob Taylor, who played for Hartlepool's youth team before joining Leeds United. Alan Stevenson was commercial manager at both Hartlepool and Albion during the 1980s, and prior to this he was 'Pool's goalkeeper (1984-86). Another 'keeper, Barry Siddall, had spells with both clubs in 1990.

HAT-TRICKS

Between 1878 to 1996, Albion players have scored well over 250 hat-tricks in first-team matches. About half have come in the Football League, 16 in the FA Cup (the last by Kevin Donovan against Aylesbury), five in the League Cup, one in the Fairs Cup, one in the Charity Shield, three in World War One games, 44 in World War Two matches and almost 60 in other competitions.

'W.G.' Richardson scored a record 12 League hat-tricks for Albion (1929-39). Jimmy Cookson and Derek Kevan both netted eight, Ronnie Allen seven, Jeff Astle six and Tony Brown, Tom Pearson and Fred Shinton five each.

A goal for Bobby Cram, one of his hat-trick against Stoke City in 1964.

Richardson also scored two FA Cup hat-tricks and a further 12 during World War Two. 'Ike' Clarke (10) and Harry Jones (8) were Albion's other main hat-trick heroes in World War Two.

'Jem' Bayliss claimed most FA Cup hat-tricks for Albion – three.

Astle hit two hat-tricks in the League Cup; Allen was a three-goal hero in the FA Charity Shield against Wolves in 1954 and Tony Brown notched Albion's only hat-trick in a European competition, scoring three times in the Fairs Cup against DOS Utrecht in 1966.

Tom Pearson notched Albion's first Football League hat-trick against Bolton Wanderers (h) on 4 November 1890.

'Jem' Bayliss grabbed Albion's first FA Cup hat-trick v Old Westminsters (h) on 13 February 1886.

And Jeff Astle had the pleasure of securing Albion's first League Cup treble v Coventry City (h) on 10 November 1965.

Two Albion defenders have scored hat-tricks in First Division matches. Sid Bowser achieved the feat from the centre-half position against Bradford City (h) on 27 September 1919 and right-back Bobby Cram netted three times against Stoke City (h) on 12 September 1964. Each player netted two penalties in their trebles.

'W.G.' Richardson scored a First Division hat-trick in three minutes for Albion against West Ham United at Upton Park on 7 November 1931.

Two years later, in September 1933, Richardson notched three goals in nine minutes of a home League game against Derby County.

Bobby Blood scored a hat-trick in five minutes in Albion's away game with Nottingham Forest on 3 March 1923; Bryan Robson netted three times in 12 minutes for Albion against Ipswich Town (h) on 16 March 1977, and Andy Hunt scored a rapid-fire hat-trick in nine minutes (78th-86th) on his home League debut for Albion against Brighton on 3 April 1993.

Lee Ashcroft secured the first League hat-trick of his career in the space of eight minutes playing for Albion against Tranmere Rovers at

Bobby Blood, scored three goals against Nottingham Forest in March 1923.

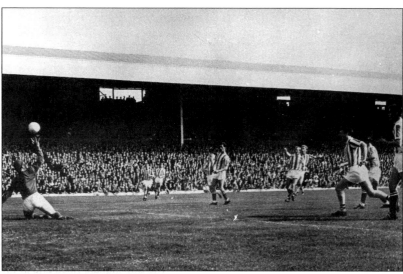

The Hawthorns on 30 April 1995, Charlie Wilson's hat-trick for Albion v West Ham (h) on 15 November 1924 came in an 11 minute spell and the same player followed up with another rapid-fire treble (inside 15 minutes) v Birmingham (h) on 6 February 1926.

Three of Jimmy Cookson's six goals for Albion against Blackpool in September 1927 were obtained during an eight-minute spell early in the second half, and his last four goals in this game were scored in 13 minutes (57-70).

John Thomas scored his first and only hat-trick for Albion in a 5-3 second leg League Cup win away at Valley Parade against Bradford City on 4 October 1989.

'W.G.' Richardson hit four hat-tricks in season 1936-37 to equal similar feats previously achieved by Fred Shinton in 1906-07 and Jimmy Cookson in 1927-28. Shinton's tally included three four-timers.

Six hat-tricks were registered in Albion's 23-0 Staffordshire Cup win over Burton Wanderers on 1 February 1890. Billy Bassett recorded two (6 goals) and other trebles were scored by Tom Pearson, George Evans, Bill Woodbine and Charlie Perry.

Albert Lewis (v Burnley 1904), Billy Jordan (v Gainsborough Trinity 1907) and Alf Bentley (v Burnley 1913) all scored hat-tricks on their League debuts for Albion; Kevin Donovan netted a treble on his FA Cup debut v Aylesbury United in 1992 and Tony Brown did likewise v DOS Utrecht on his 'European' Cup debut. (See DEBUTS).

'Dixie' Dean netted his last and record-breaking 37th League hat-trick v Albion at Goodison Park on 7 November 1936.

Tom Pearson (4 goals) and Billy Bassett (3) scored hat-tricks in Albion's 12-0 League win over Darwen in April 1892.

Roddy McLeod and Bassett scored hat-tricks in Albion's 8-0 League win v Wolverhampton Wanderers (a) in December 1893.

'W.G.' Richardson and Jack Mahon netted trebles in Albion's 8-1 win over Blackburn Rovers (h) in January 1936 and Ronnie Allen and Derek Kevan were hat-trick heroes as Albion beat Birmingham City 7-1 (a) in an Easter League game in April 1960.

A record seven League hat-tricks were scored by four Albion players in season 1906-07 – Fred Shinton (4), Tom Dilly, Fred Buck and Billy Jordan one apiece.

HAWTHORNS, The

The Hawthorns was the first Football League ground built this century, with work commencing on a large site directly on the Handsworth/Smethwick/West Bromwich border in mid-May 1900.

It was completed inside four months – in readiness for the official opening on 3 September 1900.

The lease on Albion's previous ground in Stoney Lane expired in 1899, and at the time it was one of the worst grounds in the Football League. However, being unable to finalise details on a new ground, the lease was renewed for

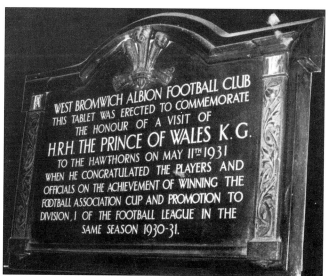

Plaque commemorating a royal visit to The Hawthorns.

a further 12 months, thus allowing enough time for the ground committee, with Harry Keys a key member, to search for a suitable site to build Albion's new stadium.

On 14 May 1900, the club's seal was affixed to a 14-year lease of the field that was to become known as The Hawthorns.

Why The Hawthorns? On the surveyor's map, the area surrounding the 'ground' was referred to as 'Hawthorns Estate' and hawthorn bushes had flourished there at one time. Therefore, it seemed an apt and obvious choice of

The Birmingham Road End in 1978-79.

The £2.5 million Halfords Lane Stand.

name. The land itself had a marshy look about it when building work commenced, and there was a brook flowing nearby which formed the boundary between Smethwick, Handsworth and West Bromwich. But this did not deter work and in no time at all the ground was ready for use.

Initially, the field of play sloped dramatically from the Halfords Lane/Birmingham Road corner, across and down towards the Smethwick End/now Rainbow Stand corner.

Over the years, though, the playing area itself has been built-up and now there is a gradual slope of just 2ft 4ins Bearing this in mind, there haven't been too many waterlogged pitches over the years with only three League games being abandoned (once they had started) owing to the state of the pitch – those against Bury in 1925, Luton Town in 1958 and Aston Villa in 1965 (all in the old First Division). There have been other matches called off through fog, poor light and falling snow. (See ABANDONED GAMES).

Hawthorns Calendar 1900-96

1900 Ground officially on Monday, 3 September 1900 for the First Division game between Albion and Derby County. At the time The Hawthorns could house 35,500 fans, and there were 20,104 present on the opening day to see Steve Bloomer (County) score the first goal, with 'Chippy' Simmons equalising for Albion.

1904 The old Stoney Lane stand, known as 'Noah's Ark' which had been transferred to The Hawthorns, burned down on Guy Fawkes' Night!

1905 Half-time scoreboard installed for the first time.

1906 A new stand was constructed at the Smethwick End.

1911 Main Halfords Lane stand overhauled; banking increased on the Handsworth side.

1912 Following a mini subsidence, the Hawthorns pitch was completely returfed.

1913 Albion purchased the freehold of The Hawthorns for just £5,350.

1914 Halfords Lane stand extended.

1920 Concrete terracing installed and a concrete wall was constructed to replace the wooden fencing surrounding the playing area.

1923 The embankment on the Handsworth side (opposite the main stand) was extended further back and the roof heightened.

1924 Ground capacity officially put at 65,000.

1931 Terracing all round ground finally completed and tip-up seats were put in the wing-stands. The nearby Hawthorns Halt railway station on the Great Western Line was opened on Christmas Day.

1934 A new stand with 750 extra seats was completed at the Smethwick/Halfords Lane corner. This brought the capacity of The Hawthorns up to nearly 66,000.

1935 A new oak-panelled tea-room was constructed.

1939 The wooden roof over the Halfords Lane stand was dismantled and replaced by asbestos sheeting which rested on five giant steel stanchions. The roof was also extended outwards to the front of the terraces.

1940-45 Owing to the war, very little work was carried out on the ground.

1947 A new block of turnstiles was erected on the Handsworth side behind the Woodman Corner.

1949 The wooden terraces in front of the main Halfords Lane stand were replaced by concrete and 750 extra seats were installed in the stand itself. The first electronic turnstile aggregator to be installed on a Football League ground in Britain was housed at The Hawthorns.

1950 A new directors' box was provided and the club's offices and dressing rooms were modernised.

1951 Eight new turnstiles were introduced at the Smethwick End.

1957 Floodlights were installed at the ground for the first time at a cost of £18,000.

1958 A wing stand (at the West Bromwich/Birmingham Road End) was added to the Halfords Lane stand.

1961 A new car park for some 600 vehicles was opened off Middlemore Road (behind the Handsworth Road stand). By 1964 they were four car parks within 800 yards of the ground.

1964 The Rainbow Stand, costing £40,000, was erected on the Handsworth side. It contained over 4,000 tip-up seats and was paid for with funds from the Development Association. The 'old' Handsworth stand was transferred across to cover the terracing behind the Birmingham Road goal.

1965 The first Throstle Club (for supporters) was opened next to The Hawthorns.

1967 Buffet bars inside the ground were renovated at a cost of £20,000.

Work is almost complete on the new-look Birmingham Road End.

1968 The Hawthorns Halt railway station was closed down.

1969 First-ever 'Open Day' for supporters held at The Hawthorns.

1970 Floodlighting renovated four-fold to fall in line with colour TV transmissions.

1976 Fourteen executive boxes installed in front of the Rainbow Stand and an extra 750 paddock seats were also put in.

1977 Executive box complex completed. Terracing reconstructed at the Smethwick and Birmingham Road Ends and new crush-barriers erected.

1979 Work started on the new £2.5 million stand to accommodate 4,500 spectators on the Halfords Lane side of the ground. This was built in two phases, 1979-82, and included 26 executive boxes.

1983 The Hawthorns Throstle Club (next to ground) was closed down. A large electronic scoreboard was erected on the front of the stand at the Smethwick End (this was removed in 1985).

1985 Smethwick End stand re-roofed. New safety measures installed at the ground.

1986 Crowd control video system installed at the ground.

1988-92 Major safety work carried out throughout the ground following the tragedies at Valley Parade and Hillsborough.

1989 Sponsors' Lounge opened in the corner of the Halfords Lane stand next to the Birmingham Road terraces.

1990 The Hawthorns pitch was completely returfed for only the second time in 90 years. Sods of turf were then sold to supporters as souvenirs.

1991 In February, a major pipe-burst caused thousands of pounds worth of damage in the Halfords Lane complex. In December, television pictures of Albion's away FA Cup-tie with Leyton Orient were beamed back to The Hawthorns on two giant screens which were erected in front of the main stand.

1992 The roof was removed from above the Smethwick End terracing as plans were put into motion to redevelop the ground and make it into an all-seater stadium.

1994 Birmingham Road terracing dug up as work continued on redeveloping The Hawthorns. Albion kicked-off the 1994-95 season with five away League games as the ground redevelopment came to a conclusion.

1995 Worked completed on Albion's all-seater stadium (including a new set of floodlights priced at £88,000) at a combined cost of £4.15 million, of which the club received £2,097,000 from the Football Trust.

The 'new' modernised Hawthorns was officially opened for the First Division League visit of Bristol City on Boxing Day (Albion won 1-0).

1995 The Hawthorns Museum was officially opened by manager Alan Buckley and The Hawthorns railway station was re-opened after 27 years.

Facts and Figures

The Hawthorns is the highest League ground above sea level in the U.K. – 550 feet

The never-to-be-beaten attendance record of 64,815 at The Hawthorns was set in March 1937 when Arsenal were the visitors for a sixth-round FA Cup-tie.

In 1996 The Hawthorns' capacity was 25,296 (all-seated) with room for 1,000 fans on the terraces (if required).

The breakdown on the ground seating, including box-holders, is:

Rainbow Stand	6,084
Halfords Lane Stand	5,110
Smethwick End	5,816
Birmingham Road End	8,286
Total	25,296

NB: Add the 1,000 terraces spaces, and the overall capacity is 26,296.

There have been three major internationals played on the ground: England 2 Ireland 0 in 1922, England 4 Belgium 0 in 1924 and England 0 Wales 1 (Victory International) in 1945.

In 1914, the Football League played the Irish League at The Hawthorns, and there have also been three other representative games played on the ground: England v The South in 1920 and England v The Rest in 1928 and 1935.

There have been a number of schoolboy and youth internationals staged at The Hawthorns plus a handful of non-League Cup Finals and a League Cup Final (Albion v West Ham, second leg, 1965-66), the 1970 Watney Cup Final (Albion v Colchester United) and the first leg of the 1995-96 Anglo-Italian English Final, Albion v Port Vale. There have also been two FA Cup semi-finals: Derby County v Sheffield United in 1901-02 and Aston Villa v Wolverhampton Wanderers in 1959-60;

The club's Throstle mascot at The Hawthorns.

one other League Cup semi-final: Burnley v Swindon Town replay in 1968-69. Albion themselves have appeared in four League Cup semi-finals on their own ground: 1965-66, 1966-67, 1969-70 and 1981-82. And one Second Division Play-off semi-final: Albion v Swansea City 2nd leg, 1992-93.

The pitch size in 1996 was 115 yards long by 75 yards wide (it used to be 118 x 79).

Tony Brown played in a record 282 Football League games for Albion at The Hawthorns. He made 361 first-team appearances all told on the ground and scored 173 goals (132 in the League).

'W.G.' Richardson score more goals at The Hawthorns than any other player: a total of 216 in all first-team matches.

Well over 4,000 matches (at various levels) have been staged at The Hawthorns in the 96 years the ground has been in use. In November/December 1919, Wolverhampton Wanderers played two Second Division League games at The Hawthorns: v Barnsley (lost 4-2) and Stockport County (2-2).

Walsall played Brighton & Hove Albion in a Third Division League game at The Hawthorns in February 1970 (because the Saddlers' Fellows Park ground was waterlogged).

On 11 May 1931, HRH The Prince of Wales (later King Edward VIII and the Duke of Windsor) visited The Hawthorns to offer his congratulations to Albion on their unique 'double' achievement.

On 7 August 1944, the American and Canadian armies staged a baseball match at The Hawthorns before a 5,000 crowd.

Immediately before World War One, an athletics meeting, staged over two days, took place at The Hawthorns, and there was also a boxing tournament held there featuring the great Jimmy Wilde.

On 29 July 1977 a limited over cricket match was staged at The Hawthorns between Indian and Pakistan Test teams. The Indians won by 4 wickets and 2,641 attended. The proceeds went towards a children's charity and Imran Khan's benefit.

On 15 October 1980, the first floodlight cricket match was played at The Hawthorns when Ian Botham's XI (which included David Gower) played Warwickshire CCC in a 30 overs match, the proceeds going towards Alistair Robertson's testimonial fund.

HEASELGRAVE, Samuel Edward

Gritty inside-forward who scored 57 goals in 163 appearances for Albion between 1937 and 1945. Born in Smethwick in 1916, Sammy Heaselgrave played for several local junior sides before he joined Albion in 1934, turning professional in 1936 and making his debut a year later. A England Junior international, he was one of only four Albion players to appear in all seven wartime seasons (1939-46) when he also guested for Walsall. He left The Hawthorns for Northampton Town and later served with Dudley Town and Northwich Victoria, retiring in 1949 to go into business in Bearwood, Warley. Heaselgrave, who won the all-England bowls title in 1963, died in 1975.

HEATH, Norman Harold

A serious back and neck injury, suffered against Sunderland, robbed Norman Heath of an FA Cup Final appearance in 1954. Prior to that he had played in 169 games for Albion, making his debut in 1943. After serving in the Army, when he represented the Combined Services, he contested the goalkeeping position with Jimmy Sanders and was in brilliant form before that cruel injury at Roker Park ended his career. Born in Wolverhampton in 1924, he joined Albion from Henry Meadows FC at the age of 18 and before his death in 1983, managed the junior side, Great Barr Gunners.

HEIGHT & WEIGHT
Tallest

The tallest player ever to appear in League and/or Cup

George Reilly, Albion's 6ft 2ins striker of the 1980s.

matches for Albion has been 6ft 4¼ins 1880s goalkeeper Bob Roberts. Strikers Stewart Evans and George Reilly (1980s), defender Alf Ridyard (1930s), wing-half Peter Billingham (1960s) and Jeroen Boere (1990s) were all 6ft 3ins tall; and midfielder Carlton Palmer and defender Paul Dyson (1980s) along with 1990s goalkeepers Stuart Naylor and Nigel Spink were all 6ft 2ins tall.

Leicester City's 6ft 7ins Australian-born goalkeeper Zeljko Kalac has been the tallest player ever to appear against Albion in a competitive game (1995).

Shortest

'Wee' Tommy Magee, at 5ft 2½ins, has been the shortest player to appear in a major League or Cup game for Albion, doing so between 1919-34.

Stewart Bowen, at 5ft 3ins tall, played first-team football for Albion in the early 1990s.

Other 'short' Albion players include wingers Alf Geddes, Jimmy McLean, Jimmy Prew, Hughie Reed and Jimmy Spencer, and midfielders Wayne Dobbins, Dave Gilbert and Andy Thompson.

Syd Tufnell of Blackpool has been the shortest player to appear against Albion in a senior match – 5ft 2¾ins tall in 1931.

The Middlesbrough forward-line of Chadwick, Bruce, Yorston, Baxter and Warren v Albion in September 1934 was collectively the smallest and probably lightest ever to play in the Football League with Yorston the tallest and heaviest at 5ft 9ins and 10st 6lbs.

Albion's forward-line at Ipswich in September 1963 comprised Ken Foggo, Tony Brown, Ron Fenton, Alec Jackson and Clive Clark – average height 5ft 8ins, the smallest in the club's history (for one match).

Heaviest

The heaviest player ever to appear in Albion's first team has been goalkeeper Jimmy Adams, who weighed 14st 10lbs during the late 1930s/early 1940s.

Defender Ted Pheasant (1904-10) weighed 14st 9lbs; centre-forward Fred Shinton (1905-07) tipped the scales at 14st 7lbs; goalkeeper Nigel Spink was 14st 6lbs in 1996 and full-back Idris Bassett (1936-43) weighed in at 14st 2lbs.

The heaviest player to line-up against Albion has been goalkeeper Willie 'Fatty' Foulke, who weighed a massive 22st when he starred for Bradford City in a Second Division game at The Hawthorns in November 1906.

Lightest

Among the players who have appeared in Albion's first team weighing nine-and-a-half stones or less are Michael Lee (1956-58), Hugh MacLean (1967-74)

Hughie MacLean, lightweight utility player who weighed in at 9st 7lbs.

and Harry Parkes (1906-08 & 1914-19) – all wingers! Tommy Magee weighed 9st 12lbs and Jimmy Prew 9st 13lbs.

HEREFORD UNITED

Albion's record against Hereford:

League Cup

Venue	P	W	D	L	F	A
Home	1	0	0	1	0	1
Away	1	0	1	0	0	0
Totals	2	0	1	1	0	1

Other Matches

Away	3	1	1	1	6	10

The first meeting between the clubs was at Edgar Street on 1 November 1954 when Hereford beat a strong Albion side 10-5 in a benefit match for Reg Bowen and Jack Sankey (once of Albion).

A crowd of 4,500 saw James score four goals for Hereford.

Albion's manager Vic Buckingham was involved in a serious car accident on his way home after the match.

Albion and Hereford met over two legs in the first round of the League Cup in 1994-95, Hereford being the first team to play and win (1-0) in front of the newly-designed Smethwick End stand at The Hawthorns in the return leg.

Archie Styles, played for both Albion and Hereford United.

Players with both clubs: Colin Anderson, George Banks, Nicky Cross, Bobby Dixon, Jimmy Duggan, Bobby Gould, Chris Hargreaves, Joe Johnson, Bobby Newsome, Stewart Phillips, Jack Sankey, Cecil Shaw, Kenny Stephens, Archie Styles, George Tranter, Bert Trentham, Jock Wallace, Ernie Watson, Winston White. Tranter was player-manager of Hereford.

Also associated with both clubs: Tommy Bowen, Darren Goodall, David Lapworth, Alan Scarrott and Alan Wileman, Albion reserves who played for Hereford; Les Palmer, an Albion forward 1989-92, signed for Hereford as a non-contract player in 1996; Colin Addison, Hereford player and manager and assistant manager at Albion; Alan Ashman, Albion manager (1967-71) and assistant manager of Hereford (1983-87).

HIGGINS, Thomas

Higgins was a fine centre-half, good in the air, strong on the ground, who scored five goals in 94 games for Albion during a four-year spell at the club in the 1890s. Born in Halesowen in 1874, he joined Albion from Stourbridge at the age of 20 and a year later appeared in the FA Cup Final when Albion lost to Aston Villa. He received £5 after battling on with his heavily bandaged head in the game which Albion lost 1-0. Higgins represented the Football League on two occasions in 1896 and was set for full international honours when his career was ended prematurely in 1898 through a knee injury. He later became a licensee in Middlesbrough and died in 1916.

HODGETTS, Frank

When making his debut at the age of 16 years, 26 days, against Notts County on 26 October 1942, Hodgetts became the youngest player ever to don an Albion shirt at first-team

level. An out-and-out winger, who hugged the touchline, he went on to score 34 goals in 178 games for the club before transferring to Millwall for £6,000 in 1949, having spent seven years at The Hawthorns. Born in Dudley in 1924, Hodgetts joined Albion from Accles & Pollocks Works team and after leaving The Den in 1953 he played for Worcester City, retiring in 1957 with a snapped Achilles tendon. He coached at The Hawthorns (1958-62) and later became chairman of the Herefordshire & Worcestershire County Lawn Tennis Association. He now lives in Hagley.

HOGG, Derek

Fast-raiding outside-left who netted 12 goals in 87 games for Albion (1958-60). Born at Stockton-on-Tees in 1930, Hogg played for Lostock Hall, Chorley and Leicester City before moving to The Hawthorns for £20,000. He left Albion for Cardiff City in a £12,000 deal and later played for Kettering Town before retiring in 1965 to become a licensee, a job he held until 1995.

HONVED

Albion played against the crack Hungarian club side, Honved, in the Heysel Stadium, Brussels on 13 October 1954 in the Le Soir Festival of Football. Honved fielded seven members of the Hungarian team which had helped destroy England 6-3 at Wembley and then 7-1 in Budapest during the previous 11 months, while Albion had won the FA Cup, finished runners-up in the English First Division and had drawn 4-4 with Wolves in the annual Charity Shield game at Molineux. A crowd of 55,000 saw Honved win 5-3, coming back from a 3-1 deficit against an Albion side which played superbly well for an hour before tiring.

The 'Galloping Major' Ferenc Puskas, Czibor (2) Szonjak and Sandor Kocsis scored for Honved while Johnny Nicholls (2) and Ronnie Allen replied for Albion.

HOOD, Owen Glyn

A clever wing-half with neat footwork and quiet approach who appeared in 74 first-team games for Albion during the late 1940s. A Welshman, born in Pentwyn in 1925, Glyn Hood was once a keen rugger player before turning to

soccer. He joined Albion from Nuffield FC in 1942 and was a key member of the Baggies' promotion-winning side in 1948-49. Sadly he was forced to quit the game in 1951 through injury. He now lives in Coventry.

HOPE, Robert

A masterful midfield player with terrific vision, splendid ball skills and strong shot, who gave Albion excellent

service for 13 years. A Scot, born in Stirlingshire in 1943, Hope joined Albion in August 1959 with colleagues Ken Foggo, Campbell Crawford and Bobby Murray, all four having played for their country in three schoolboy internationals earlier that year. Hope went on to gain further caps at Under-23 and senior levels and he scored 42 goals in 403 appearances for Albion, collecting League Cup and FA Cup winners' prizes in 1966 and 1968 respectively. He netted Albion's first-ever goal in a European competition (v DOS Utrecht in 1966) and after leaving The Hawthorns in 1972, he served with Birmingham City and Sheffield Wednesday as well as playing in the NASL with Philadelphia Atoms and Dallas Tornadoes. He later had two spells as manager of Bromsgrove Rovers, scouted for Albion and neighbours Wolves and played in more than 200 Charity games for Albion All Stars (1979-94). Hope, who also ran post offices in both Birmingham and Sutton, now lives in Walsall.

HORTON BROTHERS (Ezra & John)

Between them the Horton brothers appeared in 235 League and Cup games for Albion over a period of 17 years (1882-1899), Ezra in 83 (one goal scored) and Jack 152. Ezra, born in

Jack Horton, made 152 League and Cup appearances for Albion.

West Bromwich in 1861, was a hard-tackling, resilient right-half, who starred in all of Albion's first 36 FA Cup matches. He lined up in the 1886, 1887 and 1888 FA Cup Finals, was a member of Albion's first League team v Stoke in 1888 and totalled more than 300 appearances for the club (friendlies included). He retired through injury in 1891 and four years later became a Football League referee. Ezra guested for Aston Villa in 1884 and also played in defence for the West Bromwich hockey team, becoming only the second Midlander to represent England at this sport. He died in 1939.

Jack, a schoolmaster by profession, was a robust full-back who served Albion from 1882 to 1899, playing in the club's first-ever League game in 1888 and also in the 1895 FA Cup Final. West Bromwich-born in 1866, he amassed some 250 appearances in total for the club and was unlucky not to win England honours. On his retirement he took charge of Albion's reserve team for a short while before going into business. He died in 1947, aged 80.

HOWE, Donald

Deft positioning, reliability, good pace and sound kicking were the hallmarks of Howe's overall displays for Albion and England over a number of years. Mainly as a right-back, he appeared in 379 games and scored 19 goals for Albion between 1955 and 1964 before transferring to Arsenal for £40,000. Born in Wolverhampton in 1935, he joined Albion's ranks initially in 1950 (after being on Wolves' books as an amateur) and turned professional two years later, making his debut v Everton in 1955 along with Derek Kevan. He went on to win 23 caps for his country, playing in the 1958 World Cup Finals. He also represented England 'B', the Under-23s and the Football League XI, and toured New Zealand with the FA party in 1961. He was forced to retire through injury in 1967 and was appointed coach at Highbury, later taking over as assistant manager before returning to The Hawthorns as Albion manager in 1971. During his four years in charge Albion suffered relegation

Home	1	0	1	0	1	1
Away	1	0	0	1	1	2
Totals	2	0	1	1	2	3

Albion's first League meeting with Huddersfield ended in a 2-0 away win on 24 December 1910.

The return fixture in 1911 was played at The Hawthorns on 30 April and Albion had to win to take the Second Division title. They beat Huddersfield 1-0 before a 30,000 plus crowd, skipper Freddie Buck hitting the winner from the penalty spot.

Albion recorded their best League win over Huddersfield on 23 April 1938, beating them 5-1 at home in a First Division match.

Albion also defeated Huddersfield 4-0 at home in season 1953-54 when Ronnie Allen scored a hat-trick.

Huddersfield's best win, over the reigning League champions Albion, is 5-1 at Leeds Road on 23 October 1920.

Dick Krzywicki, played for both Albion and Huddersfield Town.

Albion finished runners-up to Huddersfield in the First Division in 1924-25, the Yorkshire side taking the title by two points.

Huddersfield did the double over Albion in 1995-96, winning 2-1 at The Hawthorns and 4-1 at the Alfred McAlpine Stadium.

'W.G.' Richardson scored 13 goals (including a run of nine in ten matches) for Albion against Huddersfield.

On 23 September 1992, Kevin Donovan, Kieran O'Regan and Neil Parsley all played for Huddersfield v Blackburn Rovers (h) in a Coca-Cola Cup-tie; less than a year later all

from the First Division. In 1975 he coached Galatasary (Turkey) and then after a brief coaching spell with Leeds United, he moved back to Arsenal, initially as coach and then as manager (1984-86). Over the last ten years Howe has been a major part of the England coaching staff (at various levels) and has also coached at Bristol Rovers, Wimbledon, QPR, Barnet and Coventry City. He was manager of QPR (1989-91) and Coventry (1992), taking a coaching position with Chelsea (1992-93). (See MANAGERS.)

HUDDERSFIELD TOWN

Albion's record v Huddersfield:

Football League

Venue	P	W	D	L	F	A	Pts
Home	28	15	6	7	52	37	39
Away	28	6	7	15	31	54	21
Totals	56	21	13	22	83	92	60

three were with Albion, making their first appearance as a trio v Watford (h) on 30 October 1993.

Albion League debutants v Huddersfield: Gilbert Alsop (1935), Joe Johnson (1937), Stuart Williams (1952), Billy Brookes (1953), Maurice Setters (1955), Tony Lange (1993).

Players with both clubs: Sam Allardyce, Ian Banks, Mark Barham, Peter Butler, Jack Byers, Dennis Clarke, David Cork, Andy Dibble, Kevin Donovan, Peter Eastoe, Dick Krzywicki, Jack Mahon, Kieran O'Regan, Neil Parsley, Harry Raw, Sid Rawlings, Ronnie Robinson, David Shaw, George Shaw, Steve Walford, Paul R.Williams.

Also associated with both clubs: Tom Daley and Jason Withe were reserve players with Albion and Town, and Jesse Carver (Albion coach-manager, Huddersfield assistant trainer). Mel Eves, a loan player with Huddersfield, was with Albion briefly in 1988.

HUDSON'S FC

Albion's first recorded game (as West Bromwich Strollers) was a 0-0 draw at home against a local team called Hudson's on 23 November 1878.

A brief report of the event with team line-ups is contained in the *West Bromwich Weekly News* of 30 November 1878. The discovery of this match was first revealed in the *Albion News* of 15 December 1993.

HUGHES, Lyndon James

A former England schoolboy and youth international wing-half, Lyndon Hughes joined Albion as a trainee in 1966, turning professional in 1968. In the next seven years he scored four goals in 125 appearances for the Baggies before transferring to Peterborough United in 1975. He later assisted Kettering Town and Bromsgrove Rovers, retiring in 1982 to work in the licensed trade. Hughes, born in Smethwick in 1950, played with only one functional kidney for 20 years

HULL CITY

Albion's record against Hull:

Football League

Venue	P	W	D	L	F	A	Pts
Home	19	9	7	3	32	17	28
Away	19	4	5	10	18	33	16
Totals	38	13	12	13	50	50	44

FA Cup

Venue	P	W	D	L	F	A
Home	1	1	0	0	2	0
Away	2	0	0	2	1	3

Anglo-Scottish Tournament

Venue	P	W	D	L	F	A
Away	1	1	0	0	2	1

Other Matches

Venue	P	W	D	L	F	A
Away	2	1	0	1	5	5

Albion's best League win over Hull is 7-1 at The Hawthorns in a Second Division game on 19 April 1930.

Albion's 1-0 win at Hull on 13 May 1989 was their first on Tigers' soil in the League since 1906. Hull's best League victory over Albion is 5-1, at home, on 23 April 1910.

During Albion's first overseas tour – to Scandinavia in May 1909 – they played Hull City in two exhibition matches, winning 2-1 in Stockholm and losing 4-3 in Gothenburg.

Albion League debutants v Hull: Billy Law (1905), Harry Wilcox (1907), Amos Lloyd (1910), Billy Wollaston (1910), Jimmy Edwards (1928), Joe Mayo (1973), Stewart Evans (1986), Bobby Williamson (1986), Ronnie Robinson (1989), Phil Hawker (1990), Ugo Ehiogu (1990).

Players with both clubs: Peter Barnes, Charlie Deacey, Alan Fettis, Chris Hargreaves, Gordon Inwood, John Kaye, Gordon Nisbet, Ernie Shepherd, Gerry Summers.

Associated with both clubs: Albion reserves Derek Hood, Tom Jones, Jack Quantick, Bill Taylor and Kim Wassell played for Hull; Albion winger Jack Mahon became assistant trainer at Hull; Bob Brocklebank was an Albion scout and Hull City manager (1955-61); Gordon Dimbleby was commercial manager at Albion (1973-80) and general manager at Hull (1980-82) and Mick Brown was a Hull full-back (1958-65) and later Albion's assistant manager.

HUNT, Andrew

Tall striker, signed from Newcastle United for a bargain fee of £100,000 in 1993 after a loan spell at The Hawthorns during which time he scored a hat-trick on his Hawthorns debut. He netted again when Albion beat Port Vale in the Second Division promotion Play-off Final at Wembley. A

willing front-runner who never gives up, Hunt was born in Grays, Essex in 1970 and joined Kettering Town from Kings Lynn before switching north to St James's Park in 1991 for a fee of £150,000. He netted 14 goals in 51 games for United and then proceeded to hit the net regularly for Albion. He formed a good striking partnership with Bob Taylor and was leading marksman in season 1994-95 with 13 goals and second the following season with 17 goals. When the 1996-97 campaign started Hunt had netted 56 goals in 149 first-team appearances for Albion.

HUNT, Stephen Peter

Midfielder Steve Hunt had a superb left foot and could spray passes all over the pitch, occasionally releasing stinging shots on goal. Born in Birmingham in 1956, he spent his early days with Aston Villa and after a good spell in the NASL with New York Cosmos whom he helped win the Super Bowl in 1977 and 1978, he joined Coventry City for

£40,000. A second spell with the Cosmos (1982) was followed by another stint at Highfield Road during which time he took his appearance tally with the Sky Blues to over 200 before joining Albion for £180,000 in 1984. He scored 20 goals in 84 games whilst at The Hawthorns, leaving for his former club Aston Villa in 1986 in a deal which brought Darren Bradley to Albion. Hunt, who played twice at full international level for England as an Albion midfielder and in three games for an England XI while with Coventry, was forced to retire through injury in 1987. He then managed Willenhall Town and later coached at Port Vale and Leicester before emigrating to New York once more to become involved in the Stateside soccer scene.

INTERNATIONAL AND REPRESENTATIVE HONOURS

Before 1924 there was only one 'Ireland' team then the Republic of Ireland began separate international matches. England Under-23 ceased to play international matches in 1976-77 when the England Under-21 team was introduced.

Full, Wartime & Victory Internationals
England
A.Aldridge (1) 1887-88 v Ireland.
R.Allen (5) 1951-52 v Switzerland; 1953-54 v Scotland (1 goal), Yugoslavia; 1954-55 v Wales, West Germany (1 goal).
G.S.Ashmore (1) 1925-26 v Belgium.
J.Astle (5) 1968-69 v Wales; 1969-70 v Portugal, Scotland, Brazil, Czechoslovakia.
R.J.Barlow (1) 1954-55 v Northern Ireland.
P.S.Barnes (6) 1979-80 v Denmark, Wales; 1980-81 v Spain (sub), Brazil, Wales, Switzerland (sub).
W.I.Bassett (16) 1887-88 v Ireland; 1888-89 v Wales (1 goal), Scotland (1 goal); 1889-90 v Wales, Scotland; 1890-91 v Ireland (1 goal), Scotland; 1891-92 v Scotland; 1892-93 v Wales (1 goal), Scotland; 1893-94 v Scotland; 1894-95 v Ireland (1 goal), Scotland; 1895-96 v Ireland, Wales (1 goal), Scotland (1 goal).
A.J.Bayliss (1) 1890-91 v Ireland.
S.Bowser (1) 1919-20 v Ireland.
W.E.Boyes (2) 1931-35 v Holland; 1935-36 v Scotland (Jubilee).

A.Brown (1) 1970-71 v Wales.
J.H.Carter (3) 1925-26 v Belgium (1 goal); 1928-29 v Belgium (1 goal), Spain (2 goals).
L.P.Cunningham (3) 1978-79 v Wales, Sweden, Austria.
W.B.Elliott (2) 1943-44 v Wales (Wartime); 1945-46 v Scotland (Victory).
B.Garfield (1) 1897-98 v Ireland.
H.Hadley (1) 1902-03 v Ireland.
J.T.W.Haines (1) 1948-49 v Switzerland (2 goals).
D.Howe (23) 1957-58 v Wales, Northern Ireland, France, Scotland, Portugal, Yugoslavia, USSR (3 times), Brazil, Austria; 1958-59 v Northern Ireland, USSR, Wales, Scotland, Italy, Brazil, Peru, Mexico, USA; 1959-60 v Wales, Sweden, Northern Ireland.
S.Hunt (2) 1983-84 v Scotland (sub), USSR (sub).
D.T.Kevan (14) 1956-57 v Scotland (1 goal); 1957-58 v Wales, Northern Ireland, Scotland (2 goals), Portugal, Yugoslavia, USSR (3 times - 2 goals), Brazil, Austria (1 goal); 1958-59 v Mexico (1 goal), USA (1 goal); 1960-61 v Mexico.
T.H.Kinsell (2) 1945-46 v Northern Ireland, Wales (both Victory).
R.McNeal (2) 1913-14 v Wales, Scotland.
T.P.Magee (5) 1922-23 v Wales, Sweden; 1924-25 v Belgium, Scotland, France.
F.Morris (2) 1919-20 v Scotland (1 goal), 1920-21 v Ireland.
J.Nicholls (2) 1953-54 v Scotland (1 goal), Yugoslavia.
H.F.Pearson (1) 1931-32 v Scotland.
J.Pennington (25) 1906-07 v Wales, Scotland; 1907-08 v Ireland, Wales, Scotland, Austria; 1908-09 v Wales, Scotland, Hungary (twice), Austria; 1909-10 v Wales, Scotland; 1910-11 v Ireland, Wales, Scotland; 1911-12 v Ireland, Wales, Scotland; 1912-13 v Wales, Scotland; 1913-14 v Ireland, Scotland; 1919-20 v Wales, Scotland.
C.Perry (3) 1889-90 v Ireland; 1890-91 v Ireland; 1892-93 v Wales.
T.Perry (1) 1897-98 v Wales.
J.Reader (1) 1893-94 v Ireland.
C.Regis (4) 1981-82 v Northern Ireland, Wales, Iceland; 1982-83 v West Germany.
J.Reynolds (3) 1891-92 v Scotland; 1892-93 v Wales (1 goal), Scotland (1 goal).
W.G.Richardson (1) 1934-35 v Holland.
S.Rickaby (1) 1953-54 v Northern Ireland.
R.Roberts (3) 1886-87 v Scotland; 1887-88 v Ireland; 1889-90 v Ireland.
B.Robson (13) 1979-80 v Republic of Ireland Australia; 1980-81 v Norway, Romania (twice), Switzerland (twice), Spain, Brazil, Wales, Scotland, Hungary; 1981-82 v Norway.

R.W.Robson (20) 1957-58 v France (2 goals), USSR (twice), Brazil, Austria; 1959-60 v Spain, Hungary; 1960-61 v Northern Ireland, Luxembourg, Spain, Wales, Scotland (1 goal), Mexico (1 goal), Portugal, Italy; 1961-62 v Luxembourg, Wales, Portugal, Northern Ireland, Switzerland.
E.A.Sandford (1) 1932-33 v Wales.
G.E.Shaw (1) 1931-32 v Scotland.
J.Smith (3) 1919-20 v

Bryan Robson in England's colours.

Wales (Victory), Ireland; 1922-23 v Ireland.
D.Statbam (3) 1982-83 v Wales, Australia (twice).
W.Williams (6) 1896-97 v Ireland; 1897-98 v Ireland, Wales, Scotland; 1898-99 v Ireland, Wales.
G.Woodhall (2) 1887-88 v Wales (1 goal), Scotland.

Asa Hartford, wearing one of his Scottish international caps.

Scotland
D.M.Fraser (2) 1967-68 v Holland; 1968-69 v Cyprus.
R.A.Hartford (6) 1971-72 v Peru, Wales, England, Yugoslavia, Czechoslovakia, Brazil
R.Hope (2) 1967-68 v Holland; 1968-69 v Denmark.
W.M.Johnston (13) 1976-77 v Sweden, Wales, Northern Ireland, England, Chile, Argentina, Brazil; 1977-78 v East Germany, Czechoslovakia, Wales (twice), England, Peru.
A.McNab (1) 1938-39 v England.

Wales
S.Davies (11) 1921-22 v Scotland (1 goal), England, Ireland; 1922-23 v Scotland; 1924-25 v Scotland, Northern Ireland; 1925-26 v Scotland, Northern Ireland, England; 1926-27 v Scotland; 1927-28 v Scotland.
W.C.Davies (2) 1908-09 v England; 1909-10 v Scotland.

Welsh international George Williams.

H.E.Foukes (1) 1931-32 v Northern Ireland.
I.Jones (4) 1922-23 v England; Ireland; 1923-24 v Scotland; 1925-26 v Northern Ireland.
R.L.Krzywicki (2) 1969-70 v East Germany, Italy.
P.J.Mardon (1) 1995-96 v West Germany (sub).
A.H.Millington (3) 1962-63 v Scotland, Hungary, England.
J.P.Murphy (15) 1932-33 v England, Northern Ireland, France; 1933-34 v Scotland, England; 1934-35 v England, Scotland, Northern Ireland; 1935-36 v Scotland, England, Northern Ireland; 1936-37 v Scotland, Northern Ireland; 1937-38 v Scotland, England.
S.Powell (4) 1890-91 v England, Scotland; 1891-92 v England, Scotland.
R.R.Rees (2) 1967-68 v West Germany; 1968-69 v Italy.
W.W.Robbins (6) 1932-33 v Scotland, England, Northern Ireland (2 goals), France; 1933-34 v Scotland (1 goal); 1935-36 v Scotland.
M.R.Thomas (2) 1985-86 v Hungary, Saudi Arabia (sub).
G.E.Williams (26) 1959-60 v Northern Ireland; 1960-61 v Republic of Ireland, Scotland, England; 1962-63 v Hungary, Northern Ireland; 1963-64 v England, Scotland, Northern Ireland; 1964-65 v Scotland, Denmark, England, Greece (twice), Northern Ireland (1 goal), Italy, USSR; 1965-66 v Northern Ireland, Brazil (twice), Chile; 1966-67 v Scotland, England, Northern Ireland; 1967-68 v Ireland; 1968-69 v Italy.
S.C.Williams (33) 1953-54 v Austria; 1954-55 v England, Northern Ireland; 1955-56 v England, Scotland, Austria; 1957-58 v England, Scotland, Israel (twice), Northern Ireland, Hungary (twice), Mexico, Sweden, Brazil; 1958-59 v

Reg Ryan (dark shirt) in action for the Republic of Ireland against Austria at Dalymount Park, Dublin, in March 1953.

Scotland, England, Northern Ireland; 1959-60 v England, Scotland, Northern Ireland; 1960-61 v Republic of Ireland, Northern Ireland, Spain (twice), Hungary; 1961-62 v England, Scotland, Northern Ireland, Brazil (twice), Mexico.
D.F.Witcomb (9) 1939-40 v England (twice); 1940-41 v England (twice, 1 goal); 1941-42 v England (twice) (all Wartime); 1945-46 v Scotland (Victory); 1946-47 v Scotland, England.

Northern Ireland (& Ireland before 1924)
G.J.Armstrong (4) 1985-86 v Turkey, Romania (sub),

England (sub), France (sub).

D.Hegan (1) 1969-70 v USSR.

J.M.Nicholl (11) 1984-85 v Finland, England, Spain, Turkey; 1985-86 v Turkey, Romania, England, France, Algeria, Spain, Brazil.

R.A.Ryan (1) 1949-50 v Wales.

J.Vernon (15) 1946-47 v Wales; 1947-48 v Scotland, England, Wales; 1948-49 v England, Scotland, Wales; 1949-50 v Scotland, England; 1950-51 v England, Scotland, Wales, France; 1951-52 v Scotland, England.

D.J.Walsh (9) 1946-47 v Scotland, Wales; 1947-48 v Scotland, England (1 goal), Wales; 1948-49 v England (2 goals), Wales; 1949-50 v Wales.

P.A.Williams (1) 1990-91 v Faroe Islands (sub).

Republic of Ireland

M.J.Giles (7) 1975-76 v Turkey; 1976-77 v England, Turkey, France (twice), Poland, Bulgaria.

A.Grealish (10) 1983-84 v Poland, China; 1984-85 v Mexico, USSR, Norway, Denmark, Spain (sub), Switzerland; 1985-86 v USSR, Denmark.

M.P.Martin (10) 1975-76 v Turkey, Norway, Poland; 1976-77 v England, Turkey, France (twice), Spain, Poland, Bulgaria.

P.M.Mulligan (16) 1975-76 v Turkey, Poland; 1976-77 v England, Turkey, France (twice), Poland, Bulgaria; 1977-78 v Bulgaria, Norway, Denmark; 1978-79 v England, Denmark, Bulgaria, West Germany, Argentina.

R.A.Ryan (15) 1949-50 v Sweden, Belgium; 1950-51 v Norway (twice), Argentina; 1951-52 v West Germany (twice), Austria, Spain; 1952-53 v France, Austria; 1953-54 v France (twice, 1 goal), Luxembourg (1 goal); 1954-55 v Norway (1 goal).

R.C.Trcacy (6) 1965-66 v West Germany; 1966-67 v Spain, Czechoslovakia; 1967-68 v Czechoslovakia (1 goal); 1976-77 v France, Poland.

D.J.Walsh (14) 1945-46 v Portugal, Spain; 1946-47 v Spain (2 goals), Portugal; 1947-48 v Portugal, Spain (1 goal); 1948-49 v Switzerland, Portugal, Sweden (1 goal), Spain; 1949-50 v England, Finland, Sweden; 1950-51 v Norway (1 goal).

Canada

C.Valentine (1) 1985-86 v Honduras.

'B' Internationals
England

R.Allen (2) 1953-54 v Scotland, Switzerland. **J.Astle** (2) 1969-70 v Columbia (1 goal), Ecuador XI (3 goals).

R.J.Barlow (2) 1951-52 v France; 1952-53 Scotland.

P.S.Barnes (1) 1980-81 v USA.

B.M.Batson (3) 1980-81 v USA, Australia, Spain.

L.P.Cunningham (1) 1978-79 v Czechoslovakia.

J.R.DugDale (3) 1953-54 v Scotland, Yugoslavia, Switzerland.

A.Ford (2) 1988-89 v Switzerland (sub), Norway.

D.Howe (1) 1956-57 v Scotland.

J.P.Kennedy (3) 1951-52 v France; 1955-56 v Yugoslavia, Scotland.

S.Naylor (3) 1988-89 v Switzerland (sub), Iceland, Norway.

J.Nicholls (1) 1953-54 v Switzerland (sub).

C.Regis (3) 1978-79 v Czechoslovakia (sub); 1980-81 v USA, Australia.

B.Robson (2) 1978-79 v Austria; 1979-80 v Spain.

D.J.Statham (2) 1980-81 v USA (1 goal), Spain (1 goal).

Scotland

J.G.Dudley (J) 1953-54 v England.

Under-23 & Under-21 Internationals
England

D.G.Burnside (2) 1960-61 v Danish XI; 1961-62 v Turkey.

D.Burrows (1) 1988-89 v Sweden (sub).

L.Cantello (8) 1971-72 v East Germany; 1972-73 v Wales, Holland (twice), Denmark, Czechoslovakia; 1973-74 v Poland, Denmark.

C.Clark (1) 1960-61 v Wales.

L.P.Cunningham (6) 1976-77 v Scotland (1 goal), Finland, Norway (sub); 1977-78 v Norway, Finland (1 goal), Italy.

D.Howe (6) 1955-56 v Scotland; 1956-57 v France, Scotland; 1957-58 v Bulgaria, Scotland, Wales.

D.T.Kevan (4) 1956-57 v Bulgaria, Romania, Czechoslovakia; 1957-58 v Bulgaria.

P.W.Latchford (2) 1973-74 v Poland, Wales.

S.Mackenzie (3) 1981-82 v Norway, Scotland (twice).

R.Moses (7) 1980-81 v Norway (sub), Switzerland (twice), Republic of Ireland, Romania, Hungary; 1981-82 v Norway (sub).

J.Nicholls (1) 1953-54 v Italy.

G.J.M.Nisbet (1) 1971-72 v East Germany.

G.A.Owen (12) 1978-79 v Bulgaria, Sweden (sub); 1979-80 v Denmark, Scotland (twice, 1 goal), East Germany; 1980-81 v Switzerland (1 goal), Romania; 1981-82 v Norway (sub), Hungary; 1982-83 v West Germany (twice, 2 goals).

C.Regis (6) 1978-79 v Denmark, Bulgaria (1 goal), Sweden (1 goal); 1979-80 v Scotland, East Germany; 1982-83 v Denmark (1 goal).

B.Robson (7) 1978-79 v Wales, Bulgaria (sub), Sweden (1 goal); 1979-80 v Denmark, Bulgaria, Scotland (twice, 1 goal).

M.E.Setters (11) 1957-58 v Bulgaria, Romania, Scotland, Wales; 1958-59 v Poland, Czechoslovakia, France, Italy, West Germany; 1959-60 v Hungary, France.

D.J.Statham (6) 1977-78 v Finland: 1978-79 v Wales, Bulgaria, Sweden; 1979-80 v Denmark; 1982-83 v Greece.

Scotland

E.P.Colquhoun (1) 1967-68 v England.

R.A.Hartford (5) 1969-70 v Wales; 1970-71 v Wales; 1971-72 v England; 1972-73 v England, Wales.

R.Hope (1) 1966-67 v Wales.

R.T.Wilson (1) 1969-70 v Wales.

Wales

B.W.Hughes (3) 1976-77 v England, Scotland; 1977-78 v Scotland.

R.L.Krzywicki (3) 1966-67 v Scotland, England; 1969-70 v Scotland.

A.H.Millington (4) 1961-62 v Scotland, Northern Ireland; 1962-63 v Scotland, Northern Ireland.

G.E.Williams (2) 1959-60 v Scotland; 1960-61 v Wales.

Republic of Ireland

K.Ampadu (1) 1991-92 v Switzerland.

J.Anderson (5) 1977-78 v Northern Ireland; 1978-79 v USSR, Argentina, Hungary, Yugoslavia.

R.C.P.Treacy (1) 1965-66 v France.

Amateur Internationals
England

R.Banks (1) 1933-34 v Wales.

L.F.Cooling (1) 1924-25 v Wales.

W.C.Jordan (2) 1907-08 v France (6 goals); 1909-10 v Ireland (2 goals).

Football League Honours

R.Allcn (1) 1957-58 v Scottish League (1 goal).

J.Astle (2) 1969-70 v Scottish League (2 goals); 1970-71 v Irish League (2 goals).

H.G.Bache (1) 1914-15 v Irish League.

R.J.Barlow (5) 1952-53 v League of Ireland, Danish Combination; 1953-54 v League of Ireland; 1954-55 v League of Ireland; 1957-58 v League of Ireland.

W.I.Bassett (3) 1891-92 v Scottish League (1 goal); 1892-93 v Scottish League (1 goal); 1896-97 v Irish League.

W.E.Boyes (1) 1935-36 v Irish League (1 goal).
A.Brown (2) 1970-71 v Irish League (sub) (1 goal), Scottish League.
F.Buck (2) 1911-12 v Southern League, Irish League.
J.H.Carter (1) 1930-31 v Scottish League.
J.Crisp (1) 1919-20 v Irish League.
J.R.Dugdale (1) 1953-54 v League of Ireland.
J.Edwards (1) 1931-32 v Scottish League.
W.Groves (1) 1891-92 v Scottish League.
T.Higgins (2) 1895-96 v Scottish League; 1896-97 v Irish League.
D.Howe (6) 1956-57 v Scottish League; 1957-58 v Scottish League; 1958-59 v League of Ireland; 1959-60 v Irish League; 1960-61 v Scottish League; 1961-62 v Irish League.
A.Jackson (1) 1961-62 v Scottish League.
A.C.Jephcott (2) 1913-14 v Scottish League; 1919-20 v Irish League.
J.Kaye (2) 1965-66 v League of Ireland (2 goals), Scottish League.
D.T.Kevan (1) 1957-58 v Scottish League (3 goals).
R.McNeal (5) 1912-13 v Southern League, Irish League; 1913-14 v Southern League, Scottish League; 1914-15 v Scottish League.
F.Morris (1) 1919-20 v Scottish League (2 goals).
D.G.Nurse (1) 1902-03 v Irish League.
H.Pearson (2) 1914-15 v Irish League: 1922-23 v Irish League.
J.Pennington (9) 1906-07 v Scottish League; 1910-11 v Scottish League; 1911-12 v Southern League, Irish League, Scottish League; 1912-13 v Irish League; 1913-14 v Irish League, Southern League; 1919-20 v Scottish League.
C.Perry (1) 1892-93 v Scottish League.
T.Perry (3) 1893-94 v Irish League; 1895-96 v Scottish League; 1896-97 v Irish League.
J.Reader (3) 1891-92 v Scottish League; 1893-94 v Irish League; 1896-97 v Irish League.
J.Reynolds (2) 1891-92 v Scottish League; 1892- 93 v Scottish League.
S.Richardson (1) 1921-22 v Irish League.
S.Rickaby: (1) 1953-54 v League of Ireland.
R.W.Robson (5) 1957-58 v Scottish League; 1959-60 v Scottish League; 1960-61 v Italian League, Scottish League; 1961-62 v League of Ireland.
G.E.Shaw (1) 1963-64 v Scottish League.
B.W.Shearman (2) 1911-12 v Southern League, Irish League.
J.L.Spencer (1) 1924-25 v Irish League.
H.F.Trentham (1) 1933-34 v Irish League.
W.Williams (5) 1895-96 v Scottish League; 1896-97 v Irish League, Scottish League; 1898-99 v Irish League; 1899-1900 v Irish League.
S.Wood (1) 1932-33 v Irish League (1 goal).

Miscellaneous Representative Honours
England XI: J.Astle, W.I.Bassett, D.Howe, D.T.Kevan, C.Perry, C.Regis, R.W.Robson.
Scotland XI: F.P.Colquhoun, J.G.Dudley, D.M.Fraser, R.Hope.
Wales XI: A.Evans, S.Powell.
Republic of Ireland XI: A.Grealish, M.P.Martin, P.M.Mulligan.
Great Britain XI: J.Vernon.
Rest of United Kingdom XI: J.Vernon.
All British XI: D.F.Witcomb.
Football League XI: W.I.Bassett, A.McNab, R.McNeal, H.Pearson, J.Pennington, T.Perry, J.Reader, G.Robson.
Young England XI: A.Brown, M.E.Setters.
FA XI: W.Adams, R.Allen, G.S.Ashmore, R.J.Barlow, W.I.Bassett, D.G.Burnside, J.H.Carter, J.Cookson, J.R.Dugdale, W.B.Elliott, D.Howe, C.E.Jackman, J.P.Kennedy, D.T.Kevan, T.H.Kinsell, T.P.Magee, G.J.McVitie, F.Morris, H.Pearson, S.Richardson, S.Rickaby, R.W.Robson, M.E.Setters, G.E.Shaw.

Scottish FA XI: A.McNab.
FA Amateur XI: N.J.Whitehead.

International Trials
The term 'International Trial' used here includes fixtures such as Professionals against Amateurs, Possibles against Probables, North against South, England against The Rest, Whites against Stripes, Whites against Blues, Players against Gentlemen, England against South, England against North.
England: W.I. Bassett, A.J.Bayliss, J.H.Carter, J.Crisp, A.R.Finch, T.W.Glidden, T.Green, G.C.James, A.C.Jephcott, T.P.Magee, F.Morris, H.F.Pearson, J. Pennington, C.Perry, J.Reynolds, S.Richardson, W.Richardson, R.Roberts, E.A.Sandford, G.E.Shaw, C.Simmons, J.Smith, J.L.Spencer, W.Williams.
Scotland: J.Stevenson.

Miscellaneous Representative Honours with Other Clubs
England: A.Aldridge, W.Ashurst, M.Barham, P.S.Barnes, L.Blissett, W.E.Boyes, S.Bull, H.Chambers, C.C.Charsley, R.Crawford, W.Garraty, G.H.Holden, G.C.Hurst, U.Ehioghu, J.A.Johnson, C.Mason, A.W.Morley, W.W.Morris, C.Palmer, M.Phelan, J.Reynolds, G.Roberts, B.Robson, N.Spink, B.E.Talbot, G.F.Wheldon.
Scotland: A.R.Albiston, E.P.Colquhoun, A.Goram, A.M.Gray, W.Groves, A.B.Hannah, R.A.Hartford, J.Holton, W.M.Johnston, A.McNab, J.Millar, D.R.Speedie, D.Stewart.
Wales: A.M.Bostock, J.Butler, W.T.Butler, V.Crowe, A.Davies, J.Davies, L.C.Davies, S.Davies, W.C.Davies, A.Dibble, I.R.Edwards, K.Jones, P.A.Griffiths, A.Hughes, I.Jones, R.L.Krzywicki, A.Marriott, T.Martin, A.H.Millington, D.Nardiello, S.Powell, A.A.Rees, R.R.Rees, W.W.Robbins, R.Roberts, M.R.Thomas, G.O.Williams, S.G.Williams, D.F.Witcomb.
Northern Ireland: G.J.Armstrong, L.O.Bookman, D.A.Campbell, J.Connor, R.Crone, R.Dennison, A.Elleman, A.Fettis, D.Hegan, W.McCabe, B. McNally, J.M.Nicholl, D.Patterson, J.Reynolds, J.Taggart, J.Vernon, D.J.Walsh.
Republic of Ireland: M.J.Giles, A.Grealish, M.P.Martin, P.M.Mulligan, K.O'Regan, R.A.Ryan, R.C.P.Treacy, J.Vernon, D.J.Walsh.
Canada: L.G.Johnson, C.Valentine.
USA: K.Crow, A.Merrick.
Holland: M.C.Jol, R.Zondervan.
Rhodesia: B.Grobbelaar.
Zambia: D.Chabala.
Zimbabwe: B.Grobbelaar.
Yugoslavia: I. Katalini´c', D.Muzinic
England 'B': S.Bull, D.Burrows, U.Ehiogu, M.Eves, M.E.Forsyth, P.G.King, S.Mackenzie, A.W.Morley, D.Mortimer, G.A.Owen, C.Palmer, G.Roberts, G.A.Rowley, N.Spink, B.E.Talbot.
England XI: P.S.Barnes, I.Clarke, J.Dorsett, G.C.Hurst, J.Mahon, A.W.Morley, B.Robson.
England 'B' XI: B.E.Talbot.
England Under-23: J.Farmer, G.C.Hurst, D.J.Mills, A.W.Morley, R.W.Robson, M.E.Setters, J.Talbut.
England Under-21: L.Ashcroft, G.Bannister, P.S.Barnes, L.Blissett, P.Bradshaw, S.Bull, D.Burrows, G.A.Crooks, J.M.Deehan, A.Dickens, P.Dyson, U.Ehiogu, G.Fenton, W.Fereday, M.E.Forsyth, P.Hucker, A.E.King, A.Marriott, A.Miller, R.Moses, G.A.Owen, C. Palmer, S.Parkin, N.Reid, F.Sinclair, D.Smith, B.E.Talbot, G.L.Thompson, C.Whyte.
England (amateur): H.G.Bache, H.Sharratt, J.G.Shield.
Young England: R.A.Gould, J.Talbut
England Semi-Professional: S.Hodson, G.Phillips.
Football League: W.Ashurst, W.E.Boyes, T.Broad, S.Bull, D.Burrows, H.Chambers R.Crawford, G.Dorsett, A.Evans, A.Flewitt, B.Grobbelaar, D.Hogg, G.C.Hurst J.Reynolds, F.W.Rouse, G.A.Rowley, C.E.Shaw, G.F.Wheldon.
Football League Division Two: S.Bull, D.R.Goodman.

Barclays League Division One: D.R.Goodman.
Football League XI: P.S.Barnes, G.C.Hurst, G.A.Owen, B.Robson.
Great Britain (amateur): H.Sharratt.
Football Alliance: R.Roberts.
Third Division South: S.F.Steele.
Third Division North: R.V.Cutler, R.A.Ryan.
Southern League: E.Bradley, A.Geddes, A.Lewis, H.Parkes, W.Thompson, H.M.Wilcox.
Southern League XI: A.Geddes, A.McKenzie.
FA XI: W.Ashurst, N.W.Bassett, S.Bull, I.Clarke, R.Crawford, S.Hodson, D.Howe, S.Lilwall, J.Mahon, G.Phillips, M.E.Setters, G.T.Summers
FA International Trials: W.Ashurst, H.Chambers, W.Garraty, J.A.Johnson, B.Rankin, J.Reynolds, B.Robinson.
Scotland Under-23: A.M.Gray, J.Holton, W.M.Johnston, M.Murray, D.Stewart.
Scotland Under-21: A.R.Albiston, A.Goram, R.A.Hartford, G.J.Hogg, B.Rice, D.R.Speedie, J.Tortolano.
Scotland (amateur): M.Murray, D.R.Speedie.
Scotland XI: A.Goram.
Scottish League: L.Bell, A.B.Hannah, W.M.Johnston, P.S.McKennan, J.Millar.
Scottish League XI: J.M.B.Wallace.
Scottish International Trials: W.Groves, J.Millar.
Wales Under-23: R.R.Rees, M.R.Thomas.
Wales Under-21: A.Dibble, I.R.Edwards, D.Nardiello, A.A.Rees, M.R.Thomas.
Wales (amateur): A.Hughes.
Welsh FA XI: W.W.Robbins.
Welsh League: I.Jones, W.Taylor.
Welsh International Trials: A.Davies, L.C.Davies.
UK-Ireland-Denmark XI: M.J.Giles.
Ireland-Northern Ireland XI: G.Armstrong, J.M.Nicholl, J.Vernon.
Northern Ireland XI: J.Armstrong, J.M.Nicholl.
Northern Ireland 'B': R.Dennison, D.Patterson.
Northern Ireland Under 21: A.Fettis, J.M.Nicholl, D.Patterson.
Irish League: S.Bowser, G.B.Drury, P.S.McKennan, J.Vernon, D.J.Walsh.
All Ireland XI: M.J.Giles, M.P.Martin, P. M.Mulligan.
Republic of Ireland XI: J.Anderson, M.J.Giles, A.Grealish, M.P.Martin, P.M.Mulligan, R.C.P.Treacy.
Republic of Ireland Under-23: M.P.Martin, P.M.Mulligan.
Republic of Ireland Under-21: K.Ampadu, A.O'Dwyer.
Republic of Ireland (amateur): M.P.Martin.
League of Ireland: J.Dainty, J.McStay, M.P.Martin, P.M.Mulligan, R.C.P.Treacy.
League of Ireland XI: J.Dainty, S.Lynex, R.C.P.Treacy.
Holland 'B': M.C.Jol, R.Zonderan.
Holland Under-23: M.C.Jol.
Holland Under-21: M.C.Jol, R.Sneekes, R.Zonderan.
Malaysian FA XI: R.Crawford.

International & Representative Records

First International Cap: Goalkeeper Bob Roberts, England against Scotland at Blackburn, 29 March 1887.
First Major Representative Honour: Goalkeeper Bob Roberts, North against South, in London, 26 January 1884.
Youngest International: Billy Bassett (19 years 2 months) against Ireland, 7 April 1888.
Most Capped Albion Player: Full-back Stuart Williams with 33 Welsh appearances between 1954 and 1962. After leaving Albion for Southampton he gained a further ten Welsh caps between 1962 and 1965. He captained Wales on 14 occasions.
Most Capped Player to Represent Albion: Former Albion midfielder Bryan Robson, up to the end of the 1991-92 season, had appeared in a total of 90 full internationals for England. Right-back Jimmy Nicholl made 73 appearances for

Northern Ireland (1976-86) and holds the distinction of being the most capped player ever to wear Albion colours. Robson left The Hawthorns after winning 13 full caps (to 1981).
Most Internationals on Albion's Books: Nine, in 1933-34 (Sandford, Pearson, Shaw, Carter and Magee of England and Robbins, Foulkes, Griffiths and Murphy of Wales) and in 1935-36 (Sandford, Pearson, Shaw, Carter, Boyes and Richardson of England and Robbins, Foulkes and Murphy of Wales).
Most Players in an International Team: Four, in 1976-77 (Giles, Martin, Mulligan and Treacy for the Republic of Ireland against France at Dublin and against Poland, also at Dublin).
International Captains: Jesse Pennington (England), Stan Davies, Jimmy Murphy, Graham Williams and Stuart Williams (Wales), Jack Vernon (Ireland), and John Giles, Mick Martin. Paddy Mulligan and Tony Grealish (Republic of Ireland) have each captained their respective countries while on Albion's books. Vernon also skippered the United Kingdom XI. Jesse Pennington, Billy Williams, Ray Barlow, Don Howe and Bobby Robson have captained the Football League representative side while Gary Owen and Cyrille Regis have led out the England Under-21 team. Doug Fraser was skipper of the Scotland XI which toured Israel, Hong Kong, Australia, New Zealand and Canada in 1967. Asa Hartford captained the Scotland Under-23 team whilst with Albion, and Don Howe and Maurice Setters captained England Under-21 during the 1950s. Joe Kennedy was skipper of England 'B' during the 1950s.
Debut Goals: Seven Albion forwards have scored on their first international appearance – all for England: George Woodhall (1888), Fred Morris (1920), Joe Carter (1926), Jack Hines (1948), Johnny Nicholls (1954), Derek Kevan (1957) and Bobby Robson (1958). Haines and Robson both scored twice, Haines against Switzerland in 1948 and Robson against France in 1957. In an amateur international in 1908, centre-forward Billy Jordan scored six goals against France on his debut. In his first full appearance for Wales, against Malta in season 1978-79, former Albion centre-forward Ian Edwards of Chester scored four goals.
Most Goals In Representative Football: Jimmy Cookson scored 24 times in 11 matches on the FA tour of Canada in 1931.
Consecutive Appearances: Between 1907 and 1920 Jesse Pennington made nine consecutive appearances against Scotland and between 1889 and 1896, Billy Bassett played for England against Scotland on eight consecutive occasions. When England defeated Scotland for the third successive year in 1893, Bassett was one of four England players who were each awarded a special international cap. Between October 1957 and November 1959 Don Howe's 23 England appearances were consecutive.
Successful Partnerships: Between March 1907 and April 1914 Sam Hardy (Aston Villa), Bob Crompton (Blackburn Rovers) and Jesse Pennington formed a resolute last line of defence for England in 14 internationals. Crompton and Pennington played at full-back together in 23 England internationals.
Dual Internationals: Albion's right-half of the early 1890s, John 'Baldy' Reynolds, was capped by both Ireland and England. Before he signed for Albion he had appeared five times in the Irish national side while with the Distillery and Ulster clubs but on arriving at Stoney Lane it was discovered that he was born at Blackburn and thus eligible to play for England. He was subsequently chosen eight times for England while with Albion and Aston Villa. Other Albion 'dual' international players were Dave Walsh, Reg Ryan and Jack Vernon, all whom played for both Northern Ireland and the Republic of Ireland.

IPSWICH TOWN

Albion's record against Ipswich:

Football League

Venue	P	W	D	L	F	A	Pts
Home	24	9	5	10	43	35	24
Away	24	5	5	14	22	51	16
Totals	48	14	10	24	65	86	40

FA Cup

Venue	P	W	D	L	F	A
Home	1	0	1	0	1	1
Away	2	0	0	2	1	6
Totals	3	0	1	2	2	7

League Cup

Venue	P	W	D	L	F	A
Home	1	1	0	0	2	0
Away	1	0	1	0	1	1
Totals	2	1	1	0	3	1

Simod Cup

Venue	P	W	D	L	F	A
Away	1	0	0	1	1	2

When Albion beat Ipswich Town 6-1 at The Hawthorns on 9 March 1963, Derek Kevan scored a hat-trick, this being his last League game for the club before transferring to Chelsea.

Ipswich whipped Albion 7-0 at Portman Road in a League game on 6 November 1976.

Albion gained revenge for that heavy defeat by winning the return fixture at The Hawthorns in March 1977 by 4-0, Bryan Robson scoring a hat-trick.

John Wark scored four goals for Ipswich in their 6-1 demolition of Albion in October 1982.

Former Albion striker John Deehan scored a hat-trick in Ipswich's 4-3 League win at The Hawthorns in September 1986.

Albion came back to beat Ipswich 3-2 at Portman Road in a First Division game on New Year's Day 1972 after being 2-0 down with 20 minutes to play.

Tony Brown scored the first of his recording breaking number of goals for Albion on his League debut at Ipswich in September 1963 (won 2-1).

One of Albion's two FA Cup defeats was their 3-1 reverse in the 1978 semi-final tie at Highbury. Albion's Mick Martin was sent-off in this game and earlier skipper John

Bobby Hope's free-kick beats the Ipswich Town defensive wall in a League Cup match at The Hawthorns in 1969.

Wile was led off with a severe head wound after clashing with future Albion boss Brian Talbot as the Ipswich man scored the first goal.

Albion League debutants v Ipswich: Tony Brown (1963), Len Cantello (1968), Roger Minton (1970), Bobby Gould (1971), Ian Benjamin (1980), David Arthur (1981), Carl Valentine (1984), Craig Madden (1986), Mel Rees (1991), Nigel Spink (1996).

Players with both clubs: Gilbert Alsop, Ian Collard, Ray Crawford, John Deehan, Mark Grew, Graham Harbey, Danny Hegan, Kevin Steggles, Brian Talbot, Romeo Zondervan.

Also associated with both clubs: Bobby Robson played for Albion (1956-62) and later managed Ipswich (1969-82) and Cyril Lea was an Ipswich player and later became Albion's youth team coach (1989-94).

ISLE OF MAN INTERNATIONAL FOOTBALL FESTIVAL

In July 1996, Albion competed in the Isle of Man International Football Festival along with five other teams. The six entrants were split into two groups of three, Albion opposing Port Vale and Wigan Athletic in Group 'B' while Bohemians, Isle of Man and Wrexham played in group 'A'.

JACKSON, Alec

A local lad who made good, Jackson was born at Tipton, deep in the heart of the Black Country in 1937, and in ten years at The Hawthorns (from 1954) he scored 52 goals in 208 first-team appearances for Albion, mainly as a winger, although he did play many times as an inside-forward. A skilful ball player, who made a scoring debut at Charlton six months after joining Albion from W.G.Allen's FC, and represented the Football League v the Scottish League in 1962, he was sold to Birmingham City for £12,500 in 1964. He later served with Walsall and thereafter assisted a number of non-League clubs including Nuneaton Borough, Kidderminster Harriers, Warley, Oldbury Town, Warley Borough, Darlaston, Blakenhall and Rushall Olympic, finally hanging up his boots in 1990 after playing in some 150 Charity games for Albion All Stars. He currently lives and works in Tipton.

JAMES, George

James was a real character, short, stocky, fearless and mighty dangerous in front of goal. He scored 57 times in 115 League and Cup games for Albion during his nine years at The Hawthorns. Born in Oldbury in 1899, he joined the club from Bilston United in 1920 and left The Hawthorns for Reading in 1929. In a home League game against Nottingham Forest in 1924, he scored the fastest ever goal by an Albion player, netting just five seconds after kick-off. An England trialist the following year, James went on to score 69 goals in 83 games for Watford after leaving Reading in 1930. On his retirement in 1933 he became a West Bromwich licensee, and he died in the town in 1976.

JEPHCOTT, Alan Claude

Quality outside-right, fast and clever, whose career was ended prematurely in 1923 after breaking his leg against Aston Villa in September 1922, an injury from which he never fully recovered. Born in Smethwick in 1891, Jephcott played for Brierley Hill before joining Albion in 1911, and at the end of his first full season at The Hawthorns, he lined up in the 1912 FA Cup Final against Barnsley, collecting a loser's medal. Then, in the first season after the World War One, he was a prominent member of Albion's League championship winning team. An England Junior international, Jephcott represented the Football League and also played for an England Select XI. He scored 16 goals in 190 appearances for Albion before he was forced to quit at the age of 31. In 1934, after coaching locally, he became an Albion director and remained on the Board until his death in 1950.

JOHNSON, Joseph Alfred

Joe Johnson was a star performer on the opposite wing to Stan Matthews with Stoke City before transferring to Albion for £6,500 in 1937. And he continued to do the business at The Hawthorns, scoring 47 goals in 145 games for Albion before leaving the club for Hereford United in 1946. An England international (five caps), Johnson was born in Grimsby in 1911 and played for Scunthorpe United and Bristol City prior to his Stoke days. After leaving Hereford, he served with Northwich Victoria, and retired in 1950. Later, he returned to West Bromwich to take over the cafe/restaurant in Dartmouth Park. During the war he guested for Crewe Alexandra, Leicester City and Notts County. He died in 1983.

JOHNSTON, William McClure

With devastating pace and the ability to beat his full-back on the outside, outside-left Willie Johnston was a welcome acquisition to Albion's forward-line at a time when the game was very defence-orientated. Born in Glasgow in 1946, Johnston was signed for a then record fee of £138,000 from Rangers in 1972 just after he had served a 67-day

suspension, and he made the first of 261 appearances for Albion (28 goals scored) against Liverpool 48 hours after arriving at The Hawthorns. Throughout his career (for clubs and country) Johnston's displays were marred by his fiery temper (he was sent-off 15 times in all). He was banished from Scotland's 1978 World Cup squad in Argentina, following an allegation that he had used a stimulant. Before his move to Albion, Johnston (who won 22 full caps for Scotland and two at Under-23 level) played some great football with Rangers, helping them win League, domestic Cup and European Cup-winners' Cup honours, and in 1971, after coming on as 'sub', he netted a hat-trick of penalties against St Johnstone. On leaving Albion in 1979, he joined Vancouver Whitecaps for £100,000 and after a loan spell with Birmingham City, he returned to Ibrox Park in 1980 and later played for Vancouver Whitecaps again, Heart of Midlothian and South China. Coaching appointments with Hearts, East Fife, Raith Rovers and Falkirk followed and now Johnston is a publican in Kirkcaldy, still keeping touch with the Baggies.

JONES, Harold Joseph

A jovial, loquacious character, Harry 'Popeye' Jones was also a very courageous forward who feared no one. Aggressive inside the penalty-area, he hit 104 goals in 169 first-team games for Albion between 1933 and 1943 before injury and illness forced him into an early retirement. Born near Haydock Park racecourse in 1911, and signed from Preston North End, Jones was in terrific form during World War

John Kaye, in confrontation with Bobby Gould of Wolves. Gould, of course, was later to serve Albion as a player and a manager.

Two, netting 47 goals in 40 outings. He also guested for Blackburn Rovers and Everton in the mid-1940s, playing in goal for the Merseysiders in one match. He was awarded the Royal Humane Society Testimonial Medal after diving into a Haydock canal to save a child from drowning in 1932. Jones died in 1957.

JONES, Stanley George
Big, burly, strong-tackling centre-half who gave Albion excellent service between 1960 and 1968 during which time he scored three goals in 267 appearances. Born at Highly, Salop, in 1938, Jones played for Walsall before and after serving with Albion and was once an amateur with

Wolverhampton Wanderers. He won a Fourth Division championship medal with the Saddlers in 1960. Towards the end of his career Jones assisted Burton Albion, Kidderminster Harriers (as player-manager) and Hednesford Town, later coaching Coleshill Town before becoming Walsall's trainer (1980-87) and assisting Albion All Stars in Charity matches. Jones now lives in Walsall and runs a sports-outfitters business.

KAYE, John
'Yorky' Kaye was an out-and-out goalscorer when he joined Albion for £44,750 from Scunthorpe United in 1963. He teamed up with Jeff Astle the following year and netted regularly until being switched to a defensive position by manager Alan Ashman in 1968. From that moment on, until he left The Hawthorns for Hull City in 1971 in a £28,000 deal, he performed supremely well, taking his appearance tally to 361 and his goals haul to 54. A League Cup and FA Cup winner with Albion in 1966 and 1968 respectively, and a League Cup loser in 1967 and 1970, Kaye played twice for the Football League Representative XI and was twice voted Midland Footballer of the Year (1966 and 1970). On his retirement as a player at Boothferry Park in 1974, he was appointed coach, taking over as manager later in the year. He then became assistant manager at Scunthorpe United, managed Goole Town in 1979 and in 1992 was appointed assistant manager at Brigg Town. In 1996 he was back at

Wembley when Brigg won the FA Vase Final. Kaye was born in Goole in 1940.

KENNEDY, Joseph Peter
A truly wonderful centre-half who, in the mid-1950s, formed a terrific middle-line with Jimmy Dudley and Ray Barlow as his colleagues.

Born in Cleator Moor near Whitehaven in 1925, Kennedy played his early football with Workington Town before having trials with Brentford and Millwall. He then turned out for non-League Freelands FC and Altrincham, and was signed by Albion in 1948, quickly helping the Baggies win promotion from Division Two. Kennedy gained a FA Cup winners' medal when he replaced injured right-back Stan Rickaby against Preston in 1954. He skippered Albion several times and won England 'B' honours as well as playing for the FA XI. He was named as reserve for the England senior side at least six times. Kennedy scored four goals in 397 appearances for Albion until 1961, when he moved to Chester, later becoming player-manager of Stourbridge. He collapsed and died whilst working at Brockhouse Ltd in 1986.

KEVAN, Derek Tennyson
Powerhouse centre-forward who scored 173 goals in 291 appearances for Albion during a 10-year association with the

club, finishing as joint top marksman in the First Division in 1961-62. A fine header of the ball, Derek Kevan, born in Ripon in 1935, played for Bradford before joining the Baggies soon after his manager at Park Avenue, Vic Buckingham, had taken over at The Hawthorns. He made a great start to his Albion career, netting twice on his debut v Everton and he cracked in a hat-trick on his last League appearance v Ipswich. Scorer of eight goals in 14 internationals for England, Kevan also gained Under-23 and Football League recognition and was one of his country's few stars in the 1958 World Cup Finals. He left Albion for Chelsea in a £50,000 deal in 1963, and later played (and scored) for Manchester City, Crystal Palace, Peterborough United, Luton Town, Stockport County, Macclesfield Town, Boston United, Stourbridge and Ansells FC, as well as Albion All Stars, whom he also managed. In the 1980s, he worked on the Albion Lottery and now lives and works in Birmingham.

KIFFORD, John

A stern, resolute full-back, good with both feet, Jack Kifford scored eight goals in 99 games for Albion during the early part of the century. A fine penalty-taker who hardly missed from the spot, he was signed from Portsmouth in 1901, having previously played for Scottish clubs Paisley and Abercorn, Derby County and Bristol Rovers. He helped Albion win the Second Division title in his first season at The Hawthorns and left Albion in 1905 for Millwall, later assisting Carlisle United and Coventry City before retiring in 1909 to join Fred Karno's Circus. Kifford was sent-off playing for Albion against Aston Villa in 1903 and his punishment was a six-week ban. Born in Paisley, Glasgow in 1878, he died in 1955, aged 77.

KINSELL, Thomas Henry

Another extremely fine full-back who was as strong as an ox and never shirked a tackle. Born in Cannock, Staffs. in 1921, Harry Kinsell was recruited by Albion as a 14 year-old and taken on as a professional in 1938. He played throughout the war and afterwards helped Albion win promotion to the First Division before leaving The Hawthorns in 1949 for Bolton Wanderers who paid £12,000 for his signature. A junior international when a teenager, Kinsell was capped twice by England at the end of the war, and he also represented the FA XI, as well as guesting for Blackpool, Mansfield Town, Middlesbrough and Southport during the hostilities, gaining a League War Cup runners-up medal with the Seasiders in 1944. After Bolton, he played for Reading and West Ham United before dropping out of the League to assist Bedford Town, retiring in 1957. Harry now lives with his wife in Brierley Hill, West Midlands.

LATCHFORD, Peter William

Goalkeeper Peter Latchford came from a footballing family – his brothers Dave and Bob kept goal for Birmingham City

and scored goals for Blues, Everton, Swansea City and England respectively. Peter was born in Birmingham in 1952 and played 104 times between the posts for Albion during his six years with the club, 1969-75. Signed from Sutton Coldfield Town, he contested the number-one spot with John Osborne and Jim Cumbes and came through with flying colours, collecting two England Under-23 caps in the process. He left The Hawthorns for Celtic (after a loan spell at Parkhead) and went on to serve the Glasgow club for 12 years, making over 300 appearances and winning medals in both League and Cup competitions north of the border. He played for Clyde in 1987-88 before retiring to run a farm in Ayrshire. Before establishing himself as a footballer Latchford represented England at basketball!

LEE, George Thomas

George 'Ada' Lee was the first player to score 100 goals for his home-town team, York City, doing so between 1936 and 1947. He then moved to Nottingham Forest from where he joined Albion for £12,000 in 1949. He went on to give

George Lee is just foiled by Burnley's England goalkeeper Colin McDonald in 1956.

Albion tremendous service as a fast-raiding outside-left with a cracking shot. He scored 65 goals in 295 games for the Baggies, helping them win the FA Cup in 1954. He moved from The Hawthorns to Lockheed Leamington in 1958, and later played for Vauxhall Motors, returning to Albion as trainer (1959-63) before taking over a similar position with Norwich City with whom he stayed until 1987 as reserve-team trainer and scout. Lee died four years later, aged 71.

LEE William

A vital member of Albion's Second Division championship winning side in 1902, centre-forward Billy Lee went on to score 25 goals in 76 games for the club in a three-year period. Born in West Bromwich in 1878, Lee, who won junior international caps for England as a teenager, played for several local sides before joining The Hawthorns staff in 1901 from Bournville Athletic. After a loan spell with Bournemouth Wanderers, he left Albion for Portsmouth in 1904 and later assisted Chesterfield Town, New Brompton and Darlaston, retiring in 1911. He died in 1934.

LEEDS CITY

Albion's record against City:

Football League

Venue	P	W	D	L	F	A	Pts
Home	6	6	0	0	15	3	12
Away	6	2	1	3	7	8	5
Totals	12	8	1	3	22	11	17

FA Cup

	P	W	D	L	F	A
Away	2	2	0	0	3	0

Other Match

	P	W	D	L	F	A
Away	1	1	0	0	5	0

Albion were the first team to play a League match at Elland Road, doing so against Leeds City on 9 September 1905 and winning 2-0 in the Second Division.

Albion's best League win against City is 5-0 at The Hawthorns on 8 September 1906 when Freddie Buck and Fred Shinton both scored twice. Albion also beat City 5-0 in their first-ever meeting (a friendly match) on 4 February 1905.

Albion League debutants v City: Joe Dorsett (1908), Harry Dicken (1909), Bobby McNeal (1910), Len Moorwood (1911).

Players with both clubs: Bill Ashurst, Arthur Watson.

LEEDS UNITED

Albion's record against United:

Football League

Venue	P	W	D	L	F	A	Pts
Home	35	18	5	12	58	43	45
Away	35	8	9	18	37	61	25
Totals	70	26	14	30	95	104	70

FA Cup

	P	W	D	L	F	A
Home	3	2	1	0	7	4
Away	2	0	0	2	0	7
Totals	5	2	1	2	7	11

League Cup

	P	W	D	L	F	A
Home	1	0	1	0	0	0
Away	3	1	1	1	4	3
Totals	4	1	2	1	4	3

Other Matches

	P	W	D	L	F	A
Home	1	1	0	0	3	1
Away	1	0	1	0	1	1
Totals	2	1	1	0	4	2

'W.G.' Richardson scored a hat-trick in Albion's 6-3 League win over United at The Hawthorns on 6 October 1934 – their best win of the 26 recorded so far.

United's best League victory over Albion is 5-1 at Elland Road on 10 February 1971.

In February 1967, Leeds crushed Albion 5-0 in a fourth-round FA Cup-tie at Elland Road – Albion's heaviest defeat in the competition.

Leeds virtually condemned Albion to the Second Division

Johnny Giles (10) in action for Albion against his former club, Leeds United in 1976. The Leeds player is Tony Currie.

by beating them 3-1 at Elland Road on 2 April 1927. When it was 1-1 Albion missed a penalty and Leeds went on to score twice in the last four minutes. But they too went down with Albion!

There have been crowd disturbances at two League games involving Albion and Leeds. The first was at Elland Road on 17 April 1971 when a disputed goal scored by Jeff Astle sparked off a pitch invasion by the home fans, and the second was at The Hawthorns on the evening of 18 May 1982 when visiting Leeds supporters smashed down the boundary wall behind the Smethwick End goal during Albion's 2-0 win – a victory which dumped United into Division Two (See CROWD DISTURBANCES).

Albion's first away win in the Football League Cup competition was at Elland Road on 13 October 1965 when they beat United 4-2 on their way to lifting the trophy at the first attempt.

Albion and Leeds met each other no fewer than seven times in season 1978-79 – twice in the First Division, three times in the League Cup and twice in the FA Cup, both the latter games taking place at The Hawthorns! Leeds had been made to play any home FA Cup-tie away that season and after drawing 3-3 in a fourth-round game on Albion soil, the replay was again staged at The Hawthorns and this time Albion won 2-0, John Wile scoring a terrific goal.

Albion beat Leeds United 3-1 in Johnny Giles' testimonial match at The Hawthorns on 22 October 1975. Derek Dougan guested and scored for Albion that night.

Tony Brown scored his record-breaking 209th League goal for Albion in their 3-1 victory at Leeds on 14 October 1978.

Albion League debutants v United: George Bytheway (1927), Tommy Green (1934), Davey Burnside (1957), Graham Smith (1971), Peter Hucker (1988), Brian Talbot (1988), Steve Walford (1989).

Played with both clubs: Peter Barnes, Martin Dickinson, Johnny Giles, Jack Mahon, Andy McCall, Carlton Palmer, Ronnie Robinson, Bob Taylor, Mickey Thomas, Imre Varadi, Frank Waterhouse, Chris Whyte.

Stuart Naylor was an amateur with Leeds United at the start of his career and striker Paul Williams had trials with

Brian Whitehouse scores for Albion against Leicester City at The Hawthorns in 1958.

Leeds and later played for Albion. Defender Neil Parsley was a Leeds reserve 1988-90 and later joined Albion; Don Howe played for and then managed Albion and later coached at Leeds (1975-77). Norman Hunter served Leeds as a player from 1960 to 1976 and was coach in 1988 after being Giles' assistant at Albion (1983-85).

LEICESTER CITY (FOSSE)

Albion's record against Leicester:

Football League

Venue	P	W	D	L	F	A	Pts
Home	44	25	9	10	93	49	62
Away	44	15	10	19	64	79	42
Totals	88	40	19	29	157	128	104

FA Cup

	P	W	D	L	F	A
Home	1	0	0	1	2	5
Away	2	0	0	2	1	3
Totals	3	0	0	3	3	8

League Cup

	P	W	D	L	F	A
Home	2	2	0	0	3	1
Away	2	1	1	0	1	0
Totals	4	3	1	0	4	1

Anglo-Scottish Cup

	P	W	D	L	F	A
Away	1	0	0	1	1	2

Anglo-Italian Cup

	P	W	D	L	F	A
Away	1	0	1	0	0	0

Other Matches

	P	W	D	L	F	A
Home	11	8	2	1	32	17
Away	14	4	1	9	24	41
Totals	25	12	3	10	56	58

Albion's biggest League win over Leicester is 6-0, in a First Division match at The Hawthorns on 13 March 1965.

Albion also won 6-4 at home on 25 September 1954 (when Johnny Nicholls scored a hat-trick in front of 48,422 fans); 6-2, again at home, on 12 April 1958 (a hat-trick here for Bobby Robson); 5-0 also at The Hawthorns, on 5 September 1959 and 5-0 again, this time at Filbert Street on 7 May

1977, when Albion played some of their best football in years.

Leicester beat Albion 6-2 at Filbert Street in a League game on 6 May 1933 (Arthur Maw netting a hat-trick) and then defeated Albion 6-3 at home in another First Division game on 12 February 1955. Ex-Baggies' star Arthur Rowley scored a hat-trick for City this time, who duly avenged that heavy defeat suffered on Albion soil earlier in the season.

By winning their penultimate Second Division League game 3-0 at Filbert Street on 5 May 1949, Albion gained promotion to the top flight.

On 9 April 1996, defender Paul Raven headed an injury-time winner to give relegation-threatened Albion a 2-1 win at Filbert Street over play-off chasing Leicester.

Albion's heaviest home defeat in the FA Cup is 5-2, suffered at the hands of Leicester Fosse (City was adopted in 1919) on 14 January 1905 in an intermediate round tie. In a 16 minute period in the first half Fosse's outside-left Arthur Mounteney scored a hat-trick.

In a Wartime League Cup-tie on 2 January 1943, Leicester crushed Albion 9-0 at Filbert Street with Denis Cheney a hat-trick hero this time.

A late strike by Allan Clarke gave Leicester a 1-0 FA Cup semi-final victory over Albion at Hillsborough on 29 March 1969.

After leaving Albion for Fulham, Arthur Rowley then joined Leicester and he went on to score 251 League goals in 303 First and Second Division matches for the Filbert Street club. Rowley holds the record for most League goals ever scored – 434.

While on loan at Leicester in 1983, Peter Eastoe broke his jaw and was sidelined for a lengthy period.

Albion League debutants v City/Fosse: Jimmy Stringer (1905), Fred Nicholls (1905), Tom Dilly (1906), Frank Waterhouse (1909), Bob Finch (1926), Sammy Cox (1948), John Kaye (1963), Terry Simpson (1963), Jeff Astle (1964), Paul Dyson (1986), Darren Bradley (1986), Arthur Albiston

(1988), Stacey North (1988), John Paskin (1988), Neil Cartwright (1989), Andy Marriott (1989), Graham Fenton (1994), Phil King (1995).

Played with both clubs: Ian Banks, Tony Brien, Ally Brown, Nicky Cross, Laurie Cunningham, Peter Eastoe, Ike Evanson, Billy Garraty, Mark Grew, Jackie Haines, Billy Harper, Derek Hogg, Steve Lynex, Peter McKennan, Roddy McLeod, Arthur Randle, Arthur Rowley, Fred Shinton, Arthur Smith, David Speedie, David Walker, Gavin Ward, Winston White, Harry Wilcox.

Also associated with both clubs: Jock Wallace played in goal for Albion and later managed City (1978-82); Gerry Summers was an Albion 1950s wing-half who later became coach with City; Dick Graham was a player with City in 1939 and a trainer with both clubs (Albion 1956-58); goalkeeper John Farmer was on loan to both Albion and Leicester (from Stoke); winger Gordon Wills was an Albion reserve before playing League football for Leicester; Steve Hunt played for Albion (1980s) and later coached at Filbert Street; Paul R. Williams was a Leicester trainee who had a loan spell with Albion in 1993 while at Coventry; Paul Kerr spent a loan period with both clubs in 1994, and Cyril Lea was a coach at Filbert Street and The Hawthorns in the 1980s.

LEYTON ORIENT

Albion's record against Orient:

Football League

Venue	P	W	D	L	F	A	Pts
Home	14	11	2	1	31	8	25
Away	14	5	6	3	16	12	16
Totals	28	16	8	4	47	20	41

FA Cup

Home	1	1	0	0	2	0	
Away	2	0	0	2	2	4	
Totals	3	1	0	2	4	4	

Albion have encountered the London club under three different guises – Clapton Orient, Leyton Orient and Orient.

The first meeting was a Second Division game on Christmas Day 1905 at The Hawthorns which ended 1-1.

Albion's best League win over Orient followed the next season – a 5-1 home victory on 6 October 1906 when Fred Shinton scored four times.

Orient's best win over Albion was 2-0 at Brisbane Road in a Second Division match on 17 November 1973.

Orient played in Division One for the first time in 1962-63 and Albion beat them in both games: 2-1 at The Hawthorns and 3-2 at Brisbane Road.

Orient have twice beaten Albion in the FA Cup in London by the same scoreline of 2-1 – in January 1985 and December 1991. The latter tie was beamed 'live' back at The Hawthorns on a giant video-screen.

Albion League debutants v Orient: Henry Hancock (1909), Charlie Deacey (1910).

Players with both clubs: Dick Bourne, Eddie Connelly, Laurie Cunningham, Reg Davies, Ike Evenson, Allan Glover, Tony Grealish, Joe Mayo,

Allan Glover, played for both Albion and Leyton Orient.

Mel Rees, Keith Smith, Colin West, Brian Whitehouse.

Also associated with both clubs: players Ted Lewis and Brian Wood (both Albion reserves); Ernie Shepherd (Albion winger, Orient coach/physiotherapist); Arthur Rowe (scout for both clubs); Charlie Hewitt (Albion player, Orient manager: 1946-48); Sid Glidden (1920s Albion reserve later Orient trainer); Gary Campbell was an Albion trialist in 1989 and Orient first teamer in 1990.

LIFE MEMBERS

In 1996 only two men held the position of Life Members of West Bromwich Albion: Alan Everiss, JP, former secretary and director, and Dr Roger O.Rimmer, M B Ch B, former club doctor, both of whom have given the club excellent service with Mr Everiss an Albion stalwart since 1933 (See LONG SERVICE).

Life Member Fred Everiss (right) welcomes Dave Walsh to The Hawthorns in 1946.

The other individuals who have been made Life Members of Albion are: William Isaiah Bassett (player, director, chairman); Dan Nurse (player, director); Jesse Pennington (player, coach, scout); Fred Everiss (secretary, director); Mrs Clara Everiss; Harry Keys (director, chairman); Ephraim Smith (assistant secretary, secretary), Tom Harris Spencer (director), Mayor H.Wilson Keys (director, chairman) and Horace Thursfield (director).

L.W. (Dave) Welsh, founder of the West Bromwich Albion Supporters Club Organisation, was also a Life Member of the Club.

NB: Shareholders and directors can nominate a person for life membership of the club. The outcome (accepted or refused) is arrived at after all the votes have been cast.

LINCOLN CITY

Albion's record against Lincoln:

Football League

Venue	P	W	D	L	F	A	Pts
Home	8	6	2	0	23	6	14
Away	8	6	0	2	15	5	12
Totals	16	12	2	2	38	11	26

FA Cup

Home	1	1	0	0	3	2	
Away	2	1	0	1	2	3	
Totals	3	2	0	1	5	5	

Autoglass Trophy

Away	1	1	0	0	2	1	

Other Matches

Home	1	1	0	0	4	1	
Away	1	1	0	0	6	1	

Albion's record League win over Lincoln is 5-0, achieved at The Hawthorns on 8 September 1948 during their Second Division promotion-winning campaign. Irish international Dave Walsh scored a hat-trick.

Five goals (four by Albion) were scored in the last 11 minutes of a Second Division match between the clubs at The Hawthorns on 12 December 1907. Albion won 5-2 despite missing a penalty.

Lincoln's best win over Albion came in a third-round FA Cup-tie at Sincil Bank on 7 January 1961 when over 14,000 fans saw them triumph 3-1.

Albion hit ten goals in two friendly matches against Lincoln in a six-week period in 1887, winning 4-1 at home and 6-1 away.

Albion League debutants v Lincoln: Arthur Crump (1910), Walter Walker (1910), Bobby Barker (1948).

Players with both clubs: Bill Ashurst, Gary Bannister,

Jimmy Campbell, John Chadburn, Roy Finch, Dave Gilbert, Percy Freeman, Bill Garraty, Freddie Haycock, Simeon Hodson, Ernie Hoyland, Dick Krzywicki, Stuart Naylor, Shane Nicholson, Harry Raw, Jack Rix, Gary Strodder, John Thomas, Trevor Thompson, Arthur Watson, Alan Webb.

When Naylor joined Albion from Lincoln in February 1986, he was the club's costliest goalkeeper at a fee of £110,000.

Albion reserves also associated with Lincoln: Steve Burke, David Campbell, Mark McCarrick, Bobby Murray, Barry Siddall, Colin Withers.

Geoff Hudson played for Lincoln (1965-66) and was later Albion's trainer and Mick Brown was a player with City (1967-68) and assistant manager at Albion.

LIVERPOOL

Albion's record against Liverpool:

Football League

Venue	P	W	D	L	F	A	Pts
Home	54	19	16	19	79	63	54
Away	54	9	17	28	48	94	35
Totals	108	28	33	47	127	157	89

Test Matches

Venue	P	W	D	L	F	A
Home	1	1	0	0	2	0
Away	1	0	0	1	0	2
Totals	2	1	0	1	2	2

FA Cup

Venue	P	W	D	L	F	A
Home	6	2	1	3	6	7
Away	4	2	2	0	5	3
Totals	10	4	3	3	11	10

League Cup

Venue	P	W	D	L	F	A
Home	2	1	1	0	2	1
Away	2	0	1	1	2	3
Totals	4	1	2	1	4	4

Other Matches

Venue	P	W	D	L	F	A
Home	1	1	0	0	5	2
Away	1	0	0	1	1	5
Totals	2	1	0	1	6	7

Albion's biggest League win over Liverpool is 6-1 at The Hawthorns in a First Division game on 1 February 1936 ('W.G.' Richardson claimed a hat-trick).

Albion won the club's first ever meeting 5-0 on 15 September 1894. Albion also defeated Liverpool 5-2 at Anfield on 27 October 1951 and by the same scoreline at The Hawthorns on Christmas Day 1953. Albion's outside-right Frank Griffin scored twice in each of those last two First Division games and he also claimed two goals in a 3-0 Albion win on 27 September 1952.

Liverpool have inflicted three 5-0 League defeats on Albion – two at Anfield – on 15 September 1900 and 28 September 1935 – and one at The Hawthorns on 23 March 1985. They have also twice beaten Albion 4-0, the last occasion being on 13 September 1980 on Merseyside.

Liverpool have achieved 12 League 'doubles' over Albion.

Albion beat Liverpool 2-0 at Stoney Lane in the decisive fourth and final Test Match at the end of the 1895-96 season to ensure they remained in the First Division.

Albion ousted Liverpool at the third attempt in the sixth round at neutral Maine Road (2-1) on their way to winning the FA Cup in season 1967-68.

Jesse Pennington played his first and last League games for Albion against Liverpool (1903-22).

Albion League debutants v Liverpool: Scott Vigrow (1896), George Reid (1897), Josiah Nock (1898), Jesse Pennington (1903), William Bowen (1915), Ted Shore (1915), Ernie Watson (1922),

David Burrows, played for both Albion and Liverpool.

Derek Kevan's match-winner for Albion against Liverpool at The Hawthorns in October 1962.

Francis Corbett (1926), 'Bos' Trevis (1934), Jack Mahon (1935), Cecil Shaw (1936), Les Horne (1949), Ray Fairfax (1963), Willie Johnston (1972), David Mills (1979), Peter Eastoe (1982), Andy Thompson (1985).

Players with both clubs: Fred Buck, David Burrows, John Chadburn, Harry Chambers, John Durnin, Charlie Hewitt, David Speedie.

Goalkeeper Bruce Grobbelaar was with Albion briefly in 1978 before going on to make over 600 appearances for Liverpool (1981-94). Paul Mardon had trials with Liverpool earlier in his career, and Jimmy Hagan started his career as a junior at Anfield, later becoming an England international and Albion's manager: 1963-67. Tony Kelly, a much-travelled midfielder, began his career as an apprentice with Liverpool in 1980 and later played for Albion (1987-89).

LIVERPOOL CHARITY CUP
On 5 November 1895 Albion were invited to play Everton (away) for the Liverpool Charity Cup. A 5,000 evening-time crowd saw Everton win 4-1 under electric lighting!

LOCAL RIVALRY
Apart from Aston Villa, Birmingham City (as Small Heath) and Wolverhampton Wanderers, all of whom became members of the Football League and are dealt with elsewhere in this A-Z, Albion had three main rivals during the 1880s and 1890s – Wednesbury Old Athletic (who played at The Oval, Wednesbury), St George's (who were also known as Mitchell's St George's and Birmingham St George's) from Cape Hill, and Aston Unity from deep in Villa territory.

George Holden played for both Wednesbury Old Athletic and Albion and was an England international.

This is Albion's record in games against those three teams:

Team	Home						Away						Totals					
	P	W	D	L	F	A	P	W	D	L	F	A	P	W	D	L	F	A
Old Athletic	12	9	2	1	35	19	13	7	2	4	29	18	25	16	4	5	64	37
St George's	8	4	2	2	19	9	10	6	1	3	18	17	18	10	3	5	37	26
Aston Unity	7	7	0	0	26	1	4	3	0	1	8	3	11	10	0	1	34	4

Old Athletic
Albion's record win over Old Athletic is 7-1 in a home FA Cup-tie on 15 October 1887 and their heaviest defeat is 5-2 (also at home) in a friendly on 1 October 1883.

Albion also met Old Athletic in FA Cup-ties in December 1884 (won 4-2), and November 1885 (won 3-2).

Albion beat Old Athletic 4-0 to win the Dudley Charity Cup Final in 1892.

Two outstanding forwards who joined Albion from Old Athletic were 'Jem' Bayliss and George Holden, both of whom played for England, Bayliss in 1891 and Holden in 1881 and 1884.

St George's
Albion met St George's three times in FA Cup action winning each time – 1-0 on 15 January 1887 (at Aston), 1-0 on 5 November 1887 (away) and 3-0 on 31 January 1891 (also away).

St George's (nicknamed The Dragons) trounced Albion 7-1 in a friendly at Fentham Road, Birchfield on 23 September 1883.

Albion's best win over St George's is 4-0 in a Birmingham

Cup-tie on Christmas Eve 1887 and in a friendly on 1 September 1891.

Albion's finest acquisition from St George's was utility forward Tommy Green in 1885.

Aston Unity
Albion were usually far too good for Unity and only lost once in 11 starts.

Albion's best win is 7-0 in a friendly on 19 December 1885. They also won 5-0 at Stoney Lane in the last meeting between the clubs on 5 February 1887.

Albion beat Unity 4-1 at home in a first-round FA Cup-tie on 31 October 1885.

The scorer of Albion's first ever League goal, outside-left Joe Wilson, was a former Aston Unity player.

LONG SERVICE
Here is a list of personnel who have been associated with West Bromwich Albion Football Club for 40 or more years:

65 years   Joe Reader (player, coach, steward) 1885-1950
63 years   Alan Everiss, JP (clerk, assistant secretary, secretary, shareholder, director, Life Member) 1933-96
55 years   Fred Everiss, JP (clerk, secretary, director) 1896-1951
54 years   Ephriam Smith (clerk, assistant secretary, secretary) 1906-60
53 years   Tommy Glidden (player, director, shareholder, coach) 1926-79
53 years   Reg Mason (ground attendant, programme seller, checker, steward) 1926-79
53 years   Dan Nurse (player 1901-05, director/Life Member 1910-59)
51 years   Billy Bassett (player, shareholder, director, chairman) 1886-1937
50 years   Fred Dowler (player, checker, steward) 1881-1931
46 years   Albert Simkins (checker, steward) 1950-96
44 years   Major H.Wilson Keys, MC TD (director, chairman, president) 1930-74

Kitman Dave Matthews (right) pictured here in 1972 in The Hawthorns boot room with Bobby Hope, joined Albion in 1961.

Among other people who have given Albion 25 years or more service are Fred Reed (37 years), Claude Jephcott (32), 'W.G.' Richardson (29) and Fred Horne (25), all former players who also held other jobs within the club; Dr Roger Rimmer (38 years as medical officer 1958-1996; Office/administration/staff: Dave Matthews (35 years as kitman/manager, 1961-96), Tony Matthews (34, as amateur player, statistician, historian, curator, 1962-96), Jim 'W' Gaunt (33, as director and president 1951-84), Sir Ernest J.Spencer (33, as president, 1904-37), Sir Bert Millichip (32, as director, chairman, president 1964-96), Ronald Hocknull (31, as steward 1965-96) and Louis Nurse (27, as scout, director 1922-48).

LOVETT, Graham

Lovett's career as a powerful midfield player, was ended by the second of two serious car smashes – he recovered from the first but not from the second (See: CASUALTIES). When

he first broke into Albion's League side in the mid-1960s, it was said that he would become the 'new Duncan Edwards'. Sadly, he never reached the heights expected of him, and it was nothing to do with football! Birmingham-born in 1947, Lovett joined Albion straight from school in 1964 and he went on to score nine goals in 156 appearances for the club, having outings in both the 1966 League Cup and 1968 FA Cup Finals. After a loan spell with Southampton, he quit League football in 1972 (two months before his 25th birthday) and played locally for Worcester City, Solihull Borough, Greaves FC and Albion All Stars before retiring in 1986. He now works for the *Express & Star* , based in Cannock.

LUTON TOWN

Albion's record against Luton:
Football League
Venue	P	W	D	L	F	A	Pts
Home	18	13	2	3	37	12	32
Away	18	6	5	7	18	25	19
Totals	36	19	7	10	55	37	51

FA Cup
Home	1	1	0	0	4	0	

Other Matches
Home	5	4	1	0	20	5	
Away	5	5	0	0	22	12	
Totals	10	9	1	0	42	17	

The first meeting between the clubs was a friendly at Dallow Lane, Luton on 30 December 1891 which Albion won 4-0.

Albion's best League win has been 4-0 – achieved twice – both at The Hawthorns in First Division matches: on 23 February 1957 and 24 October 1959.

Luton crushed Albion 5-1 at home in a First Division match on 14 December 1957 and so ended the Baggies' 17 match unbeaten League run.

A then record crowd of 7,000 saw Albion beat the Hatters' 1-0 in an FA Cup-tie at Luton on 30 January 1897. This was the game in which Albion arranged for a special train to take defender Tom Perry to Luton (from Birmingham)!

Albion scored 17 goals in four games against Luton during

the wartime season of 1939-40, winning 3-1 twice at The Hawthorns and 5-4 and 6-3 at Kenilworth Road. Harry Jones scored a hat-trick in both games at Luton and in the second 3-1 win at The Hawthorns.

'W.G.' Richardson netted six of Albion's goals (including five in 25 minutes: 55th-79th inclusive) in a 10-1 win over Luton on 22 November 1941. Eight of Albion's goals came in the space of 32 second-half minutes.

When Albion lost 3-2 at Luton on 3 May 1994, four goalkeepers were used in a League match for the first time; both first choice 'keepers, Stuart Naylor (Albion) and Juergen Sommer (Luton) were injured and replaced by Tony Lange and Andrew Petterson respectively. In the eighth minute of injury time both Gary Strodder (Albion) and Mitchell Thomas (Town) were sent-off for fighting.

Albion League debutants v Luton: Meynell Burgin (1938), Billy Elliott (1938), Geoff Richards (1946), Gilbert Williams (1947), Joe Kennedy (1949), Derek Hogg (1958), Mike Phelan (1994), Craig Herbert (1994), Brett Angell (1996)..

Players with both clubs: Jack Bannister, Lewis Bedford, Ian Benjamin, Louis Bookman, Eli Bradley, Eddie Connelly, Andy Dibble, William Ford, Tony Godden, Tony Grealish, Billy Gripton, Abe Jones, Derek Kevan, Andy King, Magnus Nicholson, Stacey North, Bruce Rankin, Imre Varadi.

Also associated with both clubs: Brian Whitehouse (Albion player in 1950s, Luton trainer 1968). Andy King returned to Luton on the Commercial side (early 1990s) until his appointment as Mansfield manager in November 1993. Paul Holsgrove had trials with Albion in 1989 and played for Luton Town in 1991.

MACKENZIE, Stephen

MacKenzie was Albion's most expensive midfield player when he joined the club for £650,000 in 1981, just two months after scoring one of the finest volleyed goals ever seen in a Wembley FA Cup Final – for Manchester City

against Spurs. A hard-working footballer with good ability, he was born in Romford in 1961 and played for Crystal Palace before moving to Maine Road for £250,000 in 1979. A member of Palace's successful youth teams of 1977 and 1978, his transfer to City caused quite a stir at the time, for he'd not played in any first-team games for the London club before Malcolm Allison splashed out half-a-million for his signature. MacKenzie played in 15 England youth internationals as a teenager and later added Under-21 and 'B' caps to his collection. After scoring 25 goals in 184 games for Albion, he left The Hawthorns for Charlton Athletic in 1987 for £200,000, being re-united with ex-Albion star Garth Crooks. In later years MacKenzie played for Shrewsbury, Willenhall Town and Stafford Rangers.

McLEOD, Roderick

Roddy McLeod was a grand little player, full of energy, commitment and ability, who scored a goal every three games for Albion – 65 in 185 first-team matches between 1891 and 1897. Born in Stirlingshire in 1872, he played for Partick Thistle for two years before moving to Albion, and

at the end of his first season with the club, he gained an FA Cup winners' medal, later playing in the losing Final of 1895 against the same team, Aston Villa. He teamed up brilliantly with Billy Bassett on Albion's right-wing and helped set up just as many goals as he scored. McLeod left Albion for Leicester Fosse and later played for Brighton United, Southampton and Brentford, with whom he won a Southern League championship medal in 1901. He quit football in 1906 to go and work in a brewery in London, but retired with rheumatoid arthritis, a legacy from his playing days. He died in 1931.

McNAB, Alexander

'Sandy' McNab was a pint-sized, flame-haired wing-half whose tackling was done judiciously without him ever

losing his poise or his temper! Brave and determined in everything he did, he helped Sunderland win the FA Cup in 1937 before joining Albion for £6,750 the following year. He played throughout the war and accumulated a total of 186 appearances for Albion (four goals) before transferring to Newport County for £1,000 in 1946. Later he assisted Dudley Town and Northwich Victoria before retiring in 1952 to become a West Bromwich publican. Capped twice by Scotland (1937-39), he represented the wartime Football League XI and toured Canada and USA with the Scotland party in the summer of 1939. He skippered Albion during the hostilities (when he also guested for Newport County, Nottingham Forest, Northampton Town and Walsall) and collected a Midland Cup winners' medal in 1944. McNab, who was born in Glasgow in 1911, played outside-left at school and was a grocer before joining Sunderland in 1932. He died in 1962, at the age of 50.

McNALLY, Bernard Anthony

An industrious midfielder who scored 23 goals in 282 League games for Shrewsbury Town before joining Albion for £385,000 in 1989. He went on to serve at The Hawthorns for six years, amassing a further 189 appearances and 14 more goals, and helped Albion win promotion to the First Division in 1993. Capped five times by Northern Ireland, McNally, who was born in Shrewsbury in 1963, was given a free transfer by manager Alan Buckley in 1995 and joined Vauxhall Conference side, Hednesford Town.

McNEAL, Robert

Bobby McNeal was a stylish left-half, who distributed the ball well, defended astutely and was always determined and competitive out on the park. Born in County Durham in 1891, he played for Hobson Wanderers before embarking on an excellent career with Albion which saw him score ten goals in 403 senior appearances between 1910 and 1925. He helped Albion win

the Second Division title in 1911, and reach the FA Cup Final the following season, and after the war he was a key member of their League championship winning side in 1920. A guest player with Fulham, Middlesbrough, Notts County and Port Vale during the hostilities of 1914-18, McNeal was capped twice by England, and he also represented the Football League five times. He was an Albion regular for 12 years and missed only eight matches in four seasons (1919-23). Injury eventually forced him into an early retirement in 1925 at the age of 34 and he chose to go into the licensed trade in West Bromwich. McNeal died in 1956.

MAGEE, Thomas Patrick

'Wee' Tommy Magee, the smallest player ever to don an Albion shirt at 5ft 2½ins , was signed by the club while serving in the trenches in France during World War One, putting pen to paper early in 1919. Seven months after signing he made his Football League debut against Oldham Athletic at the age of 20. And at the end of his initial full season at The Hawthorns he collected a First Division championship winners' medal. Born in Widnes in 1899, Magee started as an outside-right and switched to inside-right and then to right-half, the position where he made his name, going on to appear in 434 games for Albion and scoring 18 goals. Capped five times by England, he twice toured Canada with the FA (in 1926 and 1931) and is the only Albion player to date to have won both a League champ-ionship and FA Cup winners' medal while serving with the club, collecting the latter prize

in 1931. After 15 years dedicated service, Magee finally left The Hawthorns in 1934 to become player-coach of Crystal Palace, later taking over as player-manager-coach at Runcorn before leaving football in 1947. He died in 1974.

MAHON, John

Scorer of 44 goals in 123 games for Albion, Jack Mahon has one of the best scoring records by an Albion winger in the club's history. A resourceful, fast-raiding, very mobile and clever outside-right, Mahon replaced Tommy Glidden and gave Albion excellent value for money after his £4,000 transfer from Leeds United in 1935. Born in Gillingham in 1911, and previously with Doncaster Rovers, he stayed at The Hawthorns for three years before moving to Hudders-field Town. He guested for Aldershot, Bradford City, Chelsea, Halifax, Leeds, Millwall, QPR, Reading, Tor-quay United and West Ham during the war and played for York City in 1945-46, before

returning to Elland Road as coach. He took over as trainer at Hull City in 1953 and then coached in Sweden for eight years. Mahon unfortunately broke his leg on his debut for Huddersfield, but regained full fitness and toured South Africa with the FA party in 1939, playing in one Test Match. He was also a very fine club cricketer, and scored three centuries.

MANAGERS
(Also caretaker-managers & assistant managers)

Fred Everiss (born West Bromwich 1882) – Effectively Albion's first manager. Although assuming the title of club secretary in 1902, it was he, in the main, who looked after the team's affairs up until 1948 (See EVERISS FAMILY).
Here are brief details of Albion's managers since 1948:

Arthur John Smith (born Monmouth 1911) – Hawthorns trialist aged 16 and player with Wolverhampton Wanderers (1929-34), Swindon Town (1934-37) and Chelsea (1937-44). Guested over 70 times for Albion during World War Two and then coached at Molineux (1946-48). Albion's first-ever official manager (22 June 1948 to 17 April 1952), he left The Hawthorns to become Reading's boss (to 1954). Took Albion to promotion from Division Two in 1948-49. A Welsh wartime international v England, 1940, he later became a Dorset hotelier. Smith died in 1975, aged 63.

Jesse Carver, seen here in his playing days with Newcastle United, was Albion's manager for a short period in 1952. He later proved a successful coach in Italy.

Jesse Carver (born Liverpool 1911) – England schoolboy international centre-half who played for Blackburn Rovers (1930-36), Newcastle United (1936-39) and Bury (1939-40) before becoming assist-ant trainer of Huddersfield Town (1946-47). He coach-ed with the Dutch FA (1947) and in Italy with Marzotto, Lazio, Juventus and Valdagno prior to acting as Albion's manag-er-coach (18 April to 9 December 1952). After leaving The Hawthorns he coached Torino, later AS Roma (manager 1953-55), Coventry City (manager June to December 1955), Lazio (coach 1956-58), Inter Milan (coach), Sweden (World Cup coach 1958), Tottenham Hotspur (train-er-coach October 1958 to March 1959), Genoa (coach), Portugal (coach 1959-61), USA (coach 1962-63). He took Juventus to the Italian League title in 1950.

Victor Frederick Bucking-ham (born Greenwich, London, 1915) – Bromley then Tottenham Hotspur full-back (1934-49) and Eng-land wartime international (2 caps), later Middlesex County FA (coach 1946-51), Oxford University (coach 1951) and Pegasus (coach 1951), then Bradford Park

Vic Buckingham, Albion's manager when they won the FA Cup in 1954.

Albion manager Jack Smith (left) discusses tactics with Reg Ryan, trainer Arthur Fitton, Jack Vernon, Dave Walsh and trainer 'W.G.' Richardson in 1948.

Gordon Clark, succeeded Buckingham as Albion's boss.

Avenue (manager 1951-52), Albion (manager 2 February 1953 to 18 June 1959), later managerial appointments with Ajax (two spells 1959-61 & 1964-65), Plymouth Argyle (1961), Sheffield Wednesday (1961-64), Fulham (1965-68), Ethnikos (Greece) (1968-69), FC Barcelona (1969-71) and Sevilla (1972). Led Albion to runners-up in the First Division and to FA Cup victory in 1953-54, leaving the club after their Canada/USA tour in 1959. He died in Worthing in 1994, aged 79.

Gordon Vincent Clark (born Guisborough 1917) – Full-back with Goldthorpe United, Southend United (1935-36), Manchester City (1936-46), Waterford (player-manager) and Hyde United (player-manager); then Distillery (manager 1949), Aldershot (manager 1949-55), Albion (as chief scout 1955, manager: 9 July 1959 to 11 October 1961), Sheffield Wednesday (assistant manager 1961-64), Peterborough United (manager 1964-67), Arsenal (chief scout 1976-77), Fulham (assistant manager 1977), Philadelphia Fury (coach 1978-79), Queens Park Rangers (assistant manager 1979-80). He joined Buckingham at Sheffield Wednesday and took Peterborough United

Archie Macaulay (right) makes his point to Bobby Robson, Derek Kevan, Stan Jones and Jock Wallace in 1960.

to League Cup semi-finals (v Albion) in 1965-66.

Archibald Renwick Macaulay (born Falkirk, 1915) – Scottish international wing-half (7 full and six wartime caps) who played for Camelon Juniors, Glasgow Rangers (1934-37), West Ham United (1937-46), Brentford (1946-47), Arsenal (1947-50) and Fulham (1950-53). Thereafter Guildford City (manager 1954), Dundee (coach 1956-57), Norwich City (manager 1957-61), Albion (manager 19 October 1961 to 2 April 1963), Brighton & Hove Albion (manager 1963-68). Later traffic warden in Brighton. Represented Scotland in wartime internationals, played for a Great Britain XI, won a War League Cup medal in 1940 with West Ham and gained League championship and Cup winners' medals with Rangers before leading Norwich City to League Cup success in 1962 and Brighton to the Fourth Division title in 1965. He died in 1993.

James Hagan (born Washington, Co. Durham 1917) – England schoolboy and full international inside-forward (one senior cap, 16 wartime caps); Albion trialist 1933, Washington Colliery FC, Liverpool (1932-33), Derby County (1933-38) and Sheffield United (1938-58). Then Peterborough United (manager 1958-62), Albion (manager 10 April 1963 to 3 May 1967), Manchester City (scout 1968-69), Benfica (manager 1970-73), Kuwait (coach 1974-75), Sporting Lisbon (manager 1975-77), FC Porto (manager 1978-79), Boavista (manager 1979), Vitoria Setubal (manager, also 1979). Hagan guided Peterborough from the Midland League into the Football League and saw Albion twice reach the League Cup Final, winning in 1966, losing in 1967.

George Alan Ashman (born Rotherham, 1928) – Centre-forward with Sheffield United (amateur 1946-47),

Alan Ashman, Albion's manager for four years following Jimmy Hagan.

Nottingham Forest (1948-51) and Carlisle United (1951-58); then Penrith (coach 1959-61), Carlisle United (manager 1963-67), Albion (manager 23 May 1867 to 2 July 1971), Olympiakos (manager 1971-72), Carlisle United (manager 1972-75), Workington (manager 1975-77), Manchester United (scout 1977-78), Walsall (manager 1978), Derby County (chief scout 1979, assistant manager 1982), Hereford United (assistant manager 1983-87), Plymouth Argyle (scout), Notts County (scout), Mansfield Town (scout), Derby County (scout), Telford United (scout). Guided Albion to FA Cup glory in 1968 and to runners-up in the 1970 League Cup Final.

Albion manager Don Howe signs centre-forward Bobby Gould from Wolves in 1971. Gould also became an Albion manager.

Donald Howe (born Wolverhampton 1935) – Player with Wolverhampton Wanderers (amateur 1949-50), Albion (1950-64), Arsenal (1964-67) and England (23 caps). Coach and assistant manager at Highbury before becoming Albion manager (9 July 1971 – 6 April 1975), Howe later coached in Turkey and Saudi Arabia, at Leeds United, Arsenal (again), Chelsea and QPR, also managing at Loftus Road and Coventry as well as being a key figure on the England coaching staff. (See HOWE, Donald).

John Michael Giles (born Dublin 1940) – Played for St Columbus, Dublin City (later Munster Victoria), Stella Maris, Leprechauns FC and Home Farm and in the Football League with Manchester United (1956-63) and Leeds United (1963-75), becoming player-manager of Albion (19 June 1975 to 27 May 1977). Later player-manager of Shamrock Rovers (1977-83), guested for Philadelphia Fury (1978) and coached Vancouver Whitecaps (1980-83) prior to second spell as Albion manager (13 December 1983 to 29 September 1985). Won 60 caps for the Republic of Ireland, whom he also managed (1973-80). Won medals with both Manchester United and Leeds in England and Shamrock Rovers in Ireland, and guided Albion to promotion from Division 2 in 1975-76 (See GILES, John).

Ronald Allen (born Fenton, Stoke-on-Trent ,1929). Player with Port Vale (1944-50), Albion (1950-61) and Crystal Palace (1961-65). Later coach and then manager of

Ronnie Allen, the great Albion favourite who had two spells as manager at The Hawthorn, seen here with a Manager of the Month award.

Wolverhampton Wanderers (1965-68), manager of Athletic Bilbao (1969-71), Sporting Lisbon (1972-73), Walsall (1973), Albion (22 June to 22 December 1977), Saudi Arabia (National team 1978), Panathiniakos (1980) and Albion manager again (26 July 1981 to 30 June 1982). Later returned to Albion as coach (1990s). Won five England caps and led Bilbao to victory in Spanish Cup (See ALLEN, Ronald).

Ronald Franklin Atkinson (born Liverpool 1939). Player with BSA Tools FC (1954), Wolverhampton Wanderers (junior 1955), Aston Villa (reserve 1956-59) and Headington United/Oxford United (1960-71), Then player-manager of Kettering Town (1971-74), Witney Town manager (1974), Cambridge United (1974-78), Albion (12 January 1978 to 9 June 1981), Manchester United (1981-86), Bolton Wanderers (coach 1986), Albion manager for second time (3 September 1987 to 12 October 1988), Atletico Madrid (coach 1988-89), Sheffield Wednesday (manager 1989-91), Aston Villa (manager 1991-94), Coventry City (manager 1995-96). Won Wembley Cup Finals with Manchester United, Sheffield Wednesday and Aston Villa.

Ronald M.Wylie (born Glasgow 1933) – Inside-forward with Clydesdale Juniors (1946-47), Notts County (1948-58), Aston Villa (1958-65) and Birmingham City (1965-70). Coach at Villa Park and Coventry City, becoming assistant manager at Highfield Road; soccer adviser in Cyprus, Bulova (Hong Kong as manager 1981-82), then Albion manager (27 July 1982 to 13 December 1983); Aston Villa (reserve team coach-manager 1986-87) and scout for several clubs in late 1980s. Appointed Community Officer at Villa Park 1990. Won Second Division championship 1960 and League Cup

Ron Atkinson, pictured here during his first spell as manager of West Brom.

Ron Wylie, Albion boss for the first half of the 1982-83 season.

Ron Saunders, pictured leaving The Hawthorns in September 1987.

Nobby Stiles, one of the stars of England's 1966 World Cup victory who managed Albion for four months in 1985-86.

Brian Talbot, a former Albion player who took charge for just over two years.

1961 with Villa; Midland Footballer of the Year 1965.

Norbert Peter Stiles (born Manchester 1942) – Wing-half with Manchester United (1957-71), Middlesbrough (1971-73) and Preston North End (1973-74). Manager at Deepdale (1974-78) and assisted his brother-in-law Johnny Giles at Vancouver Whitecaps (1981-83), before Albion coach, then assistant manager and finally manager (15 October 1985 to 14 February 1986). He later returned to Old Trafford as coach under Alex Ferguson. Gained 28 England caps, a World Cup winners' medal (1966), a European Cup winners' medal (1968) and League and Cup medals at club level with Manchester United.

Ronald Saunders (born Birkenhead 1932) – Prolific goalscorer with Everton (1951-56), Tonbridge (1956-57), Gillingham (1957-58), Portsmouth (1958-64), Watford (1964) and Charlton Athletic (1965-67). Manager of Yeovil Town (1967-68), Oxford United (1969), Norwich City (1969-73), Manchester City (1973-74), Aston Villa (1974-82), Birmingham City (1982-86) and Albion (14 February 1986 to 1 September 1987). Led Norwich, Manchester City and Villa to Wembley League Cup Finals in successive seasons (1973-74-75), Villa winning the trophy. He also guided Villa to the Football League championship in 1981.

Brian Ernest Talbot (born Ipswich 1953). Midfield player with Ipswich Town (1968-79), Arsenal (1979-85), Watford

(1985-86), Stoke City (1986-88), Albion (for £15,000 in 1988). Caretaker manager at The Hawthorns (13 October to 1 November 1988), manager (2 November 1988 to 8 January 1991). Later with Fulham, Aldershot (manager 1991), Sudbury Town (1992) and Hibernians (Malta, 1993-96). Won six England caps and FA Cup winner with both Ipswich and Arsenal in successive seasons. Scored six goals in 83 appearances for Albion.

Robert Anthony Gould (born Coventry 1946) – Centre-forward with Coventry City 1962-68), Arsenal (1968-70), Wolverhampton Wanderers (1970-71), Albion (signed for £66,666: 1971-72), Bristol City (1972-73), West Ham United (1973-75), Wolverhampton Wanderers (1975-77), Bristol Rovers (1977-78) and Hereford United (1978-79). Also

Bobby Gould, another former Albion player who had a spell as manager of the club. He is currently the manager of the Welsh national team.

Aalsund of Norway (player-coach 1978), Charlton Athletic (coach 1979), Chelsea (assistant manager 1979-81), Wimbledon (non-contract player-coach 1981), Aldershot (assistant manager 1981), Bristol Rovers (manager 1981-83), Coventry City (manager 1983-84), Bristol Rovers (manager 1985), Wimbledon (manager 1987-90), QPR (coach 1990-91),

Ossie Ardiles, Albion's first and so far only foreign-born manager.

Albion (manager 26 February 1991 to 5 May 1992), Coventry City (manager 1992-93), Wales national team (manager 1995-96). FA Cup winner with West Ham (1975) and Second Division championships with Coventry (1967) and Wolves (1977) as a player, and FA Cup winner with Wimbledon (1988) as manager. Scored 19 goals in 60 appearances for Albion.

Osvaldo Cesar Ardiles (born Cordoba, Argentina 1952). Midfield player with Red Star (Cordoba), Instituto de Cordoba (1975), FC Huracan (1975-78), Tottenham Hotspur (signed for £325,000, 1978-88), Paris St Germain (loan 1982-83), Blackburn Rovers (loan 1988), Queens Park Rangers (1988-89), Fort Lauderdale Strikers (1989), Swindon Town (manager 1989-91). Then Newcastle United (manager 1991-

Keith Burkinshaw, who signed Ardiles for Spurs and later succeeded the Argentinian as Albion's manager.

92), Albion (manager 8 May 1992 to 18 June 1993), Tottenham Hotspur (manager season 1993-94), Deportiv Guadelajara (coach 1995), Shimizu S-Pulse of Japan (manager, 1996). Ardiles was a World Cup winner with Argentina (1978), an FA Cup winner twice with Spurs (1981 & 1982) and he guided Albion to promotion from Division Two via Wembley Play-off Final in 1993.

Keith H.Burkinshaw (born Higham 1935). After playing for Denaby United, Wolverhampton Wanderers (amateur), Liverpool (1953) and Workington (1957) he managed the latter club (1964-65), Scunthorpe United (1965-66) and then coached in Zambia (1968) before becoming assistant coach and then first-team coach at Newcastle United. In 1975 he was appointed coach at Tottenham, moving up to manager (1976-84). After a coaching spells in Bahrain and in Portugal with Sporting Lisbon, and spells as manager of Gillingham and chief scout at Swindon Town, he became Albion's assistant manager to Ardiles: (May 1992-June 1993), then manager (2 July 1993 to 16 October 1994). Burkinshaw led Spurs to the Second Division championship in 1978, to two

FA Cup triumphs (1981 & 1982), League Cup success, also in 1982, and UEFA Cup glory in 1984.

Alan P.Buckley (born Mansfield 1951). A goalscoring forward with Nottingham Forest (1966-73), Walsall (1973-78

Alan Buckley, did well as Grimsby's boss before taking over at The Hawthorns.

& 1979-86) and Birmingham City (1978-79), he was player-manager of the Saddlers (1982-85) and became manager in 1986. Thereafter he played briefly for Stourbridge and Tamworth (1986) and then took over as Kettering Town manager (1986-88), Grimsby Town (manager 1988-94), Albion (manager 20 October 1994 to date). Guided Grimsby from the fourth to the second (now first) Division in successive seasons (1990-91).

Caretaker Managers
Former Albion player Brian Whitehouse (7 April to 14 June 1975).

Centre-half John Wile (23 December 1977 to 11 January 1978)

Midfielder Brian Talbot (13 October to 1 November 1988)

Ex-England star Stuart Pearson (9 January to 25 February 1991).

Assistant Managers
Since the late 1970s, the manager of Albion has seemingly always had an assistant who was also listed as a coach at The Hawthorns, among them Colin Addison and Mick Brown (to Atkinson), Gerry Summers (to Allen), Nobby Stiles (to Giles), Stuart Pearson (to Talbot), Keith Burkinshaw (to Ardiles) and Arthur Mann (to Buckley).

Player to Manager
Albion players who later became professional League club managers (wartime guests not included): Sam Allardyce (Preston, Blackpool), Ronnie Allen (Wolverhampton Wanderers, Walsall, Athletic Bilbao, Sporting Lisbon, Albion, Panathinaikos), Ron Bradley (Olympiakos, Scunthorpe United), Vic Crowe (Aston Villa, Portland Timbers), Stan Davies (Rotherham United), Albert Evans (Coventry City), Ronnie Fenton (Notts County), Doug Fraser (Walsall), Johnny Giles (Albion, Vancouver Whitecaps, Shamrock Rovers), Bobby Gould (Bristol City, Bristol Rovers, Wimbledon, Albion, Coventry City), Harry Hadley (Merthyr Town, Chesterfield), Asa Hartford (Stockport County, Shrewsbury Town), Charlie Hewitt (Chester, Millwall, Leyton Orient, Spennymoor United, Crystal Palace), Don Howe (Albion, Coventry City), Geoff Hurst (Chelsea), John Kaye (Hull City), Andy King (Mansfield Town), Albert Lindon (Charlton Athletic, Merthyr Town), Jack Manners (Hartlepool United), Paddy Mulligan (Galway Town), Jimmy Nicholl (Raith Rovers, Millwall), Harry Parkes (Newport County, Chesterfield, Lincoln City, Mansfield Town, Notts County), Garry Pendrey (Birmingham City), Bobby Robson (Vancouver Royals, Fulham, Ipswich Town, PSV Eindhoven, Sporting Lisbon, FC Porto, Barcelona), Bryan Robson (Middlesbrough), Arthur Rowley (Shrewsbury Town, Sheffield United, Southend United), Maurice Setters (Doncaster Rovers), Ernie Shepherd (Southend United), Gerry Summers (Oxford United, Gillingham), Kenny Swain (Wigan Athletic), John Talbot (KV Mechelen), Ray Treacy (Drogheda United), Jock Wallace (Berwick Rangers, Glasgow Rangers, Leicester City, Motherwell, Colchester United), John Wile (Peterborough United), Bill Williams (Maidstone United), Graham Williams (Cardiff City), Stuart Williams (Stavanger).

MANCHESTER CITY
Albion's record against City:

Football League

Venue	P	W	D	L	F	A	Pts
Home	55	29	16	10	105	57	75
Away	55	15	7	33	85	133	37
Totals	110	44	23	43	190	190	112

Test Matches

Home	1	1	0	0	6	1
Away	1	0	1	0	1	1
Totals	2	1	1	0	7	2

FA Cup

Home	3	2	0	1	6	2
Away	1	0	1	0	1	1
Totals	4	2	1	1	7	3

League Cup

Home	1	1	0	0	4	2
Away	2	0	0	2	2	4
Totals	3	1	0	2	6	6

FA Charity Shield

Away	1	0	0	1	1	6

Other Matches

Away	2	0	1	1	4	6

In the course of time Albion have had some harrowing experiences when visiting Manchester City – a seven-goal hammering, three six-goal defeats, two five-goal reversals and a cluster of four-goal losses.

Their heaviest League defeat came on 16 April 1938, when City won a First Division game 7-1, Eric Brook scoring four times including two first-half penalties. At the end of this season both Albion and City were relegated.

When Albion lost 6-2 at Maine Road on 5 September 1936, all eight goals were scored in a frantic first-half.

City beat Albion 6-1 at home in a First Division match on 19 November 1921, five of their goals coming in the last 32 minutes.

Albion's best League win is 9-2, achieved at The Hawthorns, also in the First Division, on 21 September 1957, when City's 'M' plan was torn to shreds. There were

Peter Barnes (left) and Gary Owen, both left Manchester City to join Albion.

six different scorers for Albion with outside-right Frank Griffin netting his only hat-trick for the club.

Albion beat City 7-2 at Maine Road in a League game on New Year's Day 1934. City had a nervous young goalkeeper named Frank Swift between the posts that day and he was helpless as 'W'G.' Richardson scored a hat-trick for the Baggies.

In September 1960, a nine-goal thriller at The Hawthorns ended in a 6-3 win for Albion in the First Division with Ronnie Allen claiming a hat-trick – his last for the Baggies. Allen, in fact, scored a record 13 goals for Albion in senior games v City.

Three years later, a midget-sized Albion attack ran rings round City when recording a 5-1 League victory at Maine Road on 27 April 1963.

Albion 'doubled up' over League champions-to-be Manchester City over the Christmas period in 1967-68, winning 3-2 at The Hawthorns and 2-0 at Maine Road.

Albion crushed City 6-1 in a Test Match at Stoney Lane on 20 April 1896 to retain their First Division status. City remained in Division Two.

On a foggy afternoon in January 1958 Albion roasted City 5-1 in a third-round FA Cup-tie at The Hawthorns.

Albion, the FA Cup holders, were hammered 6-1 by

Jeff Astle scores against Manchester United in August 1968 as goalkeeper Alex Stepney looks on.

League champions City in the annual Charity Shield game at Maine Road in August 1968 before a 35,000 plus crowd. Albion's 'keeper John Osborne was injured during the game and Graham Williams took over between the posts.

Albion League debutants v City: Stan Davies (1921), Arthur Fitton (1922), Jimmy Dudley (1949), Stan Rickaby (1950), Fred Brown (1955), Bobby Robson (1956), Jack Bannister (1960), Tony Millington (1961), Ron Bradley (1962), David Cross (1976), Steve MacKenzie (1981), Tony Lowery (1981).

Kenny Stephens made his Albion debut in a League Cup-tie v Manchester City in 1966.

Players with both clubs: Peter Barnes, Tommy Broad, David Cross, Andy Dibble, George Dorsett, Joe Dorsett, Frank Dyer, Tony Grealish, Henry Hancock, Asa Hartford, Robert Hopkins, Derek Kevan, Steve MacKenzie, Ken McNaught, Gary Owen, Bruce Rankin, Nicky Reid, Imre Varadi.

Also associated with both clubs: Jimmy Hagan managed Albion (1963-67) and later became a City scout; John Deehan was a player with Albion and player-coach with City; Irish international David Campbell had trials with both clubs; goalkeeper Barry Siddall was on loan at City in 1986 and Albion in 1990; Ron Saunders managed both City and Albion and full-back Arthur Mann played for City (including an appearance against Albion in the 1970 League Cup Final) and later became assistant manager at The Hawthorns (appointed in 1995).

MANCHESTER UNITED

Albion's record against United:

Football League

Venue	P	W	D	L	F	A	Pts
Home	50	26	11	13	98	72	65
Away	50	11	13	26	65	102	35
Totals	100	37	24	39	163	174	100

FA Cup

Home	3	1	2	0	5	4
Away	3	1	1	1	6	3

Other Matches

Away	2	1	0	1	3	3

Albion and United were involved in several memorable matches between 1955 and 1985 with many high-scoring encounters including record victories for both clubs over each other.

Albion's best League win over United is 6-3 at The Hawthorns on 29 April 1968, in front of a 45,992 crowd with thousands more gaining entrance illegally. Two days earlier Albion had qualified for the FA Cup Final while United were chasing the First Division championship and were soon to become European Cup winners. Albion played brilliantly with Jeff Astle scoring a hat-trick.

Other impressive Albion League wins over United since 1955 include a 4-3 triumph at The Hawthorns on 26 October 1957, when the turnout was close to 53,000; another 4-3 home success on 6 March 1971 when Tony Brown cracked in a glorious hat-trick; two successive 4-0 First Division romps at The Hawthorns in October 1976 (this being Albion's 3,000th League game) and October 1977 and a thrilling 5-3 victory at Old Trafford on 30 December 1978 when Len Cantello, Cyrille Regis and Laurie Cunningham all scored superb goals.

United's best League win over Albion came at Old Trafford on the evening of 8 April 1970 when they romped to a 7-0 victory.

Tony Brown scored a record 12 goals for Albion in League and Cup games against United.

United crushed Albion 5-1 at The Hawthorns on 21 September 1985 as the Baggies struggled at the start of their worst-ever season. Alan Brazil scored twice for the 'Reds.'

When Albion lost 4-1 to United at their Bank Street ground, Clayton, in October in 1893, the sequel to the

Remi Moses joined United as part of the Bryan Robson transfer deal in 1981.

match was a libel case against Mr William Jephcott of the *Birmingham Daily Gazette* who criticised the rough tactics of the home side (See MISCELLANEOUS).

On 16 September 1911, reigning Division Two champions Albion, beat First Division champions United, 1-0 at The Hawthorns.

When Albion defeated United 5-1 in a First Division home game on 19 December 1925, four of the Baggies' goals came in an 11-minute spell with centre-forward Stan Davies scoring with two blistering 25-yard efforts.

United whipped Albion 5-1 at Old Trafford in mid-December 1951 after Ronnie Allen had given the visitors a 12-second lead!

Albion's 2,000th game in the Football League was celebrated with a 3-1 win over United on 29 November 1952.

The two League games between the teams in 1966-67 produced 15 goals – United winning 5-3 at Old Trafford (they were 5-1 up after 22 minutes) and 4-3 at The Hawthorns.

After drawing 0-0 at home with United in a third-round FA Cup-tie on 7 January 1939, Albion went to Old Trafford for the midweek replay and won 5-1, with Harry Jones netting twice.

Soon after the Munich air disaster, on 1 March 1958, United drew 2-2 with Albion in a sixth-round FA Cup-tie at The Hawthorns and then won the replay with a late goal from Colin Webster before 60,523 fans at Old Trafford. Three days later Albion returned to Old Trafford and beat United 4-0 in a League game with 63,278 spectators present this time!

Albion knocked United out of the FA Cup in 1977-78 by winning a home fourth round replay 3-2 after a 1-1 draw at Old Trafford when United equalised in the last minute.

Albion League debutants v United: John Burns (1893), Bill Harper (1901), Arthur Randle (1901), Ted Pheasant (1904), Sammy Peters (1905), Herbert Varney (1905), Jack Mann (1914), Jimmy Poxton (1927), Gerry Summers (1955), Bobby Dixon (1959), Campbell Crawford (1963), Alistair Robertson (1969), Stewart Woolgar (1972), David Shaw (1973). Nicky Cross (1981), Paul Barron (1983), Stuart Naylor (1986). Naylor conceded a hat-trick to Jesper Olsen on his debut as Albion lost 3-0.

Players with both clubs: Arthur Albiston, Jack Banks, Peter Barnes, Garth Crooks, Laurie Cunningham, Arthur Fitton, Johnny Giles, Graeme Hogg, Mick Martin, Remi Moses, Jimmy Nicholl, Mike Phelan, Billy Richards, Bryan Robson, Maurice Setters, Arthur Smith, Jimmy Stanton, Mickey Thomas.

Richards scored United's first goal after they had changed their name from Newton Heath in 1902 and when Robson left Albion for United in 1981 it was a then record fee (for both clubs) of £1.5 million (Moses, valued at £500,000, was transferred as part of the same deal).

Also associated with both clubs: Ron Atkinson managed United after Albion; Stuart Pearson and Nobby Stiles played for United and later served with the Albion management team; wing-half Jimmy Murphy starred for Albion in the 1930s and later became United's assistant manager (to Matt Busby) and then manager (1958); Brian Whitehouse played for Albion (1950s) and was later coach at Old Trafford; goalkeeper Peter Hucker was on loan to Albion and United (late 1980s); Albion reserve Jim Holton played 69 games for United (1970s); Mick Brown was assistant manager at both clubs (under Atkinson); 1950s Albion trainer, Tommy Jones, was once a player with United and Nobby Stiles, Bobby Charlton and George Best guested for Albion in testimonial matches. Andy Comyn was a United junior in 1986.

MANNERS, John Albert

Tough-tackling centre or left-half, who spent nine years with Albion before World War One, scoring seven goals in 209 appearances. Born at Morpeth in 1878, he joined Albion from Morpeth Harriers in 1904 and left The Hawthorns for Hartlepools United in 1913, the club he later managed (1925-27). He helped Albion win the Second Division championship in 1911, but missed out on an FA Cup Final appearance the following year, having lost his place in the side through injury. He died in 1946.

MANSFIELD TOWN

Albion's record against Mansfield:

Football League

Venue	P	W	D	L	F	A	Pts
Home	1	1	0	0	2	0	3
Away	1	1	0	0	3	0	3
Totals	2	2	0	0	5	0	6

Anglo-Scottish Cup

| Home | 1 | 0 | 1 | 0 | 1 | 1 | |

Autoglass Trophy

| Away | 1 | 1 | 0 | 0 | 1 | 0 | |

Other Matches

Home	3	2	0	1	9	6	
Away	4	1	2	1	10	11	
Totals	7	3	2	2	19	17	

Albion first met Mansfield in a Football League South wartime game on 26 November 1940, beating them 4-0 at The Hawthorns.

Albion lost 6-2 away to the Stags in another wartime fixture on 8 March 1941.

And 'W.G.' Richardson scored seven of Albion's 14 wartime goals against Mansfield.

The first competitive matches took place in Division Two in 1992-93, Albion winning 2-0 at home and 3-0 at Field Mill on their way to promotion.

Striker James McCue made his Albion first-team debut in the Autoglass Trophy game in 1992.

Kevin Kent, one of 16 players to have appeared for both Albion and Mansfield Town.

Players with both clubs: George Banks, Luther Blissett, Tony Brien, George Bytheway, John Chadburn, Simeon Hodson, Kevin Kent, Tony Lowery Noel Luke, Brian Macready, Dennis Martin, Steve Parkin, Imre Varadi, Arthur Watson, Ike Webb, Bill Williams.

Don Bradley played only two wartime games for Albion but went on to make 386 League appearances for Mansfield (1949-62), a record bettered by Sandy Pate in 1978.

Also associated with both clubs: Albion 1900s winger Harry Parkes was Mansfield's manager: 1936-38; Albion reserves Russell Allen, Stan Brierley, Jack Lewis and George Sharpe all played for Mansfield; John Jarman was Albion coach-trainer and assistant manager at Mansfield, while Andy King, a midfielder with Albion in the 1980s, became Mansfield's manager in 1993.

MARDON, Paul Jonathan

Albion manager Alan Buckley paid Birmingham City £350,000 for Mardon's services in November 1993 and he immediately became a firm favourite with The Hawthorns' fans with series of outstanding performances at the heart of the defence alongside Paul Raven. He was  soon made captain and in 1995 was chosen to play for Wales (managed by former Albion player and boss, Bobby Gould) against Germany in Cardiff. Born in Bristol in 1969, Mardon played his early football with Liverpool (trialist), Bristol City and Doncaster Rovers (on loan) going to St Andrew's in 1991. He suffered a serious facial injury towards the end of the 1994-95 season, which caused him to miss the last seven matches. He is now close to the 100 mark in senior games for Albion.

MARTIN, Michael Paul

Son of Con Martin, the former Aston Villa and Republic of Ireland defender of the 1940s and 50s, Mick followed his

father and became an Eire international, winning 52 full caps (1971-83) as well as Under-23 honours and amassing

well over 500 League and Cup appearances as a professional. Born in Dublin in 1951, he was a star junior with Reds United, Home Farm and Bohemians before joining Manchester United in 1973. He moved to Albion, initially on loan, for £30,000 in late 1975, and went on to score 15 goals in 115 games for the Baggies, helping them win promotion to the First Division at the end of his first season at The Hawthorns when assisting his manager Johnny Giles in the midfield engine room. Martin left Albion for Newcastle United for £100,000 in 1978, and later served with Vancouver Whitecaps, Wolves (on loan), Cardiff City, Peterborough United, Rotherham United and Preston North End, before retiring in 1987 when he returned to St James' Park as coach (to 1990).

MASSEURS/PHYSIOTHERAPISTS/TRAINERS

Albion's first masseur was T.H. 'Bill' Gopsill who was at The Hawthorns immediately after World War One before

Early Albion action, dating from 1882 and probably a practice match.

moving up to first-team trainer in 1922. He looked after Albion's League championship winning side of 1919-20. He died suddenly in 1927.

Since World War Two, Fred Pedley (1950-65), Tom Jones (1966-71), Richard Roberts (1971), George Wright (1971-79), Roberts (again 1979-83), Graham Doig, John McGowan, Colin Saunders, Danny Thomas, and Paul Mitchell have all held the position of Albion trainer/physiotherapist (See Trainers below).

NB – The physiotherapist also acted as trainer from 1971 onwards.

Trainers

It was not until 1883 that Albion first appointed an official trainer – Dick Oxenbould of the Tipton Harriers Athletic Club – who even then was employed on a 'casual basis'.

Later on in the year, Birchfield Harrier, Joey Law, also a Salter's employee, was employed as permanent trainer, earning 2s 6d (13p) per week which was later increased to 5s (25p) and then 7s 6d (38p).

For a time Law was assisted by Walter Nicholls, but in 1886, he was replaced by Jack Paddock, who eventually took over from Law, when he went north to 'join' Burnley as their first-team trainer.

Jack Paddock, Albion's trainer from 1889 to 1891.

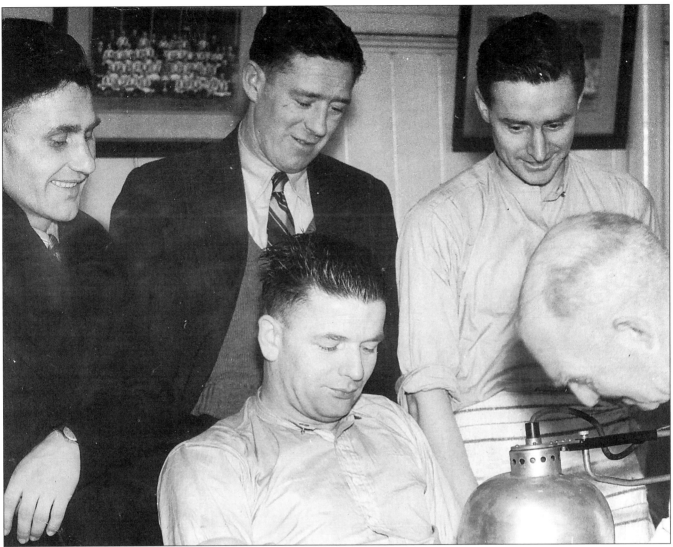

Albion trainer Fred Reed attends to Peter McKennan in 1948, as Len Millard, Jack Vernon and Dave Walsh look on.

Albion's first-team trainers 1883 to date:

Joey Law	1883-89
Jack Paddock	1889-91
William Brierley	1901-04
Jimmy Millar	1904-05
Bill Barber	1905-22
Tom 'Bill' Gopsill	1922-27
Fred Reed	1927-50
Arthur Fitton	1950-56
'Dick' Graham	1956-60
George Lee	1960-61
Wilf Dixon	1961-64
John Jarman	1964-65
Albert McPherson	1965-67
Stuart Williams	1967-69
Jimmy Dunn	1969-71
George Wright	1971-80
Richard Roberts	1980-83
Colin Saunders	1983-84
George Wright	1984-86
Graham Doig	1986-89
John McGowan	1989-92
Danny Thomas	1992-95
Paul Mitchell	1995-96

Albion prepare for pre-season training in July 1954, under 'W.G' Richardson and Arthur Fitton.

Assistant trainers have included: Walter Nicholls, Jimmy Painter (1888-98), Bill Barber (1900-05), Harry Bell (1906-07), Ernest Jones (1907-08), Bob Crone (1908-09), Ted Paddock (1909), Sammy Guest (1939-44), Sammy Short (1930-46), 'W.G' Richardson (1946-48), Arthur Fitton (1948-50), Fred Pedley (1950), Wilf Dixon (1959-60) and John Jarman (1961-64).

Bill Barber, who spent 22 years with Albion (1900-22), started off on 5 shillings (25p) a week and when he retired in 1922 he was earning £5 a week. He was granted a benefit match v Wolverhampton Wanderers in

John Jarman, Albion's trainer in 1964-65. Jarman went on to hold a number of important coaching and training positions.

Albert McPherson, Albion trainer from 1965 to 1967.

May 1921 – the only one Albion have ever arranged for a trainer!

Sam Guest was trainer to six Albion Central League championship winning teams in the 1920s and '30s.

Former Albion outside-left of the 1930s, Walter Robbins, was the Welsh national team trainer in the 1950s.

Albion's longest-serving trainer, Fred Reed, 23 years in office, was spongeman for both the 1931 and 1935 FA Cup Finals and when promotion was gained from the Second Division in 1948-49.

John Jarman later became the FA's Midland Director of Coaching.

George Wright was trainer-physiotherapist-assistant manager under manager Don Howe in 1971.

Albion's reserve defender Craig Herbert acted as first-team trainer-physiotherapist in a friendly game at Cheltenham in 1995.

George Wright, Albion trainer 1971-80 and 1984-86.

Paul Mitchell, physiotherapist 1995-96.

Training 'honours':

Jack Paddock	Football League (v Irish League)	1896-97
Bill Barber	Football League (v Scottish League)	1908-09
	Football League (v Irish League)	1914-15
'Bill' Gopsill	FA XI (v Oxford University)	1922-23
	England (v Wales)	1922-23
	England (v Belgium)	1924-25
Sam Guest	Belgium (v England)	1924-25
	FA XI (v Staffordshire)	1926-27
	The Rest (v England)	1927-28 & 1934-35
Fred Reed	England (v The Rest)	1927-28 & 1934-35
	Football League (v Irish League)	1934-35
	England (v Wales)	1945-46

MATCHES

Congested Fixture List

At the end of the 1911-12 campaign Albion were forced to play seven matches in the space of ten days owing to early season postponements coupled with a long FA Cup run.

Their programme went as follows (Albion's score given first in each case):

Sat	20 April 1912	v Barnsley (FA Cup Final)		0-0
Mon	22 April 1912	v Everton (away, League)		0-3
Wed	24 April 1912	v Barnsley (FA Cup Final replay)		0-1
Thur	25 April 1912	v Blackburn R. (away, League)		1-4
Fri	26 April 1912	v Bradford City (home, League)		0-0
Sat	27 April 1912	v Sheffield wed. (home, League)		1-5
Mon	29 April 1912	v Oldham Athletic (home, League)	0-0

Notwithstanding the great number of matches played in so short a time, Albion finished the season in ninth position in the First Division, dropping only five places during those hectic ten days.

For the game with Everton on 22 April, Albion put out their reserve side and although all but two of the 11 participating players had previously lined up in the senior side, they were fined £150 by the Football League for the 'Offence' of fielding an under-strength team.

Two in One Day

Albion have played two first-team matches on the same day on two separate occasions. On 16 March 1891, they defeated Warwick County (home) 6-0 in a Birmingham Cup-tie and also beat Sheffield Wednesday 2-1 in a friendly.

Then, on 14 August 1973, Albion defeated Rhyl 3-1 away and simultaneously lost 3-0 at Colchester United, both in pre-season friendlies.

Most in a Season

Albion's first XI fulfilled a total of 76 matches in season 1978-79 – 42 League, eight UEFA Cup, six FA Cup, three League Cup, two Tennent-Caledonian, eight testimonials, two friendlies and five on tour.

Their full record was:

Venue	P	W	D	L	F	A
Home	31	18	9	4	57	24
Away	45	19	15	11	76	49
Totals	76	37	24	15	133	73

The previous highest number of games was 67 in 1891-92.

The most FA Cup games played by Albion in a season is ten (1967-68).

Albion met neighbours Aston Villa eight times in 1892-93, winning two, drawing two and losing four.

Albion played 35 friendly matches in 1887-88.

Longest

The longest game played by Albion was their wartime Midland Cup Final (2nd leg) against Nottingham Forest at The City ground on 6 May 1944 which lasted 128 minutes (90 minutes normal time, 20 minutes extra-time and then eight more minutes of sudden-death time which ended when Albion scored the decisive goal to win the trophy 6-5 on aggregate (4-3 at Nottingham after a 2-2 draw at The Hawthorns in the first leg).

The longest FA Cup-tie involving Albion was played in season 1952-53 when a fourth round clash with Chelsea went to a second replay, the Londoners finally going through after 420 minutes of football! The results of the games were 0-0, 1-1 (aet), 1-1 (aet) and 0-4.

In the League Cup, Albion have played in three games all of which went to a second replay (300 minutes) – against Leeds United in 1978-79, v Preston North End in 1980-81 and West Ham United in 1981-82 (See FOOTBALL LEAGUE CUP).

Unbeaten Run
From 14 October 1978 to 15 January 1979, Albion played 21 first-team matches without defeat – a club record. The run comprised 13 League games, 2 FA Cup-ties, 4 UEFA Cup-ties and 2 testimonials (See FOOTBALL LEAGUE for other sequences).

MIDDLESBROUGH
Albion's record against 'Boro:
Football League

Venue	P	W	D	L	F	A	Pts
Home	37	20	9	8	61	36	50
Away	37	5	9	23	28	63	19
Totals	74	25	18	31	89	99	69

FA Cup

Home	1	1	0	0	1	0
Away	2	1	0	1	1	1
Totals	3	2	0	1	2	1

Other Matches

Away	3	0	1	2	3	10

Albion (as FA Cup holders) lost their first-ever game against Middlesbrough, 7-2 away at Linthorpe Road in a friendly on 7 September 1892.

Albion's best League win over 'Boro is 6-3 at The Hawthorns in a First Division match on 5 January 1935.

David Mills, Britain's first half a million pound player when he was transferred from Middlesbrough to Albion in 1979.

Albion also won 5-2 at home on Boxing Day 1935 when 'W.G.' Richardson scored four times. In fact, Albion scored 20 home League goals against Middlesbrough between 1933 and 1938 yet managed only three at Ayresome Park!

'Boro's best League win over Albion is 4-0 at The Hawthorns in a Second Division match on 16 March 1974.

On 7 May 1938, Middlesbrough defeated an injury-hit Albion side 4-1 at home to ensure the Midlanders' relegation to Division Two, Mick Fenton scoring all 'Boro's four goals.

David Mills became the first half-a-million pound footballer in British history when he was transferred from Middlesbrough to Albion for £516,000 in January 1979.

Albion League debutants v 'Boro: Sid Corfield (1904), Bill Richardson (1928), Jack Screen (1935), Freddie Cox (1953), Romeo Zondervan (1982), Stewart Phillips (1988), Neil Parsley (1993). Cyrille Regis scored a superb goal on his First Division debut at The Hawthorns v 'Boro, having earlier netted when making his first-team bow for Albion v Rotherham in a League Cup-tie.

Players with both clubs: Mark Barham, Bob Crone, Arthur Davies, Andy Dibble, Charlie Hewitt, Abe Jones, Peter McKennan, David Mills, Alonzo Poulton, Stan Rickaby, Dick Roberts, Bryan Robson (player-manager of 'Boro), Jack Taggart, Willie Thompson.

Also associated with both clubs: Nobby Stiles played for 'Boro and later managed Albion; Paul Kerr played for 'Boro and was on loan to Albion from Port Vale and Mike Kelly was a goalkeeping coach with both clubs.

MILLARD, Leonard
After starting his career as a centre-forward and then playing as a wing-half, Len Millard became a resolute left-back, who went on to appear in 627 first-team games for Albion, scoring 18 goals. Born in Coseley, near Wolverhampton, in 1919, he joined The Hawthorns staff as an amateur in 1937 after serving with Wallbrook, Coseley Town, Bilston Town and Sunbeam FC. He became a professional in 1942 and took over the number-three shirt from Harry Kinsell towards the end of Albion's 1948-49 Second Division promotion campaign. Five years later, at the age of 35, Millard skippered Albion to victory over Preston in the FA Cup Final, marking Tom Finney out of the game. He continued to play first-team football until 1957 and the following year quit the club to become manager of Stafford Rangers (1958-61). Sadly Millard had a leg amputated in 1989 and is now resident in his native Coseley, although confined to a wheelchair.

MILLWALL
Albion have met Millwall under three different guises: Millwall Rovers, Millwall Athletic and Millwall, and their record against the London club is:
Football League

Venue	P	W	D	L	F	A	Pts
Home	14	6	4	4	21	16	18
Away	14	3	4	7	19	24	10
Totals	28	9	8	11	40	40	28

FA Cup

Away	1	1	0	0	1	0

League Cup

Home	2	2	0	0	6	1
Away	1	0	0	1	0	3
Totals	3	2	0	1	6	4

Full Members' Cup

Away	1	0	0	1	0	2

Other Matches

Home	1	1	0	0	3	1
Away	4	2	0	2	7	5
Totals	5	3	0	2	10	6

Albion recorded their best League win over Millwall on Boxing Day 1929, beating them 6-1 at The Hawthorns in a Second Division match. 'W.G.' Richardson made his Albion debut in this game, scoring once and making another two.

On 3 December 1938, Albion beat Millwall 5-1 (away) in a Second Division game, two goals coming from Harry Jones who was described in the London press as a 'human rocket.' Millwall had former Hawthorns' favourite Harold Pearson in goal,

Millwall's best win over Albion is 4-1. They achieved this scoreline twice – at The Hawthorns on Boxing Day 1987 and at The Den on 6 October 1990.

Andy Hunt scored a hat-trick in Albion's 3-0 home win over Millwall on 22 March 1993.

After losing the first leg of a 2nd round League Cup-tie at Millwall by 3-0 in October 1983, Albion played magnificently in the return fixture three weeks later to win 5-1 (5-4 on aggregate). The game at The Hawthorns was marred by crowd trouble caused by travelling Millwall supporters. Defender John Smith had his only first-team game for Albion in the away leg at Millwall.

A crowd of just 967 witnessed the Full Members' Cup-tie between the clubs at Millwall in October 1986. Young defender Sean Hayward made his only appearance for Albion in this game.

In a friendly match against Millwall (Athletic) at New Cross on 28 April 1894, England international winger Billy Bassett became the first Albion player ever to be sent-off – dismissed in the second-half for 'unparliamentary language'.

Albion League debutants v Millwall: 'W.G.' Richardson (1929), Harry Raw (1931), Billy Gripton (1939), David Rushbury (1974), Paul Edwards (1994), Jeroen Boere (1994).

Players with both clubs: Sam Allardyce, Gerry Armstrong, Allan Crowshaw, Reg Davies, Alf Dean, Arthur Flavell, George Garratt, Alf Geddes, Frank Hodgetts, Tony Kelly, Jack Kifford, Archie McKenzie, Harold Pearson, Jimmy Poxton, Sid Rawlings, Arthur Smith.

Also associated with both clubs: Peter Burridge, Steve Burke and Jimmy Whitehouse (Albion reserves, Millwall League players); Paul Kerr (Millwall player, later on loan to Albion), Charlie Hewitt, Albion player (1908-10), Millwall manager (1936-40/1948-56); Peter Hucker, an on loan goalkeeper with Albion (1988) was with Millwall (1989-90); Paul Holsgrove, who had trials with Albion in 1989, was on Millwall's books (1992-94).

MISCELLANEOUS

Albion reached the Final of every competition they entered in 1887-88: the FA Cup (won), The Staffordshire Senior Cup, the Birmingham Cup, the West Bromwich Charity Cup (won), and the Walsall Cup (won). Albion's record in Cup competitions this season was superb: played 23, won 19 (10 at home), drew 2 and lost 2. Goals: 78 'for' and 19 'against'.

At Warwick races on 30 March 1925, a horse called King Throstle won the opening race while the second event was won by a horse named Top of the League. That same afternoon, Albion beat Sheffield United 2-1 to go to the top of the First Division – a most remarkable coincidence.

In January 1953, Albion's first team were leading the First Division with 33 points from 26 games. Simultaneously, their reserve side were at the foot of the Central League with 15 points from 25 games.

In March 1894, Newton Heath (now Manchester United) sued Mr William Jephcott and the *Birmingham Daily Gazette* for £500 libel damages after the journalist had criticised the rough play of the Lancashire club. Several Albion players gave evidence on behalf of Mr Jephcott, but Newton Heath won the case – only to be awarded the lowest possible damages – one farthing! Both clubs had to bear their own costs.

In 1897 'Jem' Bayliss, skipper of Albion's 1888 FA Cup Final winning team, read his own obituary in a local newspaper. A rumour spread that Bayliss had died of typhoid fever at his Great Bridge home (it was even confirmed at the Albion offices where the directors were holding a meeting). The paper carried an article contradicting the story the following day.

The two longest footballing campaigns Albion have ever participated in were both of 11 months' duration: 1886-87 – (19 July to 20 June) and 1965-66 (7 July to 5 June).

MORRIS, Frederick

Morris was a strongly-built, courageous forward, who scored 118 goals in 287 games for Albion, whom he served before, during and after World War One. Born in Tipton in 1893, he

played for Ball Street Primitives, Tipton Victoria and Redditch before joining The Hawthorns staff in 1911. He netted a goal on his debut v Sunderland a year later and in the first season after the war set a new club record by scoring 37 goals as Albion won the First Division championship. Morris, a junior international, went on to gain two full England caps and also represented the Football League and the FA. In 1922 he became the first Albion player to reach 100 League goals. He guested for Fulham and Watford in wartime and left The Hawthorns for Coventry City in 1924, later assisting Oakengates Town. He retired in 1930 and died in Great Bridge in 1962.

MULLIGAN, Patrick Martin

Right-back Paddy Mulligan was an expert on the overlap and was never really given a difficult time by a winger at club or international level. He joined Albion from Crystal Palace in 1975 and in his four years at The Hawthorns amassed 132 appearances, scoring two goals. He helped Albion win promotion from the Second Division and formed a fine triangle on the field of play with his manager, Johnny Giles, and Mick Martin, all three Republic of Ireland internationals. In his career Mulligan gained a total of 51 full caps and also played in schoolboy internationals and for the League of Ireland. He won four FAI Cup-winning medals (1965-69), came on as 'sub' for Chelsea when they won the the European Cup-winners'

Cup in 1971 and also took part in the 1972 League Cup Final at Wembley. Born in Dublin in 1945, Mulligan played for Stella Maris, Home Farm (two spells), Bohemians, Shamrock Rovers (two spells), Boston Beacons (in the NASL) and Chelsea prior to moving to Selhurst Park in 1972. After leaving Albion he returned to Shamrock Rovers and in 1980-81 was assistant manager of the Greek club, Panathinaikos, later taking over as manager of Galway Rovers. Mulligan quit football in 1982 and began an accountancy/insurance business.

MURPHY, James Patrick

Known as 'Spud' by his colleagues, Welshman Jimmy Murphy was a vigorous attacking wing-half, who took over from Tommy Magee in Albion's League side in the early 1930s. A glutton for hard work, he gave Albion excellent service and appeared in 223 first-class games for the club between 1928 and 1939. Born in Ton Pentre in 1908, he played for several junior teams in South Wales before signing for Albion. Capped by his country 15 times, he lined up for Albion in the 1935 FA Cup Final and on leaving the club he signed for Swindon Town, later assisting Morris Commercial FC. After the war, he was appointed coach at Manchester United, and became assistant manager to Matt Busby in 1955, taking over as team manager for a short period following the Munich air disaster in 1958. He was the Welsh national team manager from 1956 to 1963, leading his country in the 1958 World Cup Finals. In 1982 he became scout and football adviser at Old Trafford and remained in close association with the Lancashire club until his death in 1989.

NAYLOR, Stuart William

Stuart Naylor was manager Ron Saunders' first signing for Albion, joining for a club record fee for a goalkeeper of

£110,000 from Lincoln City in 1986. A Yorkshireman, born in Leeds in 1962, he had trials with Leeds United as a lad and played for Yorkshire Amateurs before signing for Lincoln in 1978. Loan spells with both Crewe Alexandra and Peterborough United preceded his move to The Hawthorns. Tall, strongly built, with good reflexes, Naylor was capped by England at youth level and in 1989 represented his country's 'B' team on three occasions. During his time at Sincil Bank, he turned out at centre-forward in a game v Newport County in 1982. In 1995 Naylor created an Albion record, having appeared in more games for the club than any other goalkeeper (354+1 League, 13 FA Cup, 22 League Cup, 20 'other' Cups and 53+2 friendlies) for a total of 462+3. He was granted a testimonial in 1995-96 (v Coventry City) and released by Albion on a free transfer at the end of that season. Naylor's father (Bill) and uncle (Tommy) played for Oldham Athletic between 1948 and 1959.

NEWCASTLE UNITED

Albion's record against United:

Football League

Venue	P	W	D	L	F	A	Pts
Home	49	24	15	10	100	60	64
Away	49	14	11	24	70	101	39
Totals	98	38	26	34	170	161	103

FA Cup

Home	3	2	0	1	4	5

League Cup

Away	1	1	0	0	1	0

Texaco Cup

Home	1	1	0	0	2	1
Away	1	0	0	1	1	3
Totals	2	1	0	1	3	4

Other Matches

Away	6	3	1	2	12	12

Albion first opposed Newcastle (West End) before the Football League was formed – beating them 5-1 in a friendly match on 3 April 1888 in the North-East.

Albion's best League win over United is 7-3 at St James' Park in a First Division match on 16 September 1953. That evening a crowd of over 58,000 saw Johnny Nicholls score a hat-trick as Vic Buckingham's side turned on a magnificent display of attacking football.

George McVitie made his Albion debut against Newcastle in 1970.

Albion also beat United 6-0 at The Hawthorns on 5 September 1960 with Alec Jackson a hat-trick hero this time. Before this game Albion had suffered five successive League defeats.

On 27 September 1902 Albion registered a sensational 6-1 home win over United who had not previously conceded a goal that season!

Tony Brown netted a hat-trick in Albion's 6-1 home League win over United in April 1967 and two years later Albion again beat the Geordies, this time by 5-1.

Ronnie Allen scored a hat-trick in Albion's 3-0 League win at Newcastle on 2 January 1956, and two years earlier he netted all three goals when Albion knocked United out of the FA Cup in a classic home fifth-round tie on 20th February 1954 when the gate was 61,088 – a record for a Cup game at The Hawthorns.

United won 3-0 on Albion soil in the fifth round, on the way to their 1974 FA Cup Final defeat by Liverpool.

United's best League win over Albion is 5-1, achieved four times, three at home: 21 November 1931, 14 September 1938 (Cairns scored four goals) and 26 November 1949 and once at The Hawthorns, 1 November 1989.

Albion lost four and drew four of their first eight League games away at Newcastle (1898-1914).

Albion League debutants v United: Tom Newall (1913), Louis Bookman (1914), Alonzo Poulton (1914), Ivor Jones (1922), Arthur Gale (1932), Bill Tudor (1938), Ernie Hoyland (1938), Andy Aitken (1959), George McVitie (1970), Robbie Dennison (1985), Carlton Palmer (1985), Sam Allardyce (1989).

Players with both clubs: Stan Allan, Harry Brown, Eddie Connelly, Wayne Fereday, Andy Hunt, Tom Hutchinson, Dennis Martin, Mick Martin, David Mills, Bob Pailor, George Reilly, Dick Roberts, Mark Robinson, Colin Suggett, John Trewick, Imre Varadi.

Also associated with both clubs: Albion reserves John Anderson and Steve Carney both went on to play for Newcastle, Anderson winning 15 caps for Northern Ireland. Kenny Wharton was on loan at The Hawthorns from Newcastle in 1989; Ossie Ardiles managed both clubs in the 1990s; Keith Burkinshaw was assistant manager and manager of Albion (1992-94) having earlier been on United's coaching staff (1968-75); Jesse Carver was a 1930s defender with United and later Albion's coach/manager (1952); Maurice Setters, an Albion player (1955-60) was later chief scout at United and Mick Martin was Newcastle coach (1987-90).

NEWPORT COUNTY

Albion's record against County:

Football League

Venue	P	W	D	L	F	A	Pts
Home	1	0	1	0	2	2	1
Away	1	1	0	0	7	2	2
Totals	2	1	1	0	9	4	3

Other Matches

	P	W	D	L	F	A
Home	1	1	0	0	6	0
Away	2	1	0	1	4	2
Totals	3	2	0	1	10	2

Albion first encountered Newport in the Football League South transitional season of 1945-46, winning 3-0 at Somerton Park and 6-0 at The Hawthorns when Ike Clarke hit a hat-trick.

The following season, Clarke scored four more goals in Albion's 7-2 win at Newport in a Second Division match

Albion League debutants v County: Ray Barlow (1946), John Tighe (1947).

Players with both clubs: Paul Bradshaw, Simeon Hodson, Kevin Kent, Billy Lunn, Sandy McNab, Jack Mann, Harry Parkes, Sammy Richardson, Walter Robbins, Trevor Thompson, Paul A. Williams, Doug Witcomb, Harry Wright.

Colin Addison, managed Newport County and had two spells as assistant manager at The Hawthorns.

Parkes was Newport's first manager after World War One (1919-22) and during the 1919-20 season he played in goal at Plymouth (lost 3-0).

Also associated with both clubs: former Albion reserve Tudor Martin played for Newport in 1929-30 and hit five goals in a 10-0 win over Merthyr Town (away) in April 1930. He scored a record 34 goals for the Welsh club that season before transferring to Wolves. Billy Arch, Alf Hickman, Jim Southam and Frank White, all Albion reserves, later played for Newport, Hickman appearing in their Third Division South championship-winning side of 1938-39. Colin Addison was assistant manager and coach at Albion and manager of Newport County (1977-78).

NICHOLLS, John

One of Albion's finest post-war marksmen, Johnny Nicholls netted 64 goals in 145 appearances for the club. He formed a splendid partnership with Ronnie Allen as Albion took runners-up spot in the First Division and won the FA Cup in 1953-54. Born in Wolverhampton in 1931, he had trials with Albion and Wolves while playing local football with Heath Town United and in 1950 was taken on at The Hawthorns, turning professional the following year. He stayed with Albion until 1957, having gained two full England caps and others at 'B' and Under-23 levels. He later served with Cardiff City, Exeter City, Worcester City, Wellington Town, Oswestry and GKN Sankey's as well as the Albion All Stars before retiring in 1973. He died of a heart attack on his way home from the Albion-Middlesbrough game in April 1995.

NICKNAMES

West Bromwich Albion have four nicknames in common use: 'Albion', the 'Baggies', the 'Throstles' and 'West Brom', the latter being mainly used outside the Midlands!

'Throstle' is the Black Country name for a thrush, and it seems likely that this nickname derived from these speckled-breasted birds which frequented the area around Dartmouth Park, West Bromwich before the turn of the century and indeed, were plentiful in the hawthorn bushes when Albion first moved to their present ground in 1900. For years the club's official crest has depicted a thrush perched on a sprig of hawthorn, thus incorporating the name of the ground as well! No one can reproduce or use this crest without written authority from the Secretary of West Bromwich Albion Football Club.

No one really knows when or from where, the 'Baggies' arrived. This nickname – used with affection by the avid supporters of the club – was not around before 1904 and explanations have been varied as to how it was adopted.

Some references indicate that 'Baggies' may well have been introduced to the terraces in 1905 after fans had gone round public houses collecting much-wanted funds for the club in small bags (baggies).

The nickname could have been chosen after full-back Amos Adams, a full-back with thick-set thighs which made his baggy shorts look ever larger than they really were! One day a fan shouted out 'Baggy' and that name may well have stuck!

Players' Nicknames

Several players acquire a nickname during their career and listed here are a few of the more 'interesting' appertaining to Albion stars: 'Peggy' (Lee Ashcroft), 'The King' (Jeff Astle); 'Benno' (Martyn Bennett), 'Snobby' (Alf Bentley), 'Titty' (Wally Boyes), 'Bomber' (Tony Brown), 'Chippy' (Clive Clark), 'Chuck' (Charlie Drury), 'Jason' (Kevin Donovan), 'Iron' (Jimmy Edwards), 'Bungo' (Alun Evans). 'Jasper' (Alf Geddes), 'Diddy' (Dave Gilbert) 'Ironsides' (Ezra Horton), 'Popeye' (Harry Jones), 'Yorky' (John Kaye), 'The Tank' (Derek Kevan), 'Ada' (George Lee), 'Shack' (Jack Lovatt), 'Shuv' (Graham Lovett), 'Snowy'

Albion's 'Three Degrees' – Laurie Cunningham, Cyrille Regis and Brendon Batson, pictured in 1978-79.

(Harry Lowery), 'Sandy' (Alex McNab), 'Captain Mardon' (Paul Mardon), 'Spud' (Jimmy Murphy), 'Bruiser' (Stuart Naylor), 'Poacher' (Johnny Nicholls), 'Peerless' (Jesse Pennington). 'Cock' (Ted Pheasant), 'Baldy' (John Reynolds), 'Pop' (Bryan Robson), 'Steel' (Billy Richardson), 'Ginger' (Billy – W.G. – Richardson), 'Salt' (Jack Sankey), 'Trigger' and 'Super Bob' (Bob Taylor), 'Darkie' (George Timmins), 'Rubber' (Willie Thompson), 'Tucker' (John Trewick), 'Bos' (Arthur Trevis), 'Puffer' (Frank Waterhouse), 'Scrumpy' (Clive Whitehead), 'Ironclad' (Billy Williams), 'Tug' (Charlie Wilson), 'Spry' (George Woodhall) and 'Splinter' (Stan Wood)

Ronnie Allen and Johnny Nicholls were known as the 'Terrible Twins' in 1953-54 and in the 1930s the Albion half-back line of Sankey, Richardson and Edwards was referred to as 'Salt', 'Pepper' and 'Mustard.' Brendon Batson, Laurie Cunningham and Cyrille Regis were known as the 'Three Degrees' and Cunningham was also described in the press as the 'Black Pearl'.

NISBET, Gordon James Mackay
Gordon Nisbet joined Albion as a goalkeeper and made his League debut in that position – but thereafter he made another 166 appearances for the club (scoring one goal) as a thoughtful and composed right-back, having being successfully converted into a defender by manager Don Howe. Born at Wallsend-on-Tyne in 1951, Nisbet played for Willington Boys' Club and joined Albion in 1968 after trials with Blackpool, Leicester City, Preston and Sunderland. He conceded three goals on his debut against Coventry City in 1969 and after lining up in a number of outfield positions for

the reserves, he played at right-back in the senior side for the first time away at Arsenal in December 1971. He made good progress and won an England Under-23 cap within a year. Nisbet left Albion for Hull City in a £30,000 deal in 1976 (after the arrival of Paddy Mulligan) and later appeared in more than 300 games in seven years with Plymouth Argyle (1980-87). A season with Exeter City followed, then he signed for Ottery St Mary's, returning to Plymouth as youth team coach in 1991. He acted as caretaker-manager for a time at Home Park and in 1995 was appointed manager of Barnstaple Town.

NORTHAMPTON TOWN
Albion's record against Northampton:
Football League

Venue	P	W	D	L	F	A	Pts
Home	1	0	1	0	1	1	1
Away	1	1	0	0	4	3	2
Totals	2	1	1	0	5	4	3

FA Cup

Away	1	1	0	0	3	1

League Cup

Home	1	0	1	0	1	1
Away	2	2	0	0	7	3
Totals	3	2	1	0	8	4

Other Matches

Home	13	11	2	0	54	18
Away	12	1	3	8	16	30
Totals	25	12	5	8	70	48

Albion's first game against Northampton was an away friendly on 4 April 1899 which they lost 6-1.

When Albion beat Northampton 4-3 in the first League game between the clubs at The County Ground on Friday evening, 10 September 1965, they went to the top of the First Division. Jeff Astle scored a hat-trick in this game (his second in seven days) and Albion used their first ever League substitute, Graham Lovett replacing the injured Kenny Foggo.

On 6 December 1941, Albion whipped Northampton 7-0 in a Regional League game, Peter McKennan netting a hat-trick on his debut. In this same game Billy Elliott equalled Harry Jones' club record by scoring in his 11th consecutive match.

In another high-scoring war match, Albion defeated North-ampton 6-0 at The Hawthorns on 17 March 1945, Ike Clarke claiming a hat-trick this time.

Albion's first visit to Northampton's new Sixfields Stadium was for the second leg of a first round Coca-Cola Cup-tie on 23 August 1995. They won 4-2 after being held 1-1 at home in the first leg when defender Tony Brien made his debut for Albion.

Martin Singleton played for both the Baggies and the Cobblers.

Players with both clubs: Norman Aldridge, Ian Benjamin, John Cole, Fred Cook, Ray Fairfax, Dave Gilbert, Frank Griffin, Sammy Heaselgrave, Roy Hunter, Dick Krzywicki, Albert Lewis, Harry Lowery, Hugh Morrow, Mick Perry, Sid Rawlings, George Reilly, Jack Sankey, Martin Singleton, Garry Thompson, Bob Ward.

Also associated with both clubs: Albion reserves Barry Cooke, Ted Duckhouse, Colin Lyman, Jim Southam and Kim Wassall later played for Northampton; Dick Graham was a Northampton goalkeeper and later Albion trainer and Gordon Dimbleby was commercial-manager and secretary at both clubs, and current Albion secretary, Dr. John Evans, was part-time secretary of Northampton Town (1986-89).

NORTHWICH VICTORIA

A Football League club in the 1890s, Northwich Victoria have played Albion in three friendly matches: on 3 October 1885 (Albion lost 2-1), on 25 September 1886 (Albion won 2-1) and on 30 September 1891 (Albion won 5-0).

England international left-wingers Peter Barnes and Joe Johnson played for both clubs, as did Scottish international wing-half Alex 'Sandy' McNab, who was player-manager of the Vics. Len Cantello played for Albion (1967-79) and Altrincham (1982 and 1986). Stuart Pearson, Bobby Gould's assistant at Albion in the early 1990s, was also coach and player-manager at Northwich and Mark McCarrick, an Albion reserve, was on Victoria's book in 1991.

NORWICH CITY

Albion's record against City:

Football League

Venue	P	W	D	L	F	A	Pts
Home	12	5	4	3	16	12	15
Away	12	3	4	5	16	18	11
Totals	24	8	8	8	32	30	26

FA Cup

Home	3	3	0	0	5	0

League Cup

Home	2	0	2	0	1	1
Away	2	0	0	2	0	5

Texaco Cup

Home	1	1	0	0	5	1

Other Match

Away	1	1	0	0	3	2

City were members of the Southern League when they met Albion for the first time, losing a 2nd round FA Cup-tie at The Hawthorns 1-0 on 2 February 1907.

A crowd of 3,109 – the lowest at The Hawthorns for a competitive game for nine years – saw Albion inflict a 4-2 defeat on Norwich in a Second Division game on 29 April 1939 – the last League game before World War Two. This is Albion's best win over City and George Banks scored twice on his debut for the Baggies.

Norwich's best League win over Albion is 4-1 at The Hawthorns in a First Division match on 21 November 1995.

Norwich beat Albion 1-0 in a vital relegation battle at The Hawthorns on 21 April 1973. Albion were relegated.

Cyrille Regis scored a hat-trick when Albion beat Nor-wich 3-1 (away) in a First Divis-ion match on 25 September 1982.

Regis had earlier scored a memorable goal to give Albion a 1-0 fifth-round FA Cup victory over Norwich at The Haw-thorns in February 1982.

The 'other' match was a testimonial played at Spalding United in October 1980 when John Deehan, later to join Norwich, scored a hat-trick in Albion's 3-2 win.

John Deehan scored a hat-trick for Albion against Norwich City in a testimonial match on Spalding United's ground in 1980 and later played for and managed the Canaries.

Albion League debutants v Norwich: George Banks (1939), Barry Cowdrill (1980), Noel Luke (1983), Alan Fettis (1995). Players with both clubs: Mark Barham, Geoff Barnsley, Ron Bradley, David Cross, John Deehan, Jimmy Edwards, Kenny Foggo, Asa Hartford, Gerry Howshall, Mike Phelan, Colin Suggett, Steve Walford, Brian Whitehouse.

John Deehan, besides playing for both clubs, also managed Norwich (1994-95); Archie Macaulay and Ron Saunders managed both clubs; Albion's 1950s outside-left George Lee was later Norwich's trainer/coach (1963-87) and Gordon Bennett was Albion's secretary (1986-89) before becoming youth development officer at Carrow Road; Albion reserve winger Bill Taylor (1920-21) played for Norwich in 1931.

NOTTINGHAM FOREST

Albion's record against Forest:

Football League

Venue	P	W	D	L	F	A	Pts
Home	51	27	9	15	107	79	66
Away	51	19	11	21	78	84	50
Totals	102	46	20	36	185	163	116

FA Cup

Home	6	1	4	1	9	8
Away	8	3	3	2	18	11
Totals	14	4	7	3	27	19

(The abandoned FA Cup-tie of 1973 has not been included)

League Cup

Home	1	1	0	0	3	1
Away	2	1	0	1	4	8
Totals	3	2	0	1	7	9

Anglo-Scottish Cup

Away	1	0	0	1	2	3

Other Matches

Home	7	4	2	1	16	8
Away	6	3	1	2	14	13
Totals	13	7	3	3	30	21

In the very first meeting between the clubs – the final of the Wednesbury Charity Cup at Perry Barr on 19 May 1883 – Forest beat Albion 5-3 and Tinsley Lindley, their centre-forward scored four goals. Two minutes before half-time in this game, Albion's skipper John While broke his leg (See CASUALTIES).

Albion registered their best-ever League victory over Forest in the very last match staged at Stoney Lane on 16 April 1900. Albion won 8-0 that day with Billy Walker scoring a hat-trick.

Forest quickly gained revenge for that defeat by whipping Albion 6-1 at The Hawthorns on 20 October 1900.

Two more 6-1 Forest victories were gained on 7 October 1899 (Division One) and in a 2nd round first leg League Cup clash at The City Ground on 6 October 1982. Albion won the return leg 3-1, but went out 7-4 on aggregate.

Max Murray, made his debut against Forest in 1962.

Forest won 5-0 at The Hawthorns on 8 February 1984 when Albion conceded a penalty and an own-goal, and they were 5-1 victors on the same ground on 1 September 1979.

Albion ran up one of the biggest FA Cup semi-final victories of all-time when, in a continuous blizzard, they beat Forest 6-2 in a second replay on 9 March 1892. Albion's outside-right Billy Bassett had a hand in all his side's goals, laying on a hat-trick for his opposite winger Alf Geddes.

Albion knocked Forest out of the FA Cup in a fourth-round replay in January 1958, winning 5-1 at The City Ground with only ten men. Maurice Setters had gone off early in the game when the scores were level at 1-1. The teams had drawn 3-3 five days earlier.

Albion and Forest met each other four times in the fourth round of the FA Cup in 1972-73, Albion finally winning 3-1 at neutral Filbert Street. The second game at The City Ground was abandoned in the 79th minute through fog (See ABANDONED MATCHES).

Forest lost only once in 62 games between 1977 and 1979 – the team to beat them was Albion, who won a sixth-round FA Cup-tie 2-0 at The Hawthorns on 11 March 1978, Cyrille Regis scoring a superb goal.

George James is believed to have scored the fastest League goal at The Hawthorns – five seconds after kick-off for Albion against Forest in the First Division match on 15 December 1924. James added three more afterwards to help Albion to a 5-1 victory.

Tony Brown was another four-goal hero for Albion in their 4-1 Second Division victory over Forest (away) on 12 January 1974. Brown scored a record 14 goals for Albion in games against Forest.

Albion's famous Cup and promotion winning side played together for the first time in a League game against Nottingham Forest at The City Ground on 29 November 1930 when they ran out 6-1 winners.

Albion won the Midland War Cup in season 1943-44, beating Forest 6-5 in the two-legged Final (See GAMES, longest, and WARTIME FOOTBALL).

Albion were undefeated in nine League visits to Forest between 1948 and 1964.

Albion beat Forest 3-2 in a League Cup-tie at Meadow Lane, home of Notts County, in 1968 (Forest's City Ground had been damaged by fire).

Albion League debutants v Forest: Alf Dean (1897), Jack Knowles (1897), Billy Walker (1899), Sammy Legge (1906), Dick Pike (1939), Charlie Evans (1946), Arthur Taylor (1948), Arthur Smith (1948), Ernie Shepherd (1948), Max Murray (1962), Bill Williams (1965), John Osborne (1967), Barry Donaghy (1973), Paul Mardon (1993), Paul R.Williams (1993).

Players with both clubs: Stan Allan, Gary Bannister, Enos Bromage, Meynell Burgin, Alf Dean, Ike Evenson, Alan Fettis, Ross Fielding, Doug Fraser, Harry Hadley, Asa Hartford, George Lee, Andrew Marriott, Ronnie Rees, Brian Rice, Ben Shearman, Kenny Swain, Sam Timmins.

Associated with both clubs: David Campbell (Albion trialist, Forest player); Ronnie Fenton (Albion player, Forest assistant manager-coach); Alan Ashman and Alan Buckley were both Forest players who later became Albion managers); Colin Lyman and Ernie Peers (Albion reserves, Forest players).

NOTTS COUNTY

County are the oldest Football League Club (founded in 1862) and this is Albion's full record against the Magpies:

Football League

Venue	P	W	D	L	F	A	Pts
Home	30	17	9	4	74	41	46
Away	30	6	7	17	29	54	20
totals	60	23	16	21	103	95	66

FA Cup

Home	3	2	1	0	8	2
Away	3	1	0	2	4	6
Totals	6	3	1	2	12	8

Anglo-Scottish Cup

Home	1	1	0	0	3	1

Other Matches

Home	7	6	0	1	28	6
Away	5	0	1	4	7	17
Totals	12	6	1	5	35	23

The first meeting between the clubs took place three years before League football was introduced, County winning a friendly match 4-3 at Trent Bridge on 14 November 1885.

When Albion won the First Division championship in 1919-20, their biggest victory was 8-0 at home against Notts County on 25 October. Freddie Morris scored five goals in this, Albion's best-ever win over County.

County's biggest League win over Albion is 8-1 at home on 19 November 1892.

All of Albion's goals in their emphatic 5-0 League win over County at The Hawthorns on 12 April 1924, were scored in the space of 18 minutes.

In an important League game at Meadow Lane on 6 March 1976, goals by Willie Johnston and Joe Mayo gave Albion a 2-0 win over County and put them on the road to promotion from Division Two.

In wartime football Albion beat County 8-1 in a home Midland Cup-tie on 11 January 1941. Five weeks later County defeated Albion 4-0 in a first round, first leg League Cup game, but Albion stormed back to win the 2nd leg on 22 February by 5-0 to pull off a terrific victory.

Albion League debutants v County: Albert Millard (1888),

Harry Hadley (1898), Joseph Connor (1898), Amos Adams (1899), George Williams (1900), Stan Allan (1911), Ben Shearman (1911), Arthur Cook (1911), Teddy Rooke (1924), Len Darnell (1926), Stan Wood (1928), Jimmy Adams (1929), Les Palmer (1990), Tony Rees (1994). Harry Parkes made his Albion debut in an FA Cup-tie v County in 1907.

Players with both clubs: Lee Ashcroft, Bill Ashurst, Jeff Astle, Kevin Bartlett, Ian Benjamin, Wally Boyes, James Burns, Peter Butler, John Chadburn, Frank Cresswell, Bob Crone, Andy Gray, Mark Grew, Simeon Hodson, Graeme Hogg, Roy Horobin, Phil King, Paul Reece, Graham Smith, Keith Smith, Gary Strodder, Arthur Watson.

Also associated with both clubs: David Campbell (Albion trialist, County player); Albion reserves Colin Lyman, Pat Regan, Steve Burke and Gordon Wills later played for County; Ron Wylie was an inside-forward with County (1949-58) and later Albion manager, and Arthur Mann played for County (1972-79) and was appointed Albion's assistant manager in 1994.

NUMBERING OF PLAYERS

In the same year that players were numbered in the FA Cup Final for the first time – 1933 – so Tottenham Hotspur made the proposal that players should also be numbered in Football League games. Spurs' proposal was defeated, but six years later, at the League's annual meeting, the idea was finally adopted with the voting 24-20 in favour.

Albion players first wore numbered jerseys for the Football League Jubilee Fund game against Aston Villa (away) on 19 August 1939 – and they have worn numbers ever since. In 1969-70, numbers were sewn on to the players' shorts as well as on their shirts, but this venture lasted only a couple of years.

NURSE, Daniel George

Dan Nurse was a powerful right-half who was instrumental in helping Albion win the Second Division title in 1901-02. Not always at ease when opposed by an intricate dribbler, he was, however, a very efficient player going forward. He skippered Albion for three seasons at the turn of the century and went on to score four goals in 88 appearances for the club after joining from Wolverhampton Wanderers in 1901. Born in West Bromwich in 1873, and a former Princes End and Coseley player, Nurse led by example. He represented the Football League in 1902-03, but two years later was forced to retire through injury. He became an Albion director in 1910, staying in office until 1927, having been elected a life member of the club in 1920 (in recognition of his sterling efforts to help keep Albion in existence during the summer of 1910). He died in 1959, aged 85.

OLDHAM ATHLETIC

Albion's record against the Latics:

Football League

Venue	P	W	D	L	F	A	Pts
Home	24	10	10	4	27	18	34
Away	24	5	5	14	22	38	17
Totals	48	15	15	18	49	56	51

Simod Cup

Venue	P	W	D	L	F	A	
Away	1	1	0	0	3	0	

Other Matches

Venue	P	W	D	L	F	A	
Away	3	2	0	1	3	5	

Albion lost their first game against Oldham, going down 2-1 in a Second Division fixture at Boundary Park on 14 September 1907.

Albion's biggest League win over the Latics is 3-0 on 21 March 1921 in an away First Division match.

Latics' best League win over Albion is 5-0 at Boundary Park on 1 January 1930.

Albion won their first League game after World War One, beating Oldham 3-1 at The Hawthorns on 30 August 1919.

In goal for the visitors was Howard Matthews, who was the son of the former Albion 'keeper of the 1880s.

Tony Brown scored the most important Albion goal against Oldham – the 55th minute match-winner at Boundary Park on 24 April 1976 which gave Albion a 1-0 victory and with it promotion to the First Division.

On 1 October 1921, 16-year-old Charlie Wilson made his debut in a League game at Oldham, becoming the youngest-ever player to appear for Albion in a competitive match (See AGE).

Albion were one of only a handful of teams to win two games on Oldham's plastic

Carl Valentine, played for Albion and the Latics.

pitch during the 1980s. They triumphed 3-0 in a Simod Cup-tie played there in 1987, and a year later were 3-1 victors in a Second Division game.

Albion League debutants v Oldham: Ike Evenson (1907), William Jackson (1913), Tommy Magee (1919), Andrew Smith (1919), Charlie Wilson (1921), Jimmy Cookson (1927), Mick Martin (1975), Don Goodman (1987), Steve Lynex (1987), Tony Kelly (1987), Ian Banks (1989), Adrian Foster (1990), Tony Brien (1995).

Players with both clubs: Tommy Broad, David Cross, Mark Grew, Henry Hancock, Bill Harris, Asa Hartford, Fred Leedham, Peter McKennan, George McVitie, David Shaw, Ray Treacy, Carl Valentine.

Also associated with both clubs: Andy Goram was Albion's reserve goalkeeper before joining Oldham (1981-87) and then going on to to play for Hibernian (1987-91), Rangers and Scotland, and Bill Asprey was a defender with Oldham and later coach at The Hawthorns.

OSBORNE, John

One of Albion's finest post-war goalkeepers, Osborne appeared in 312 competitive matches during his 11 years at The Hawthorns (divided into two spells). Alert and intelligent (both as a footballer and in quizzes!), courageous and commanding, he suffered several hand injuries during the early part of his career, which resulted in a strip of plastic being inserted into one of his fingers, hence his title 'The bionic goalkeeper'. Born in Barlborough, Derbyshire in 1940, 'Ossie' won England schoolboy honours as a wing-half

John Osborne collects the ball during the 1968 FA Cup Final.

before being converted into a quality goalkeeper at Chesterfield, the club which has produced many good custodians over a period of years. He was signed by Albion manager Jimmy Hagan for £10,000 early in 1967 and over the next five years contested the number-one spot with Dick Sheppard, Jim Cumbes, Peter Latchford and Graham Smith. He helped Albion win the FA Cup in 1968 and two years later was in their 1970 League Cup losing side. In 1973 'Ossie' quit Albion to run a sports business but returned to The Hawthorns after six months. He had a loan spell with Walsall before regaining his first-team place in 1975. He was in peak form when Albion won promotion in 1976, keeping 22 clean sheets and conceding only 33 goals – a club record. He left The Hawthorns in 1978 to join Shamrock Rovers (managed by his former boss, Johnny Giles) and thereafter acted as goalkeeping cover with several English clubs. In 1983-84 he managed non-League Corinthians FC, working also for the Sandwell Mail before becoming commercial manager of Worcestershire County Cricket Club.

OVERSEAS OPPOSITION

Albion's first overseas tour took them to Denmark and Sweden in 1909 and since then the club has been involved in competitive and friendly matches in 36 different countries: Abu Dhabi (1980), Argentina (1966), Austria (1961), Bahrain (1980), Belgium (1946, 1954, 1968, 1974), Brazil (1966), Canada (1959, 1969, 1981), China (1978), Cyprus (1982), Denmark (1909, 1979), East Germany (1979), Gibraltar (1992), Holland (1964, 1966, 1972, 1982, 1983), Hong Kong (1978, 1984), Italy (1967, 1970, 1971, 1980, 1993, 1995), Kenya (1968), Kuwait (1981), Luxembourg (1946), Norway (1969), Peru (1966), Portugal (1978, 1987), Republic of Ireland (1932, 1953, 1975, 1989, 1990), Rumania (1968), Saudi Arabia (1977), Spain (1958, 1971, 1977, 1978, 1979, 1981, 1982), Sweden (1909, 1972, 1981, 1984), Switzerland (1981), Syria (1978), Tanzania (1968), Tunisia (1985), Turkey (1978), Uganda (1968), Uruguay (1966), USA (1959, 1965, 1969, 1981, 1990), USSR (1957), Yugoslavia (1972, 1979, 1980).

At Stoney Lane and The Hawthorns, Albion have received visits from clubs in 21 different countries: Austria, Belgium, Canada, China, Czechoslovakia, East Germany, France, Holland, Israel, Italy, Japan, Malta, Portugal, Rumania, South Africa, Spain, Sweden, Switzerland, Turkey, USSR, Yugoslavia.

Joe Kennedy heads clear against FC Zenit during Albion's tour of the USSR in 1957. The Albion goalkeeper is Fred Brown.

Overseas competitions in which Albion have participated include the New York International Tournament (1965), the Brussels Le Soir Festival of Football (v Honved 1954), the Palo Alto International Tournament (1969), the Anglo-Italian Tournament (1970, 1971, 1993 and 1995), the Swedish Orendscupen Tournament (1969 and 1972), the Trofeo Costa Blanca (1977), the Trofeo Teresa Herrera (Spain 1979), the Trofej Marjan Tournament (Yugoslavia 1980), Sevilla International Tournament (1981), Barcelona International Tournament (1982) and the San Jose Cup (1990).

Albion's tour party for the USA and Canada in 1959. From left to right are Ronnie Allen, Derek Hogg, Alec Jackson, Davey Burnside, Graham Williams, Clive Jackman, Archie Styles, Bobby Cram, Chuck Drury, Keith Smith, Bobby Robson (on steps on bus), Joe Kennedy, Dick Graham, Brian Whitehouse, Ray Potter, Stuart Williams, Maurice Setters and Ray Barlow with his daughter.

And of course Albion appeared in the European Fairs Cup in season 1966-67, the European Cup-winners' Cup in 1968-69 and the UEFA Cup in 1978-79, 1979-80 and 1981-82.

Albion had provisionally arranged a close season tour to Germany in 1954 (after their FA Cup triumph) but this was postponed due to international call-ups and injuries to key players.

Facts & Figures

First match v overseas opposition: 27 October 1888 v The Canadians (home) 1-0

Biggest home win: 11-6 v Kaffirs (h) 22 November 1899

Biggest away win: 15-0 v Alberta All Stars (in Calgary) 27 May 1959

Heaviest defeat: 0-6 v Polonia Bytom (in New York) 25 July 1965

Albion were undefeated in three tour games in USSR in 1957 and became the first professional team from Britain to win in this country.

Albion scored 59 goals in nine games during their tour of Canada and USA in 1959.

As FA Cup holders, Albion toured East Africa in 1968 and were undefeated in six matches.

In May 1978 Albion became the first professional European club side to win in China.

The furthest Albion have played away from The Hawthorns is at Shanghai in the People's Republic of China in May 1978 – some 7,800 miles from West Bromwich.

In a Trofeo Costa Blanca match in Alicante, Spain, in August 1977, two Albion players, John Wile and Mick Martin and their manager Ronnie Allen, were all sent-off. This was the first time in the club's history that two first-team players had been dismissed in the same game.

Mexican international striker Hugo Sanchez scored five goals in Real Madrid's 6-1 victory over Albion in the San Jose Cup in America in May 1990.

The largest crowd ever to watch Albion play in an overseas match – 95,300 – assembled in Belgrade for the UEFA Cup clash with Crvena Zvezda (Red Star) on 7 March 1979.

Up to the end of the 1995-96 season, Albion's complete record abroad (v overseas clubs) is:

P	W	D	L	F	A
129	63	32	34	299	170

OVERSEAS PLAYERS

Alexis Suave, a Gibraltese, was the first 'overseas' footballer to play for Albion, doing so in a Birmingham Cup game against Notts Rangers on 23 January 1890. Albion won the tie and Suave scored a hat-trick in this his only outing for the club!

Here is a list of the other 'overseas-born' players who have been associated with Albion:

Player	Birthplace	With Albion
Fred Waterfall	New York, USA, 1895	1913-14
Jack Hemming	Alice Springs, Australia, 1886	1905-08
Alex Kirally	Budapest, Hungary, 1940	1960-61
Milton Labhaya	Born Nigeria, 1958	1973-74
Glen Johnson	Vancouver, Canada, 1951	1969-72
Marl Leetion	Johannesburg, South Africa, 1956	1972-75
Cyrille Regis	Maripiasoula, French Guyana, 1958	1977-84
Brendon Batson	Grenada, West Indies, 1953	1978-84
Patrick Wasmuth	Durban, South Africa, 1956	1977-78
Bruce Grobbelaar	Durban, South Africa, 1958	1978-79
Ivan Katalinic	Belgrade, Yugoslavia, 1951	1979-80
Maarten Jol	The Hague, Holland, 1956	1981-84
Romeo Zondervan	Paramaribo, Surinam, 1959	1982-84
Jimmy Nicholl	Hamilton, Canada, 1956	1984-86
Kevin Crowe	USA, 1964	1985-86
Drazen Muzinic	Split, Yugoslavia, 1953	1979-80
Vetle Andersen	Kristiansand, Norway, 1964	1989-90
John Paskin	Capetown, South Africa, 1962	1988-89
David Chabula	Zambia, 1967	1990-91
Frank Talia	Australia, 1970	1991-92
Januscz Gora	Poland, 1969	1991-92
Alan Giamattei	Italy, 1970	1992-93
Alister Roper	America	1993-94
Phillip Gyau	Nigeria, 1970	1993-94
Francois Ndanga*	Kinshaha, Belgian Congo 1963	1993-94
Augustine Equavon	Nigeria, 1970	1993-94

Jeroen Boere	Arnhem, Holland, 1967	1994-95
Richard Sneekes	Amsterdam, Holland, 1968	1995-96

* Full name: Francois Danga-Tumba

Goalkeeper Bruce Grobbelaar became a Zimbabwean international who made 628 League and Cup appearances for Liverpool (1981-94) before transferring to Southampton.

Both Jol and Zondervan were capped by Holland, the latter going on to make over 250 appearances for Ipswich Town. Albion paid £250,000 for Jol and £225,000 for Zondervan and both players were bought from Twente Enschede.

Right-back Nicholl, who was capped 73 times by Northern Ireland, also played for Manchester United (1973-82), Sunderland, Toronto Blizzard, Rangers and Dunfermline Athletic before becoming manager of Raith Rovers and then Millwall (1996).

Dutch international Maarten Jol.

Midfielder Sneekes, also played for Ajax, and joined Albion from Bolton Wanderers for £400,000 in March 1996. He scored in each of his first three League games for Albion.

Striker Boere also played for Go Ahead, West Ham United, Portsmouth and Crystal Palace before joining Southend United for £180,000 in 1996.

Left-back Alberto Tarantini, a 1978 World Cup winner with Argentina, guested for Albion in Len Cantello's testimonial match 12 months later. In 1996 Tarantini was charged with alleged possession of drugs.

Ossie Ardiles, an Argentinian team-mate of Tarantini in 1978, managed Albion for the 1992-93 season (See MANAGERS).

Outside-right Ryzard Krzywicki was born in Penly, Flintshire in 1947. His father was Polish, his mother Welsh, and he went on to play for Wales.

Ivan Katalinic, Albion's Yugoslavian international.

OWEN, Gary A.

A ball-playing midfielder with good skills and excellent vision, Owen had seven seasons at The Hawthorns during which time he scored 26 goals in 229 appearances for Albion. Born in St Helen's in 1958, he played his early football with Eccleston Youth Club and Warrington & District Boys before joining Manchester City in 1972, becoming a professional in 1975. Four years later and already an established England Under-21 international (he won 22 caps at this level), Owen was transferred to Albion for £465,000 and quickly became a favourite with the supporters. Unfortunately towards the end of his Baggies' career he suffered with injuries (including a fractured shin bone at West Ham) and finally left the club in 1986 for the Greek side, Panionios, later playing for Sheffield Wednesday and Apoel Nicosia. He retired in 1990 and became an art dealer in North Staffordshire/Cheshire.

Gary Owen, scored 26 goals in 229 appearances for Albion.

OXFORD UNITED

Albion's record against United:

Football League

Venue	P	W	D	L	F	A	Pts
Home	8	7	1	0	18	6	20
Away	8	3	4	1	10	7	12
Totals	16	10	5	1	28	13	32

Other Matches

	P	W	D	L	F	A
Away	2	1	1	0	4	3

Oxford, initially known as Headington United, first met Albion in a Second Division game at The Hawthorns on 8 December 1973. Albion won 1-0 with a goal by substitute David Shaw.

Albion's best win over United is 3-0 – at home on 28 September 1974 (also in Division Two).

United have beaten Albion just once in the League – at The Manor Ground on 20 April 1974.

Oxford's first League fixture in the top flight was against Albion at The Hawthorns on 17 August 1985. The result was a 1-1 draw – and this point was the only one Albion obtained in the opening ten games of that season!

Albion League debutants v Oxford: Garth Crooks (1985), Imre Varadi (1985), Craig Shakespeare (1990).

Players with both clubs: Norman Aldridge, Gary Bannister, Bobby Barker, John Durnin, Peter Hucker, Mickey Lewis, Paul Reece, John Trewick, Imre Varadi.

Also associated with both clubs: Ron Atkinson skippered Oxford both in the Southern League and Football League and later had two spells as Albion's manager; wing-half Gerry Summers played for Albion in the 1950s and was Oxford manager from 1969 to 1975; Ron Saunders managed Oxford in 1969 and Albion 1986-87; Mick Brown was a coach, assistant manager, then manager at Oxford (1970s)

Mickey Lewis (stripes) played for both Oxford and Albion. Here he is in opposition to Brighton's Tony Grealish, who later joined the Baggies.

and later assistant manager at Albion, and Matt Keeble was a reserve player with both clubs.

PAILOR, Robert

Bob Pailor was a hefty centre-forward with good pace, a powerful shot and strong heading ability. He averaged a goal

every two games for Albion (scoring 47 in 92 games) and was a key figure in their front-line during the six years leading up to World War One. He played a leading role during the run up to the 1912 FA Cup Final which ended in defeat at the hands of Barnsley. Born in Stockton-on-Tees in 1887, Pailor served with St Oswald's FC and West Hartlepool before joining Albion in 1908. He was transferred to Newcastle United in 1914 and actually made his debut for the Geordies against Albion! He spent a season at St James' Park before retiring with a kidney complaint. He later became a bookmaker and unfortunately went blind. He died in 1976.

PALMER, Carlton Lloyd

A tall, long-striding utility player who looked international class from a very young age, eventually going on to win full England honours as a midfielder. Born in Rowley Regis, West Midlands in 1965, Palmer played for a number of local teams (Netherton and Dudley Town included) before joining Albion on YTS forms in 1983, turning professional a year later. He made rapid progress after his League debut in 1985 (at Newcastle) and went on to score five goals in 140 games for Albion up to 1989 when he was sold to Sheffield Wednesday for £750,000. From Hillsborough he moved to Leeds United for £2.8 million in 1994 and during 1996 took his senior appearances to past the 500 mark including 18

full caps, five at 'B' team level and four Under-21s. He played for Leeds in the 1996 Coca-Cola Cup Final v Aston Villa.

PARTNERSHIPS
(See also PLAYERS)

In season 1919-20, Albion's defence of Hubert Pearson, Joe Smith, Jesse Pennington, Sammy Richardson, Sid Bowser and Bobby McNeal played together in 32 of the 42 League games and in one FA Cup-tie – a club record.

Albion fielded an unchanged team in 12 consecutive League games between 31 August and 9 November 1929.

Albion's forward-line of Colin Suggett, Tony Brown, Bobby Gould, Ally Brown and Asa Hartford remained unchanged for 18 consecutive matches from 6 September to 18 November 1972.

Tony Godden, Paddy Mulligan, Derek Statham, Tony Brown, John Wile and Alistair Robertson, wearing nos. 1-6, played in 18 successive League matches as a unit from 10 September to 27 December 1977.

England internationals Joe Smith and Jesse Pennington were full-back partners for Albion in 229 League games between 1910 and 1922 – a club record. George Shaw and Bert Trentham played at full-back together in 211 League games (1930-36).

John Wile and Alistair Robertson were Albion's defensive pairing in 573 games between October 1970 and May 1983 (404 League, 35 FA Cup, 39 League Cup, 12 European and 83 'others').

PEARSONS, (Harold Frederick & Hubert Pryor)

Between them, the goalkeeping Pearsons (Hubert and his son Harold) amassed a total of 680 first-team appearances for Albion over a period of 30 years (1908-37 inclusive). Their careers at The Hawthorns overlapped and as a family

Harold, who was also born in Tamworth in 1908, played for Belgrave United, Two Gates FC, Nuneaton Borough and Tamworth Castle prior to signing for Albion in 1925. He left the club for Millwall in 1937 and guested for West Ham United in the 1939-40 season. He later coached at The Hawthorns (1948-52) before becoming an Albion scout (1953-55). Harold died in West Bromwich in 1994.

NB: Former Birmingham and England goalkeeper Harry Hibbs (also born in Tamworth) was a cousin of Harold...and they opposed each other in that 1931 FA Cup Final at Wembley.

PEARSON, Thomas

Tom Pearson was a quality marksman who topped the club's scoring charts in the first five seasons of League Football, 1888-93. A brilliant inside-left, he had endurance, resilience and shooting power, and in 171 League and Cup appearances for the club, netted 88 goals (100 in all matches) and in fact, he missed only 14 matches (all through injury) during his six seasons with Albion. Born in West Bromwich in 1866, he joined Albion from the local Sandwell club in 1886 and played in three FA Cup Finals, 1887, 1888 and 1892, collecting winners' medals in the last two. Unfortunately he was forced to retire prematurely through injury (1894) and was a virtual cripple at the age of 30. Pearson died in West Bromwich in 1918.

PEMBERTON, James Henry Arthur

A strong, competent right-back, who gained a regular place in Albion's League side immediately after World War Two,

Top: **Hubert Pearson, scored two penalties for Albion despite being a goalkeeper.**

Right: **Harold Pearson tipping the ball over the bar during the 1931 FA Cup Final against Birmingham.**

they won a full set of club medals while playing professionally. Hubert, a fine line 'keeper, agile with a good pair of hands, who actually scored two penalties in 1911-12, was a member of Albion's First and Second Division championship-winning sides and their victorious FA Charity Shield team. Harold, who stood 6ft 2in. tall and weighed almost 14 stones, had an enormous pair of hands, could kick long and true and was brave and commanding inside the penalty-area. He played in Albion's 1931 FA Cup-winning XI and then in Millwall's 1939 Third Division South championship-winning team. Hubert also represented the Football League and the FA and Harold gained a junior international cap and made one full England appearance (v Scotland in 1932).

Hubert was born in Tamworth in 1886 and played for Kettlebrook Oakfield, Tamworth Castle and Tamworth Athletic before spending 20 years with Albion (1906-26). He retired after handing over his duties to George Ashmore and became a licensee in West Bromwich. He died in Tamworth in 1955.

and went on to hold his position for four years until suffering a crippling knee injury at Villa Park on the opening day of the 1950-51 campaign. Sadly he never played again – handing over the number-two shirt to Stan Rickaby. Jim Pemberton, born in Wolverhampton in 1916, played for Round Oak FC and Brownhills Albion before moving to The Hawthorns as an amateur in 1937, signing professional forms a year later. During the war, while serving as a Lance Corporal in the Royal Fusiliers based in North Africa and Italy, he played regularly for the Army and on his return became a permanent fixture in Albion's senior side, helping them win promotion to the First Division in 1949. He retired as a player in 1951 and when he died in Wolverhampton in 1995 he was almost completely blind.

PENALTIES

The penalty-kick was first introduced by the Irish FA in

Peter Barnes netting from the spot in Albion's 2-0 win at Coventry in March 1980.

1890. The English adopted it in September 1891 and immediately brought it into operation in the Football League.

Penalty Shots
The first penalty awarded to Albion was against Aston Villa in a home friendly match on 11 January 1892. Tom Pearson missed the kick by shooting over the bar.

Albion's first League penalty came in their Division One home game against Nottingham Forest on 3 April 1893. This time John Reynolds successfully netted from the spot to earn his side a 2-2 draw.

Reynolds was Albion's first recognised penalty-taker, scoring for the first time from the spot in a Bass Charity Cup-tie against Stoke (home) on 27 February 1893.

The first penalty conceded by Albion in a League match was away to Wolverhampton Wanderers on 19 September 1891. Fortunately Harry Allen, the home centre-half, skied the ball over the bar and Albion went on to win the game 4-3.

The first penalty scored against Albion in a League game was by Jock Campbell for Sunderland on 24 October 1891 on Wearside.

Roddy McLeod was the first player to miss a penalty for Albion in an FA Cup-tie – failing against Blackburn Rovers at Stoney Lane on 27 January 1894. (Albion lost 3-2).

'Chippy' Simmons was the first player to score a League penalty at The Hawthorns – for Albion against Chesterfield on 9 September 1901.

Bobby Blood (v Tottenham Hotspur in a home League game in 1921) and Cyrille Regis (v Rotherham United in a League Cup-tie, in 1977) both scored penalties on their Albion debuts.

Albion's Fred Buck netted a match-winning penalty against Huddersfield Town in the last League game of the 1910-11 season, and the 1-0 victory clinched the Second Division championship.

The most penalties awarded to Albion in a season is 14

(all matches) in 1957-58. Ronnie Allen scored from nine; Don Howe from two and Derek Kevan one. Allen missed the others! In 1919-20 Albion's centre-half Sid Bowser scored eight penalties.

Tony Brown beat Allen's club record of nine penalties when he netted ten in 1977-78 (seven in the League, two in the FA Cup and one in the Tennent-Caledonian Cup).

Before joining Albion, Willie Johnston scored a hat-trick of penalties for Glasgow Rangers against St Johnstone in a game at Muirton Park on 6 November 1971 – this after coming on as a substitute.

Goalkeeper Hubert Pearson scored from two penalty-kicks for Albion in home League games against Bury and Middlesbrough in 1911-12. Albion won both matches 2-0 and 3-1 respectively.

Goalkeeper Jim Sanders saved 28 penalties during his playing career (1940-59). As an Albion player (1945-58) he stopped 20 spot-kicks, including nine in season 1948-49 when promotion was gained to the First Division.

Full-back Cecil Shaw had a 100% record off the spot as a Wolves player, but after joining Albion from Molineux, he missed his first penalty for the Baggies, hitting a post in an away FA Cup-tie at Coventry in February 1937.

Derek Kevan scored one penalty for Albion, the last goal of a 9-2 home League win over Manchester City in September 1957.

Ronnie Allen became only the third player to score a penalty in an FA Cup Final at Wembley – for Albion v Preston in 1954.

Albion were beaten 4-3 in a penalty shoot-out by Colchester United in the Watney Cup Final of 1971; 3-1 by Southampton in the semi-final of the Tennent-Caledonian Cup in 1978 and 5-4 by Chelsea in the Southern Area semi-final of the Full members Cup in 1985.

Albion have registered one penalty shoot-out triumph – 4-1 over Birmingham City at St Andrew's in the English semi-final of the Anglo-Italian Cup in 1996.

Blackburn Rovers' full-back Bill Eckersley scored an 86th minute penalty to knock Albion out of the FA Cup in 1952.

Albion missed two penalties in home League games against Leeds United in 1959, Swindon Town (1989) and Port Vale (1991). The latter deprived the team of a much-needed win at a crucial stage in the season!

Tony Brown is Albion's most successful penalty-taker in the club's history, netting 55 times from the spot out of 63 kicks taken. His 50th conversation was against Aston Villa in a League game at The Hawthorns on 25 November 1978. He missed two penalties against Manchester United and two against Leicester.

Albion's main penalty-takers over the years: John Reynolds (1893), Billy Williams (1896-1901), Jack Kifford (1902-03), George Dorsett (1903-04), Ted Pheasant (1904-06), Fred Buck (1907-11), Sid Bowser (1919-22), Stan Davies (1923-25), Tommy Glidden (1926-28), George Shaw (1928-32), Teddy Sandford (1934-36), Cecil Shaw (1937-39), Dave Walsh (1946-49), Ronnie Allen (1951-60), Don Howe (1961-64), Bobby Cram (1964-67), Tony Brown (1967-80), Peter Barnes/Gary Owen (1980-83), Garry Thompson (1983-84), Derek Statham (1984-85), Steve Hunt/George Reilly (1985-87), Tony Morley/Brian Talbot/Colin Anderson/Bernard McNally/Don Goodman/Graham Roberts (1990-91), Craig Shakespeare (1991-92) and from 1993 to date Lee Ashcroft/Ian Hamilton/Bob Taylor/Andy Hunt have all been handed the job with Ashcroft the most successful.

PENNINGTON, Jesse

One of the greatest names in the annals of West Bromwich Albion Football Club, Jesse 'Peerless' Pennington was a superbly equipped left-back, scrupulously fair in his play, hardly ever committing a foul. Beautifully balanced, sure-

footed, with tremendous kicking ability, he was never given the run-around by a winger, and besides being a wonderful captain, he was also a dedicated sportsman and a clubman of the highest calibre. Born in West Bromwich in 1883, he was missed by Aston Villa, and played for Dudley Town before joining Albion in 1903. His debut came at Liverpool six months later and for the next 19 years he was an automatic choice in the side, going on to amass 496 first-team appearances. He was a vital member of Albion's Second Division championship-winning side of 1910-11 and their 1912 FA Cup Final team 12 months later and then skippered Albion to the Football League championship in 1919-20. In between times he won 25 England caps (1907-20), represented the Football League on nine occasions, played for an England XI five times, and also starred in five international trials. He skippered both club and country and his partner in 23 of his 25 outings for England was the Blackburn Rovers' full-back Bob Crompton. Pennington had a minor disagreement with Albion in 1910 (over pay) and

signed for Kidderminster Harriers! But that dispute was soon settled and he was back with Albion in double-quick time. In 1913 Pennington was the subject of an attempt at bribery, but the police quickly sorted things out and the culprit was duly sentenced to six months imprisonment (See BRIBERY). After retiring in 1922 Pennington became a soccer coach at Malvern College. He then scouted for Wolverhampton Wanderers (1938-39) and Albion (1950-60). In 1969 he was made a life member of West Bromwich Albion FC – a fitting tribute to a king-size footballer. Pennington died at Kidderminster in 1970.

PERRY FAMILY

There have been eight members of the Perry family associated with West Bromwich Albion Football Club since 1884 – five brothers (all players) Charles, Walter, Thomas, Edward and William; then two more players, Arthur and his brother Eric (sons of Charlie) and since 1977, Douglas, son of Arthur. In fact, there was a sixth brother, Frank, who was employed at Salter's spring works but never played football, while Arthur had two more sons, Ernest and Charles, who again didn't take to football.

Charlie Perry – Born in West Bromwich in 1866, and a teenage player with West Bromwich Strollers (not Albion), he played 219 games and scored 16 goals for Albion between 1884 and 1896. A tall, polished centre-half, with poise and fine positional sense, he won three England caps and also played for the Football League XI as well as starring in the 1886, 1887, 1888 and 1892 FA Cup Finals for Albion. He

Charlie Perry, played in four FA Cup Finals for Albion.

missed the 1895 Final through injury. He was a regular member of Albion's first team for nine years and on his retirement (in 1896) was made a director. He later became a licensee in West Bromwich, the town where he died in 1927.

Walter Perry – Born in West Bromwich in 1868, he was an inside-forward who scored seven goals in 15 games during two separate spells with Albion (1886-89 and 1894-95). He also served with West Bromwich Excelsior (1885),

Wolverhampton Wanderers, Warwick County and Burton Swifts (between his days at Albion) and Burton Swifts (again) at the end of his career. He retired in 1900 and was later appointed Albion's reserve-team manager (1906-07). He then became a League linesman (1909-12). Walter died in West Bromwich in 1928.

Tom Perry – Born in West Bromwich in 1871, he started his career with Christ Church FC in 1886 and played also for West Bromwich Baptist and Stourbridge before signing for Albion in 1890. He remained at the club until 1901, accumulating 291 appearances and scoring 15 goals. He won one England cap and played three games for the Football League (1894-98). He was Albion's

Walter Perry, scored seven goals in 15 games for Albion and was later reserve-team manager.

right-half in the 1895 FA Cup Final and joined Aston Villa after leaving The Hawthorns. He retired in 1903 and went into business in West Bromwich. Ironically Tom died in the town two weeks after his brother, Charlie.

Edward Perry – Born in West Bromwich in 1878, he was a reserve defender with Albion for two seasons 1899-1901 and played minor football after leaving The Hawthorns. He died circa 1950.

Arthur Perry – Albion's full-back in 81 League and Cup games during the 1920s. Strong in the tackle, he partnered both Joe Smith and Dicky Baugh and was always totally committed. Born in West Bromwich in 1897, he joined Albion from West Bromwich Baptist in 1921, and within two years gained a junior international cap. He stayed six years at The Hawthorns before transferring to Wellington Town, later playing for and also managing Brierley Hill. He then took charge of Dudley Town in 1935 before retiring from football two years later. He became an Albion scout, a position he held until 1951. He died in West Bromwich in 1977.

Bill Perry – Born in West Bromwich in 1900, he played

Arthur Perry, 81 League and Cup games for Albion in the 1920s.

for Albion's third and fourth teams as utility forward in the 1920s and later served with Dudley Town. He died circa 1970.

Eric Perry – Born in West Bromwich in 1907, and an amateur throughout his life, he had two spells with Albion as a defender: 1923-26 and 1930-32, but never played in the first team. In between times he served with Wellington Town, Willenhall and Bilston United and in 1932 joined Coventry City. He played 43 games during a two-year spell

at Highfield Road before ending his footballing career with Dudley Town (1935-37). Thereafter he concentrated on playing cricket for West Bromwich Dartmouth and Staffordshire, and if he'd been a 'pro' he would have surely played for England as a batsman, for he was highly rated by Douglas Jardine, a Test Match captain. His career with Dartmouth ran from 1923 to 1951, and he scored 16 centuries and took five wickets in an innings on nearly 30 occasions. He also played golf for Staffordshire and was a county golfer up until the age of 58. He died in March 1988.

Doug Perry – The youngest son of Arthur, he has been an Albion shareholder since the death of his father in 1977 and now runs a motorcycle shop in West Bromwich.

PETERBOROUGH UNITED
Albion's record against Peterborough:

Football League

Venue	P	W	D	L	F	A	Pts
Home	2	2	0	0	7	0	6
Away	2	0	1	1	0	2	1
Totals	4	2	1	1	7	2	7
League Cup							
Home	2	1	0	1	2	4	
Away	3	2	0	1	7	4	
Totals	5	3	0	2	9	8	
Texaco Cup							
Away	1	0	0	1	1	2	
Anglo-Italian Cup							
Home	1	1	0	0	3	1	
Other Match							
Away	1	1	0	0	2	0	

Albion first met Peterborough in season 1965-66, when they were paired together in the semi-final of the League Cup.

Martin Pike, on the books of both Albion and Peterborough.

Albion won the first-leg 2-1 at The Hawthorns on 1 December, and then took the second leg a fortnight later at London Road by 4-2 with Tony Brown netting a hat-trick. Former Albion manager Gordon Clark was boss of 'Posh' at the time and Vic Crowe, an amateur at The Hawthorns in the 1950s, was their skipper.

Two years later 'Posh' gained their revenge for that 6-3 aggregate defeat by knocking Albion (the FA Cup holders) out of the League Cup 2-1 at home on 25 September 1968. A youthful John Wile was the star of the home defence that night – and two years later he joined Albion! Peterborough also eliminated Albion from the League Cup in 1988-89, winning a second-round tie 3-2 on aggregate which included an impressive 3-0 victory at The Hawthorns. Neil Parsley made his debut for Albion in the Anglo-Italian Cup game in 1993.

Players with both clubs: Ian Benjamin, Paul Bradshaw, Tony Godden, Harry Guy, Gary Hackett, Roy Horobin, Lyndon Hughes, Tony Kelly, Derek Kevan, Noel Luke, Mick Martin, Alan Merrick, Tony Millington, Stuart Naylor, Tony Rees, Ronnie Robinson, Terry Simpson, Keith Smith, John Wile. Graham Easter made his only Albion appearance as 'sub' v Peterborough in the Littlewoods Cup in September 1988 while defender Chris Whyte made his senior debut for Albion against 'Posh' in that same Cup-tie.

Also associated with both clubs: Gordon Clark and Jimmy Hagan managed both clubs; John Wile played for and managed both clubs, being in charge at The Hawthorns on a caretaker basis and at London Road (1983-86). Five Albion reserves, Colin Brookes, Tom Daley, Bobby Downes, Martin Pike and Sid Glidden, later played for 'Posh.'

PHEASANT, Edward

Ted 'Cock' Pheasant was a real tough guy. As strong as an ox, he feared no one. He weighed well over 14 stones, and could play at either centre-half or centre-forward, always giving manly performances. Born in Darlaston in 1877, he

played for Wednesbury Excelsior and Wednesbury Old Athletic before joining Wolverhampton Wanderers in 1896. He scored 19 goals in 168 appearances whilst at Molineux, transferring to Albion in 1904. In 1899 he was selected to represent the Football League but declined the offer and played in a League game for Wolves instead. He went on to score 22 goals in 152 outings for Albion, up to 1910, when he moved to Leicester Fosse. Sadly he died two weeks later of peritonitis, aged 33.

PLAY-OFFS (League)

After a nail-biting second-half to the 1992-93 campaign, Albion qualified for the Second Division promotion Play-offs by finishing fourth in the final League table. In the semi-final they were paired with Swansea City, playing the first leg at The Vetch Field on 16 May 1993. Backed by 4,000 supporters in a crowd of 13,917, Albion played well below par and were beaten 2-1, but that crucial 'away' goal (courtesy of City's Andy McFarlane) was certainly a boost to morale when the second leg was played three days later at The Hawthorns. On a special night, in front of a 26,045 all-

ticket crowd (paying over £150,000 at the gate) Albion ran out winners by 2-0 (Andy Hunt and Ian Hamilton the scorers) and so booked their place in the Wembley Final against Port Vale.

Two players – Micky Mellon (Albion) and City's Colin West, himself a former Baggies man – were both sent-off, and as a result the unfortunate Mellon missed the final!

Over 42,000 Albion fans flocked to Wembley on Sunday 30 May 1996 to cheer on Ossie Ardiles' men and at the end of the day it was Albion who celebrated promotion, beating Vale 3-0, Hunt, Nicky Reid and Kevin Donovan the scorers. Vale were reduced to ten men in the second-half when defender Peter Swan was dismissed after a 'professional' foul on Bob Taylor. Albion's team at Wembley was: Tony Lange; Reid, Steve Lilwall; Darren Bradley, Gary Strodder, Paul Raven; Donovan, Hamilton, Taylor, Hunt and Bernard McNally. Subs: Gary Robson and Simon Garner. The official attendance was 53,471.

PLAYERS

In 118 years of playing football, competitively or otherwise, Albion have utilised well over 1,500 players in their first team. If you add to that total the vast number of reserves, juniors and wartime guests who have turned out for the club at various levels, then the amount of footballers who have donned the Albion colours since 1878 is in the region of 4,000 – probably nearer 4,500.

Guest Players

During World War One (1915-19) Albion recruited only a handful of guest players in the few fixtures they fulfilled, but during World War Two (1939-46), a total of 42 guests turned out in the 298 matches which Albion contested, and listed here, in A-Z order, are those guests:

Birmingham City's England goalkeeper Gil Merrick, who guested for Albion during World War Two.

Jack Acquaroff (Norwich City), Matt Armstrong (Aberdeen), Harry Ashley (Darlington), George Billingsley (Aston Villa), Alan Brown (Huddersfield Town), Ken Butler (Birmingham University), James Bye (Birmingham), Don Dearson (Birmingham), Peter Doherty (Manchester City), Maurice Dunkley (Manchester City), Len Duns (Sunderland), George Edwards (Aston Villa), Lester Finch (Barnet), Ted Goodall (Bolton Wanderers), Tommy Green (Coventry City), W.Griffiths (Bury), Billy Guest (Blackburn Rovers), Eddie Hapgood (Arsenal), George Hardwick (Middlesbrough), Jimmy Jinks (Millwall), Sam Jones (Blackpool), Harry Lane (Plymouth Argyle), Jack McDonald (Bournemouth), Norman Male (Walsall), George Marks (Arsenal), George May (Dulwich Hamlet), Gil Merrick (Birmingham), Peter McKennan (Partick Thistle), Jimmy McCormick (Tottenham Hotspur), Harry Parkes (Aston Villa), Billy Price (Huddersfield Town), Walter Quinton (Birmingham), Jimmy Sanders (Charlton Athletic), Laurie Scott (Arsenal), Jack Shelton (Walsall), Hedley Simms (Wellington Town), Tom Smalley (Northampton Town), Jack Smith (Chelsea), Jack Smith (Sheffield United), Les Smith (Brentford), Billy Walsh (Millwall), Tom Wood (Newport County).

NB: Frank Manders (Norwich City) guested for Albion reserves and was tragically drowned in Sutton Coldfield in March 1942.

George Best in Albion's colours, as a guest player in Jeff Astle's testimonial game in 1974.

McKennan and Sanders both joined Albion after the war as players; Ashley, Green and Male had been professionals at The Hawthorns before the hostilities and Chelsea's Jack Smith returned to manage Albion in 1948.

Occasionally, in testimonials/benefit matches in particular, players are 'invited' to take part in the action and since the mid-1970s internationals Bobby Charlton, Derek Dougan, Nobby Stiles, Carlton Palmer, Bryan Robson, Alberto Tarantini and George Best have all worn Albion's colours in games at The Hawthorns.

In 1972 goalkeeper John Farmer (Stoke City) 'guested' for Albion during their tour of Sweden and against Feyenoord in Holland.

And the Wolves defender, Charlie Mason, 'guested' for Albion in the 'Championship of the World' game against Renton in 1888.

In contrast, Albion themselves allowed players to 'guest' for other clubs during World War Two, among them: 'Ike' Clarke, Eddie Connelly, Jimmy Duggan, Cliff Edwards, Billy Elliott, Charlie Evans, Sammy Heaselgrave, Bill Harris, Eric Jones, Harry Jones, Harry Kinsell, Harry Lowery, 'Sandy' McNab, Bobby Newsome, Arthur Rowley, Jack Sankey, Danny Smith, Bill Tudor, Lew Twigg and Doug Witcomb.

Most-travelled Player
Sidney Glidden, born 1907 in Sunderland and brother of Albion's 1930s skipper Tommy, won England schoolboy honours as a teenager and joined Albion as an amateur in 1923. After leaving The Hawthorns in 1928 he played for Halifax Town, Worcester City, Doncaster Rovers, York City, Peterborough & Fletton United, Newport County, Loughborough Corinthians, Larne (Ireland), Wigan Athletic, Blyth Spartans, Hyde United, Reading, Colwyn Bay (player-manager) and Hereford United. He retired in 1939 and was a PT instructor during the war, before taking over as trainer at

Leyton Orient. He next became a physiotherapist with the Stoke-on-Trent Education Committee, combining the job with that of player-manager of Congleton Town. In 1952 he was appointed Stoke City's trainer and quit football in 1955 having been associated with 21 different clubs in 25 years. He died in 1980.

Short Service
Other than loan players, trialists and guests, of all the professional footballers to have signed for Albion, inside-right Stan Steele has the undistinguished tag of being the

Stan Steele, spent just 108 days with Albion in 1961.

one who has stayed the shortest time with the club. He was signed from Port Vale on 16 March 1961 and returned to Vale Park three months and 17 days later having made just one League appearance for the Baggies (at Blackburn).

Ian Banks joined Albion from Bradford City on 27 March 1989 and left the club for Barnsley on 24 July 1989.

Full-back Willie McCullum spent four and a half months with Albion (15 January-30 May 1891). Winger Ted Burton was at The Hawthorns under four months (1 March-30 June 1905) and those who have spent five months with Albion include: Ernie Ford (1922-23), Billy Johnstone (1889-90), Peter McKennan (1947-48), Jack Parry (1895) and Charlie Shaw (1888).

Several amateur footballers have also been associated with Albion for relatively short periods of time, among them: Billy Folks (1904), Sid Oliver (1888-89) and John Rea (1894-95).

Longest Named Player

In the mid-1930s Albion's reserve centre-half boasted no fewer than seven Christian names. He was Arthur Griffith

'Bos' Trevis, despite his nickname the Albion player with the longest name in the club's history.

Stanley Sackville Redvers Trevor Boscowen Trevis. His colleagues called him 'Bos' and he made one senior appearance, against Liverpool in 1934. He is also the longest-named player in Football League history.

Shortest Named Player

John Rix, an Albion wing-half (1927-39) has the honour of being the shortest named professional footballer to represent the club.

Irishmen

When Albion played Chesterfield in a home Second Division match on 7 April 1947, they had four Irish-born players in their line-up: Jack Vernon, Reg Ryan, Dave Walsh and Billy Lunn. In reserve was Irish goalkeeper John Tighe.

When Johnny Giles was player-manager at The Hawthorns (1975-77) his staff included

Jack Rix, the Albion player with the shortest name.

fellow Irishmen Mick Martin, Paddy Mulligan, Ray Treacy, John Anderson, Ray Cooke and Paddy Kelly. Giles, Martin, Mulligan and Treacy – all full internationals – played together for the first time in the League v Derby County (a) on 25 September 1976. Anderson also went on to win senior caps.

Ray Treacy, one of four Irish internationals in the same Albion team.

Four Irish players – Gerry Armstrong, Robbie Dennison, Tony Grealish and Jimmy Nicholl – were registered with Albion in 1985.

A total of 23 'Irishmen' have played League football for Albion since 1888 – Armstrong, Louis Bookman, Tony Brien, Joe Connor, Bob Crone, Dennison, Alan Fettis, Giles, Grealish, Lunn, Bernard McNally, Martin, Hugh Morrow, Mulligan, Nicholl, Kieran O'Regan, Ryan, Jack Taggart, Tighe, Treacy, Vernon, Walsh and Paul A.Williams.

Williams, in fact, was the last Albion player to be capped by Northern Ireland.

Darren Patterson, an Albion reserve defender (1986-89) went on to win eight full caps for Northern Ireland (1994-96).

Johnny Giles has been the only Irishman to manage Albion (1975-77 & 1984-85).

Detailed in the Arsenal-Albion matchday programme of 21 December 1977 were nine Irishmen: Mulligan, Giles, Martin and Treacy for Albion and Rice, Nelson, O'Leary, Brady and Stapleton of Arsenal. All nine may well have figured in that League game but bad weather caused it to be postponed!

Scotsmen

When Albion signed goalkeeper Dave Stewart from Leeds United in November 1978, he became the 50th Scottish-born player to be registered with the club as a professional.

Nine of Albion's Scottish players of 1969-70. Left to right are Hughie Reed, Asa Hartford, Bobby Hope, David Hogg, Doug Findlater, Ray Wilson, Doug Fraser, Mark Cowan, Ally Robertson, Hugh MacLean and Jim Holton.

George Dudley joined Albion from the Vono Sports Club (Tipton) in November 1937 and in doing so became the first Scot to be associated with The Hawthorns club for 30 years. Tom Dilly had been the last in 1907 – and it is said that the absence of Scottish-born players was not merely chance, but the result of a definite policy, backed by club chairman Mr William Isaiah Bassett (who died in April 1937).

At the start of the 1967-68 season Albion had as many as nine Scottish-born League players on their books: Bobby Hope, Kenny Foggo, Eddie Colquhoun, Ray Wilson, Asa

Hartford, Dennis Martin, Hugh MacLean, Doug Fraser and Hughie Reed. And by 1969-70 the number of Scots on Albion's books had risen to 15 – one-third of the club's playing staff – an all-time record.

Over 60 Scottish-born players have represented Albion in senior competitions over the years, the following in the last ten years: Arthur Albiston, Andy Gray, Graeme Hogg, James McCue, Micky Mellon, George Reilly, Brian Rice, Alistair Robertson, David Speedie and Bobby Williamson.

Albion have had two Scottish-born managers – Archie Macaulay (1961-63) and Ron Wylie (1982-83).

For players who have served with Albion and with Scottish League clubs see SCOTTISH CONNECTION.

Welshmen

Albion fielded an all-Welsh half-back line for the Second Division League game against Burnley on 17 September 1938 – Jimmy Murphy, Bill Tudor and Doug Witcomb.

More than 40 Welshmen have played League football for Albion, including four Davies's – Arthur, Llewellyn, Bill and Stan.

Welsh international full-backs Graham and Stuart Williams (not related) played together in competitive games for Albion and in major internationals for their country. Stuart Williams won a record 33 caps while with Albion (See INTERNATIONALS).

Graham Williams, one of over 40 Welshmen to appear in Albion's colours. He played alongside fellow Welsh international Stuart Williams, who was no relation.

Andy Dibble, Paul Mardon, Tony Rees and Mickey Thomas were all capped by Wales in the last ten years and all played for Albion.

Jack Smith is the only Welshman to have managed Albion (1948-52).

North-East Born Players

Around 50 footballers from the North-East of England (known as the 'Hotbed of Soccer') have been associated with Albion over the years, among them full internationals Bill Ashurst, Bobby McNeal, 'W.G.' Richardson, Stan Rickaby, Bryan Robson and Bobby Robson.

Others who have won intermediate and representative honours include: Barry Donaghy, Tommy Glidden, Derek Hogg, David Mills, Gordon Nisbet, Gary Robson, Colin Suggett and John Trewick.

Ian Collard, Bobby Cram, Ronnie Fenton, Eddie Readfern, Fred Richardson and John Wile were six more North-East born, post-1945 players who starred for Albion.

Ronnie Fenton, one of the many Albion players recruited for the North-East 'Hotbed of Soccer'.

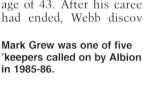

Goalkeeper Bob Ward, before Steve Lynex he was the most recent West-Bromwich-born player to appear for the Baggies.

Local Born Players

Winger Steve Lynex was the last West Bromwich-born player to appear in Albion's League side (1987-88). Prior to Lynex, it had been goalkeeper Bob Ward (1976-77).

Carlton Palmer (born in Rowley Regis, two miles from West Bromwich) played for Albion's League XI between 1985 and 1989.

There have now been almost 90 West Bromwich-born players registered with the Albion as professionals (1885-1996) and in the early years virtually every member of the first-team squad came from within a three or four-mile radius of the club's headquarters. When Albion won the FA Cup in 1888, every player in that side was a purely local-born (and bred) footballer.

Players – most, least used in a season

The fewest number of players used by Albion in a full 42-match League season is 17 – in 1977-78 and 1978-79.

The most players called up for duty in a full campaign has been 33 – in 1904-05 and 1985-86.

In the wartime season of 1942-43 Albion fielded 54 players in total, 43 in the Football League South – a club record.

Most Players in One Match

The most players used by Albion in one match is 21 – in a friendly against the Army at Aldershot Military Centre on 16 May 1983. The recognised team played in the first half and their second XI counterparts took the field after the break. Only goalkeeper Mark Grew played for the duration of the game and Alan Webb, who had appeared in the first 45 minutes, later came on as substitute. Albion won 5-0.

Goalkeepers

Albion's first registered goalkeeper was Sam Biddlestone (1879), although Bob Roberts played in the club's first recorded game v Hudson's in 1878.

Roberts was Albion's first full international – capped by England v Scotland in 1887. He also played in three successive FA Cup Finals: 1886-87-88.

Joe Reader, who succeeded Roberts, is the only player to appear on three different home grounds for Albion – Four Acres, Stoney Lane and The Hawthorns.

Hubert Pearson is the goalkeeper who served Albion longest: 20 years – 1906-26.

Ike Webb (an Albion League 'keeper: 1901-04) came out of retirement to play in World War One games for the club at the age of 43. After his career had ended, Webb discov-

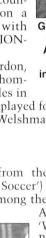

Mark Grew was one of five 'keepers called on by Albion in 1985-86.

ered he had been playing for some years with a fractured skull.

All of Tony Millington's first five League games for Albion in 1961 ended in draws (a unique record).

In 1962-63 Millington paid two visits with Albion to Molineux and conceded a total of 15 goals – seven in a First Division game and eight in a Central League match!

John Osborne conceded a club record low of 33 League goals in 42 Second Division matches in 1975-76. He also kept 22 'blank' sheets.

Four goalkeepers – Bob Roberts, Hubert Pearson (2), Jock Wallace and Jimmy Sanders – all scored goals for Albion in first or second team matches.

Albion fielded three different 'keepers in successive League games at the start of the 1969-70 season – John Osborne, Gordon Nisbet and Jim Cumbes.

Stuart Naylor made more senior competitive appearances (409+1) than any other Albion goalkeeper (1986-96).

Albion called on five different goalkeepers in all competitions in 1985-86 – Paul Bradshaw, Tony Godden, Mark Grew, Stuart Naylor and David Powell.

Full-backs

The first Albion full-back to win a full England cap was Albert Aldridge v Ireland in 1888.

Jesse Pennington has been the longest-serving Albion full-back of all-time, playing 496 games for the club between 1903 and 1922.

Joe Smith and Pennington were full-back partners in 229 League games for Albion (1910-22).

The Shaws – George and Cecil (not related) – were Albion's full-backs in 15 League games in 1937 and 1938.

The Williamses – Graham and Stuart – played as full-back partners for Albion and Wales in the late 1950s.

Bobby Cram scored a hat-trick from the right-back position for Albion against Stoke City in a League game at The Hawthorns on 12 September 1964.

Albion's captains in the 1954, and 1968 FA Cup Finals were both left-backs – Len Millard and Graham Williams.

Derek Statham is the only Albion full-back to score on his League debut v Stoke City (away) on 18 December 1976.

Centre-backs

The tallest defender ever to play for Albion has been 1930s star Alf Ridyard, who stood 6ft 3ins tall.

Fred Buck, at 5ft 3ins has been the smallest centre-half in Albion's history (1911-14) and the smallest ever to appear in an FA Cup Final (1912).

Sid Bowser became the first Albion defender to score a hat-trick – doing so from the centre-half position in a home League game against Bradford City on 27 September 1919.

Alf Ridyard. at 6ft 3ins the tallest defender to play for Albion.

Wing-halves

Right-half Tommy Magee – the smallest player ever to appear in a League game for Albion (See HEIGHT) made his Albion debut in 1919 just months after signing for the club in the trenches of a French battlefield during World War One.

Lanky wing-halves were commonplace in football circles during the period 1945 to 1965 – and two of the tallest wing-halves ever to don an Albion shirt were Ray Barlow at 6ft 2ins) and Peter Billingham (6ft 3ins). Carlton Palmer (6ft 2ins) played wide midfield in the late 1980s.

Tony Brown (wearing number-four) scored a record 23 goals from a 'wing-half' position for Albion in 1968-69.

Goalscorers

Albion have always had a regular goalscorer in their first team every decade since the club joined the Football League, among them (listed in A-Z order): Ronnie Allen (1950-61), Jeff Astle (1964-74), Billy Bassett (1886-99), 'Jem' Bayliss (1884-92), Alf Bentley (1913-22), Bobby Blood (1921-24), Tony Brown (1963-80), Joe Carter (1921-36), Clive Clark (1961-69), Jimmy Cookson (1927-33), Stan Davies (1921-27), Billy Elliott (1938-51), Tommy Glidden (1922-36), Don Goodman (1987-92), Andy Hunt (1993-96), George

Dave Walsh, a prolific goalscorer for Albion after World War Two.

James (1920-29), Harry 'Popeye' Jones (1933-43), Derek Kevan (1953-63), Billy Lee (1901-04), Fred Morris (1911-24), Bob Pailor (1908-14), Tom Pearson (1886-92), Cyrille Regis (1977-84), 'W.G.' Richardson (1929-45), Fred Shinton (1906-08), 'Chippy' Simmons (1898-1907, two spells), Bob Taylor (1992-96), Dave Walsh (1946-50).

Wingers

Some of the quickest wingers to have played for Albion in League and Cup action were Billy Bassett, Lewis Bedford, Clive Clark, Billy Elliott, Dick Krzywicki, Willie Johnston and Hughie Reed.

Clive Clark scored a club record 32 goals for Albion from the outside-left position in season 1966-67 (19 League, 8 League Cup, one FA Cup, one Fairs Cup, three friendly).

Outside-left Ernie Shepherd played for three different clubs in season 1948-49 and each one won promotion from its respective Division – Albion and Fulham (Division Two) and Hull City (Division Three North).

Outside-left George Dorsett made his League debut for Albion on 4 January 1902. Twelve games later – 0n 29 March 1902 – he was on the losing side for the first time. A club record from debut day to first defeat: 11 matches.

Graham Williams started his Albion career as a outside-left (in 1955) and later became a Welsh international left-back.

Harry Kinsell played 158 games for Albion, all but one as a full-back. His third last appearance was at outside-left v Fulham in March 1949.

PLYMOUTH ARGYLE

Albion's record against Argyle:

Football League

Venue	P	W	D	L	F	A	Pts
Home	12	4	3	5	18	22	12
Away	12	1	4	7	13	23	6
Totals	24	5	7	12	31	45	18

FA Cup

Home	2	1	0	1	3	3	
Away	1	1	0	0	5	1	
Totals	3	2	0	1	8	4	

League Cup

Home	1	1	0	0	1	0	
Away	1	0	0	1	0	2	
Totals	2	1	0	1	1	2	

Other Matches

Home	1	1	0	0	5	2
Away	2	1	0	1	6	3

Argyle have an impressive League record against Albion and three of their 12 victories have been big ones: 5-1 at Home Park on 31 January 1931 (during Albion's epoch making season); 5-2 at The Hawthorns on 19 April 1947 and 5-2 (again on Albion soil) on 12 April 1993, at a time when the Baggies were in sight of the Play-offs. Steve Castle scored a hat-trick in 32 minutes for Argyle.

Albion's best League win over Argyle has been 4-2 at home on 31 December 1938, when Cecil Shaw ripped a hole in the net with a block-busting penalty.

Albion did the double over Argyle when gaining promotion from the Second Division in 1948-49 – winning 3-0 at home and 2-1 away, Dave Walsh scoring in both matches.

Geoff Barnsley, played for both Albion and Plymouth Argyle.

Albion scored twice in the last five minutes to earn a 3-3 draw at Plymouth in a Second Division game on 12 September 1987. Former Scottish international Andy Gray celebrated his Baggies' debut with two goals.

Albion twice knocked Argyle out of the FA Cup in the third round in the space of three years – winning 3-2 at The Hawthorns on 9 January 1960 (when Derek Kevan scored a hat-trick) and 5-1 Home Park on 5 January 1963.

Albion League debutants v Argyle: Norman Aldridge (1947), Roy Finch (1947), Andy Gray (1987). Stacy Coldicott made his first competitive appearance for Albion in a Coca-Cola Cup-tie v Plymouth Argyle (1992).

Players with both clubs: Kwame Ampadu, Jack Banks, Geoff Barnsley, Paul Barron, Fred Buck, Davey Burnside, Wilf Carter, John Chadburn, Andy Comyn, Jimmy Cookson, Stewart Evans, Ike Evenson, George Garrett, Les Horne, Alan Miller, Gordon Nisbet, Sid Rawlings, Hughie Reed, Arthur Smith, Kevin Summerfield, Billy Thompson, Paul R.Williams, Harry Wilcox.

Also Associated: Albion reserves David Campbell, Mick McCartney, Adrian Littlejohn and Luke Tinkler also played first-team football for Argyle; Vic Buckingham managed Albion (1953-59) and Argyle (1963).

PORTSMOUTH

Albion's record against Pompey:

Football League

Venue	P	W	D	L	F	A	Pts
Home	27	20	2	5	65	25	46
Away	27	12	9	6	42	40	36
Totals	54	32	11	11	107	65	82

FA Cup

Home	1	1	0	0	2	0
Away	3	2	0	1	3	3
Totals	4	3	0	1	5	3

Other Matches

Home	2	2	0	0	5	1
Away	5	1	0	4	5	11
Totals	7	3	0	4	10	12

Albion's first encounter with Portsmouth was a friendly match (away) on 10 December 1904. Pompey won 3-2.

Albion first opposed Portsmouth at competitive level in 1931 – beating them 1-0 in a fifth-round FA Cup-tie at Fratton Park on 14 February and 1-0 in a League Division One game later in the year, on 26 September. 'W.G.'

Richardson scored the winner in that Cup-tie – one of 15 goals he netted against Pompey.

Albion's best League victory over Pompey is 6-2, away, on 17 September 1958.

Portsmouth cruised to a 6-1 victory in a one-sided First Division game at muddy Fratton Park on 14 December 1954 – their best win at any level over Albion.

Portsmouth achieved back-to-back League championship triumphs in seasons 1948-49 and 1949-50. In the latter campaign they succumbed in both games against Albion, losing 3-0 at The Hawthorns and 1-0 at Fratton Park.

Albion beat the reigning League champions Portsmouth 5-0 at home on 9 September 1950 playing some excellent attacking football, and they repeated that scoreline on 20 October 1951 by producing a similar display of all-action soccer.

On their way to winning the FA Cup in 1968, Albion ousted Portsmouth 2-1 in a fifth-round tie at Fratton Park in front of a sell-out crowd of 42,642.

Goalkeeper Reg Davies made his Albion debut against Portsmouth in 1954.

Twelve years earlier, in January 1956, Albion won a fourth round match at The Hawthorns 2-0 before a near 60,000 crowd.

Albion's first-ever Sunday League game saw them draw 1-1 away at Portsmouth in Division Two on 3 February 1974.

Lee Ashcroft's headed goal gave Albion a 1-0 win at Portsmouth on the last day of the 1993-94 season – and the three points gained kept the Baggies in the First Division! Two goals by Dutchman Richard Sneekes gave Albion a 2-0 win at Portsmouth on 30 March 1996 to keep up the Baggies' fine record at Fratton Park – only one League defeat in 14 visits there since 1955.

Albion League debutants v Pompey: Reg Davies (1954), Brian Whitehouse (1956), Jimmy Campbell (1958), Clive Jackman (1958), Paul Raven (1989), Gary Hackett (1990), Gary Strodder (1990), Peter Butler (1996).

Players with both clubs: Kevin Bartlett, Jereon Boere, Fred Brown, Jimmy Campbell, Ike Clarke, Ian Collard, Fred Cook, Ray Crawford, Reg Cutler, John Durnin, Kenny Foggo, Fred Haycock, Graeme Hogg, Eric Jones, Jack Kifford, Billy Lee, Alan Miller, Ray Potter, Ken Swain, Fred Wheldon, Clive Whitehead, Bill Williams, George Young.

Also associated with both clubs: Brett Angell (Pompey trainee 1986), Ron Saunders was a Pompey goalscorer (1958-64) and later Albion manager, and Jasper Yuell was an Albion reserve and Pompey League player (1946-52). Mike Kelly, Albion coach in the early 1980s, had a brief coaching spell at Portsmouth before his arrival at The Hawthorns.

PORT VALE

Albion's record against the Vale:

Football League

Venue	P	W	D	L	F	A	Pts
Home	12	5	4	3	21	11	14
Away	12	3	0	9	14	29	7
Totals	24	8	4	12	35	40	21

Play-off Final

Wembley	1	1	0	0	3	0

FA Cup

Home	1	1	0	0	2	1
Away	1	1	0	0	2	1
Totals	2	2	0	0	4	2

Jimmy Dudley's equaliser against Port Vale in the 1954 FA Cup semi-final at Villa Park.

League Cup

Home	1	1	0	0	1	0
Away	1	0	1	0	2	2
Totals	2	1	1	0	3	2

Anglo-Italian Cup

Home	1	0	1	0	0	0
Away	1	0	0	1	1	3
Totals	2	0	1	1	1	3

Albion first met Vale on 19 April 1884, beating them 6-0 in a friendly at Burslem.

Albion's best League win is 4-1 – achieved twice at The Hawthorns on 28 April 1906 and 6 April 1931 (both games in Division Two).

When Vale whipped Albion 8-1 in the Potteries on 9 March 1929, all five home forwards found the net. The nine goals were scored between the 22nd and 76th minutes.

With five minutes remaining of a third-round FA Cup-tie at The Hawthorns in January 1935, Vale led Albion 1-0. But late goals from Arthur Gale and 'W.G.' Richardson gave Albion an undeserved 2-1 victory, and they went all the way to Wembley!

First Division Albion faced Third Division North Vale in the 1954 FA Cup semi-final at Villa Park on 27 March before a full-house crowd of 68,221. A shock looked on the cards when Albert Leake put Vale ahead on 40 minutes, but a lucky equaliser from Jimmy Dudley and a disputed penalty by ex-Vale man Ronnie Allen sent Albion through to Wembley 2-1.

Albion beat Port Vale 3-0 at Wembley in the Second Division Play-off Final of 1992-93, Andy Hunt, Nicky Reid and Kevin Donovan the scorers before a crowd of 53,471 (See PLAY-OFFS).

In season 1995-96 Vale reached the Final of the Anglo-Italian Cup by defeating Albion 3-1 on aggregate in the two-legged English Final (See ANGLO-ITALIAN CUP).

Albion League debutants v Vale: Isaiah Turner (1904), Harold Jones (1906), Jack Rix (1928), Daryl Burgess (1989), Gary Hackett (1980), Kevin Donovan (1992).

Players with both clubs: Ronnie Allen, Harry Aston, Peter Barnes, Kevin Bartlett, Bobby Blood, Louis Bookman, Alistair Brown, Nicky Cross, Reg Davies, Wayne Ebanks, Mark Grew, Ezra Horton, Jack Horton, Tony Kelly, Kevin Kent, Derek Monaghan, David Mountford, Jack Paddock, Stan Steele, Kevin Steggles, Alan Webb, Colin West, Winston White.

Also associated with both clubs: Albion reserves Sid Glidden, Welsh internationals Phil Griffiths and Keith Jones, Paul Kerr, Colin Lyman, Tim Rawlings, Albert Titley and 'Monty' Wilson all played first-team football for Vale; Bobby Downes (Albion reserve) and Steve Hunt (Albion League player) became coaches at Vale Park; John Westmancoat was secretary of Albion and Vale and Ray Fairfax was a full-back with Albion and Vale's secretary (late 1980s); Bill Asprey played for Vale (1967-68) and later became coach at The Hawthorns. Keith Leonard, a coach with Albion in 1986-87, played on loan with Vale (1973-74) and current Albion youth coach, Richard O'Kelly, was a Vale forward (1986-87) and later the club's community liaison officer.

POTTER, Raymond John

Albion manager Vic Buckingham signed Ray Potter on a free transfer from Crystal Palace in 1958 and in the next nine years the Beckenham-born goalkeeper appeared in 238 first-team games for the club, collecting a League Cup winners' prize in 1966.

Potter was 22 when he joined Albion and he gained a first-team place four months after moving from London. An unspectacular 'keeper, he had a safe pair of hands and rarely let the side down. After being replaced by John Osborne, he left The Hawthorns for Portsmouth in 1967. He announced his retirement three years later and became assistant

Goalkeeper Ray Potter, 238 senior appearances after joining the Baggies on a free transfer.

commercial manager of Colchester United, a position he held for two months prior to taking over as P.R.O./secretary of Bournemouth. In 1975 he returned to Fratton Park as administration officer, but in 1988 was out of football and working for a bakery in Hampshire.

PRESIDENTS

The position of president of West Bromwich Albion Football Club is an honorary one and does not confer a seat on the Board, although in the case of Mr Jim Gaunt, he occupied a dual role as a director and Club president for a year (1974-75).

Albion Club Presidents over the years have been:

George Salter	September 1882 – August 1904
Sir Ernest J. Spencer	September 1904 – July 1937
The Earl of Dartmouth	August 1937 – February 1958
Walter W. Hackett	September 1958 – April 1964
Major H. Wilson Keys	August 1964 – September 1974
James W. Gaunt	September 1974 – August 1984
F. A. 'Bert' Millichip	August 1984 to date

PRESTON NORTH END

Albion's record against fellow League founder-members Preston:

Football League

Venue	P	W	D	L	F	A	Pts
Home	43	19	11	13	71	58	51
Away	43	12	12	19	51	77	36
Totals	86	31	23	32	122	135	87

FA Cup

	P	W	D	L	F	A
Home	2	2	0	0	3	0
Away	5	3	0	2	9	9
Totals	7	5	0	2	12	9

League Cup

	P	W	D	L	F	A
Home	2	1	1	0	2	1
Away	2	1	1	0	2	1
Totals	4	2	2	0	4	2

Other Matches

	P	W	D	L	F	A
Home	8	4	2	2	17	12
Away	7	0	1	6	5	26
Totals	15	4	3	8	22	38

Two of the game's giants in the 1880s were Preston North End and West Bromwich Albion and clashes between the two always drew great interest from the sporting public.

The teams met as early as October 1883 when Preston won a home friendly match by 3-1.

Albion lost two more friendlies at Preston by 7-0 in May and early December 1886, but over Christmas 1886, Albion defeated North End 5-1 at Stoney Lane to set the scene for a titanic FA Cup semi-final showdown on 5 March 1887. Albion pulled out all the stops and beat the 'Invincibles' 3-1. Tom Pearson scored twice and goalkeeper Bob Roberts produced a superb display which earned him his first England cap.

The following season Albion and Preston both won through to the FA Cup Final at The Oval on 24 March 1888. It was Albion who came out on top (again), winning 2-1 against the odds with goals from George Woodhall and skipper 'Jem' Bayliss to lift the trophy for the first time. Preston had asked to be photographed with the Cup before

kick-off but London referee Major Marindin said 'No' and he was right! (See FA CUP).

Season 1888-89 saw the baptism of the Football League, and Preston gained sweet revenge for that Oval defeat by twice overcoming Albion in the League matches, winning 3-0 at home and 5-0 at Stoney Lane (this being their joint record win over Albion). They also accounted for Albion 1-0 in the FA Cup semi-final before a capacity crowd at Sheffield – on their way to clinching the double.

Albion and North End were relegated for the first time at the end of the 1900-01 season, and after losing their first-ever match in Division Two 1-0, Jimmy McLean, later to become a Preston half-back, scored Albion's first goal in this Division in a 3-1 home win over North End on 7 September 1901.

On 10 April 1937, Preston knocked Albion out of the FA Cup, beating them 4-1 at Highbury. This defeat came just two days after the death of The Hawthorns' chairman, Mr W.I.Bassett.

Albion's next major victory over Preston came in the FA Cup Final at Wembley on 1 May 1954. That day two goals by Ronnie Allen and a late effort from Frank Griffin brought them a 3-2 success (See FA CUP).

Albion achieved their best League win over North End at The Hawthorns on 2 January 1960, winning 4-0 before 24,000 fans.

Albion League debutants v Preston: Tom Perry (1890), Tom McCulloch (1891), Willie McCullum (1891), John Castle (1891), Chris Charsley (1891), Len Humpage (1894), Jack Parry (1895), Arthur Watson (1896), Arthur Smith (1901), George Dorsett (1902), Arthur Swift (1914), Roland James (1920), Dickie Baugh (1925), Dicky Dale (1928), Teddy Sandford (1930), Harry Lowery (1938), Geoff Barnsley (1955), Clive Clark (1961).

Players with both clubs: Sam Allardyce, Lee Ashcroft, Clive Clark, Stan Davies, Graham Easter, Fred Fenton, Arthur Fitton, Willie Hendry, Harry Jones, Jim McLean, Mick Martin, Tony Morley, Sid Rawlings, Bethel Robinson, John Thomas, Ray Treacy, Paul A.Williams, Harry Wilcox.

Also associated with both clubs: Nobby Stiles played for Preston (1973-75) and later became Albion's coach and then manager; Albion's chief scout Norman Bodell (1986-94) was a Preston North End coach in the 1970s; Albion reserve goalkeeper Barry Siddall (1990) played for Preston in 1992 and ex-Baggies' defender Sam Allardyce was caretaker manager at Deepdale (1993-94).

PROFESSIONALISM

Professionalism in football was very much frowned upon by the authorities in the 1880s, but eventually the FA officials came to realise that the paying of players could not be prevented. The Birmingham FA followed the official line for a while and suspended several local players for alleged professionalism, among them Tommy Green, who was later to play in Albion's 1886 FA Cup Final team. The authorities relented in 1885, however, and on 17 March of that year, the Albion committee appointed Henry Jackson and Tom Smith to represent the club at an FA meeting in London six days later to consider the question of the payment of players.

At Anderton's Hotel, London, on 20 July 1885, the Football Association legalised the remuneration of players, and Albion wasted no time in adopting professionalism, a committee meeting resolving on 11 August 1885 that the club should be registered as professional.

Albion's pioneer professionals received 10s (50p) a week, but were not given training expenses nor was loss of time allowed. This sum of money was not all that generous when one considers the discomforts players of that Victorian era had to put up with, such as poor dressing-room facilities (invariably damp, dimly lit and often without a bath), long

Len Millard and Tom Finney shake hands before the 1954 Albion-Preston FA Cup Final.

hours spent in draughty railway carriages travelling to and from away matches, having to work on a Saturday morning prior to a home game and then having to take the field on a cold day without having had a square meal.

Albion's first professionals included: 'Jem' Bayliss, George Bell, Harry Bell, Abel Tom Bunn, George Bushell, Harry Green, Tommy Green, Ezra Horton, Arthur Loach, Charlie Perry, Bob Roberts, George Timmins and George Woodhall.

PUBLIC LIMITED COMPANY

West Bromwich Albion Football Club became a Public Limited Company on 11 April 1996. Two new shares issues were introduced to supporters.

• 8,335 Premier shares (including a Premier certificate,

authentically signed by six Albion all-time greats) at £3,000 each.

• 8,335 'A' Ordinary shares at £500 each.

The holders of a Premier share certificate is entitled to an Albion season ticket for admission to The Hawthorns for each of eleven successive seasons commencing with the 1996-97 campaign.

At a poll it was agreed that every person holding either (a) a Premier share or (b) an 'A' ordinary share, will be entitled to one vote per share.

The share issue was partially underwritten by High House Ltd, which guaranteed that the Albion club would receive £2.5 million whether all the 16,670 new shares were issued or not.

It was also stated that West Bromwich Albion plc would not be quoted on the Stock Exchange.

The club's new address was given as WBA FC, Tom Silk Building, Halfords Lane, West Bromwich, B71 4BR.

NB: Albion first became a Limited Liability Company in August 1891 when a total of 495 shares were issued.

QUEEN'S PARK RANGERS

Albion's record against Rangers:

Football League

Venue	P	W	D	L	F	A	Pts
Home	8	3	3	2	10	7	9
Away	8	3	1	4	10	8	7
Totals	16	6	4	6	20	15	16

FA Cup

	P	W	D	L	F	A
Home	1	1	0	0	3	2
Away	1	0	0	1	0	1
Totals	2	1	0	1	3	3

League Cup

	P	W	D	L	F	A
Home	1	1	0	0	2	1
Away	1	0	0	1	2	3
Totals	2	1	0	1	4	4

Other Matches

	P	W	D	L	F	A
Away	2	2	0	0	6	2

Albion lost their two most important matches against Rangers – going down 2-3 in the 1967 League Cup Final at Wembley (See LEAGUE CUP) and then succumbing 1-0 in the FA Cup semi-final at Highbury in 1981. This latter game was decided by a second-half goal by Clive Allen who deflected Ally's Robertson's clearance past 'keeper Mark Grew.

The teams first met in League action in season 1948-49. Albion won 2-0 away and drew 1-1 at home, on their way to promotion.

On 28 December 1969 Albion inflicted a 4-0 defeat on Rangers at Loftus Road in a First Division match.

The first encounter between the teams was a friendly at Rangers' Harvist Road ground on 8 January 1898, which Albion won 4-1.

Albion League debutants v Rangers: Lyndon Hughes

Tony Morley made his Albion debut against QPR in 1983.

(1968), Tony Morley (1983), Steve Bull (1986).

Players with both clubs: Gary Bannister, Paul Barron, Clive Clark, Jimmy Dugdale, Peter Eastoe, Wayne Fereday, Allan Glover, Adam Haywood, Peter Hucker, Andy King, Billy Law, Alf Ridyard, Ernie Shepherd, Garry Thompson, Billy Thompson, Ike Webb, Fred Wheldon, Bill Williams.

Also associated with both clubs: Albion 1930s reserve Reg Banks later played for Rangers; Colin Anderson was on loan with Rangers (1985) before joining Albion; Gordon Clark was Albion manager (1959-61) and assistant manager at Rangers (1979-80); Don Howe was an Albion player and manager before coaching at Rangers and Mike Kelly was goalkeeping coach at The Hawthorns and Loftus Road. Steve Burke, an occasional Rangers first-team forward (1979-86) was an Albion reserve in 1986.

RANDLE, Arthur John

A junior international right-half in 1901, Arthur Randle went on to amass 143 appearances for Albion (two goals

scored) in the next seven years before transferring to Leicester Fosse in 1908. He left The Hawthorns under a cloud after losing his place to Sammy Timmins. Born in West Bromwich in 1880, he played for Oldbury Town and Darlaston as a teenager before moving to The Hawthorns where he became a superb passer of the ball as well as having a fine tactical brain. He died of cancer in Coventry in 1912.

RAVEN, Paul Duncan

A talented defender who has formed fine partnerships with Daryl Burgess, Gary Strodder and Paul Mardon during his

time with Albion. Strong in the tackle, commanding in the air, Raven has good pace and ability on the ground, and reached the milestone of 200 appearances for Albion during the 1995-96 campaign. Born in Salisbury in 1970, he joined Albion from Doncaster Rovers for £150,000 in 1989 and has since had a loan period back at Belle Vue. An England schoolboy international, he helped Albion win the 1993 Play-off Final at Wembley.

READER, Josiah

Rated one of the finest goalkeepers in the game during the 1890s, Joe Reader had marvellous reflexes, was a safe handler and used the fly-kick to good effect. He played in 370 games for Albion over a period of 16 years from 1885, having joined the club straight from school. Born in West Bromwich in 1866, he starred in both the 1892 and 1895 FA Cup Finals against Aston Villa, collecting a winners' medal in the former. The only Albion player to appear on the club's three major home grounds – Four Acres, Stoney Lane and The Hawthorns – he won one England cap and also represented the Football League and League XI. He retired in 1901 to become a trainer-coach at Albion, and was later steward at The Hawthorns until 1950, spending 65 years in total with the club (See LONG SERVICE). He died in West Bromwich in 1954.

READING

Albion's record against Reading:

Football League

Venue	P	W	D	L	F	A	Pts
Home	10	8	0	2	22	6	20
Away	10	5	3	2	21	15	16
Totals	20	12	3	3	43	21	36

FA Cup

Home	1	1	0	0	2	0	

League Cup

Home	1	0	0	1	2	4	
Away	2	0	1	1	2	4	
Totals	3	0	1	2	4	8	

Other Matches

Away	4	0	1	3	7	13	

The first meeting between the clubs was a friendly at Elm Park on 16 November 1901, Albion forcing a 1-1 draw.

Albion's best League win over the Royals is 5-0 at The Hawthorns on 30 March 1929.

On 17 November 1928, Albion lost 5-3 at Reading, despite a hat-trick from Jimmy Cookson, who scored a total of 12 goals in all games against the Royals, including four on 21 January 1928 (won 5-3).

Percy Freeman, played for Albion and Reading.

Reading knocked Albion out of the Coca-Cola Cup in 1995-96, winning 5-3 on aggregate after taking the second leg 4-2 at The Hawthorns.

Albion, League Cup Finalists the two previous seasons, were beaten 3-1 by Reading in this competition on 13 September 1967 before a near 19,000 Elm Park crowd. One of the Reading stars that evening was former Albion reserve winger Alan Scarrott.

Albion League debutants v Reading: Fred Leedham (1928), Martin Singleton (1986), Paul Barron (1989). Dennis Gordon made his debut for Albion in an FA Cup-tie v Reading in 1948.

Players with both clubs: Paul Barron, John Chadburn, Len Darnell, Percy Freeman, George James, Arthur Kelsey, Harry Kinsell, Alonzo Poulton.

Also associated with both clubs: Albion reserves George Irwin, Jack Lewis, Jim McIlvenney, Gary Phillips, Alan Scarrott and Jimmy Whitehouse all played for Reading; Jack Smith managed both clubs and Sid Glidden was an Albion reserve and later Reading trainer (13 years).

REED, Frederick William Marshall

Fred Reed was a loyal and dedicated servant to West Bromwich Albion Football Club. A rugged, no-nonsense centre-half, he made 157 appearances at first-team level and a similar number for the reserves between 1912 and 1927 (scoring five senior goals). On his retirement, he was appointed trainer at The Hawthorns, a position he held until 1950. Born at Scotswood-on-Tyne in 1894, he played

Fred Reed shakes hands with Sheffield United skipper Billy Gillespie in 1925.

for Lintz Institute before signing for Albion. He eventually replaced Sid Bowser in the Baggies' League side and when he called it a day (through injury) he handed over the pivotal duties to Teddy Rooke. Reed guested for Newcastle United during World War One, and died in West Bromwich in 1967.

REFEREES (and umpires)

West Bromwich-born David Asson, an Albion reserve in 1898-99, became a Football League referee in 1914. Seven years later he officiated in the Football League v Southern League representative game and was linesman for the 1922 FA Cup Final between Huddersfield Town and Preston North End. The following year he was given the honour of refereeing the first-ever Wembley Cup Final when an estimated 200,000 fans entered the stadium to watch Bolton Wanderers beat West Ham United 2-0.

Former Albion players Arthur Smith and John Whitehouse joined the list of League referees in 1902 and 1903 respectively and reserve goalkeeper Joe Matthews and inside-forward Walter Perry became a League linesmen in 1909-10.

Prior to the introduction of match linesmen, umpires were appointed for League and Cup games in England; several ex-Albion players were official club umpires, among them goalkeeper Bob Roberts and forwards Billy Bisseker and Willie Lines, who sadly lost his sight while still playing for the club (1886). Mr Joe Noons was one of the first Albion umpires, officiating in the early 1880s.

Charlie Lines, a relative of Willie, and an amateur with Albion in 1909, was a Football League referee between 1911-36. He took charge of two FA Cup semi-finals and the 1929 Amateur Cup Final between Ilford and Leyton.

Two early Albion secretaries – Louis Ford and W.Pierce Dix – were both referees, the former during the early 1900s, the latter as early as 1880. Pierce Dix, in fact, refereed the 1881 FA Cup Final and the 1885 international between Scotland and Ireland in Glasgow.

Cecil Shaw, Albion's full-back (1936-47) refereed in the Oldbury & District Leagues in 1959-60.

On 25 August 1884, during Andy Hunter's benefit match (Albion v Aston Villa), referee Jack Ridell was insulted and promptly walked off the pitch in a 'huff.' Saturday Night reporter Joe Gilbert took over his duties. Villa won the game 3-2.

On 20 February 1960, referee Jack Husband collapsed during the half-time interval of the Leicester City-Albion FA Cup-tie at Filbert Street. He died on his way to hospital.

One of Albion's goals in a 13-1 friendly win over Swansea FC (away) on 20 April 1899 was 'scored' inadvertently by referee Tom Kinney who diverted Billy Bassett's shot past the 'keeper.

In the 1930s the 'two referee' system was considered by the Football League management committee – one official in each half of the field.

The plan was put into action in the England v The Rest representative match at The Hawthorns on 27 March 1935. It was a reasonable success and a second game was arranged, this time between Albion and a Football League XI at the same venue on 8 May 1935. Neither referee was over-worked as the League XI won 9-6, but the plan was regarded a failure at the next annual meeting and when the proposal was put forward again in 1937, it was immediately rejected.

REGIS, Cyrille

Regis spent seven splendid years at The Hawthorns during which time he scored 112 goals in 302 appearances. A strong, forceful striker with power in both feet and head, he was a big favourite with the Baggies' fans. Some of his strikes were quite brilliant individual efforts, and he found the net when making his debut in five different competitions for the club – a unique record. Born in Maripiasoula, French Guyana in 1958, he joined Albion from non-League Hayes for a bargain £5,000 in 1977 (spotted by Ronnie Allen) and before he left for Coventry City (for £300,000 in 1984) he won five full England caps, three at 'B' team level and six with the Under-21 side and played in three Cup semi-finals with Albion. Voted PFA Young Footballer of the Year in 1979, he was runner-up to Steve Perryman in the Footballer of the Year awards in 1982 and whilst with Coventry he gained an FA Cup winners' medal (1987) and collected three more Player of the Year awards in the Midlands. After Coventry he played for Aston Villa, Wolverhampton Wanderers and Wycombe Wanderers before joining Chester City in 1995. The only player ever to appear in League matches for four West Midland clubs (Albion, Coventry, Villa and Wolves), Regis reached three personal milestones in 1994-95 – 150 League goals and 200 goals in all games, and 700 senior appearances at club level.

REYNOLDS, John

Known affectionately as 'Baldy' Reynolds, this highly-talented right-half who knew every trick in the book, was capped by two different countries – Ireland and England! He played in five internationals for Ireland in the 1880s before it was confirmed that he was English, having been born in

Blackburn in 1869! He later added eight more caps to his collection in a white shirt instead of a green one! Reynolds was a reserve with Blackburn Rovers in 1884-85 and served with the East Lancashire Regiment in Ireland before joining Albion in 1891 after spells with Distillery and Ulster (gaining an Irish Cup winners' medal). He helped Albion win the FA Cup in 1892 (scoring in a 3-0 win over Aston Villa) and after hitting six goals in 46 games for the club (including Albion's first penalty) he left for neighbours Villa in 1893 and scored on his debut for his new club against his old one, Albion! Then two years later he won a second FA Cup medal when Villa beat Albion in the 1895 Final. He also helped Villa twice lift the First Division championship. Later in his career Reynolds played for Celtic (with whom he won Scottish League honours), Southampton, Bristol St George, Stockport County and Willesden, retiring in 1905. He also coached in New Zealand and guested for Droitwich Town in 1891. Reynolds died in 1917.

RICHARDSON, Samuel

Brother of Bill Richardson (overleaf) Sammy was a wing-half mainly noted for his work-rate and physical strength. He

was also a fine passer of the ball and scored one goal in 212 appearances for Albion whom he served before, during and after World War One. Born in West Bromwich in 1892, he signed for Albion from Great Bridge Celtic in 1913 and gained a regular place in the first team in 1919, collecting a League championship winning medal at the end of that immediate post-war season. He later represented the Football League and the FA XI and was replaced in Albion's middle line by Tommy Magee who had played in front of him during the early 1920s. Richardson left The Hawthorns in 1927, signing for Newport County, later assisting Aldershot before retiring in 1931. A guest player for Coventry City during the war, he died in West Bromwich in 1959.

RICHARDSON, William

Although a shade casual at times, Bill Richardson was a splendid centre-half, unflagging, good in the air with a strong, determined tackle. He and his brother Sammy were together at The Hawthorns briefly, Bill also joining Albion

Bill Richardson in action during the 1931 FA Cup Final.

from Great Bridge Celtic in 1926. He stayed until 1937 during which time he amassed a fine record of 352 appearances at first-team level, scoring one goal (v Wolves in 1935). A key figure in Albion's double-winning side of 1931, he also played in the 1935 FA Cup Final and was part of two terrific half-back lines, first with Tommy Magee and Jimmy Edwards as his partners and then with Jimmy Murphy to his right. West Bromwich-born (in 1908), Richardson played for Swindon Town, Dudley and Vono Sports before retiring in 1941. He died in 1985.

RICHARDSON, William 'G'.

On his day 'W.G.' Richardson had few equals and no superiors in the art of snapping up half-chances which fell to him inside the penalty area. He was so alert and seemed to know, instinctively, where the ball would land after it had left a colleague's foot. A terrific centre-forward, he depended on his alertness rather than his strength and will go down as being one of Albion's greatest-ever marksmen, netting 328 goals in 444 first-team appearances for the Baggies between 1929 and 1945. Born at Framwellgate Moor, County Durham, in 1909, and a former bus driver, he joined Albion from Hartlepools United at a time when the Baggies were seeking to bolster up their attack in readiness for a promotion push from Division Two. 'Ginger' Richardson (the 'G' was added to distinguish him from centre-half Bill Richardson) settled in

immediately and the goals started to flow freely (See GOALS). He hit the net regularly during the 1930s, grabbing four goals in five minutes at West Ham in November 1931 to equal a League record. A vital cog in Albion's double-winning side, he also played in the 1935 Cup Final, and in that same year was capped by England (v Holland). After a terrific wartime campaign, when he guested for Derby and Walsall as well as notching 100 goals for Albion, Richardson left The Hawthorns to have a season with Shrewsbury. He returned as Albion's trainer-assistant coach in 1946 and was still on The Hawthorns' payroll when he collapsed and died playing in a charity match in Birmingham in 1959. Richardson's son, Brian, was an Albion reserve in the 1950s.

RICKABY, Stanley

Stan Rickaby was an accomplished right-back who took over from Jim Pemberton in 1950 and handed over his duties to Don Howe in 1955. During the intervening five years, the Stockton-on-Tees-born, raven-haired defender, who was signed from Middlesbrough by Albion boss Jack Smith for a mere £7,500, accumulated 205 appearances in the number-two shirt, scoring two goals (both terrific shots from some distance). He was capped once by England, but sadly missed the 1954 FA Cup Final through

injury. He left The Hawthorns to become player-manager of Poole Town and later served with Weymouth and Newton Abbot Spurs before emigrating to Australia in 1969. Rickaby now lives in Perth and celebrated his 72nd birthday back in the Midlands in 1996.

ROBBINS, Walter William

Hard-shooting outside-left who scored 31 goals in 91 appearances for Albion after joining the club from his home town club Cardiff City in 1932 for £3,000. Born in 1910, he played initially for Ely United, and was capped 11 times by his country, also touring Canada with the Welsh FA in 1929. A big favourite with the Cardiff fans, he helped the Ninian Park club win the Welsh Cup in 1930 and later in life was trainer when City won promotion in 1947 and 1952. He also trained the Welsh national side (1950s). Robbins, with tree-trunk legs and cannonball shot, left Albion in 1939 for Newport County, moving back to Ninian Park (as trainer) in 1945. In 1958 he was appointed chief scout of Swansea Town, later becoming assistant manager at Vetch Field before reverting back to chief scout in 1971. He retired in 1978 through ill-health and died a year later in Swansea. Albion played a testimonial match for Robbins at Vetch Field in 1971.

ROBERTS, Robert John

Albion's first international footballer, Bob Roberts was a giant of a man standing a fraction over 6ft 4ins tall, just the right size for a goalkeeper although in his early days he did play as a full-back! He had tremendous reach, could deal  comfortably with high crosses and always got the better of onrushing forwards who chose to challenge him for possession. He wore size 13 boots, could kick long distances (he was credited with a goal in an FA Cup-tie against Derby Junction in 1886 with a huge punt downfield) and during his two spells with Albion amassed well over 400 appearances (in all games), 84 in major competitions. Born in West Bromwich in 1859, he was a founder member of the club and appeared in three successive FA Cup Finals (1886-87-88). He gained three full England caps and also played for the Football Alliance and in three international trials. His first spell with Albion ended in 1890 and after a season with Sunderland Albion he returned to West Bromwich for another term before ending his career with Aston Villa. On his retirement in 1893, Roberts went into business in the North-East where he remained for the rest of his life. He and right-half Ezra Horton were the only players to feature in Albion's first FA Cup-tie and the club's first Football League game. Roberts died in Byker, Newcastle in 1929.

ROBERTSON, Alistair Peter

Ally Robertson gave Albion 18 years tremendous service as

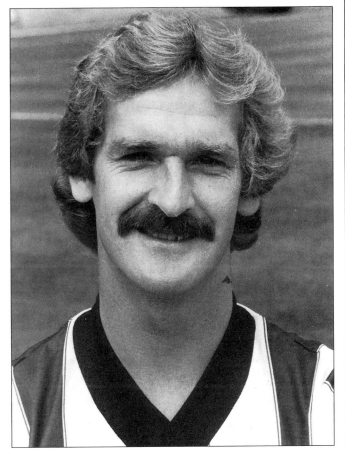

a rugged, hard-tackling, no-nonsense defender. He formed a superb partnership with John Wile and they played together in more than 570 games for the club. Born in Philipstoun, Scotland in 1952, and a pupil at Linlithgow Academy, Robertson joined Albion from Uphall Saints in 1968, turning professional a year later when he also made his senior debut against Manchester United before a 45,000 Hawthorns' crowd. He unfortunately suffered a broken leg in 1970, but on regaining full fitness he became a regular member of Albion's first team, going on to accumulate 626 senior appearances, scoring 12 goals. Indeed, Robertson played in a total of 729 first-team matches for the Baggies – the second highest appearance-maker in the club's history (behind Tony Brown). As a youngster he played in four schoolboy internationals for his country and added six youth caps to his collection with Albion. In 1979 he passed Jimmy Dudley's record of 166 consecutive League appearances for Albion. Robertson left Albion in 1986, joining neighbours Wolverhampton Wanderers on a free transfer. He spent four years at Molineux, helping Wolves gain promotion from the Fourth to the Second Division and also win the Sherpa Van Trophy at Wembley. He then had brief spells as manager of both Worcester City and Cheltenham Town before retiring in 1993 to become a car salesman, based in West Bromwich.

ROBSON BROTHERS (Bryan & Gary)

Between them Bryan and Gary Robson served Albion for 21 years, amassing combined totals of 531 senior appearances and 81 goals. **Bryan**, born in Witton Gilbert, County Durham in 1957, joined Albion in 1972 after playing for both Washington schools and Chester-le-Street boys. He turned professional at the age of 17 and made his debut in 1975, quickly establishing himself in the side, being able to play in a number of positions. In the end it was in midfield where he made his name, going on to win England recognition. In six years' of first-team action for Albion, he scored 46 goals in 249 outings before moving to join his former boss, Ron Atkinson, at Manchester United in 1981 for a then British record fee of £1.5 million plus fellow midfielder Remi Moses (valued at £500,000). At Old Trafford, Robson became a superstar, leading United to three FA Cup Final victories (1983, 1985 and 1990). He was also a key figure in two Premiership championship triumphs and starred in United's 1991 European Cup-winners' Cup success. He won 90 full caps for England (13 with Albion), gained seven at Under-21 level and played in three 'B' internationals. He scored exactly 100 goals in 467 appearances for the Reds up to 1994, when he became player-manager of Middlesbrough, leading the Teesiders  into the Premiership in 1995. In this same year he was also appointed to England's coaching staff.

Gary Robson joined Albion during the year his elder brother left for United. Born in Pelaw, County Durham in 1965, he played his early football with Whitehill Boys and Chester-le-Street schools, and in 1980 had trials with Newcastle United. He went on to score 35 goals in 282 first-team appearances for Albion, lining up in a number of

Bryan Robson, joined Manchester United in a record £1.5 million deal which included another Albion player, Remi Moses.

positions from right-back to outside-left! He played for the Football League in 1989 and after helping the Baggies win promotion to the First Division in 1993, he left The Hawthorns for Bradford City, moving to non-League Gateshead in 1995. Both Bryan and Gary were granted testimonials – the former by United (1991) and Gary by Albion (1994). A third Robson brother, **Justin**, played for Newcastle United and appeared for Albion as a 'guest' in Gary's testimonial match v Aston Villa in 1994.

ROBSON, Robert William

Robson was a stylish wing-half or inside-forward who scored 61 goals in 257 appearances for Albion between 1956 and 1962. Born in Sacriston, County Durham in 1933, he was an amateur with Middlesbrough and had trials with Southampton before joining Fulham in 1950. He was part of a superb forward-line at Craven Cottage which included Bedford Jezzard and Johnny Haynes and it was his goalscoring ability which promoted Albion manager Vic

Buckingham to pay £20,000 for his services in the mid-1950s. Robson settled in well at The Hawthorns, teaming up with Ronnie Allen and Derek Kevan. He won the first of his 20 full England caps in 1957 and participated in the 1958 World Cup Finals. After six excellent years with Albion he returned to Fulham for £20,000 and left the London club in 1967 after taking his League record to 583 appearances and 133 goals. Thereafter he became deeply involved in football

coaching and management – Oxford University (trainer-coach 1965-66), Vancouver Royals (player-manager 1967), Fulham (manager 1968), Chelsea (scout, part-time coach 1968-69), Ipswich Town (manager 1969-82), England ('B' team manager 1978-82, senior manager 1982-90), PSV Eindhoven (1990-92), Sporting Lisbon (1992-93), FC Porto (1994-96), Barcelona. He led Ipswich to FA Cup and UEFA Cup Final victories in 1978 and 1981 respectively, and Porto to a Portuguese Cup triumph in 1994 and to the country's League title in 1996.

ROCHDALE

Rochdale have been a Football League club since 1921 and are one of only two current League teams Albion have yet to meet in competitive football (the other being Scarborough). Over the years there have been a number of players who have been associated with both Albion and Rochdale (at various levels) and they are: Barry Cowdrill, Stan Davies, Bobby Downes, Jack Haines, Ted Huntley, Noel Luke, Winston White, Jack Whitehouse, and Paul A.Williams. Albion's chief scout Norman Bodell (1986-94) was a Rochdale defender (1958-62).

Barry Cowdrill, played for Albion, Rochdale and Rotherham.

ROTHERHAM UNITED

Albion's record against United:

Football League

Venue	P	W	D	L	F	A	Pts
Home	1	0	1	0	2	2	1
Away	1	1	0	0	2	0	3
Totals	2	1	1	0	4	2	4

FA Cup

Home	2	2	0	0	7	0
Away	1	0	1	0	0	0
Totals	3	2	1	0	7	0

League Cup

Home	1	1	0	0	4	0

Other Matches

Home	1	1	0	0	2	1
Away	1	1	0	0	4	0
Totals	2	2	0	0	6	1

The first time the clubs met was in the fourth round of the FA Cup at The Hawthorns on 30 January 1954. On a frosty pitch, Albion put on the style and won 4-0 with Ray Barlow in brilliant form.

Cyrille Regis scored twice (one a penalty) on his senior debut for Albion in a 4-0 League Cup victory over Rotherham at The Hawthorns on 31 August 1977.

After a 0-0 draw at Millmoor on 7 January 1984, Albion won their third-round FA Cup replay at home four days later 3-0, with Tony Morley scoring twice.

Albion League debutants v Rotherham: Luther Blissett (1992); League Cup debut: Cyrille Regis (1977).

Players with both clubs: Ian Banks, Tony Brien, Barry Cowdrill, Stan Davies, Stewart Evans, Tony Grealish, Eric Robinson, Ronnie Robinson, Ben Shearman, Imre Varadi, Bobby Williamson.

Also associated with both clubs: Albion reserves David Campbell, Martin Pike and Ernie Pattinson all played League football for United; Albion 1950s star Maurice Setters was United's assistant manager (1984-85); Geoff Hudson was player-coach with United (1966) and Albion trainer (1970-72); Norman Hunter was 1980s coach at Albion and later manager of Rotherham (1985-87); Mick Martin, Albion midfielder of the 1970s, had trials with Rotherham in 1990.

RUSSIA (USSR)
Albion toured the Soviet Union in the summer of 1957,

Albion take the field against FC Zenit during their tour of Russia in 1957.

playing three matches, winning two and drawing one. When defeating Dynamo Tbilisi 3-0 in Georgia on 7 June, they became the first British professional side to win behind the Iron Curtain.
Here are details of those three tour games:
2 June v FC Zenit 1-1
Scorer: Kevan. *Att:* 80,000
7 June v Dynamo Tbilisi 3-0
Scorers: Horobin, Kevan (2). *Att:* 35,000
12 June v CDKA (Russia Red Army) 4-2
Scorers: Whitehouse, Kevan (2), Griffin. *Att:* 80,500

The Russian Red Army side visited The Hawthorns for an international friendly on 29 October 1957 (See FLOODLIGHTS).

On a rainy evening a crowd of 52,805 saw an 11-goal thriller, Albion winning 6-5 with goals from Kevan (2), Allen (pen.), Robson, Griffin and Howe. Allen missed a second spot-kick.

RYAN, Reginald Alphonso
Reg Ryan was a stocky, mobile player who started his career as a wing-half and ended as an inside-forward. A consistent performer for Albion during the first ten years after World War Two, he made 272 first-team appearances and scored 31 goals, helping Albion win promotion to the First Division in 1949 and the FA Cup five years later. Born in Dublin in 1925, he played Gaelic football in Ireland before moving to Blackpool, and then to Coventry, signing for the Highfield Road club in 1944 after trials with Sheffield United. He was transferred to Albion the following year, and was later joined by fellow countrymen Jack Vernon, Billy Lunn, John Tighe and Dave Walsh. Winner of 17 full international caps (16 with the Republic of Ireland, one with Northern Ireland), Ryan, nicknamed 'Jumbo' by his colleagues, joined Derby County for £3,000 in 1955 and gained a Third Division North championship medal in his second season at The Baseball Ground. He also represented the Third Division North against the South. He returned to Coventry

in 1958 and retired two years later to work in the pools department at Highfield Road, switching to do a similar job at Albion in 1961. Thereafter he became a scout, first with Albion and later with Hereford United, Derby County, Leeds United and Aston Villa. He now lives in Sheldon.

SANDERS, James Albert
Jim Sanders turned out to be a very consistent goalkeeper after his career had been placed in jeopardy; he was invalided out of the Air Force during the war after suffering serious back and neck injuries when his fighter bomber was shot down in Europe. Born in Hackney, London in 1920, Sanders played for Longlands FC and Charlton Athletic before moving to The Hawthorns, initially as a guest, in 1945. He also guested for Chelsea, Fulham, Southampton and West Ham during the hostilities. He stayed with Albion for the next 13 years, amassing 391 appearances and helping Albion win the FA Cup in 1954, after coming into the side late in the season when regular 'keeper Norman  Heath was injured at Sunderland. Sanders also starred in Albion's promotion-winning side of 1948-49 when he saved nine penalties, and during his career he drew up a terrific record of stopping spot-kicks (See PENALTIES). On leaving Albion in 1958, Sanders had a season with Coventry City and later played for Hinckley Athletic. He retired in 1960 to become a publican and later a hotelier. He now lives in retirement in Tamworth.

SANDFORD, Edward Albert

When Teddy Sandford joined Albion in 1929, there was an abundance of inside-forward talent at The Hawthorns, but he quickly made his mark, gained a first-team place within a year and went on to become a truly great footballer, appearing in 317 games for the Baggies and scoring 75 goals. Born in Handsworth, less than a mile from The Hawthorns in 1910, Sandford played for the Birmingham Carriage Works and Smethwick Highfield before signing for Albion. He was the youngest member of Albion's 1931 double-winning side and was only 22 when he won his only England cap. Three years later he scored in the 1935 FA Cup Final, and in 1937, having been converted to a centre-half, he skippered Albion against Arsenal when a record crowd of almost 65,000 packed into The Hawthorns for a sixth-round Cup-tie. Sandford, strong, with a powerful shot, left Albion for Sheffield United in 1939.

He worked and played for Morris Commercial during the early part of the war, retiring in 1943. From 1950-57 he was an Albion coach and later scouted for the club (1961-67). Nephew of former Albion 1900s centre-half 'Abe' Jones, Sandford died in Birmingham in 1995.

SANKEY, John

Jack Sankey was an industrious, highly efficient wing-half or inside-forward who let the ball do most of the work! His overall play was characterised by some powerful long-distance shooting and during his time at The Hawthorns he hardly ever had a bad game. Born in Moulton, Cheshire in 1912, he joined Albion from Winsford United in 1930 but had to wait four years before making his debut. Once in the side, he stayed and became a very important member of the first team, going on to score 27 goals in 290 appearances. He left The Hawthorns for Northampton Town in 1945 and guested for Walsall in 1946 prior to transferring to Hereford United the following year. He became assistant trainer-coach at Edgar Street (1953-54) and was Albion coach from 1955-64 and then scout for a season before retiring to work in a cycle factory in Handsworth. He died in Birmingham in 1985.

SCARBOROUGH

Albion have yet to play Scarborough (a Football League club since 1987) at any level, but three players have served with both clubs – outside-left George Lee, a star of Albion's successful 1953-54 side, Ronnie Robinson and Christian Hargreaves.

SCOTTISH CONNECTIONS

Here are details of personnel who have been associated with both Albion and Scottish League clubs. (Those indicated * did not play first-team League football while at The Hawthorns):

Aberdeen: Jack Beynon*, Andy Dibble, Doug Fraser, Gary Hackett.

Airdrieonians: Mark Cowan*, Scott Vigrow, Jock Wallace.

Albion Rovers: George Dudley, Danny Hegan.

Alloa Athletic: Willie Johnstone, Stuart Romaines*.

Arbroath: Tom Dilly, Willie Johnstone.

Ayr United: Alistair Love*, Dave Stewart*, Scott Vigrow.

Berwick Rangers: Stuart Romaines*, Jock Wallace.

Celtic: Willie Groves, Peter Latchford, Willie McCullum, Ebenezer Owers, John Reynolds. (Mick Martin coach).

Clyde: Jock Cameron, Mark Cowan*, Peter Latchford, Archie McKenzie, Max Murray, Ebenezer Owers. Walter Jack manager.

Clydebank: Bobby Williamson.

Cowdenbeath: Gerry Adair*, Ken McNaught (trial).

Dumbarton: Laurie Bell, Eddie Connelly, Archie McKenzie, Hugh MacLean, Willie McCullum, Stuart Robertson*, Jimmy Stevenson, George Young.

Dundee: Arthur Albiston, Alf Dean, Charlie Donnachie, William Ford, Archie Macaulay (coach), Stewart McLaren*, Brian Rice, Scott Vigrow.

Dundee United: Andy Gray, John Paskin (trial).

Dunfermline Athletic: Gerry Adair*, Vetle Andersen, Ken McNaught (coach), Bobby Murray*, Jimmy Nicholl.

East Fife: Willie Johnston (coach).

East Stirling: Mark Leetion*.

Falkirk: Andy Aitken, Jimmy Fowler*, Willie Johnston (coach), Alistair Love*, Brian Rice, Stuart Robertson*, Stuart Romaines*, Billy Thomas*.

Hamilton Academical: Billy Thomas*, Scott Vigrow, James Weir*.

Heart of Midlothian: Eli Bradley, Tom Dilly, Graeme Hogg, Willie Johnston, Stewart McLaren*, Joey Tortolano*, Jimmy Varty. Albion's assistant manager Arthur Mann (1994-96) played for Hearts.

Hibernian: Gerry Adair*, Andy Aitken, Laurie Bell, Andy Goram*, Willie Groves, Peter McManus, Brian Rice, Joey Tortolano*.

Dave Stewart, one of three Albion players to have appeared for Ayr United.

Billy Thomas, played for Albion and Morton.

Andy Gray, a much-travelled striker whose clubs included Albion and Glasgow Rangers.

Kilmarnock: Bobby Williamson.

Meadowbank Thistle: Gerry Adair*, Mark Leetion*.

Morton: Billy Thomas*, Stewart MacLaren.

Motherwell: Stewart MacLaren*, Jock Wallace (manager).

Partick Thistle: George Elmore, Danny Hegan (trial), Alistair Love*, James McCue, Billy McDonald, Roddy McLeod, Peter McKennan, James Weir*.

Queen of the South: Charlie Evans (guest), George McVitie.

Queen's Park: Max Murray.

Raith Rovers: Andy Aitken, Willie Johnston (coach), Jimmy Nicholl, Stuart Romaines*.

Stewart MacLaren, also played for Motherwell.

Rangers: Andy Goram*, Andy Gray, Willie Johnston, Billy McDonald, Jimmy Millar, Max Murray, Jimmy Nicholl, Graham Roberts, Jock Wallace (manager), Colin West, Bobby Williamson, George Young. Albion manager Archie Macaulay played for Rangers.

Renton: Andrew Hannah*.

St Mirren: Harry Clements.

Stirling Albion: Bobby Murray*.

Third Lanark: Laurie Bell, Harry Clements, Archie McKenzie, Max Murray. Former Albion secretary W. Frank Heaven was secretary of Third Lanark in 1904-05.

Matches

Albion have played against the following Scottish clubs at various levels – Clyde (v Albion Reserves 1980), Dumbarton, Dundee, Dunfermline Athletic, Heart of Midlothian, Hibernian, Kilmarnock, Meadowbank Thistle (v Albion Reserves 1981), Morton, Motherwell, Rangers, Renton, St Mirren and Third Lanark.

SCUNTHORPE UNITED

Albion's record against United:

FA Cup

Venue	P	W	D	L	F	A
Home	2	1	1	0	1	0
Away	1	1	0	0	3	1

Other Match

Away	1	0	1	0	0	0

Scunthorpe were in the Fourth Division when they first met Albion in a third-round FA Cup-tie at The Hawthorns on 2 January 1971. Inspired by a young Kevin Keegan, the Irons forced a 0-0 draw. The replay took place nine days later at The Old Show Ground, where Albion came out on top by 3-1.

The other Cup-tie was a fourth round clash on Albion soil on 1 February 1984. Mickey Forsyth scored the winner – his only goal for Albion.

Players with both clubs: Jack Bannister, Wally Boyes, David Cork, Sammy Cox, Tony Ford, Dave Gilbert, Ian Hamilton, Joe Johnson, John Kaye, Dick Krzywicki. Kaye later returned to United to become coach.

Also associated with both clubs: Albion 1950s defender Ron Bradley was Scunthorpe's manager (1973-74) and Bruce Collard, an Albion 1960s reserve, later played for United. Goalkeeper Ron Green played for Scunthorpe (1986-88) after a loan spell at Albion. Keith Burkinshaw, Albion's manager 1993-94, was a Scunthorpe defender (1965-68).

SECRETARIES

Albion's secretaries: 1880-1996

1880-81	John Bisseker
1881-82	John While
1882-83	Arthur E.Eld and F.Seymour (joint secretary)
1883-84	Arthur E.Eld (Hon. secretary), Joseph Hughes (Hon. financial secretary)
1884-90	Tom Smith (Hon. general secretary)
1884-85	John Homer (Hon. financial secretary)
1885-87	Thomas Foster (Hon. financial secretary)
1887-90	Louis Ford (Hon. financial secretary)
1890-92	Louis Ford (general secretary), W.Pierce Dix (Hon. financial secretary)
1892-94	Henry 'Swin' Jackson (general secretary)
1892-95	Clement Keys (financial secretary)
1894-95	E.Stephenson (general secretary)
1895-96	Clement Keys
1896-1902	W.Frank Heaven
1902-48	Fred Everiss
1948-60	Ephriam 'Eph' Smith
1960-80	Alan Everiss
1980-84	Anthony E.Rance
1984-85	Gordon H.Dimbleby
1985-86	John Westmancoat
1986-89	Gordon Bennett
1989-96	Dr John J.Evans

Secretarial notepad

Albion's first treasurer was Joseph Hughes, who was followed by William Bisseker (1882-84) and James Couse (1884-85).

Albion's assistant secretaries have included: 'Eph' Smith (1911-48), Alan Everiss (1948-60), Fred Horne (1960-74) and Ray Fairfax (1974-79).

Tom 'Razor' Smith represented Albion at a number of important football meetings in London during the 1880s, and had a big say in the introduction of professionalism. He travelled 4,000 miles in 1886-87 on Albion business. A George Salter's employee, he was also a player for the club in the early days.

'Eph' Smith, secretary 1948-60.

W.Pierce Dix was a leading figure in Sheffield footballing circles between 1875 and 1888 and a referee of note who, in 1883, when a vice-president of the Football Association, umpired the Staffordshire Cup Final (with Lionel King) between Albion and Stoke (See REFEREES).

Albion's first full-time paid general secretary (with a salary of £50 a year) was Louis Ford (appointed in 1890). Ford was responsible for bringing many fine players to the club including Willie Groves, Roddy McLeod and John Reynolds. An Albion committee member and then director (1892-96), he was an FA Councillor (1890-93), member of the Football League management committee and vice-president of the League from 1894 to 1897. In 1900 he became a League referee. He was also secretary of Walsall (1896-1900) and Leicester Fosse (1914).

'Swin' Jackson was a Staffordshire and West Bromwich Dartmouth cricketer who was later secretary of Leicester Fosse and Luton Town before emigrating to Canada where he became a parish registrar and postmaster until his death in 1930.

W.Frank Heaven was also a Dartmouth cricketer who gave the Albion six years unstinting service before he resigned over a disagreement with the directors in 1902. He was just 23 when he was appointed secretary in 1896. He spent the 1904-05 season with Third Lanark but on

Gordon Dimbleby, Albion secretary 1984-85.

John Westmancoat, Albion secretary 1985-86.

Gordon Bennett, Albion secretary 1986-89.

Dr John Evans, Albion secretary since 1989.

returning south he died tragically on Boxing Day 1905 when still only 32 years of age.

Clement Keys (1895-96) was the first Albion secretary placed in sole charge of the club's administration.

Between 1902 and 1980 the position of Albion secretary was held by three members of the same family – Fred Everiss, 'Eph' Smith (Fred's brother-in-law) and Alan Everiss (Fred's son) (See EVERISS FAMILY).

Tony Rance was commercial manager and secretary of Bristol City before joining Albion and later he became assistant secretary and general manager of Wrexham.

Gordon Dimbleby also served (as secretary-commercial manager etc.) with Northampton Town, Hull City, Wolverhampton Wanderers and Chelsea.

John Westmancoat also held the secretary's job at Walsall, Birmingham City and Port Vale. He died in January 1992.

Gordon Bennett was employed by Bristol Rovers as secretary and later managing director before moving to Albion. He left to become youth development officer at Norwich City.

Dr John Evans was secretary of Nuneaton Borough prior to his appointment at Albion. He was also part-time secretary of Northampton Town (1986-89).

SENDINGS-OFF

The first player to be sent off whilst representing West Bromwich Albion was one of the most famous footballers of the 1880s and 90s – England international William Isaiah Bassett. He was dismissed for using 'unparliamentary language' – saying "You don't understand the bally game" during Albion's friendly at Millwall in April 1894.

Here are the details of all sendings-off involving Albion players (and manager) at competitive level:

Football League

Joe Reader	v Bolton Wanderers	(a)	13 April 1895
Abraham Jones	v Stoke	(a)	21 October 1899
Jack Kifford	v Aston Villa	(a)	12 September 1903
Stan Davies	v Sheffield United	(a)	4 December 1926
Joe Carter	v Blackburn Rovers	(h)	19 September 1931
Teddy Sandford	v Blackburn Rovers	(a)	30 January 1932
Teddy Sandford	v Tottenham Hotspur	(a)	17 March 1934
Wally Boyes	v Middlesbrough	(a)	1 January 1937
Derek Hogg	v Leeds United	(a)	27 December 1958
Maurice Setters	v Sheffield Wednesday	(a)	31 October 1959
Clive Clark	v Aston Villa	(a)	6 October 1962
Graham Williams	v Aston Villa	(a)	17 October 1964
Dick Krzywicki	v Manchester City	(a)	4 October 1969
Len Cantello	v Sheffield Wednesday	(a)	10 March 1970
Willie Johnston	v Swindon Town	(a)	8 September 1973
David Shaw	v Portsmouth	(a)	3 February 1974
Willie Johnston	v Bristol City	(h)	16 November 1974
Ray Wilson	v Oxford United	(a)	15 March 1975
Len Cantello	v Chelsea	(h)	20 August 1975
Johnny Giles	v Luton Town	(a)	13 December 1975
John Wile	v Hull City	(a)	21 February 1976
Paddy Mulligan	v Stoke City	(a)	18 December 1976
Alistair Robertson	v Coventry City	(a)	13 December 1980
Steve MacKenzie	v Middlesbrough	(a)	9 March 1982
Cyrille Regis	v Aston Villa	(h)	8 May 1982
Gary Owen	v Notts County	(a)	15 May 1982
Maarten Jol	v Luton Town	(a)	18 December 1983
Garry Thompson	v Wolverhampton W	(a)	28 April 1984
Cyrille Regis	v Sunderland	(a)	8 September 1984
Alistair Robertson	v Watford	(h)	8 December 1984
Martyn Bennett	v Stoke City	(a)	12 March 1985
Jimmy Nicholl	v Stoke City	(a)	12 March 1985
Steve Hunt	v Coventry City	(a)	28 September 1985
Jimmy Nicholl	v QPR	(h)	9 November 1985
Martin Dickinson	v Southampton	(h)	29 March 1986
Carlton Palmer	v Leeds United	(h)	6 December 1986
Garth Crooks	v Ipswich Town	(a)	3 March 1987
Martyn Bennett	v Blackburn Rovers	(a)	22 August 1987
Tony Kelly	v Swindon Town	(h)	29 August 1987
Tony Morley	v Crystal Palace	(a)	8 September 1987
Robert Hopkins	v Huddersfield Town	(a)	26 March 1988
Don Goodman	v Plymouth Argyle	(a)	24 August 1988
Stewart Phillips	v Barnsley	(a)	8 October 1988
Carlton Palmer	v Portsmouth	(a)	3 December 1988
Robert Hopkins	v Bradford City	(a)	18 February 1989
Carlton Palmer	v Bradford City	(a)	18 February 1989
Graham Harbey	v Oxford United	(a)	8 September 1990
Paul Raven	v Bristol City	(a)	2 February 1991
Gary Bannister	v Plymouth Argyle	(h)	13 March 1991
Frank Sinclair	v Exeter City	(a)	28 December 1991
Darren Bradley	v Torquay United	(h)	29 February 1992
Paul Williams	v Peterborough Utd	(a)	11 April 1992
Darren Bradley	v Chester City	(h)	18 April 1992
Simon Garner	v Barnsley	(a)	14 August 1993
Ian Hamilton	v Tranmere Rovers	(a)	2 November 1993
Daryl Burgess	v Bolton Wanderers	(h)	6 November 1993
Paul Raven	v Oxford United	(a)	12 April 1994
Gary Strodder	v Luton Town	(a)	3 May 1994
Gary Strodder	v Luton Town	(a)	3 May 1994
Bob Taylor	v Southend United	(a)	27 December 1994

FA Cup

Willie Johnston	v Everton	(h)	30 January 1974
Mick Martin	v Ipswich Town	(SF)	8 April 1978
Darren Bradley	v Coventry City	(h)	18 January 1995

League Cup

Willie Johnston	v Brighton & H.A.	(h)	22 September 1976
Len Cantello	v Leeds United	(n)	2 October 1978
Alistair Brown	v West Ham United	(a)	1 December 1981

The scene which led to the sending-off of Albion's Willie Johnston and Bristol City's John Emanuel at the Hawthorns in 1974.

Maarten Jol	v Tottenham Hotspur	(SF h)	3 February 1982
Gary Owen	v Aston Villa	(h)	30 November 1984
Martin Dickinson	v Derby County	(a)	24 September 1986
Gary Strodder	v Bristol City	(a)	5 September 1990

League Play-Offs

Mickey Mellon	v Swansea City	(h)	19 May 1993

European Cup-winners' Cup

Ronnie Rees	v Dinamo Bucharest	(a)	13 November 1968

UEFA Cup

Alistair Brown	v Carl Zeiss Jena	(h)	3 October 1979

Autoglass Trophy

Stacy Coldicott	v Torquay United	(h)	9 February 1992

Anglo-Italian Cup

Carl Heggs	v Cosenza	(a)	22 December 1993
Paul Mardon	v Reggiana	(h)	8 November 1995

Wartime Football

Eddie Connelly	v Coventry City	(h)	23 March 1940
Eddie Connelly	v Coventry City	(h)	9 November 1940

Bass Charity Vase

George Reilly	v Burton Albion	(a)	22 July 1987

Birmingham Cup

Tom Hutchinson	v Small Heath	(SF)	18 March 1895

FA Youth Cup Final

Asa Hartford	v Sunderland	(a)	3 May 1969
Jim Holton	v Sunderland	(a)	3 May 1969

Tour/Friendly Games

Graham Lovett	v Uruguyan select XI	(a)	22 May 1966
Graham Lovett	v Flamengo (Brazil)	(a)	5 June 1966
Graham Williams	v Uganda National XI	(a)	29 May 1968
Asa Hartford	v East African XI	(a)	5 June 1968
John Wile	v FC Hercules	(a)	14 August 1977
Mick Martin	v FC Hercules	(a)	14 August 1977
Ronnie Allen (manager) v FC Hercules		(a)	14 August 1977
Derek Statham	v Sevilla	(a)	21 August 1981
Don Goodman	v Swansea City	(a)	16 August 1990

Seeing 'Red'

Kifford received a six-week suspension for his offence in 1903.

Sandford was the first Albion player to be sent off twice.

Ally Brown's dismissal in the UEFA Cup-tie v Carl Zeiss Jena in 1979 was effected during the half-time interval. He was alleged to have elbowed an opponent as the players were leaving the field.

Goodman was sent-off in the friendly at Swansea in 1990 for allegedly head-butting Andy Legg.

Willie Johnston was sent off 15 times times during his eventful career – four times with Albion, seven with Glasgow Rangers, twice with Hearts and once with Scotland and Vancouver Whitecaps.

Frank Sinclair was sent off in only his fourth game for Albion.

Archie Styles (Everton) was sent off with Johnston for fighting during that FA Cup-tie in 1974 and John Emanuel (Bristol City) accompanied Johnston to the dressing room later that same year.

Johnston's dismissal against Brighton in a League Cup-tie in 1976 came after he had aimed a kick at the referee!

Eddie Connelly was sent off seven times in his career. He was suspended *sine die* by the FA after his second wartime dismissal when playing for Albion in 1940. But he appealed against the decision and was back in action after 11 months. He was the last Albion player to be sent off at The Hawthorns for 34 years.

When Mick Martin was dismissed in the 1978 FA Cup semi-final at Highbury, he became the first player to be sent off at this stage of the competition for more than 40 years.

Alistair Robertson was sent off in the tunnel at the end of the game against Watford in December 1984 (along with future Albion striker George Reilly).

In the League Cup semi-final first leg game in 1982, Albion's Jol was ordered off along with Tottenham's Tony Galvin for fighting.

When Bennett and Nicholl were dismissed at The Victoria Ground in 1985, Stoke's Bertschin also saw 'red' (dismissed with Bennett). This was the first time two Albion players had been sent off in the same League match.

Two Bradford City players (Leigh Palin and West Bromwich-born David Evans) were dismissed in a League game at The Hawthorns in May 1987, and Barnsley had substitute Sean Dunphy sent-off in a League game on the same ground on 11 November 1989. (Albion won 7-0).

Palmer (Albion) and the Leeds duo of Ian Snodin and John Stiles (son of Nobby) were sent off in the space of six minutes (either side of half-time) during the League game at The Hawthorns in December 1986. Palmer and Snodin went off together for fighting.

Along with Bradley, two Torquay United players – Justin Fashanu (for illegal use of elbow) and Wes Saunders (fighting with Bradley) – were also sent off in the game in February 1992. The referee was Ted Parker (Preston) who also booked seven players in this same fixture.

When dismissed at Barnsley in 1993, Simon Garner became the first Albion substitute ever to be sent off and the first Albion player to receive his marching orders on the opening day of a League season.

George Reilly was sent off for head butting an opponent after just three minutes of the Base Charity Cup-tie at Burton in 1987. This is the earliest sending off of an Albion player, while the latest was Strodder's dismissal at Bristol City in the League Cup of 1990 (16 minutes into added time).

When Patsy Gallacher (Sunderland) was ordered off in a League game against Albion at The Hawthorns on 6 April 1935 for 'ungentlemanly conduct', another 37 years passed before the next visiting player was dismissed on Albion soil – Peter Cormack of Liverpool taking an early bath on 9 December 1972.

Three Albion players – Maurice Setters (England Under-23), Mick Martin (Republic of Ireland) and Willie Johnston (Scotland) have been sent off while representing their country in internationals.

Aidan Davison was the first goalkeeper ever to be sent off at The Hawthorns – dismissed for a 'professional' foul playing for Bolton Wanderers against Albion in a First Division game on 6 November 1993.

On 10 November 1973, two former Albion players – Ken Stephens (Bristol Rovers) and Doug Fraser (Walsall) – who lined up in the 1968 FA Cup semi-final v Birmingham City, were sent off for fighting in a Third Division match at Fellows Park.

Albion have had four players sent off in Football League matches at The Victoria Ground (Stoke).

On 30 April 1995, Tranmere Rovers defender Dave Higgins was sent off against Albion in a League match at The Hawthorns. Eleven days earlier he had been dismissed while playing in a Pontins League game for Rovers on the same ground.

Several former Albion players have been sent-off while playing against Albion: John Durnin (Oxford United, 1991), Colin West (Swansea City, 1993), Dave Barnett (Birmingham City, 1993) and Imre Varadi (Rotherham United, 1993).

Players sent off playing against Albion who subsequently signed for the Baggies include: Tony Morley (Aston Villa,

1982), George Reilly (Watford, 1984), Simon Garner (Blackburn Rovers, 1987) and Tony Ford (Stoke City, 1988).

Among the Albion players sent off in reserve team games are defender Ernie Pattinson and winger Jimmy Poxton (in the same fixture v Sheffield Wednesday, away, October 1927); goalkeeper Fred Brown (at Molineux in February 1956); striker David Cross (v Everton 1984-85); forward Imre Varadi (v Hull City 1985-86); centre-half Martyn Bennett (v Port Vale 1986-87); 'keeper Mel Rees (twice in successive seasons at Blackpool 1990-91 and Blackburn Rovers 1991-92); defender Paul Raven and striker Colin West (in the same match at Rotherham in 1991-92); midfielder Steve Parkin (v Bolton Wanderers 1991-92); centre-back Gary Strodder (v Sheffield United 1994-95) and defender Rob Hayter (v Nottingham Forest 1996) (See CENTRAL LEAGUE).

Suspension
The first Albion player to receive a suspension from the Football League for misconduct was centre-forward Willie Hendry, who was reported to the League for fighting with a Bolton player (Sneddon) on 5 November 1888. Both players were suspended for a month in December of that year.

Willie Johnston joined Albion in December 1972 after having just finished a 67-day suspension, imposed by the Scottish FA.

SETTERS, Maurice Edgar
Maurice Setters was a tough-tackling, bandy-legged, crew-cut wing-half or inside-forward who also filled in at full-

back and centre-half during a playing career which spanned 20 years. Born in Honiton, Devon in 1936, he joined Exeter City in 1952, transferred to Albion for £3,000 in 1954. After scoring ten goals in 132 games for the Baggies, he moved to Manchester United for £30,000 in 1960. Setters gained England schoolboy honours and went on to win one youth cap and 16 at Under-23 level, also playing for the FA XI and Young England. He helped United win the FA Cup (1963) and after leaving Old Trafford he had spells with Stoke City, Coventry and Charlton Athletic before becoming Doncaster Rovers' manager (1971-74). Setters then coached at Sheffield Wednesday and was assistant manager at Rotherham United and chief scout with Newcastle United before spending nine years as assistant manager (to Jack Charlton) of the Republic of Ireland national team.

SHAW, Cecil Ernest

Teak-tough full-back who scored 14 goals (most of them penalties) in 251 games for Albion between 1936 and 1947. Mansfield-born in 1911, Cecil Shaw played for Rufford Colliery (Notts) prior to joining Wolverhampton Wanderers in 1930. He made 183 appearances during his six years at Molineux before teaming up with his namesake, George, at The Hawthorns. Able to withstand any challenge, Shaw was one of only a handful of footballers to serve with Albion before, during and after World War Two. He left the club for Hereford United and retired in 1949, later refereeing in local Leagues as well as scouting for Albion. He died in Handsworth, Birmingham, in 1977.

SHAW, George Edward

No relation to Cecil, George Shaw was also a full-back, and a very good one at that, who netted 11 goals in 425 appearances for Albion during his 12 years at the club (1926-38). Born in Swinton in 1899, he played for Rossington Main

Colliery, Doncaster Rovers (two spells), Gillingham and Huddersfield Town before moving to The Hawthorns for £4,100. An FA Cup winner in 1931 and finalist four years later with Albion, Shaw helped Huddersfield take the First Division championship three seasons running in the mid-1920s. He gained one England cap (v Scotland in 1932) and also played for the Football League and the FA XI, touring Spain in 1929 and Canada in 1931. An ex-naval man, he joined Stalybridge Celtic as player-manager (from Albion) and later played for and coached Floriana of

Malta. On his retirement in 1951 he went to live near Doncaster where he died in 1973.

SHEARMAN, Benjamin

A useful outside-left, quick off the mark who was surprisingly accurate with his centres. Born in Lincoln in 1884, Shearman played for Worksop Town, Rotherham Town and Bristol City before joining Albion in 1911. At the end of his first season at the club he appeared in the FA Cup Final, having twice represented the Football League. He spent eight years with Albion during which time he scored 18 goals in 143 outings. He left The Hawthorns for Nottingham Forest in 1919 and later served with Gainsborough Trinity before becoming trainer-coach of Norton Woodseats (1932-37). He died in 1958.

SHEFFIELD UNITED

Albion's record against United:

Football League

Venue	P	W	D	L	F	A	Pts
Home	43	22	8	13	74	48	56
Away	43	9	14	20	38	63	33
Totals	86	31	22	33	112	111	89

FA Cup

Home	3	3	0	0	13	3	
Away	3	0	2	1	2	4	
totals	6	3	2	1	15	7	

League Cup

Home	1	1	0	0	2	1	

Texaco Cup

Home	1	1	0	0	1	0	
Away	1	0	1	0	1	1	
Totals	2	1	1	0	2	1	

Other Matches

Away	2	0	0	2	0	4	

Albion's first visit to Bramall Lane for a friendly match with United on 19 April 1892 ended in a 3-0 defeat.

Albion's best win over United is 7-1 in a fourth-round FA Cup-tie at The Hawthorns on 26 January 1935. 'W.G.' Richardson scored a hat-trick in gale-force conditions.

Albion's best League win over the 'Blades' is 4-0 – achieved twice, each time at home – on 31 March 1923 (Division One) when Welsh international Stan Davies claimed a hat-trick and on 4 November 1987 (Division Two) when four different forwards figured on the scoresheet.

Between 1903 and 1934 Albion won only once in 15 League and Cup visits to Bramall Lane.

A record crowd of 57,197 saw United beat Albion 2-0 in a sixth-round FA Cup-tie at Bramall Lane on 7 March 1925.

Albion's outside-right Frank Griffin broke his right leg during his side's 4-1 fifth-round FA Cup replay victory over United at The Hawthorns on 19 February 1958.

Martin Dickinson, played for the Baggies and the Blades.

When Albion did the 'double' over United in 1995-96 (3-1 at home and 2-1 away) their victory at Sheffield was the first there in 30 years.

Albion League debutants v United: Tom Hutchinson (1894), Billy Newall (1894), Billy Williams (1894), Arthur Smith (1899), Billy Folks (1904), Sam Richardson (1915), Sid Hatton (1920), Ernest Ford (1923), George Shaw (1926), Harold White (1938), Mickey Fudge (1963), Asa Hartford (1968), Peter Latchford (1972), Wayne Dobbins (1986), Graeme Hogg (1987), Steve Parkin (1989), Bernard McNally (1989), John Thomas (1989).

Players with both clubs: Brett Angell, Ian Benjamin, Dick Bourne, Eddie Colquhoun, Martin Dickinson, Willie Hendry, Ken McNaught, Mel Rees, Teddy Sandford, Gerry Summers, Imre Varadi, Arthur Watson, Paul A.Williams.

Also associated with both clubs: Stewart Evans was a United apprentice who later played League football with Albion; Jack Driscoll, Adrian Littlejohn and Martin Pike were Albion reserves who later made United's first XI and Dave Bradford played competitive football with United and Central League football with Albion. Arthur Rowley played for Albion (1940s) and managed United (1968-69); Jimmy Hagan played for United (1938-58) and managed Albion (1963-67) and Dennis Mortimer played for United and was an Albion coach (1990s); Albion first-team trialist Mel Eves (1988) was a League player with United (1984-86).

SHEFFIELD WEDNESDAY
Albion's record against Wednesday:
Football League

Venue	P	W	D	L	F	A	Pts
Home	48	15	16	17	78	71	46
Away	48	12	6	30	69	104	30
Totals	96	27	22	47	147	175	76

FA Cup

Home	3	2	0	1	5	4
Away	6	3	1	2	11	8
Totals	9	5	1	3	16	12

Other Matches

Home	3	1	1	1	6	6
Away	4	2	1	1	7	5
Totals	7	3	2	2	13	11

Wednesday beat Albion 6-0 in the first-ever League meeting between the clubs on 2 January 1893 – and ever since that day the Owls have certainly had the better of the exchanges, winning nearly half of the 96 encounters at League level, 17 of them on Albion soil.

Albion's best win is also 6-0, at Stoney Lane on 22 April 1895. Albion had to win this final League game of the season by this precise scoreline to avoid playing in the dreaded Test matches! There were rumours that the result had been 'fixed.'

Albion's 1,000th game in the First Division saw them beat Wednesday 2-0 at The Hawthorns on 11 February 1933.

After being three times in arrears, Albion eventually won a nine-goal thriller in front of a near 60,000 crowd at Hillsborough by 5-4 on Boxing Day 1952. Two Wednesday players – Curtis and Gannon – conceded own-goals while Kenny diverted Nicholls' effort past his own 'keeper. In the return game at The Hawthorns 24 hours later, 52,681 fans saw Wednesday win 1-0.

Jeff Astle scored a hat-trick in Albion's 4-2 home win over Wednesday on 4 September 1965 – his first treble for the club.

Albion were 2-0 down at home to Wednesday on 13 February 1954, but they bounced back to win the game 4-2.

Albion beat Wednesday 2-0 in the FA Cup semi-final of 1895 but 40 years later the Owls gained sweet revenge by

Albion's line-up which met Sheffield Wednesday in the 1935 FA Cup Final. Back row (left to right): Fred Everiss (secretary), Fred Reed (trainer), Harry Raw, Harold Pearson, Joe Carter, George Shaw, Claude Jephcott (director). Middle row: 'W.G.' Richardson, Teddy Sandford, Bill Richardson, Billy Bassett (chairman), Tommy Glidden, Jimmy Edwards, Bert Trentham. Front row: Stan Wood, Jack Sankey, Wally Boyes, Harry Jones, Jimmy Murphy.

defeating Albion 4-2 in the Wembley Final, when Ellis Rimmer scored twice in the dying minutes of an excellent contest.

Albion lost 1-0 to Leicester City in the 1969 FA Cup semi-final at Hillsborough.

One of Tony Brown's finest goals was scored in a third-round FA Cup-tie at Hillsborough in January 1970. The Owls still won 2-1.

Albion League debutants v Wednesday: Bob Crone (1893), Billy Smith (1903), Ernie Edwards (1913), Harry 'Popeye' Jones (1935), Norman Heath (1947), Harry Guy (1950), Michael Lee (1956), Bob Ward (1975), Ian Edwards (1975), David Burrows (1986), Mark Robinson (1986). Roddy McLeod made his debut for Albion in an FA Cup-tie v Wednesday in 1891.

Players with both clubs: Gary Bannister, Lewis Bedford, Laurie Bell, Harry Burton, George Drury, Bobby Hope, Phil King, David Mills, Gary Owen, Carlton Palmer, George Reid, David Rushbury, Craig Shakespeare, George Simpson, Garry Thompson, Imre Varadi, Colin West, Charlie Wilson, Doug Witcomb.

Also associated with both clubs: Jim Driscoll, Colin Gregson and Jim Holton were all Albion reserves and Wednesday League players; Ron Atkinson and Vic Buckingham managed both clubs; Gordon Clark was Albion manager and later Wednesday assistant manager; Maurice Setters was an Albion player and Wednesday coach; George Irwin was Albion's reserve 'keeper, who later became Wednesday's trainer; Tony Brien, an occasional first-teamer with Albion, made one appearance for Wednesday in the 1995 Inter-Toto Cup competition; Tommy Jones was a trainer at both clubs and Bill Asprey coached at The Hawthorns and Hillsborough.

SHINTON, Frederick

Nicknamed 'Appleyard' and 'Tickler' Fred Shinton was a very sporting character who played with dash and tenacity.

A courageous centre-forward, he scored 46 goals in just 68 games for Albion, including three four-timers in a haul of 26 in 21 outings in 1906-07. Born in Wednesbury in 1883, he played for Wednesbury Old Athletic and Hednesford Town before joining Albion in 1905. He stayed at The Hawthorns for two and a half years, leaving for Leicester Fosse in late 1907. After being top-scorer in Division Two in 1909-10 with 31 goals he went on to play for Bolton Wanderers and Leicester (again) before retiring through ill-health in 1912. He died in 1923.

SHREWSBURY TOWN

Albion's record against Shrewsbury:

Football League

Venue	P	W	D	L	F	A	Pts
Home	4	3	0	1	9	3	9
Away	4	2	1	1	5	3	7
Totals	8	5	1	2	14	6	16

League Cup

	P	W	D	L	F	A	
Home	1	1	0	0	2	1	
Away	1	0	1	0	3	3	
Totals	2	1	1	0	5	4	

Autoglass Trophy

	P	W	D	L	F	A	
Home	1	1	0	0	4	0	

Other Match

	P	W	D	L	F	A	
Away	1	0	1	0	1	1	

When Albion, under Brian Talbot's leadership, defeated Shrewsbury 4-0 at home on 2 January 1989 they went to the top of the Second Division.

Shrewsbury came back from 3-0 down to force a draw in the first leg of a 2nd round League Cup-tie at Gay Meadow on 16 October 1981 – this being the first-ever meeting between the clubs.

The first season the teams met at League level (1986-87) Town 'doubled up' over Albion, winning 1-0 at home and 2-1 at The Hawthorns (Division Two).

Arthur Rowley, played for Albion and later appeared for and managed Shrewsbury.

Albion's 4-0 win over Town in the Autoglass Trophy on 22 October 1991 was witnessed by just 6,992 fans.

Albion League debutants v Town: Ken Swain (1988), Chris Whyte (1988).

Players with both clubs: Mark Barham, Bobby Barker, Gary Hackett, Asa Hartford, Robert Hopkins, Tony Kelly, Steve Mackenzie, Bernard McNally, John Paskin, Gary Piggott, Tony Rees, Arthur Rowley, Kevin Summerfield, Mickey Thomas. As player-manager Rowley scored 152 League goals for Shrewsbury (1958-65).

Associated with both clubs: Dave Butler, Jim Driscoll, Mike Gibson, Ron Green Jim Holton, Gary Leonard, Vic Robinson and Ray Russell were all Albion reserves who later played in Shrewsbury's first team. Gavin Ward was a Shrewsbury reserve who later kept goal for Albion's first team, and current Albion assistant manager Arthur Mann was a Shrewsbury player in 1979.

SIMMONS, Charles

'Chippy' Simmons had the honour of scoring Albion's first League goal at The Hawthorns – the equaliser to Steve

Bloomer's opener for Derby County in a First Division match on 3 September 1900. An upright player, good on the ball with a fair turn of speed and an excellent right-foot shot, he had two spells with Albion and in all netted 81 goals in 193 appearances. Born in West Bromwich in 1878, Simmons played for Oldbury Town and Worcester Rovers before joining Albion in 1898. He spent six years with the club and then had a season with West Ham United, returning to The Hawthorns for his second spell which lasted two more seasons. After that he did well with Chesterfield Town before joining Wellington Town, later playing in Canada with Royal Rovers (1910-11). On his retirement in 1922, Simmons returned to West Bromwich where he took over a pub, having learnt the trade initially in 1909. He died in Wednesbury in 1937.

SIMOD CUP

Albion competed in the Simod Cup for two seasons: 1987-88 & 1988-89, playing three matches, all away from home. Their full record in the competition is:

Venue	P	W	D	L	F	A
Away	3	1	0	2	6	7

Albion defeated Oldham Athletic on the plastic pitch at Boundary Park by 3-0 in their first match in the competition on 10 November 1987. The attendance was a meagre 1,841.

A crowd of 5,998 saw West Ham United defeat Albion 5-2 at Upton Park on 9 November 1988 with their centre-forward Leroy Rosenior scoring four goals.

SMITH, Joseph

Black Country born and bred, Joe Smith came from Netherton and served Albion before, during and after World War One. He played his early football with Netherton St Andrew's, Darby End Victoria and Cradley St Luke's, joining Albion in 1910 at the age of 20. In the next 16 years he developed into one of the finest right-backs in the country. He appeared in 471 games for Albion without ever scoring a goal. He helped the team win the Second Division title in 1911, reach the FA Cup Final the following year and then carry off the League championship crown in 1920, when he missed only two games as partner to Jesse Pennington. Smith also won junior international honours in 1909 and

he went on to play in two full and one Victory internationals for the full England team. Described as a 'right-back strategist' Smith had a strong tackle for a relatively small man, and he was so consistent, being absent from just five First Division games out of a possible 252 between 1919 and 1925. He guested for Everton and Notts County in the war and left The Hawthorns in 1926 to join Birmingham. He was player-manager of Worcester City for three years – 1929-32 – and on his retirement became a licensee in Dudley. Smith died in a Wolverhampton hospital in 1956.

SNEEKES, Richard

When long-haired midfielder Richard Sneekes moved to The Hawthorns from Bolton Wanderers for £400,000 in March 1996, Albion were deep in relegation trouble, but the Dutchman proceeded to score ten goals in 13 games during the last two months of the season to lift the Baggies to First Division safety and in doing so became a cult hero at The Hawthorns. Born in Amsterdam in October 1968, Sneekes played for Ajax Amsterdam as a 16-year-old in

Holland's premier League, being the youngest player ever to represent the club at senior level (a record since beaten by Clarence Seedorf). He was capped 22 times for his country's youth team and twice at Under-21 level before leaving Ajax to play for two more Dutch sides, FC Volendam (1987) and Fortuna Sittard (1990), later assisting Lugano (Switzerland) on loan before being sold to Bolton for £200,000 in 1994. He scored 11 goals in 69 games whilst at Burnden Park, helping the Wanderers reach the Carling Premiership.

SOUTHAMPTON

Albion's record against the Saints:

Football League

Venue	P	W	D	L	F	A	Pts
Home	25	16	4	5	38	21	38
Away	25	2	10	13	25	44	14
Totals	50	18	14	18	63	65	52

FA Cup

Venue	P	W	D	L	F	A
Home	3	0	3	0	3	3
Away	5	1	0	4	5	11
Totals	8	1	3	4	8	14

Tennent-Caledonian Cup

Venue	P	W	D	L	F	A
Away*	1	0	1	0	1	1

* Played at Ibrox Park on 5 August 1978 and Saints won 3-1 on penalties.

Ally Brown scores for Albion in the 4-0 home win against Southampton in October 1979.

Other Matches

Home	1	1	0	0	5	2
Away	1	1	0	0	2	1
Totals	2	2	0	0	7	3

Albion have a poor League record at Southampton, only two wins in 25 visits: 1-0 in February 1947 (Billy Elliott the scorer) and 2-0 in August 1969, when Colin Suggett netted twice on his debut.

Albion and Southampton were promotion rivals in 1948-49 and in a crucial game at The Dell in front of a record crowd of 30,856 Albion earned a vital point which set them on their way to gaining a place in the First Division. Saints stayed down.

Albion's other victory at The Dell was a significant one when they defeated Saints 3-2 after extra-time in a fourth-round FA Cup replay in February 1968, on their way to Wembley glory.

Southampton ousted Albion from the FA Cup in season 1975-76, winning a fourth round replay at The Dell 4-0 (after a 1-1 draw).

Albion's best League win of the 18 recorded so far is 5-1 at The Hawthorns on 3 May 1930 (Division Two) when Jimmy Cookson scored four times. Albion also won 4-0 at home in October 1979.

Saints' best League win over Albion is 4-0 at The Dell (Division One) on 26 August 1967. Albion also lost 4-1 at Southampton in December 1982 and 4-3 in March 1985. Garry Thompson netted twice for the Baggies in the latter game.

In a Football League South fixture at The Hawthorns on 24 November 1945, Albion's Arthur Rowley crashed into a goalpost at the Smethwick End and snapped it in half. The game finished in semi-darkness with Albion winners by 5-1 thanks to a Billy Elliott hat-trick.

Albion League debutants v Saints: Hugh Morrow (1948), Pete Freeman (1969), Colin Suggett (1969), Danny Hegan (1969), Garry Pendrey (1979), Derek Monaghan (1980), Maarten Jol (1981), Gary Robson (1983).

Players with both clubs: James Bowden, Tommy Broad, Harry Brown, Davey Burnside, Harry Hadley, Billy Light, Graham Lovett, Roddy McLeod, John Reynolds, Terry Simpson, David Speedie, Derek Statham, Stuart Williams.

Also associated with both clubs: Yugoslav international goalkeeper Ivan Katalinic had trials with Albion (1979) and later played 48 League games for Saints (1980-82); Ian Hamilton was an amateur at The Dell (1985) and later joined Albion (1992); Frank Costello was an Albion reserve (1904-05) who later played for Saints and Mick McCartney was also a second-team player at The Hawthorns (1971-73) and a Saints first-team player (1980-81). Gerry Summers was a 1950s Albion player and Southampton scout in 1981 and Mike Kelly coached at both clubs (1980s). Bruce Grobbelaar had a few months with Albion in 1978 and kept goal for Saints in the Premiership (1994-96).

SOUTHEND UNITED

Albion's record against Southend:

Football League

Venue	P	W	D	L	F	A	Pts
Home	3	2	1	0	7	3	7
Away	3	1	0	2	5	4	3
Totals	6	3	1	2	12	7	10

The first meetings took place in 1993-94 (Division One). At The Hawthorns Southend came back from 2-0 down to earn a point at 2-2 and at Roots Hall Albion ran out 3-0 winners to register their first away victory of the season.

By winning 2-0 at home on 15 April 1995, Albion virtually saved themselves from relegation to the Second Division.

Albion League debutant v Southend: Shane Nicholson (1996).

Players with both clubs: Brett Angell, Ian Benjamin, Jeroen Boere, Peter Butler, Joe Dorsett, Kenny Foggo, Tony Forrester, Allan Glover.

Also associated with both clubs: Albion reserves Matt Dunsmore, Ray Whale, and Chris O'Neill all joined Southend (with Forrester) in 1959. Three more Albion reserves – David Hogg, Alistair Love and Tudor Martin –

Sprightly winger Tony Forrester, played for both Albion and Southend.

also played for Southend. Colin Lyman played for Southend (1933-34) before joining Albion. Arthur Rowley, an Albion player in the 1940s, managed Southend 1970-76; Ernie Shepherd played with Rowley at Albion and was later assistant manager-coach at Southend; Gordon Clark was a 1930s player with Southend and Albion scout, assistant manager and manager 1956-61; Albion reserve 'keeper in the 1920s, George Irwin, later became trainer at Southend; Wilf Dixon was a trainer at both clubs between 1955 and 1964 and Geoff Hudson was coach, manager and then general manager at Roots Hall 1968-70 and Albion coach 1970-72.

SOUTHPORT

Southport, a Football League club from 1921-78, have never met Albion at any level.

Players with both clubs: Luther Blissett, Stan Butler, Clive Clark, Jim Cumbes, Andy King.

Also associated with both clubs: Albion reserves Colin Brookes (1960s) and Pat Hilton (1970s) later played for Southport.

SPENNYMOOR UNITED

Albion defeated Spennymoor 7-1 at The Hawthorns in a third-round FA Cup-tie on 16 January 1937. All five Baggies' forwards scored that day – Sandford 2, 'W.G.' Richardson 2, Wood, Jones and Mahon – and the attendance was 23,746.

Albion forward Charlie Hewitt became player-manager of Spennymoor United when he left The Hawthorns in 1910.

In December 1995, former Albion full-back Ronnie Robinson joined United from Scarborough.

SPRING ROAD

In 1960 Albion purchased a piece of land from William Kendrick & Son for £32,000. The club's initial aim was to transform it into a training ground, which they did, building two dressing rooms and a heated gymnasium. But within a year the ground, now known as Spring Road, also became the home of Albion's third team who played in the Warwickshire Combination. In 1969 the facilities at Spring Road were modernised but in 1974 Albion's first-team squad chose to take up a new training venue at the University of Aston complex in Great Barr, mainly because of motorway noise and pollution caused by smoke from nearby foundries.

Over the next few years Albion trained at several other venues including the M & B Sports ground in Edgbaston, the GKN sports ground in Smethwick and Hope's sports ground 300 yards down the road from The Hawthorns. In October 1988 Albion sold Spring Road to Kinmain Construction for £298,000.

On 27 July 1985 Albion played a first-team friendly match at Spring Road, beating Rotherham United 2-1.

STAFFORDSHIRE CUP

The Staffordshire Cup competition was introduced in 1878 and five years later Albion, entering for the first time, won the trophy, beating Stoke 3-2 in the final (their first ever success at club level). En route to the final, which was played at Stoke on 21 April 1883, Albion ousted Bloxwich Strollers 4-0 and Aston Villa 1-0, both after replays following 3-3 draws, also St George's, who were disqualified

for fielding two ineligible players when the teams drew 2-2 and Leek White Star 8-0 in the semi-final. A crowd of 6,150 witnessed the final, when George Timmins, Fred Bunn and George Bell (with the winner) scored for Albion, who fielded this team: Bob Roberts; Harry Bell, Jim Stanton; Ezra Horton, Bunn, John While (captain); Jack Whitehouse, Harry Aston, Billy Bisseker, Timmins and G. Bell. Albion's first team played in another nine Staffordshire Cup Finals, the details being:

12 April 1884
St George's 2 Albion 1 (Loach)
10 May 1886 Replay
Albion 4* (Green, Woodhall, Bayliss) Stoke 2 (after 0-0 draw)
* Only three scorers given – one goal was attributed to a 'scrimmage'.
9 April 1887
Walsall Swifts 0 Albion 4 (Bayliss 2, Woodhall, Paddock)
28 April 1888 2nd Replay
Albion 1 (Woodhall) Wolverhampton W 2 (after 0-0 & 1-1 draws)
20 April 1889
Leek 0 Albion 2 (Wilson, Bayliss)
5 May 1898
Burslem Port Vale 1 Albion 0
26 April 1900 Replay
Burslem Port Vale 0 Albion 5 (Simmons, Walker 2, Roberts 2) (after 1-1 draw)
25 November 1901
Stoke 0 Albion 3 (McLean, Lee, Harper)
17 November 1902
Stoke 0 Albion 2 (Buck 2)

Albion's first team played in the competition until 1905. Their last tie was on 2 October of that year v Aston Villa (a), lost 4-0.

Thereafter the Staffordshire FA decreed that reserve teams could take part in the competition and Albion's second XI went on to win the trophy outright in 1924 (3-0 v Stoke); 1926 (3-1 v Stoke); 1932 (3-2 v Wolves); 1933 (2-0 v Aston Villa) and 1951 (1-0 v Wolves).

Albion's reserve team lost in the finals of 1907, 1908, 1910, 1925, 1938 and 1953.

In 1969 Albion shared the Cup with Stoke City. The sides drew 0-0 in the final which was also a Central League fixture.

Albion's record in the Staffordshire Cup (first team only):

Venue	P	W	D	L	F	A
Home	27	22	4	1	114	20
Away	41	21	6	14	91	62
Totals	68	43	10	15	205	82

Albion scored in all but one of their 27 home games.

23-0 v Burton Wanderers (h) on 1 February 1890 is Albion's best win in the competition.

Their heaviest defeat is 6-1 at Aston Villa on 10 October 1898.

STAFFORDSHIRE FOOTBALL ASSOCIATION
Grand Football Match.
FINAL TIE for COUNTY CHALLENGE CUP
VALUE 50 GUINEAS.
Winners to receive GOLD MEDALS: Losers, Silver Medals.

STOKE
v.
WEST BROMWICH ALBION.

Stoke Team.		West Bromwich Albion.	
H. WILDIN (Goal).		R. ROBERTS (Goal).	
T. STANFORD,	Backs	H. BELL,	Backs
M. MELLOR,		J. STANTON,	
H. R. BROWN,	Half Backs	E. HORTON,	
F. BETTANY,		F. BUNN,	Half Backs
E. JOHNSON,		J. WHITE,	
F. POWELL,		H. ASTON,	
G. SHUTT,	Forwards	J. WHITEHOUSE,	
P. FENNELL,		G. TIMMINS,	Forwards
W. MYATT,		G. BELA,	
F. BENNETT,		W. BISSEKER.	

Stoke have scored 42 goals to 3; West Bromwich 32 to 8 in the above competition. Special Trains from all parts. Kick-off at 4 o'clock.
ADMISSION, 6d. and 1s.
AT STOKE, SATURDAY NEXT, APRIL 21st.
Tickets to be obtained on the way to the ground.
West Bromwich Albion have only been beaten once this season and are in for the Final of the Wednesbury Charity Cup.

Team sheet for the 1883 Staffordshire Cup Final.

STALYBRIDGE CELTIC

Celtic spent just two seasons in the Football League (1921-23).

Albion have played Celtic twice at senior level, beating them 2-0 (away) in a first round FA Cup replay on 17 January 1923 (after a 0-0 draw at The Hawthorns).

Associated with both clubs: Albert McPherson played for Celtic in the 1950s and later became Albion's coach-trainer (1965 to mid '80s). Jack Gaskell and Dick Jones were 1950s Albion reserves who later played for Celtic. George Shaw, Albion's full-back from 1926-38, joined Celtic as player-manager after leaving The Hawthorns.

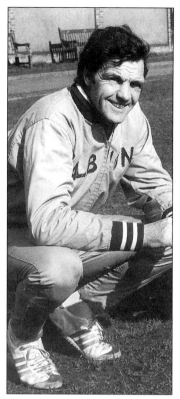

Albion's Albert McPherson played for Stalybridge Celtic in the 1950s.

STATHAM, Derek

One of the finest left-backs in England during the early 1980s, Statham was unlucky not to have received more than

the three England international caps he won, this being due to the form and consistency of Kenny Sansom. Nevertheless, Albion got excellent mileage out of the Wolverhampton-born defender, whose ball skills, attacking ability, drive and enthusiasm was admired by The Hawthorns fans. 'Dekka' scored ten goals in 378 appearances at senior level for the Baggies between 1976 and 1987 when he was transferred to Southampton for £100,000.

Statham joined Albion straight from school as a 16 year-old in 1975 and made his League debut at Stoke a year later, scoring past Peter Shilton! Winner of seven England Youth caps, one 'B' cap and six at Under-21 level, he gained an FA Youth Cup winners' medal in 1976 and helped Albion reach three Cup semi-finals and the UEFA Cup quarter-final, in the space of five seasons (1977-78 & 1981-82). He was voted Midlands' Sportswriters' 'Young Player of the Year' in 1978. From The Dell, Statham moved to Stoke City (1989), then onto Walsall (1991) and rounded off his playing career with a spell at Telford United.

STEVENSON, James

Stevenson, 6ft 2ins tall, began his career as a centre-forward and ended it as a resilient, strong-tackling centre-half. Born in Bonhill, Dumbartonshire in 1875, he played his early football in Scotland with Dumbarton Fereday and Dumbarton, joining Preston North End in 1895. Three years

later he teamed up with Bristol St George, and returned to Deepdale after a season. In 1900 Albion paid £150 for his services and he went on to score nine goals in 129 appearances in a three-year stay at The Hawthorns, helping Albion win the Second Division championship in 1902. The following season he represented the Anglo-Scots v Scotland and in 1904 moved back to Dumbarton, retiring just before World War One. He was Albion's assistant trainer for the 1914-15 season and died following a tragic accident at the Leven Shipyard in 1925.

STOCKPORT COUNTY

Albion's record against County:

Football League

Venue	P	W	D	L	F	A	Pts
Home	9	7	1	1	19	5	17
Away	9	5	2	2	11	11	12
Totals	18	12	3	3	30	16	29

FA Cup

	P	W	D	L	F	A	
Away	1	1	0	0	5	0	

Other Matches

	P	W	D	L	F	A	
Away	2	1	0	1	5	5	

Albion's best win over Stockport is 5-0 – in a fifth-round FA Cup-tie at Edgeley Park on 16 February 1935. County's skipper blundered after winning the toss, choosing to face driving rain and strong winds. Albion were unstoppable and led 5-0 at half-time with four of their goals coming in the space of nine minutes (18th-27th). After the break Albion had no difficulty in holding on to their advantage.

Albion's best League win over County is 4-2, at The Hawthorns, on 18 February 1911 (Division Two), while County's best over Albion is 5-1 at Edgeley Park (also in Division Two) on 20 February 1993. Earlier that season Albion won 3-0 at home when Simon Garner

Danny Campbell, a centre-half with both Albion and Stockport.

A goal for John Paskin in Albion's 6-0 win over Stoke in December 1988.

scored a superb goal. Albion League debutants v County: Bill Bowser (1907), Fred Rouse (1909), Stewart Bowen (1991), Dave Pritchard (1991), Stacy Coldicott (1992).

Players with both clubs: Brett Angell, Bobby Blood, Danny Campbell, Reg Cutler, Ike Evenson, Asa Hartford, Derek Kevan, John Paskin, John Reynolds, Winston White, Paul A.Williams. Hartford was player-manager of County (1987-89).

Also associated with both clubs: Albion midfielder Len Cantello later became County's coach, and four Albion reserves, Percy Anderson, Steve Burke, Alan Common and Gary Leonard also played for County. Stuart Pearson, Albion's coach in the 1980s, was earlier a coach with County.

STOKE CITY

Albion's record against Stoke:

Football League

Venue	P	W	D	L	F	A	Pts
Home	55	28	10	17	110	65	71
Away	55	9	17	29	56	104	36
Totals	110	37	27	46	166	169	107

FA Cup

Home	2	1	1	0	5	2	
Away	2	1	1	0	4	2	
Totals	4	2	2	0	9	4	

Autoglass Trophy

Away	1	0	0	1	1	2	

Other Matches

Home	23	15	3	5	70	34	
Away	29	13	9	7	59	46	
Totals	52	28	12	12	129	80	

Albion's first trophy success came in the Staffordshire Cup Final of 1883 when they beat Stoke 3-2 away (See STAFFORDSHIRE CUP).

Albion's first League game was against Stoke (away) on 8 September 1888. Albion won 2-0 to become the first team to head the new Football League table (on goal-average).

Albion's worst-ever League defeat is 10-3 – suffered at the hands of Stoke at The Victoria Ground in a First Division match on 4 February 1937. An early injury to 'keeper Billy Light didn't help Albion's cause and the home side dominated the game from the 11th minute on. Freddie

Steele helped himself to five goals with Joe Johnson (soon to move to The Hawthorns) scoring twice.

Albion also lost 5-0 at Stoke in November 1903, 4-0 in September 1937 (another hat-trick for Steele) and 5-1 in January 1953 – all League games.

Albion's best League wins over Stoke (all at home) have been: 5-1 in October 1933, 5-3 in September 1964 (when Baggies' full-back Bobby Cram scored a hat-trick), 6-2 in September 1965 (a hat-trick this time for John Kaye), 5-2 in August 1970 and 6-0 in December 1988.

Between 1989 and 1996, Albion met Stoke 13 times in League competition and once in the Autoglass Trophy – and never won a single game.

Garth Crooks scored a hat-trick for Stoke in their 3-2 League win over Albion in December 1979. Crooks later joined Albion.

Albion sealed Stoke's relegation to Division Two with a 3-1 victory at The Hawthorns in the last home game of the 1976-77 season.

When the sides were drawn together in the fifth round of the FA Cup in 1888, Stoke offered Albion £40 to switch the tie to The Victoria Ground. They were rebuffed and Albion swept to a 4-1 victory with 'Jem' Bayliss scoring all four goals.

In a wartime League Cup-tie on 19 February 1944, Stoke beat Albion 8-2 with both Steele and Tommy Sale netting hat-tricks.

Albion League debutants v Stoke: Billy Bassett, Ezra Horton, 'Jem' Bayliss, Willie Hendry, Jack Horton, Tom Pearson, Charlie Perry, Bob Roberts, George Timmins, Joe Wilson and George Woodhall (all in 1888 – the first game in the competition); Alex Ramsey (1888), John Rea (1894), John Cameron (1896), Platt Gollings (1899), Jim Stevenson (1900), Alf Owen (1904), Harry Wright (1907), Harry Boston (1929), Norman Whitehead (1934), Mike Betteridge (1950), Fred Richardson (1950), Dennis Martin (1968), Hughie Reed (1968), Derek Statham (1976), Jimmy Nicholl (1984), Simeon Hodson (1988), David Speedie (1993), Paul Agnew (1995).

Players with both clubs: George Baddeley, Gary Bannister, Paul Barron, Tommy Broad, Fred Brown, Garth Crooks, Bill Davies, Paul Dyson, Wayne Ebanks, Fred Fenton, Ross Fielding, Tony Ford, Gary Hackett, Graham Harbey, Willie

Hendry, Geoff Hurst, Joe Johnson, Tony Kelly, Steve Parkin, Paul Reece, Brian Rice, Fred Rouse, Maurice Setters, Andy Smith, Andrew 'Scottie' Smith, Derek Statham, Brian Talbot, Mickey Thomas, Isaiah Turner.

Also associated with both clubs: Ex-Albion midfielder Asa Hartford was Stoke's assistant manager in 1993-94; Brian Caswell played for Albion's reserves and later coached at Stoke; Bill Asprey had over 340 games for Stoke (1954-65) and later managed the Potters (1984-85) after coaching at Albion (1972-74); Stoke goalkeeper John Farmer 'guested' for Albion in 1972 and Sid Glidden, an Albion reserve (1925-28) was Stoke's trainer (1952-54). David Powell, an Albion reserve goalkeeper, was on loan at Stoke in 1988 and another 'keeper, Barry Siddall, on loan to Albion in 1990, earlier kept goal for Stoke (1984-86).

STONEY LANE

Stoney Lane (situated behind the Sandwell Brewery) was Albion's home ground for 15 years, 1885 to 1900, yet the club's administration was dealt with at the nearby Plough & Harrow public house and afterwards at offices in High Street, West Bromwich.

Albion moved to Stoney Lane (from Four Acres) because they wanted a more spacious ground, and the club's committee were authorised to secure the tenancy of the field which belonged to the local undertaker, Mr H.Webb, on 27 February 1885.

The lease was drawn up for an initial seven-year term at an annual rent of £28, and work started almost immediately to convert the field into a suitable pitch for Albion to play on.

The field was levelled and returfed, and ashes were spread round the perimeter of the ground which was 120 yards long by 82 yards wide. The playing area measured 110 yards by 78 – one of the largest in the area.

A wooden grandstand, with planking serving as seats, was erected. Known affectionately as 'Noah's Ark', this was on the Sandwell Road side of the ground (the brewery side). The centre of the stand had covering for 600 spectators while the

An Albion team group of 1899-1900, their last season at Stoney Lane. Back row (left to right): W.J.Paddock (trainer), H.Keys (chairman), A.Jones, A.Adams, H.Hadley, J.Reader, T.Brennand (director), W.Williams, B.Garfield, J.Banks, F.Heaven (secretary), H.Powell (director). Front row: A.Dunn, J.Paddock, C.Simmons, T.Perry, W.Walker, R.Roberts, W.Richards.

two uncovered portions at each end could house 1,500 fans. The opposite side of the ground was covered in ash, and this was gradually raised towards the back so that everyone could get a clear view of the pitch. There was no covered accommodation of any sort there.

Fencing and a boundary wall were also put in place and two simply furnished brick 'dressing tents' sporting corrugated iron roofs were also constructed, along with three refreshment stalls. Wagonettes and vehicles were permitted to drive into the ground and were stationed behind the bank at the Stoney Lane end where there were

also had five 'pay boxes'. These were found to be inefficient, so supporters gained admission by purchasing ground tickets through openings in the walls! Ground tickets could also be bought from the Plough & Harrow pub, and for big matches, neighbouring houses were also utilised to sell tickets.

The pitch had a pronounced slope towards the Stoney Lane end, and the cost of equipping the entire ground cost Albion £370.

To help cover the cost, a series of home friendly matches were arranged, starting with a fixture against a strong Scottish side Third Rifle Volunteers on 5 September 1885, which Albion won 4-1 Tommy Green scoring a hat-trick before a crowd of 2,122.

As the years rolled by so the standards at Stoney Lane slumped – simply because the Albion Directors refused to spend money on the ground which was one of the poorest in the First Division in the early 1890s.

The first season tickets at Stoney Lane cost 5s (25p) each and Albion's total gate receipts in their opening campaign there amounted to £1,190.

The first groundsman, Mr R.Russell, was paid the princely sum of 5s (25p) a week.

The usual entrance fee for games at Stoney Lane was 6d (3p).

The first League fixture at Stoney Lane saw Albion beat Burnley 4-3 on 29 September 1888.

Stoney Lane's biggest crowd – 20,977 – attended the third-round FA Cup-tie against Wolves on 2 March 1895, Albion winning 1-0 with a goal from Roddy McLeod.

Albion's last game at Stoney Lane was played on 16 April 1900 when they beat Nottingham Forest 8-0 in a First Division match before a crowd of 5,187. Billy Walker scored a hat-trick.

Preston North End were the most successful opposing team at Stoney Lane, winning five times.

Of the 27 FA Cup matches staged at the ground, none were drawn – and between 1885 and 1893 Albion were undefeated in 14 consecutive home FA Cup ties.

Albion's full playing record at Stoney Lane was:

Competition	P	W	D	L	F	A
League	170	88	33	49	343	230
FA Cup	27	23	0	4	84	26
Other Matches	155	112	26	17	469	161
Totals	352	223	59	70	896	417

* The two Test Matches of 1896 have been included under 'Other Matches'.

STRIKES (and Rebellions)
Players' Strike 1886

In January 1886, a letter was sent from the Albion committee to the club's 2nd XI players, which read: 'The committee have reluctantly been compelled, owing to the state of the funds, to discontinue paying the second team, but if the balance at the end of the season will permit, a bonus will be given to the second-team players according to the number of matches played. Of course, travelling expenses and refreshments, with payment for necessary loss of time, will be paid by the club.'

The players were so displeased that they refused to play against Small Heath Alliance reserves and the match had to be cancelled. After the first month of the season, Albion's second XI players had been on half-pay which had left them disillusioned and this action by the committee was the last straw. After a number of the malcontents had been briefly suspended they were reinstated to the team, but a few left the club at the season's end to join Crosswell's Brewery FC (later Oldbury Town).

In fact, when the Crosswell's team visited Stoney Lane to play Albion in a Walsall Cup-tie on 16 October 1886, seven

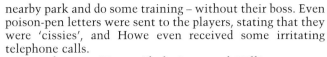

Geoff Carter, just one of the 'rebels' in 1963, when the 'tracksuit saga' led to an escalation of the problems facing Albion manager Jimmy Hagan.

members of their side were former Albion players – Matthews, Bradbury, Stanton, F.Bunn, W.Bunn, Neale and Bradley.

Transfer Rebellion 1963

On 9 December 1963, ten Albion players – Ray Potter, Don Howe, Graham Williams, Doug Fraser, Stan Jones, Terry Simpson, John Kaye, Ronnie Fenton, Bobby Hope and Clive Clark – asked for a transfer because "...we can't get on with manager Jimmy Hagan."

The other member of the first team, Alec Jackson, was already on the transfer list, and he, too, joined the rebellion!

Albion's captain Howe acted as spokeman, and said: "No one is getting any satisfaction out of his football, and we feel the main reason for this is the failure to get on with the manager. Training is too stereotyped, Mr Hagan shows a lack of understanding and imposes too many restrictions."

The upheaval went on for four days and after having their transfer requests turned down by the Albion Board on 11 December, the ten rebels finally decided to return to normal duties as professional footballers, agreeing jointly that a way was open for happy relations in the future between players and the management staff at The Hawthorns.

Mr Jim Gaunt, the Albion chairman, said at a press conference on 13 December 1963:

"This kind of situation is always arising in industry and politics, and can only be settled by give and take on both sides.

"No side has given way. It has been mutually agreed that no information other than the statement which Mr Everiss, the club secretary, will pass on to you, shall be released."

This was the statement read out by Alan Everiss:

"The players are satisfied with the interview this morning with the chairman and manager. The various points have been fully discussed and now we feel the way is open for happy relations in the future.

"We are confident that the machinery exists to iron out any troubles that may arise. The requests for transfers have been withdrawn."

Track Suit Saga 1963

On Thursday 19 December 1963, further trouble flared at The Hawthorns when nine other 'rebels' joined the ten who had asked for a transfer ten days earlier, and refused to train in shorts in bitterly cold weather. After being refused permission to wear track suits, the 21 players, again led by Howe, walked out of their Spring Road training ground at Smethwick, and went off for a special meeting.

Howe had been training with the England party at Birmingham University and when he walked into the training ground on the Thursday morning, he was met by a band of disgruntled Albion players who told him that earlier in the week (Tuesday) they had been refused permission to wear track suits on a freezing cold morning.

They asked Howe what had been agreed during England training sessions. Howe replied: "They let us use our own discretion and treated us like adults. We could wear trouser bottoms if we wished."

At the time when the Albion players staged their walk-out, the temperature in West Bromwich and surrounding area was 27.7 degrees – four degrees below freezing!

This dispute involving manager Hagan, trainer Wilf Dixon and the 21 players, went on for five days, and at one stage during the quarrel the players threatened to go into a

nearby park and do some training – without their boss. Even poison-pen letters were sent to the players, stating that they were 'cissies', and Howe even received some irritating telephone calls.

Four players – Howe, Clark, Jones and Williams – were each fined £5 by manager Hagan for refusing to train at all.

At last, on 23 December 1963, chairman Jim Gaunt announced that a settlement in the 'track-suit saga' had been reached and the following day the Albion players began their afternoon training session by lapping their practice pitch wearing sweaters and shorts. It is understood that this was their own decision!

Manager Hagan made no comment – but a brief statement, issued by the club, revealed that the players and manager had come to a mutual agreement and all was settled.

The 'extra' ten 'rebels' who joined the initial 11 transfer-seekers were: Tony Millington, Bobby Cram, Ray Fairfax, Ron Bradley, Bill Williams, 'Chuck' Drury, Ken Foggo, Geoff Carter, Mickey Fudge and Brian Macready.

Three days after the decision was made to 'return to normal duties' Albion played out a terrific 4-4 draw with Tottenham Hotspur at The Hawthorns and they followed up by winning the return fixture 2-0 in London. The track-suit rebellion was forgotten in a relatively short time.

Manager Hagan remained at The Hawthorns until 1967 and under his leadership Albion won the League Cup in 1966 and were beaten finalists in the same competition two months before his departure.

NB: In April 1964 Howe was transferred to Arsenal.

STRINGER, James

Nicknamed 'Joe' and 'Stinker', Stringer was a sound, vigilant goalkeeper, 6ft 2ins tall and over 13st in weight, who replaced 'Ike' Webb between the posts after moving to The Hawthorns from Wolverhampton Wanderers in 1905. Born in Netherton, Dudley, in 1878, he spent five years with Albion during which time he amassed 172 senior appearances. He left for Dudley Town in 1910 and on his retirement in 1912 he became trainer of Port Talbot, a position he held for four years. He remained in South Wales and died at Llanelli in 1933.

STRODDER, Gary

Resolute, no-nonsense central defender who cost Albion £190,000 from West Ham United in 1990. Born in Cleckheaton in 1965, Strodder joined Lincoln City as a professional in 1983 and moved to Upton Park in 1987 after 149 appearances for the Imps. He then played 81 games for the London club and 166 for Albion (9 goals), helping the Baggies win the Second Division Play-off Final at Wembley in 1993. He left The Hawthorns for Notts County for £145,000 in 1995.

Geoff Hurst is replaced by substitute Tony Brown against Oldham Athletic in October 1975.

SUBSTITUTES

Substitutes today play a big part in the game, and it is sometimes hard to appreciate that their use in the Football League has only been allowed since 1965 (passed at the annual meeting on 29 May of that year). Initially there was only one 'sub' allowed and that for an injured player, and in 1965-66 a total of 746 substitutes were used in League matches, Albion's contribution being eight.

In 1967 the 'injuries' proviso was lifted by the League meaning that the 'sub' could come on at any time for any player.

Only one player sat on the 'subs' bench until 1989. The League then allowed two 'subs' to be used (up to 1994) and since then, in all three major domestic tournaments (League, FA Cup and League Cup) three 'subs' have been allowed. In certain other competitions (Anglo-Italian Cup, Autoglass Trophy etc.) up to five substitutes can now be named.

Graham Lovett was Albion's first League substitute to be used v Northampton Town, away, on 10 September 1965, replacing Kenny Foggo.

Lovett was also the first Albion 'sub' to come off the bench in the FA Cup competition, taking over from Dick Krzywicki in the third-round tie at Colchester on 27 January 1968.

Krzywicki was Albion's first League Cup 'sub' to be utilised, replacing Doug Fraser against Manchester City at home in a third-round tie on 5 October 1966.

Albion's Dennis Clarke became the first substitute to appear in an FA Cup Final, taking over from the injured John Kaye at the end of normal time in the 1968 Final against Everton on 18 May.

Lovett created a hat-trick of substitute 'firsts' when he took over from the injured Jeff Astle in Albion's European Cup-winners' Cup game against RFC Brugge in Belgium on 18 September 1968.

Several players have made their senior debuts for Albion as a substitute, among them in League games: Len Cantello (1968), David Shaw (1973), David Mills (1979), Colin Anderson (1985), Carlton Palmer (1985), Kevin Donovan (1992), Andy Hunt (1993) and Mick Mellon (1993), while Mark Grew had his first game as 'sub' in the home UEFA Cup game v Galastasary in 1978.

Albion used two substitutes for the first time in a League game v Oldham Athletic (h), 15 August 1987, Carlton Palmer and David Burrows replacing Bobby Williamson and Gary Robson.

Albion's first goalkeeping 'sub' in the League was Stuart Naylor, who replaced Tony Lange against Peterborough United (away) in the 11th minute of their match on 15 January 1994.

Striker Nicky Cross made a total of 40 'sub' appearances for Albion between 1981 and 1985 (a club record).

Albion full-back Mickey Forsyth was on the pitch for only 17 seconds of the First Division game against Everton on 11 February 1984 before being substituted by Nicky Cross (Forsyth was injured). This stood as the fastest substitution in Britain until Leicester City's Iwan Roberts went off after only three seconds following a clash with Albion's Stacy Coldicott at the start of a League match at Filbert Street on 9 April 1996.

Substitute David Shaw scored with his first kick 20 seconds after coming on at the start of the second half of Albion's home Second Division match against Oxford United on 12 December 1973.

Ronnie Rees came on as 'sub' for Albion in the fourth-round FA Cup-tie at Fulham on 25 January 1969 and scored the winning goal with his first kick!

Albion manager Ron Atkinson said, after naming David Mills, his record £500,000 signing from Middlesbrough, as substitute at Norwich City on 13 January 1979: "How can I afford to risk such a costly player on a pitch like that – he might hurt himself!"

The Carrow Road surface was frost-bound that afternoon.

Both goalkeepers – Stuart Naylor (Albion) and Luton's Jurgen Sommer were substituted (by Tony Lange and Andy Petterson respectively) in a League game at Kenilworth Road on 3 May 1994. This, in fact, was the first time that all four goalkeepers had been used in a League match.

The first Albion substitute to be sent off in a League encounter was Simon Garner at Barnsley on 14 August 1993.

Former Albion midfielder Craig Shakespeare scored with his first touch of the game after coming on as a substitute for Grimsby Town in their home League game against the Baggies on 1 February 1994 (2-2 draw).

Albion first used three substitutes in a League match v Charlton Athletic (h) on 5 February 1995 – Tony Lange, Lee Ashcroft and Bob Taylor replacing Stuart Naylor, Dave Smith and Andy Hunt respectively.

SUGGETT, Colin

Suggett was only 20 years old when he became Albion's first £100,000 signing, joining the club from Sunderland in 1969. Prior to his move to The Hawthorns, the County Durham-born striker had starred in the 1966 and 1967 FA Youth Cup Finals for the Roker Park club and represented England at both Schoolboy and Youth team levels. He scored twice on

his Albion debut at Southampton and went on to net a total of 30 goals in 170 senior appearances for the Baggies which included the League Cup Final of 1970. He left Albion for Norwich City in a £70,000 deal in 1973 and two years later played in his second losing League Cup Final at Wembley. After leaving Carrow Road, he did well with Newcastle United, whom he served from 1978 to 1981 when he retired to become coach at St James' Park. He was later reserve team manager and also acted as caretaker-manager of the Geordies before leaving the club in 1991. Suggett was a keen golfer, pigeon-fancier, horse-racing buff and greyhound owner, who often gave his colleagues 'guaranteed' tips!

SUNDERLAND

Albion's record against Sunderland:

Football League

Venue	P	W	D	L	F	A	Pts
Home	62	32	15	15	116	87	83
Away	62	8	20	34	63	135	38
Totals	124	40	35	49	179	222	121

FA Cup

Home	2	2	0	0	6	3	
Away	1	1	0	0	2	1	
Totals	3	3	0	0	8	4	

Other Match

Away	1	1	0	0	5	3	

Albion's first game against Sunderland was a friendly at Newcastle Road on 3 May 1890 which they won 5-3.

Sunderland won 10 and drew two of their first 12 League games against Albion (all in Division One).

Albion's best League win of the 40 recorded so far, is 6-4

at The Hawthorns on 27 February 1937. For 30 minutes this game was goalless! Three years earlier, on 24 March 1934, Albion won 6-5 in a real ding-dong encounter.

Other big Albion wins include two 5-1 scorelines – at home on Boxing Day 1932 ('W.G.' Richardson scored a hat-trick) and at Roker Park on New Year's Day 1966 (both in the First Division).

Sunderland's best League victory over Albion is 8-1 at home on 22 October 1892. This latter encounter marked Albion's 100th League game in the competition since 1888. Sunderland also beat Albion 7-1 in the North-East in January 1896; won 5-0 at Roker Park on Christmas Eve 1921; won 5-2 at The Hawthorns and 4-0 on Wearside in 1925-26; crushed Albion 6-1 at home in September 1935 (Raich Carter scored four times); repeated that scoreline on Albion soil on 23 October 1937 (Carter netting a hat-trick this time) and again in a re-arranged First Division game in February 1977.

Albion achieved their first League 'double' over Sunderland at the 40th attempt in 1956-57, winning 2-0 at home and 4-1 away.

In a mid-week League game at Roker Park in March 1954, Albion's goalkeeper Norman Heath received paralysis to his spine and legs. He never played again (See CASUALTIES).

Tony Brown scored 12 goals for Albion in League games against Sunderland, including a hat-trick in a 4-1 home win in August 1964 when the visitors had 15 year-old Derek Forster in goal.

Albion were 2-1 victors in a thrilling third-round FA Cup-tie at Roker Park on 24 February 1912 when a record crowd of 43,383 packed into the ground.

Albion League debutants v Sunderland: Jimmy Burns (1890), Franklin Wright (1895), Arthur Flavell (1897), Jabez Foster (1898), Frank Hobson (1902), Claude Jephcott (1911), Fred Morris (1912), Nelson Howarth (1926), Hugh Foulkes (1931), Frank Griffin (1951), Grenville Jones (1954), Dick Sheppard (1965), Ray Treacy (1966), Eddie Colquhoun (1967), Wayne Ebanks (1983), Julian Darby (1995), Chris Hargreaves (1995).

Shaun Cunnington, played for Albion and Sunderland.

Players with both clubs: Sam Allardyce, Brett Angell, Peter Barnes, Jack Boyd, Frank Cresswell, Shaun Cunnington, Andy Dibble, Tony Ford, Don Goodman, Danny Hegan, Archie McKenzie, 'Sandy' Mc-Nab, Jimmy Millar, Jimmy Nicholl, Colin Suggett, 'Ike' Webb, Colin West.

Suggett became Albion's first £100,000 footballer when he transferred from Sunderland in July 1969.

Jimmy Millar played in Sunderland's first-ever League game against Burnley on 13 September 1890. He scored five goals for the Wearsiders against Fairfield in an FA Cup-tie in 1895 and netted 104 goals in 237 League games in two spells with the Roker Park club: 1890-96 and 1900-04. Millar joined Albion as player-trainer in 1904 from Chelsea.

Also associated with both clubs: Jim Holton, a second-team player with Albion (1968-71), later appeared in 15 League games for Sunderland and won 15 full caps for Scotland. Sid Glidden, an Albion reserve in the 1920s, played for Sunderland's first team in the 1930s. Barry, on loan at Albion in 1900, was Sunderland's first-team goalkeeper for six years (1976-82) making 167 League appearances.

SUPPORTERS CLUBS

West Bromwich Albion's official supporters club was founded on 4 October 1951 with an official membership of 130, and the first headquarters for enrolment was in a lorry parked opposite the main entrance to The Hawthorns in Halfords Lane. The initial club is still in existence today, operating from Westbourne Road, West Bromwich.

Throstle Clubs

On 13 April 1965, the first Throstle Club was opened at The Hawthorns, Birmingham Road (adjoining the Woodman Inn). Former Albion skipper Jesse Pennington pulled the first pint!

The building of the club was a joint operation by the Albion Development Association and local breweries at a cost of £50,000.

Five more Throstle clubs were opened over the next few years – in Halfords Lane (300 yards from the ground), in Dog Kennel Lane, Warley, in Hamstead Road, Great Barr (The Golden Throstle), in Tipton and in Lower Gornal. There is now only one in existence today – the Halfords Lane club – which is run by West Bromwich Albion themselves with former player Ally Brown as steward.

Supporters Club Branches

When West Bromwich Albion celebrated its official centenary in 1979, there were 16 branches of the supporters club spread worldwide including organisations in Australia, on the Isle of Wight and in London.

In 1996 the secretary of the 'main' branch of the WBASC (HQ Halfords Lane Throstle Club) was Alan Cleverley, and there were 26 branches: Avon & Somerset, Devon, Droitwich, East Birmingham, Boney Hay & Cannock, South Midland, Gloucester, Hitchin & District, Ireland, Kidderminster, London, Malta, Manchester, Northern, North East, Oldham, Redditch, Shropshire, South Birmingham, South Wales, Southern, Sutton Coldfield, Tamworth, Walsall, Warwick and Wednesbury, with more in the pipeline. Indeed, there were Albion supporters living in Australia, New Zealand, Scandinavia, Hong Kong, Italy and Spain.

At various times during the season former players, current players and club personnel attend individual branches and usually there is an excellent turnout.

At the end of every season, at the annual Supporters Club Player of the Year Night, a member (or representative) from each branch presents an award to an Albion player who has been voted Player of the Year by the respective branch (Daryl Burgess, Bob Taylor, Paul Mardon and Andy Hunt all won the star prize in recent years).

The London Branch of the Albion Supporters Club were the first such club/organisation to sponsor a Football League match – Albion v Bristol City at The Hawthorns on New Year's Day 1979.

The Albion Supporters Club were awarded the John White Football League Supporters Award in 1968-69 for being the best behaved supporters in the country.

Ten years later, in 1979, Albion fans received another award for good behaviour – this time from the National Federation of Supporters Clubs.

In 1974-75, the Hawthorns Away Travel Section (HATS) was inaugurated by members of the Halfords Lane Throstle Club and this was followed in the 1980s by Mammoth Tours (a travel club run by Dave Holloway).

SWANSEA CITY (TOWN)

Albion's record against Swansea:

Football League

Venue	P	W	D	L	F	A	Pts
Home	10	6	3	1	30	13	17
Away	10	1	3	6	11	21	5
Totals	20	7	6	7	41	34	22

Play-Offs

Home	1	1	0	0	2	0
Away	1	0	0	1	1	2
Totals	2	1	0	1	3	2

FA Cup

Away	1	0	0	1	2	3

Other matches

Home	2	2	0	0	12	3
Away	7	3	2	2	14	14
Totals	9	5	2	2	26	17

Albion's most significant victory over Swansea was the one they achieved at The Hawthorns on Wednesday 19 May 1993, when they triumphed 2-0 in the second-leg of the Division Two Play-off semi-final to go through to Wembley 3-2 on aggregate, having lost the first game at Vetch Field the previous Sunday. Micky Mellon (Albion) and Colin West (Swansea, ex-Albion) were both sent-off in the second-leg (See PLAY-OFFS).

The first six League meetings between the clubs (all in Division Two) produced 34 goals – in 1927-28 Albion won 5-2 at home and lost 3-2 away; in 1928-29 Albion won 5-1 at The Hawthorns and crashed 6-1 at Swansea and in 1929-30, it was Albion 6 Swansea 2 in West Bromwich and 1-0 to the Welsh side in South Wales.

Tommy Glidden scored four times in Albion's six-goal romp on 26 October 1929 – their best win over the Swans.

Cyrille Regis netted a hat-trick when the teams met for the first time in the top-flight, Albion winning 4-1 at The Hawthorns on 5 September 1981.

'W.G.' Richardson obtained five goals in Albion's 8-2 win over Swansea in a wartime Football League South game at The Hawthorns in October 1941.

Albion's first post-war League game saw them beat Swansea Town 3-2 at The Vetch Field on 31 August 1946, Dave Walsh scoring twice on his debut for the Baggies. Walsh netted in each of the next five League games to set a club record.

In the 1970s Albion twice visited Vetch Field to play Swansea in testimonial matches for former players Walter Robbins (in 1971) and Tony Millington (in 1977).

Swansea of Division Four knocked Second Division Albion out of the FA Cup in January 1987, winning a third-round tie 3-2 at The Vetch Field.

Albion League debutants v Swansea: Bill Saunders (1938), Jimmy Duggan (1946), Frank Hodgetts (1946), Harry Kinsell (1946), Len Millard (1946), Jim Pemberton (1946), Jimmy Sanders (1946), George Tranter (1946), Dave Walsh (1946), Nicky Reid (1992), Alan Dickens (1992).

Players with both clubs: Kwame Ampadu, Harry Boston, Fred Buck, Arthur Cook, Ted Crowe, Robbie Dennison, Roy Finch, Jack Haines, Carl Heggs, Ivor Jones, Amos Lloyd, Tony Millington, Stewart Phillips, Ronnie Rees, Colin West.

Also associated with both clubs: David Campbell had  trials for both clubs in the 1990s; Tudor Martin was an Albion reserve who later played for Swansea and 1930s Baggies' forward Walter Robbins later became Swansea's trainer, chief scout and then assistant manager. Albion Scottish international reserve goalkeeper Dave Stewart spent two years at Vetch Field (1980-82) after leaving The Hawthorns.

Welsh international Ivor Jones cost Albion £2,500 when they signed him from Swansea Town in 1922.

SWINDON TOWN

Albion's record against Swindon:

Football League

Venue	P	W	D	L	F	A	Pts
Home	6	3	0	3	11	11	8
Away	6	0	2	4	2	7	2
Totals	12	3	2	7	13	18	10

FA Cup

	P	W	D	L	F	A	
Home	1	1	0	0	2	0	

League Cup

	P	W	D	L	F	A	
Home	1	0	1	0	2	2	
Away	2	1	0	1	2	2	
Totals	3	1	1	1	4	4	

Other Matches

	P	W	D	L	F	A	
Away	4	3	0	1	10	5	

Albion's first played Swindon (away) in a friendly match in March 1897 and ran out winners 1-0.

The first League game between the clubs took place at the County Ground on 8 September 1973 (Division Two). Albion lost 1-0 and had Willie Johnston sent-off!

A crowd of 16,254 saw holders Albion beat Swindon 2-0 at the County Ground in a League Cup-tie on 25 October 1966 – on their way to the Wembley Final.

Peter Latchford palms away the ball during Albion's first-ever League meeting with Swindon Town, in 1973.

Albion were awarded three penalties in six second half minutes of their home League game against Swindon Town on 17 December 1989. Bernard McNally and Graham Harbey both missed from the spot before Don Goodman scored. Albion lost 2-1.

Albion lost 5-2 to Swindon in a bottom-of-the-table clash at The Hawthorns on 19 March 1995. Peter Thorne scored a second half hat-trick for Swindon who were relegated to the Second Division while Albion stayed up!

Albion League debutants v Swindon: David Powell (1988), Stacey North (1988), Tony Ford (1989).

Players with both clubs: Mike Betteridge, John Chadburn, Jimmy Cookson, Peter Eastoe, Fred Fenton, Phil King, Mark Robinson, Hughie MacLean, Jimmy Murphy, Kieran O'Regan, Ron Potter, Bill Richardson, Andrew Smith, Sid Swinden, Ray Treacy, Harry Webster.

Also associated with both clubs: Ossie Ardiles managed both clubs; Albion reserves Kenny Allen, Peter Hilton and Stan Horrocks all played for Swindon's first team, and Jack Smith played for Swindon 1934-37 and was Albion's manager:1948-52. Keith Burkinshaw was Swindon's chief scout (1989-92) before joining Albion as assistant manager.

TACTICS AND TEAM EVOLUTION

Along with Stoke and Nottingham Forest, Albion claim to have been one of the first clubs to use the basic 1-2-3-5 formation in competitive matches. This was in 1882-83. Prior to this teams used to field 12 players a side, a goalkeeper, five defenders and six forwards, although occasionally it was 1-1-4-6.

Since the 1880s, team formations have varied considerably with managers and coaches opting for different line-ups according to the competition, the opposition and the importance of the fixture itself. Over the years, besides utilising the now seemingly 'old' yet traditional line-up of goalkeeper, two full-backs, three half-backs and five forwards, Albion have also used the following formations with the goalkeeper as a permanent fixture: 2-2-6, 4-4-2, 4-2-4, 4-3-3, 1 (a sweeper) -3-4-2, 5-3-2, 5-4-1 and 5-2-3.

In match reports from yesteryear there is no mention of 'linkman', 'sweeper', 'striker', 'back-four defenders' or 'midfielders.' The common talk was of full-backs, centre-halves, inside-forwards, wingers and centre-forwards.

'Kick and rush' football was the sort of game footballers played in the early years and again in the 1950s (especially Tottenham Hotspur and Wolves). Nowadays the game is more involved, with tactical plans coming into operation weekly.

Once upon a time, Albion's philosophy down the years has been to 'attack' and play entertaining football. This is certainly what the supporter wants to see! But the modern-day style of football has become much more technical and occasionally a team has to defend in numbers or attack in force to gain the right result.

Tactical Talk

In 1886, the Albion Committee decided to nominate 16 or 17 players each month from which the first team would be chosen.

Each playing member would receive 10s (50p) per match with the remaining five or six non-playing reserves collecting 5s (25p).

One hundred years later, a first-team squad comprised anything up to 25 players (two full teams) and most of them were on the same sort of wages, with only a handful receiving slightly more because of long service and status.

On 20 April 1912, Albion played Barnsley in the FA Cup Final. Two days later they met Everton in the League and there were 11 changes in the side which had drawn 0-0 in the Final. Albion were fined £150 by the Football League for breach of the competition rules.

In 1898-99 Albion tried eight different players in the centre-forward position; six seasons later (1904-05) they called on seven and in 1907-08 a total of nine 'centre-forwards' featured in the first team, eight in successive matches – a Football League record.

In 1909-10 the club still hadn't sorted out their problem position and another six lined up during the course of the campaign.

The outside-left position caused Albion a lot of problems in 1895-96 when 11 players occupied that role. The same sort of thing happened in 1948-49, when the number-11 shirt was worn by nine different players including England international full-back Harry Kinsell.

TAGGART, John

Born in Belfast in 1872, 'Jack' Taggart was a stalwart half-back, able to play in all three middle-line positions. He always tried to pass the ball to a colleague rather than hoof it up field and during a three-year spell with Albion, he scored five goals in 93 games. He served with Belfast Distillery and Middlesbrough before joining Albion in 1893 and two years later played in the FA Cup Final defeat by Aston Villa. He left Albion for Walsall in 1896, and amassed 123 appearances in five seasons with the Saddlers before retiring through ill-health. Capped by Ireland against Wales in 1899, Taggart died of cancer in 1927, aged 55.

TALBUT, John

Oxford-born John Talbut was 26 years of age when he joined Albion for £30,000 from Burnley in 1966, and in the next five years he gave the club excellent service, appearing in

192 games and scoring one goal. A stern tackler, big 'T' played 160 times for the Turf Moor club and whilst there represented England Under-23, having earlier starred in the Durham Boys team and for his country at schoolboy level. Before leaving The Hawthorns in 1971 to become player-manager of the Belgian club KV Mechelen, he won an FA Cup winners medal (1968) and a League Cup runners-up medal (1970). On his retirement in 1974, Talbut took over as licensee of the Kup Winna bar in Mechelen and was later a leisure centre proprietor in Brussels. He still lives in Belgium.

TAYLOR, Robert

Born in Easington, County Durham in 1967, Bob Taylor joined Albion from Bristol City for £300,000 early in 1992

and quickly became a hero at The Hawthorns with his superb marksmanship. Strong and powerful, both on the ground and in the air, he is a perpetual hard-worker who was on Hartlepool United's books as a youngster. He then scored

nine goals in 42 League games for Leeds United and followed up with 50 in 106 outings in the same competition for Bristol City. He scored on his Albion debut against Brentford and in his second season with the club top-scored with 37 goals, helping Albion win promotion to the First Division via the Wembley Play-off Final. He was named Albion's captain in 1995-96, and when that campaign ended Taylor's record for Albion was 100 goals in 228 senior appearances, his 100th goal coming against Derby County on the last day of the season.

TENNENT-CALEDONIAN CUP

Albion have twice competed in the four-club Tennent-Caledonian Cup competition, hosted by Rangers at their Ibrox Park Stadium.

In August 1977, goals by Tony Brown (2), David Cross and Bryan Robson enabled Albion to beat St Mirren 4-3 and so

Lyndon Hughes (extreme left) clears his lines for Albion in the away leg of the Texaco Cup-tie against Morton in 1970.

qualify to meet Rangers in the Final. They duly defeated the hosts 2-0 with 'Player of the Tournament' Laurie Cunningham scoring both goals.

In August 1978, as holders of the trophy, Albion, after a 1-1 draw at the end of normal time, lost 3-1 on penalties to Southampton in the semi-final, and then succumbed 2-0 to Heart of Midlothian in the match for third place.

TEXACO CUP/BRITISH ISLES CUP

Albion played nine games in this short-lived competition which took place during the early 1970s.

Albion's full record in the competition is:

Venue	P	W	D	L	F	A
Home	5	3	2	0	9	3
Away	4	0	1	3	4	8
Totals	9	3	3	3	13	11

In season 1970-71, Albion lost twice to the Scottish club Morton, 2-1 away in the first game and then 1-0 at The Hawthorns, thus going out of the competition at the first hurdle.

The 1972-73 competition was sponsored to the tune of £100,000 with Albion, along with eight other Football League clubs and seven from Scotland, receiving an initial payment of £1,000. After drawing 1-1 away at Sheffield United, Albion beat the Blades 2-1 at The Hawthorns but were themselves eliminated by Newcastle United at the second stage, losing 4-3 on aggregate (2-1 winners at home, but 3-1 losers at St James' Park).

In 1974-75, the competition (with a sponsorship this time of £120,000) was re-organised into a pre-season event comprising eight regionalised groups, four in England and four in Scotland. Each participating club received £1,500. The winners of each group progressed through to the quarter-finals. Albion were in group one, but unfortunately they failed to qualify. They drew 0-0 at home with the group winners Birmingham City, beat Norwich City 5-1 and lost 2-1 at Peterborough United.

THOMPSON, Garry Linsey

Out-and-out striker, sharp and decisive on the ground, strong in the air, Garry Thompson had an excellent career, scoring well over 150 goals in more than 550 League and Cup games. He played in turn, for Coventry City (from 1977), Albion (signed for £225,000 in 1983, sold for £450,000 in 1985), Sheffield Wednesday, Aston Villa (1986-88), Watford, Crystal Palace, Queen's Park Rangers, Cardiff City and Northampton Town (1995-96). For Albion his record was 45 goals in 105 appearances and whilst at Highfield Road he played six times for England at Under-21 level. Born in Birmingham in 1959, Thompson dropped out of League football in 1996.

Garry Thompson celebrates a League Cup goal against local rivals Birmingham City at The Hawthorns in November 1984.

TORQUAY UNITED

Albion's record against Torquay United:

Football League

Venue	P	W	D	L	F	A	Pts
Home	1	1	0	0	1	0	3
Away	1	0	0	1	0	1	0
Totals	2	1	0	1	1	1	3

Autoglass Trophy

Home	1	1	0	0	2	1

Other Matches

Away	3	2	0	1	3	2

Albion's two League games against United were played in season 1991-92. Roy Hunter scored the winning goal at The Hawthorns after coming on as a substitute. Three players were sent-off in this stormy first Hawthorns meeting of the clubs: Justin Fashanu and Wes Saunders of Torquay and Darren Bradley (Albion).

In three competitive games between Albion and United, four players have been sent off, two from each side (See SENDINGS OFF).

Albion scored twice through Kevin Donovan in the last three minutes to oust Torquay from the Autoglass Trophy in 1992-93.

Albion League debutants v United: Andy Dibble (1992), Roy Hunter (1992).

Players with both clubs: Colin Anderson, Geoff Barnsley, Tony Brown, Wayne Dobbins, Elfed Evans, Stewart Evans, Adrian Foster, Paul Holmes, Phil King, Tony Lange, Garry Pendrey, Mick Perry, Dick Sheppard.

Also associated with both clubs: Scott Colcombe and Ken Allen were both Albion

Wayne Dobbins played for both Albion and Torquay United.

reserves who played League Football for United, Allen having three spells at Plainmoor, and Albion 'keeper Tony Godden was a non-contract player with United. Defender Craig Herbert spent two years at Plainmoor on the YTS before joining Albion in 1994.

TOTTENHAM HOTSPUR

Albion's record against Spurs:

Football League

Venue	P	W	D	L	F	A	Pts
Home	53	32	8	13	114	68	73
Away	53	14	14	25	56	91	45
Totals	106	46	22	38	170	159	118

FA Cup

Venue	P	W	D	L	F	A	
Home	5	3	0	2	9	6	
Away	4	0	1	3	2	9	
Totals	9	3	1	5	11	15	

League Cup

Home	2	0	1	1	0	1
Away	2	0	0	2	0	6
Totals	4	0	1	3	0	7

FA Charity Shield

Away	1	1	0	0	2	0

Other Matches

Home	5	2	1	2	12	6
Away	1	0	0	1	2	4
Totals	6	2	1	3	14	10

The first meeting between the clubs was an FA Cup semi-final at Villa Park on 8 April 1901 when Spurs, then a Southern League side, beat Albion of the First Division 4-0.

Len Millard and goalkeeper Norman Heath in action against Spurs at White Hart Lane in January 1954. Albion won 1-0.

It was goalless at half-time but then Spurs' centre-forward 'Sandy' Brown went to town and scored four times to destroy plucky Albion. The attendance was 34,979.

Albion's best League win over Spurs is 5-0 – achieved at The Hawthorns on 12 February 1927 (Division One). Stan Davies and Joe Carter both scored twice.

Four years earlier (on 8 December 1923) Carter netted all four goals when Albion beat Spurs 4-1 in a home League game.

Spurs have registered four emphatic 5-0 home wins over Albion, three of them in the First Division: in March 1951, when Len Duquemin scored a hat-trick; in April 1959 when Bobby Smith led the Londoners' charge with a four-timer and in March 1986 before a crowd of 10,841 – the lowest at White Hart Lane since 1947. The other 5-0 scoreline was in a fourth-round League Cup-tie in October 1970 when England World Cup star Martin Peters netted a hat-trick. This Cup reverse is also Albion's heaviest in this competition.

A crowd of 71,853 saw Spurs defeat Albion 3-1 in a fourth-round FA Cup-tie at White Hart Lane in January 1948. Both teams were in the Second Division at the time.

In season 1908-09 and again in 1948-49 Albion and Spurs were promotion aspirants in Division Two. Spurs pipped the Baggies for a place in the top flight in 1909, but Albion turned the tables forty years later as Spurs finished six points behind runners-up Albion.

There have been many high-scoring games between the clubs over the years at League level. Albion, in fact, have recorded five thrilling 4-3 victories – at The Hawthorns in April 1930 and in September 1938, when Harry Jones hit a hat-trick; in front of 56,552 fans at Tottenham in August 1952; and at home again in November 1958 and in April 1969, Bobby Hope scoring a superb opening goal in the latter game. Albion also ran up impressive home wins of 4-1 in March 1913, 4-0 in November 1934, 4-2 in October 1976 (after being 2-0 down) and 4-2 in May 1981 when Peter Barnes was in excellent form.

The teams shared eight goals in a tremendous 4-4 draw at The Hawthorns on Boxing Day 1963 and 24 hours later Albion caused an upset by winning 2-0 at White Hart Lane. The last 50,000 plus crowd at The Hawthorns (54,992) assembled for a fifth-round FA Cup-tie between Albion and Spurs in February 1962. Spurs won 4-2 on their way to retaining the trophy.

The 100th League meeting between the clubs was staged at The Hawthorns on 23 April 1983. Tottenham won 1-0.

Albion beat Spurs 2-0 at White Hart Lane to win the 1920 FA Charity Shield. Andy Smith scored both goals.

Spurs beat Albion 1-0 on aggregate in the semi-final of the 1981-82 League Cup competition, winning 1-0 at White

Hart Lane in the second leg. Maarten Jol (Albion) and Tony Galvin (Spurs) were both sent-off in the first leg.

The last peacetime game at The Hawthorns before the commencement of World War Two took place on 2 September 1939 when Spurs beat Albion 4-3 in a Second Division game which was subsequently declared null and void. Eric Jones (Albion) and Jack Morrison (Spurs) both scored hat-tricks.

Ray Barlow netted a hat-trick in Albion's 5-0 home win over Spurs in the Football League South transitional season of 1945-46.

Tony Brown has scored more goals against Spurs than any other Albion player – 12 – including two home hat-tricks, in a 3-0 home win in December 1966 and in a 3-1 victory four years later.

Albion League debutants v Spurs: Fred Reed (1915), Bobby Blood (1921), Harry Chamberlain (1922), Jack Boyd (1948), Tony Forrester (1958), Dennis Clarke (1966), John Talbut (1966), Laurie Cunningham (1977), Tony Godden (1977), John Deehan (1979), Mark Grew (1981), Clive Whitehead (1981), Tony Grealish (1984), Steve Hunt (1984), Paul Bradshaw (1985), Martin Dickinson (1986). George Elmore made his first senior appearance for Albion in an FA Cup-tie against Spurs in 1903 and winger Hughie MacLean made his Albion debut in a League Cup-tie against Spurs in 1971.

Players with both clubs: Gerry Armstrong, Freddie Cox, Garth Crooks, Tom Evans, Charlie Hewitt, Graham Roberts, Steve Walford.

Also associated with both clubs: Keith Burkinshaw managed Spurs 1976-84 and Albion 1993-94; Ossie Ardiles was a player (1978-88) and later manager of Spurs (1993-94) and Albion's manager in 1992-93; Vic Buckingham played for Spurs before, during and after the war, and managed Albion from 1953 to 1959; Danny Thomas played right-back for Spurs 1983-87 and was Albion's physiotherapist 1992-95; Jesse Carver managed Albion in 1952 and was Spurs' assistant coach 1958-59; Arthur Rowe played for and later managed Spurs (1949-55) and was Albion scout in 1957-58; Wilf Dixon, after being Albion's trainer in the 1960s, was Spurs' assistant manager 1974-76 and Colin Lyman, an Albion 1930s reserve, played for Spurs 1937-46.

TOURS

Albion's first overseas tour took them to Denmark and Sweden in May 1909. They played seven games, winning four and losing three. Their best victories were those of 10-0 against Gefle FC (Bill Garraty scored six times) and 8-3 over a Stockholm Select XI (Freddie Buck registered a four-timer).

Since then Albion have made further tours (also playing in tournaments overseas) to Ireland (May 1932, May 1953, July 1975, July/August 1989, August 1990), Belgium & Luxembourg (May 1946), Russia (June 1957), Canada & USA (May/June 1959, May 1969 and May 1981), Austria (May 1961), Holland (August 1964, August 1983), South America (May/June 1966 – playing games in Argentina, Brazil, Peru and Uruguay), USA (New York – July 1965), East Africa (May/June 1968, playing games in Kenya, Tanzania, and Uganda), Norway (July 1969), Yugoslavia (May 1972, August 1980), Sweden (July/August 1972), Belgium (July/August 1974), Spain (August 1977, August 1979, August 1981, August 1982), China/Hong Kong (May 1978), Syria (August 1978), Denmark (May 1979), Abu Dhabi/Bahrain (January 1980). USA (May 1990) (See OVERSEAS OPPOSITION).

TRANMERE ROVERS

Albion's record against Rovers:

Football League

Venue	P	W	D	L	F	A	Pts
Home	4	2	1	1	9	5	6
Away	4	0	1	3	4	11	1
Totals	8	2	2	4	13	16	7

Lee Ashcroft scored a hat-trick in eight minutes when Albion recorded their best League win (5-1) over Tranmere at The Hawthorns in April 1995.

Tranmere's best win over Albion is 3-1 at Prenton Park on 22 October 1938 – the first time the teams had met.

Players with both clubs: Meynell Burgin, Joe Carter, Jim Cumbes, Dicky Dale, John Thomas.

Russell Allen (son of Ronnie) played in one friendly game for Albion (1972) and later scored 44 goals in 156 League appearances for Rovers (1973-78); David Campbell had trials with both clubs in the early 1990s and Tommy Jones was a Tranmere forward (1926-29) who was later trainer-coach at Prenton Park (1946) and physiotherapist at The Hawthorns (1965-71). Mark McCarrick, an Albion apprentice in the late 1970s, was a first-team player with Tranmere (1988-91) and goalkeeper Barry Siddall, on loan to Albion in 1990, was a Tranmere loan player in 1986.

Dicky Dale played for both Albion and Tranmere Rovers.

TRANSFERS

Outgoing transfers £200,000 and above:

Player	Sold to	Date	Fee
Bryan Robson	Manchester U	October 1981	£1,500,000
Laurie Cunningham	Real Madrid	June 1979	£995,000
Peter Barnes	Leeds U	July 1981	£930,000
Don Goodman	Sunderland	December 1991	£900,000
Carlton Palmer	Sheffield W	February 1989	£750,000
David Burrows	Liverpool	October 1988	£625,000
Remi Moses	Manchester U	October 1981	£500,000
Chris Whyte	Leeds U	July 1990	£400,000
Len Cantello	Bolton W	May 1979	£350,000
Cyrille Regis	Coventry C	October 1984	£300,000
John Trewick	Newcastle U	December 1980	£234,000
Asa Hartford	Manchester C	August 1974	£225,000
David Cross	West Ham U	December 1977	£200,000
Steve MacKenzie	Charlton A	June 1987	£200,000

Peter Barnes, Albion's record buy was sold to Leeds for £930,000.

Incoming transfers £220,000 and above:

Player	Bought from	Date	Fee
Peter Barnes	Manchester C	July 1979	£748,000
Steve MacKenzie	Manchester C	July 1981	£650,000
David Mills	Middlesbrough	January 1979	£518,000
Gary Owen	Manchester C	May 1979	£465,000
John Deehan	Aston Villa	September 1979	£424,000
Paul Mardon	Birmingham C	November 1993	£400,000
Richard Sneekes	Bolton W	March 1996	£400,000
Bernard McNally	Shrewsbury T	July 1989	£385,000
Bob Taylor	Bristol C	January 1992	£300,000
Imre Varadi	Sheffield W	June 1985	£285,000
Gary Bannister	Coventry C	March 1990	£250,000
Julian Darby	Coventry C	November 1995	£250,000
Maarten Jol	Twente Enschede	October 1981	£250,000
Graham Roberts	Chelsea	November 1990	£250,000
Colin West	Sheffield W	February 1989	£250,000
Paul A. Williams	Stockport Co	March 1991	£250,000
Lee Ashcroft	Preston NE	August 1993	£225,000
Craig Shakespeare	Sheffield W	February 1990	£225,000
Garry Thompson	Coventry C	February 1983	£225,000
Romeo Zondervan	Twente Enschede	March 1982	£225,000
Shaun Cunnington	Sunderland	August 1995	£220,000

Players signed/sold for unusual fees

Ally Brown signed from Leicester City in 1972 for £61,111.
Bobby Gould bought from Wolves for £66,666 in 1971.
Gould transferred to Bristol City for £68,888 in 1972.
Bobby Hope sold to Birmingham City for £66,666 in 1972.
George McVitie signed from Carlisle United for £33,333 in 1970.
Dennis Martin was sold to Carlisle United for £22,222 in 1970.
John Trewick sold to Newcastle United for £234,567 in 1984.
Albion paid £28 to get forward Ralph Brett released from the Army (RAMC) in August 1898.

Transfer Records

How Albion's transfer record has been broken since 1921:

Player	Bought from	Date	Fee
Bobby Blood	Port Vale	February 1921	£4,000
George Shaw	Huddersfield	December 1926	£4,100
Cecil Shaw	Wolves	December 1936	£7,500
Jack Vernon	Belfast Celtic	February 1947	£9,500
Ronnie Allen	Port Vale	March 1950	£20,000
Bobby Robson	Fulham	March 1956	£25,000
John Kaye	Scunthorpe U	May 1963	£44,750
Colin Suggett	Sunderland	June 1969	£100,000
Willie Johnston	Rangers	December 1972	£138,000
David Mills	Middlesbrough	January 1979	£518,000
Peter Barnes	Manchester C	July 1979	£748,000

Foreign Connection

The following played competitive football abroad and for Albion's first team: Arthur Albiston (Norway), Sam Allardyce (Finland, USA), Vetle Andersen (Norway, Germany, Denmark), Gerry Armstrong (Spain), Jeff Astle (South Africa), Gary Bannister (Hong Kong), Mark Barham (Hong Kong), Peter Barnes (Spain, Portugal), Dave Barnett (New Zealand, Canada), Luther Blissett (Italy), Jeroen Boere (Holland), Darren Bradley (South Africa), Paul Bradshaw (Canada), Alistair Brown (Canada), Tony Brown (USA), Danny Campbell (USA, South Africa), Len Cantello (USA, Hong Kong, Holland), Neil Cartwright (Norway), Clive Clark (USA), Eddie Colquhoun (USA), Bobby Cram (USA, Canada), Ray Crawford (New Zealand, South Africa), David Cross (Canada), Jim Cumbes (USA), Laurie Cunningham (Spain, France, Belgium), Graham Easter (Norway), Peter Eastoe (Portugal), Johnny Giles (Canada), Tony Grealish (Portugal), Asa Hartford (USA), Danny Hegan (South Africa),

An early foreign export. Magnus Nicholson left Albion in 1894 and eventually joined Austria FC of Vienna, a club he later coached.

Bobby Hope (USA), Robert Hopkins (Hong Kong), Wayne Hughes (USA), Steve Hunt (USA), Geoff Hurst (South Africa, USA), Glen Johnson (Canada, USA), Willie Johnston (Canada), Maarten Jol (Holland, Germany), Andy King (Holland, Sweden), Mick Martin (Canada), Joe Mayo (Hong Kong), Alan Merrick (Canada, USA), Roger Minton (USA), Tony Morley (USA, Hong Kong, New Zealand, Australia, Holland, Malta), Paddy Mulligan (USA), Jimmy Nicholl (Canada), Magnus Nicholson (Austria), Gary Owen (Cyprus, Greece), John Paskin (Canada, South Africa, Belgium, Hong Kong), Stewart Phillips (Hong Kong), George Shaw (Malta), Chippy Simmons (Canada), John Smith (Sweden), Richard Sneekes (Holland, Switzerland), Stan Steele (South Africa), Brian Talbot (Canada), John Talbut (Belgium), Mickey Thomas (Canada), Trevor Thompson (USA), Ray Treacy (Canada), Carl Valentine (USA), Steve Walford (Hong Kong, Turkey), Winston White (Hong Kong), Chris Whyte (USA), John Wile (Canada), Bill Williams (South Africa), Paul A.Williams (South Africa), Romeo Zondervan (Holland).
NB: Barry Hughes was Albion's reserve centre-half in the 1950s and later went on to play in over 500 games in Holland.

Two Spells

Players who had two separate spells with Albion (on a permanent basis): Sid Bowser, Paul Bradshaw, Fred Buck, David Cross, Ernie Fellows, Harold Jones (goalkeeper), Sammy Legge, Albert Lewis, Steve Lynex, Tony Morley, John Osborne, John Paddock, Harry Parkes, Walter Perry, Alonzo Poulton, Bob Roberts (goalkeeper), Tom Roberts, Bethel Robinson, Charlie Simmons, Ted Smith, Ray Treacy and Harold Wright.

The following were one-time footballers with Albion who later returned to the club in a different capacity: Ronnie

Allen (manager, coach), Harry Ashley (coach, steward), Mark Ashton (Football in the Community officer), Billy Bassett (director, chairman), Harry Bell (trainer), Tony Brown (coach), Bob Crone (trainer), Cliff Edwards (director), Ray Fairfax (assistant secretary), Arthur Fitton (trainer), Johnny Giles (manager), Bobby Gould (manager), Bill Harris (scout), Ken Hodgkisson (coach, scout), Bobby Hope (coach), Fred Horne (assistant secretary), Roy Horobin (chief scout, youth development officer), Don Howe (manager), Claude Jephcott (director), Derek Kevan (Albion Development), George Lee (trainer), Dan Nurse (director), Harold Pearson (coach, scout), Jesse Pennington (scout), Arthur Perry (scout), Charlie Perry (director), Walker Perry (reserve-team manager), Joe Reader (coach, steward), 'W.G.' Richardson (assistant trainer-coach), Reg Ryan (scout, pools adviser), Jack Sankey (coach, scout), George Savage (coach), Cecil Shaw (scout), Jim Stevenson (assistant trainer), Gerry Summers (coach), George Timmins (steward, gateman), John Trewick (coach), Brian Whitehouse (coach), Billy Williams (trainer, coach), Stuart Williams (trainer).

NB – Cliff Edwards was the last ex-player to serve on the club's Board of Directors (1971-86).

Loan Players

Here is a list of players who have been on loan to Albion:

Player	His Club	Date at Albion
Kwame Ampadu	Arsenal	1991*
Brett Angell	Sunderland	1996
Colin Anderson	Torquay United	1985*
Mark Barham	Huddersfield Town	1989
Vince Bartram	AFC Bournemouth	1991
Luther Blissett	Watford	1992
Jeroen Boere	West Ham United	1994
Peter Butler	Notts County	1996
David Cork	Huddersfield Town	1988
Andy Dibble	Manchester City	1992
Alan Dickens	Chelsea	1992
John Durnin	Liverpool	1988
Graham Fenton	Aston Villa	1993
Wayne Fereday	AFC Bournemouth	1991-92*
Alan Fettis	Hull City	1995
Alf Geddes	Millwall	1895
Andy Gray	Aston Villa	1987*
Mark Grew	Ipswich Town	1986
Graham Harbey	Ipswich Town	1989*
Phil Hawker	Walsall	1991
Graeme Hogg	Manchester United	1987
Paul Holmes	Everton	1996*
Peter Hucker	Oxford United	1988
Andy Hunt	Newcastle United	1993*
Phil King	Aston Villa	1995
Andy Marriott	Nottingham Forest	1989
Mick Martin	Manchester United	1975*
Alan Miller	Arsenal	1991
Shane Nicholson	Derby County	1996*
Brian Rice	Nottingham Forest	1989
Craig Shakespeare	Sheffield Wednesday	1989*
Barry Siddall	Hartlepool United	1990
Frank Sinclair	Chelsea	1991-92
David Speedie	Southampton	1992
Kevin Steggles	Ipswich Town	1987*
Kenny Swain	Portsmouth	1978 & 1988
Steve Walford	West Ham United	1989
Paul Williams	Coventry City	1993

* Later joined Albion on a permanent basis.

Released

Numerous Albion players were released down the years by the club or were transferred after failing to make the grade. The list which follows highlights a selection of reserves or juniors who did not appear in Albion's League team but who

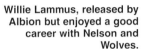

Kenny Swain, one of many players who has appeared in Albion's colours whilst on loan.

Willie Lammus, released by Albion but enjoyed a good career with Nelson and Wolves.

were successful subsequently with other clubs:-

Gerry Adair (Hibernian, Dunfermline Athletic, Cowdenbeath, Meadowbank Thistle), Russell Allen (Tranmere Rovers, Mansfield Town), John Anderson* (Preston North End, Newcastle United, Republic of Ireland), William Arch (Newport County, Grimsby Town, Hartlepools United), Dave Barnett (Barnet, Walsall, Birmingham City), Bert Baverstock (Bolton Wanderers, Blackpool), Gary Bell (Cardiff City, Hereford United, Newport County), Jack Beynon (Halifax Town, Rotherham United, Doncaster Rovers, Aberdeen), Tommy Bowen (Newport County, Walsall), Don Bradley (Mansfield Town), Jack Bridgett (Walsall), Arthur Brookes (Halifax Town), Dave Butler (Shrewsbury Town, Workington, Seattle Sounders), Bill Chambers (Burnley, Halifax Town, Bolton Wanderers, Chester), George Chapman (Brighton & Hove Albion), Scott Colcombe (Torquay United, Doncaster Rovers), Bruce Collard (Scunthorpe United), Barry Cooke (Northampton Town), Frank Costello (Southampton, West Ham United, Bolton Wanderers), Mark Cowan (Airdrieonians), Vic Crowe* (Aston Villa, Wales), Bobby Downes (Peterborough United, Rochdale, Watford, Barnsley, Blackpool), Jack Draper (Northampton Town), Jack Driscoll (Sheffield Wednesday), Ted Duckhouse (Birmingham City, Northampton Town), Graham Easter (Crewe Alexandra), Jack Edwards* (Aberystwyth Town, Wales), Jack Flavell (Walsall), Ron Floyd (Crewe Alexandra), Jimmy Fowler (Falkirk), Bill Gallier (Walsall), Mike Gibson (Shrewsbury Town, Bristol City, Gillingham), Sid Glidden (Sunderland, Port Vale, Reading), Andy Goram (Oldham Athletic, Hibernian, Rangers, Scotland), Bruce Grobbelaar* (Vancouver Whitecaps, Crewe Alexandra, Liverpool, Southampton, Zimbabwe), Harry Haddington (Walsall), Jimmy Hagan* (Derby County, Sheffield United, England), Jack Hallows (Bradford City, Barnsley), Ian Hathaway (Mansfield Town, Rotherham United, Torquay United), Pat Hewson (Gateshead), George Hickman (Halifax Town), Pat Hilton (Brighton & Hove Albion, Blackburn Rovers, Gillingham, Aldershot), Peter Hilton (Swindon Town), Jim Holton* (Shrewsbury Town, Manchester United, Sunderland, Coventry City, Scotland), John Honour (Hartlepool United), Derek Hood (Hull City, York City, Lincoln City), Stan Horrocks (Swindon Town), Barry Hughes (Blauwit, Alkmaar in Holland), Dennis Jennings (Grimsby Town, Birmingham City, Huddersfield Town), Dick Jones (Crewe Alexandra), Tom Jones (Hull City), Ernie King (Brighton & Hove Albion), Willie Lammus

(Nelson, Wolverhampton Wanderers), Keith Lawrence (Brentford), Mark Leetion (Meadowbank Thistle, East Stirling), Gary Leonard (Shrewsbury Town, Bury, Stockport County, Hartlepool United), Jack Lewis (Crystal Palace, Bournemouth, Reading), John Lewis (Mansfield Town), Adrian Littlejohn (Walsall, Sheffield United, Plymouth Argyle), Alistair Love (Southend United, Newport County, Partick Thistle, Ayr United, Falkirk), John Loveridge (Walsall), Colin Lyman (Tottenham Hotspur, Northampton Town, Notts County, Nottingham Forest, Port Vale), Mark McCarrick (Birmingham City, Crewe Alexandra, Lincoln City, Tranmere Rovers), Mick McCartney (Carlisle United, Southampton, Plymouth Argyle), Stewart MacLaren (Motherwell, Dundee, Heart of Midlothian), Tudor Martin* (Newport County, Wolverhampton Wanderers, Swansea Town, West Ham United, Southend United, Wales), Billy McDonald (Glasgow Rangers, Partick Thistle), John McIlvenny (Bristol Rovers, Reading), Bill Morris* (Wolverhampton Wanderers, England), John Morris (Walsall), Albert Newman (Walsall, Aston Villa), Darren Patterson* (Wigan Athletic, Preston North End, Crystal Palace, Luton Town, Northern Ireland), Ernie Pattinson (Rotherham United, Doncaster Rovers), Ernie Peers (Walsall, Nottingham Forest, Burton United), Eric Perry (Coventry City), Gary Phillips (Barnet, Brentford, Reading, Hereford United), Martin Pike (Peterborough United, Sheffield United, Tranmere Rovers, Bolton Wanderers, Fulham, Rotherham United), Jack Pitt (Bristol Rovers), Eli Postin (Cardiff City, Bristol Rovers, Wrexham), Jack Quantick (Hull City), Tim Rawlings (Walsall, Port Vale), Robert Roberts* (Rhosllanarchongog, Wrexham, Crewe Alexandra, Wales), Stuart Romaines (Berwick Rangers, Falkirk, Raith Rovers, Alloa Athletic), Alec Ross (Crystal Palace), Ray Russell (Shrewsbury Town, Crewe Alexandra), Alan Scarrott (Reading), Wilf Smith (Blackpool), Jim Southam (Newport County, Birmingham City, Northampton Town), Ronnie Stockin (Wolverhampton Wanderers, Cardiff City, Grimsby Town), Bill Taylor (Cardiff City, Aberdare Athletic, Hull City, Norwich City), Billy Thomas (Falkirk, Hamilton Academical, Morton), Jack Thomas (Crystal Palace), Luke Tinkler (Plymouth Argyle, Walsall), Joey Tortolano (Hibernian), Geoff Turton (Gillingham. Crystal Palace), Keith Vickers (Portsmouth, Gillingham), Wilf Vickers (Brighton & Hove Albion, Aldershot), Frank Warrilow (Millwall, Barnsley), Tom Watson (Gateshead), Trefor West (Walsall), Ray Whale (Southend United), Frank White (Coventry City, Newport County), Jim Whitehouse (Walsall, Rochdale, Carlisle United), Jimmy Whitehouse (Reading, Coventry City, Millwall), Gordon Wills (Notts County, Leicester City, Walsall), Barry Wood (Crystal Palace, Leyton Orient, Colchester United, Workington), Jasper Yeull (Portsmouth).
* These players became full internationals for the countries indicated.
NB: Arthur Rowley scored four goals in 24 League games for Albion in 1948, then went on to net another 430 in the same competition playing for Fulham, Leicester and Shrewsbury Town. Don Bradley appeared in 385 League games for Mansfield (1949-62).

Transfer Talk
Alf Ridyard was transferred from Albion to Queen's Park Rangers immediately after a milking a cow on 16 March 1938.

Harold Bache was signed by Albion's secretary/manager Fred Everiss whilst sitting at a desk teaching English in a French University near Amiens on 6 February 1914.

Between 1949 and 1968, eighteen former Albion players joined Walsall (See WALSALL for details of Walsall-Albion players).

Over a period of 10 years (1961-71) ten players left The

Hawthorns for Crystal Palace (See CRYSTAL PALACE).

On 15 January 1891 Albion signed three Scotsmen: Roddy McLeod (from Partick Thistle), Tom McCulloch (Glasgow United) and Willie McCullum (Celtic).

John Reynolds was fined £1 per week towards the end of the 1892-93 season because of 'poor form.' He was playing for a transfer to which Albion would not agree and eventually left the club under a cloud.

On 1 January 1908, a limit of £350 was placed on all transfers by the FA. Three months later this was rescinded.

The transfer deadline was first introduced in March 1911.

Albion's Joe Carter signed for Sheffield Wednesday on 6 February 1936, but the transfer was called off six days later because Carter fell and injured his knee at home.

Asa Hartford was all set to leave Albion for Leeds United in 1971 for £170,000, but the transfer fell through after doctors diagnosed that the Scottish international had a hole in the heart.

Hartford continued to play first-class football until 1990.

Albion secured the transfer of Tommy Magee in the French trenches during World War One. Magee was sent the signing-on papers and signed for the Baggies on 27 January 1919.

In March 1960, Albion had a record £42,500 bid for Denis Law (then of Huddersfield Town) turned down. Law joined Manchester City for £55,000 soon afterwards.

Tom McCulloch, one of three Scots who joined Albion in January 1891.

TRAVELLING
(See also OVERSEAS OPPOSITION)
Long trips between away matches in successive days have been made by Albion as follows:
252 miles from Tottenham Hotspur to Burnley, 2-3 April 1926
241 miles from Arsenal to Blackburn Rovers, 12-13 April 1963
226 miles from Derby County to Portsmouth, 7-8 April 1950
201 miles from Arsenal to Everton, 10-11 April 1936

On several occasions Albion played Newcastle United at home (or away) on one day and 24 hours later fulfilled the return fixture – a trip of 208 miles.

On 24 April 1912, Albion played Barnsley at Sheffield in the FA Cup Final replay, returning home after the game. The next morning they made the trip north to play Blackburn in a League match – again returning to the Midlands afterwards. On 26 April Albion entertained Bradford City, played hosts to Sheffield Wednesday the next day and ended the season with another home game against Oldham Athletic on the 29th.

TRENTHAM, Herbert Francis
Bert 'Corker' Trentham was a fine full-back, able to operate on either flank. A model of consistency, being sound rather than outstanding, he always had a handkerchief wrapped around his withered right hand, and he formed a fine partnership with George Shaw. The pair played over 230 games together in Albion's defence, lining up in both the 1931 and 1935 FA Cup Finals. Born in Chirbury in 1908, Trentham won junior international honours and joined Albion from Hereford United for £600 in 1929. In the next eight years he appeared in 272 League and Cup matches, helping Albion achieve the Cup and promotion double in 1930-31, and he also played for the Football League (1933).

Albion full-back Bert Trentham and West Ham's Vic Watson in action at Upton Park in November 1931.

He returned to Hereford on leaving The Hawthorns in 1937 and retired two years later after a spell with Darlaston to concentrate on his ironmongers' business in Birmingham. He died in 1979.

TREWICK, John

'Tucker' Trewick was a determined midfielder who gave Albion good service during an eight-year stay at The Hawthorns (1972-80). He scored 12 goals in 134 first-team appearances and helped the team win promotion in 1976.

Born in Stakeford, near Bedlington in 1957, Trewick played for Northumberland Boys prior to joining Albion and he left the club for Newcastle United for a fee of £234,567. In 1984 he joined Oxford United and played for Birmingham City for two years prior to 1989. Thereafter he had spells with Bromsgrove Rovers, Hartlepool United, Gateshead and Tamworth, returning to Albion as

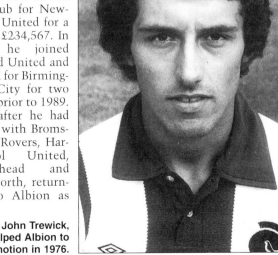

John Trewick, helped Albion to promotion in 1976.

coach in 1992. He gained Division Two championship and Milk Cup winners' medals with Oxford in 1985 and 1986, and earlier in his career played for England at both schoolboy and youth-team levels. All told Trewick amassed well over 400 appearances as a professional.

UEFA CUP

Albion have had three attempts at trying to win the UEFA Cup.

John Wile shouts instructions to his defenders while keeping a close watch on Argentinian international Mario Kempes during the UEFA Cup fourth-round first-leg match in Valencia in November 1978.

They first tried in 1978-79 when they reached the quarter-finals after eliminating Galatasary 6-2 on aggregate (winning both games 3-1), Sporting Braga 3-0 (2-0 away, 1-0 at home) and Valencia 3-1 (1-1 in Spain, 2-0 at The Hawthorns). Red Star Belgrade prevented further progress, winning 1-0 in Yugoslavia and then drawing 1-1 in West Bromwich courtesy of a late goal from Savic.

Albion's next entry into the competition was the following season (1979-80), but this time they went out at the first hurdle, beaten 4-1 on aggregate by the East German side Carl Zeiss Jena who won 2-0 at home and 2-1 at The Hawthorns.

Albion's last European exploits came in 1981-82 and again they fell at the first fence, this time bowing out to Grasshoppers of Zurich who won 1-0 in Switzerland and 3-1 at The Hawthorns to go through 4-1 on aggregate.

Albion's full UEFA Cup record:

Venue	P	W	D	L	F	A
Home	6	3	1	2	9	7
Away	6	2	1	3	6	6
Totals	12	5	2	5	15	13

Goalkeeper Mark Grew made his senior debut for Albion in the home leg of the first-round UEFA Cup-tie against Galatasary on 27 September 1978.

UNITED COUNTIES LEAGUE

This competition was short-lived, lasting one season (1893-94). It was open to Midland clubs who had been knocked out of the FA Cup at an early stage, but it lacked interest and support. Eight teams entered and were split into two groups of four. Albion, along with Small Heath, Stoke and Wolverhampton Wanderers, competed in Group 'A'.

Albion qualified for the Final after winning four of their six games: Small Heath 5-4 (a) and 3-1 (h), Stoke 5-0 (h) and Wolves 3-1 (h). They lost 5-2 at Stoke and 4-2 at Wolves.

Derby County came through from Group 'B' and met Albion in the Final at The Baseball Ground on 30 April 1895.

A crowd of 9,000 witnessed a 1-1 draw (after extra-time) but the replay was held over until 6 October when Albion had to travel to the same venue. This time they lost 2-1 in front of 6,000 fans.

Albion's full record in the UCL was:

Venue	P	W	D	L	F	A
Home	3	3	0	0	11	2
Away	5	1	1	3	11	16
Totals	8	4	1	3	22	18

UNIVERSITIES

Albion have played a number of friendly matches (at home and away) against both Oxford and Cambridge Universities and also against the Corinthians, an amateur club founded in 1882 with its players drawn exclusively from public schools and universities.

Oxford University were first encountered at Stoney Lane on 1 November 1886 when Albion were 6-1 winners, and the last fixture (at senior level) was on 6 December 1897 (1-1).

Albion first played Cambridge University on 5 December 1887 (in West Bromwich) and they won 5-0. The last meeting was on 27 November 1899 when the teams played out a 2-2 draw in Cambridge.

The Corinthians first entertained Albion at the Queen's Club (London) on 20 February 1892 when eight goals were shared in a 4-4 draw. Albion continued to play against the famous amateur side at regular intervals until 1932. On 2 February 1924, Albion won a second-round FA Cup-tie at The Hawthorns 5-0 before a crowd of 49,005.

Ron Atkinson was associated with both university city clubs – being a player with Oxford United and later manager of Cambridge United. He was manager of Albion from 1978-81 and 1987-88.

Albion's record against University sides:

Cambridge University

Venue	P	W	D	L	F	A
Home	2	1	1	0	6	1
Away	7	3	1	3	23	21
Totals	9	4	2	3	29	22

Oxford University

Venue	P	W	D	L	F	A
Home	2	1	0	1	8	4
Away	10	5	3	2	26	16
Totals	12	6	3	3	34	20

Corinthians

Venue	P	W	D	L	F	A
Home	7	5	1	1	22	11
Away	5	1	1	3	12	18
Totals	12	6	2	4	34	29

The Reverend W.C. (Billy) Jordan, an amateur centre-forward, played in Albion's 1906-07 FA Cup semi-final team against Everton (lost 2-1). Educated at St John's College, Oxford, he scored twice for an Oxford XI against Cambridge University in 1908 and besides playing for Albion, he also served with Everton and Wolverhampton Wanderers, and after retiring became a Director of Darlington. He scored eight goals in his two amateur internationals for England. Ordained in 1907, he became curate at St Clement's Church, Nechells, Birmingham in 1911 and thereafter devoted his time to the church, conducting several Sportsmens' Services up and down the country. He also served the Church at Widnes, on the Isle of Man, in Slaidburn (Yorkshire), Darlington and Belbroughton. He died in Belbroughton in 1949, aged 64.

Harold Bache was another well-known University footballer who played for Albion. The son of a former Albion Director, he was a superb all-round sportsman who was killed in action in 1916 (See BACHE, Harold Godfrey).

VERNON, John

Jack Vernon was a truly great centre-half who cost Albion a then record fee of £9,500 when he joined the club from Belfast Celtic in 1947. During the ten years prior to moving to The Hawthorns Vernon had played superbly well in Ireland and this after he had been an amateur with Liverpool! Born in Belfast in 1919, he started out with

Dundela Juniors and joined his home town club Celtic in 1937. During the war he won two Irish League championship medals (1939 and 1940) and three Irish Cup winners' medals (1941, 1943 and 1944) and he also represented the Irish League on 12 occasions between 1941

and 1946. He collected his first five full international caps (out of a total of 22) while playing in Ireland and soon after joining Albion, he lined up for the Great Britain side against the Rest of Europe at Hampden Park, and later skippered the United Kingdom XI against Wales (1951). He captained both Albion and Ireland and guided the Baggies to promotion from the Second Division in 1948-49. In his size five boots Vernon was masterful on the ground, strong in the air and a devoted professional who hardly committed a serious foul. He scored one goal (against Sheffield Wednesday in 1948) in exactly 200 games for Albion, up to 1952 when he returned 'home' to play for Crusaders. He retired in 1954 to continue his father's butchers' business in Belfast, a job he did until his untimely death in 1981.

WAGES (SALARIES)

Albion have been paying wages to their players ever since 1885 – the year the club became a professional concern.

In those far off Victorian days top class footballers could earn between 5s (25p) and 12s.6d (63p) a week...which was a lot of money at the time. As the years rolled by, so the wages were increased and by 1898, ten years after the Football League was formed, some Albion players (Billy Bassett included) were being paid £4.10s (£4.50) a week. The lowest paid professional was receiving 10s (50p).

In 1901 the Football League enforced the maximum wage regulations and these were maintained for 60 years.

The maximum wage was initially set at £4 a week, but very few Albion players received that amount immediately (relegation was suffered in season 1900-01).

Obviously as the cost of living went up, so did the players' wages and here is a chart showing the steady increase of an Albion players' weekly wage:

1910 – up to £5 a week (all year round)
1920 – up to £9 a week (all year round)
1922 – down to £8 a week (£6 close season)
1930 – down to £7 a week (£6 close season)
1945 – up to £8 a week (£7 in close season)
1947 – up to £12 a week (£10 in close season)
1951 – up to £14 a week (£10 in close season)
1953 – up to £15 a week (£12 in close season)
1957 – up to £17 a week (£14 in close season)
1958 – up to £20 a week (£17 in close season)
1961 – up to £25 a week (£20 in close season)

Since the maximum wage restriction was lifted Albion, along with virtually every other League club, have been paying players wages based on service and stature. And, although specific figures cannot be disclosed, it can be said that some players at The Hawthorns were very well paid: i.e. up to £250 a week during the 1970s, up to £500 a week in the 1980s and £1,000 plus per week in the 1990s.

Player-manager Johnny Giles, in his first season at The Hawthorns (1975-76) earned between £12,000 and £15,000.

Ron Atkinson averaged £20,000 a year in his period in charge (1978-81) and manager Ossie Ardiles' annual salary in 1992-93 was estimated at £40,000.

Manager Alan Buckley signed a contract with Albion in 1995 which indicated that his annual salary was in the region of £100,000 per annum.

WAKE MONDAY

In the closing years of the nineteenth century a local Black Country custom allowed for celebrations on Wake Monday (the first Monday in November). The local pubs laid on cheap beer and free food, and Albion took full advantage of the fact that most people in the area were on holiday by arranging a home game. From November 1887 to November 1897 Bolton Wanderers were exclusively the visitors to Stoney Lane, winning four times, losing on six occasions and drawing one of 11 matches played. Everton, Sheffield United and Stoke took over the fixture until 1900 which

was the last year in which Albion played a first-team game on Wake Monday.

WALSALL

Albion's record against the Saddlers whom they have met under four different guises – Walsall Swifts, Walsall Town, Walsall Town Swifts and Walsall:

Football League

Venue	P	W	D	L	F	A	Pts
Home	1	0	1	0	0	0	1
Away	1	0	1	0	0	0	1
Totals	2	0	2	0	0	0	2

FA Cup

Home	1	1	0	0	6	1
Away	1	0	1	0	1	1
Totals	2	1	1	0	7	2

League Cup

Home	2	1	0	1	5	4
Away	1	0	1	0	0	0
Totals	3	1	1	1	5	4

Autoglass Trophy

Home	1	1	0	0	4	0

Other Matches

Home	26	17	6	3	79	27
Away	50	20	13	17	87	82
Totals	76	37	19	20	166	109

Albion first met neighbours Walsall Swifts in an away friendly match on 28 April 1883, a game they lost 2-1.

Albion's first game against Walsall Town (who amalgamated with the Swifts in 1888) was in the Staffordshire Cup on 22 December 1883. Albion won 4-0 and Harry Aston scored all four goals.

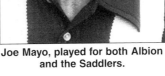

Joe Mayo, played for both Albion and the Saddlers.

On 24 September 1888, Walsall Town Swifts entertained Albion under electric lighting at their Chuckery ground. Around 7,000 spectators witnessed the 2-2 draw played out in thick mist, the game being reduced to half-an-hour each way.

'It was a pretty sight' wrote one observer. 'But play was confined to little spots and of course nothing like a full view of the game could be seen.'

The first competitive match against Walsall FC was an FA Cup-tie played at Walsall on 27 January 1900. A crowd of 9,106 saw the 1-1 draw before Albion easily won the replay 6-1 five days later.

During World War Two Albion and Walsall met on 29 occasions in various competitions. On 31 May 1941 the Saddlers thrashed Albion 10-3 at Fellows Park in what was Albion's heaviest wartime defeat. Albion's two best wartime results against Walsall were a 7-2 win on 20 January 1940 and a 7-1 victory on 15 January 1944.

Albion's first League Cup game was at home to Walsall on 22 September 1965. A then record crowd for the competition – 41,188 – saw Albion win 3-1, Tony Brown scoring twice.

It was not until season 1988-89 that Albion and Walsall first met in League action – and then both games (at The Hawthorns and Fellows Park) ended goalless.

Albion were the last team to play at Fellows Park, taking

on Walsall in a testimonial match for Peter Hart on 11 May 1990.

A crowd of 2,180 witnessed the 1-1 draw.

Albion's emphatic 4-0 win over the Saddlers in the Autoglass Trophy was achieved at The Hawthorns on 5 January 1993 before a crowd of just over 6,700.

Albion League debutants v Walsall: David Cork (1988).

Tony Lange and Scott Darton made their senior debuts for Albion against Walsall in the Autoglass Trophy (1993).

Players with both clubs: Albert Aldridge, Gilbert Alsop, Colin Anderson, David Arthur, Harry Baldwin, Lewis Bedford, Peter Billingham, Bill Bowser, Sid Bowser, Darren Bradley, Alistair Brown, Joe Carter, Joe Connor, Gary Childs, Nicky Cross, Reg Davies, Alf Dean, Tom Dilly, Jimmy Dudley, Peter Eastoe, Ernie Edwards, Doug Fraser, Tony Godden, Tony Grealish, Phil Hawker, Ken Hodgkisson, Les Horne, Alec Jackson, George Johnson, Stan Jones, Billy Law, Tony Lowery, Norman Male, Jack Mann, Joe Mayo, Jimmy McLean, John Osborne, Jack Paddock, William Paddock, Garry Pendrey, Eric Perkins, Jimmy Prew, Darren Rogers, Craig Shakespeare, Terry Simpson, Martin Singleton, Horace Smith, Derek Statham, Kenny Stephens, Kevin Summerfield, Gerry Summers, Sammy Timmins, Jack Taggart, David Walker, Dave Walsh, Joe Wilson.

NB: Besides playing for both clubs, Fraser also managed Walsall (1974-77).

The following played reserve/youth-team football for Albion and later served Walsall: Norman Allsopp, Dave Barnett, Tommy Bowen, Jack Bridgett, Peter Bunch, Jack Flavell, Bill Gallier, Darren Goodall, Harry Haddington, Adrian Littlejohn, John Loveridge, John Morris, Albert Newman, Ron Nicholls, Ernie Peers, Tim Rawlings, Bill Rotten, Luke Tinkler, Jim Whitehouse, Jimmy Whitehouse, Phil Whitehouse, Gordon Wills, Peter Woodward.

Ron Green and Jimmy Dainty were Walsall players before having brief spells with Albion.

Also associated with both clubs: Ronnie Allen (1973), Alan Ashman (1978-79) and Alan Buckley (1979-82 and 1982-86 – two spells) were managers of Walsall who also managed Albion; Dick Graham, Albion trainer 1956-58, was briefly Walsall manager in 1968; John Jarman and Albert McPherson were Walsall defenders who later joined Albion's coaching/training staff; Jim Southam, an Albion reserve full-back, became Walsall's trainer; Fred Pedley was an Albion physiotherapist and later Walsall trainer; Louis Ford (1890s) and John Westmancoat (1980s) were secretaries at both clubs; Richard O'Kelly was a Walsall striker (1979-86 and 1988) and is now coaching Albion's youth team (1996).

WALSALL CUP

Albion entered their second team for the Walsall Senior Cup in 1885-86 and from then onwards it was almost exclusively a competition for the reserves except on two occasions when the first team took over the fixtures.

On 16 October 1886 the Albion Committee chose a strong side to face Crosswell's Brewery at home because the brewers had included seven former 'Throstles' in their line-up. Albion won the game 5-2 and then left the remainder of the ties to the second team who eventually lost to Walsall Town.

In 1887-88 the second team drew twice with Oldbury Town (formerly Crosswell's Brewery) in the first round of the Walsall Cup before the Albion fielded their senior side who duly sent Oldbury packing to the tune of 5-1 (away) with 'Jem' Bayliss scoring a hat-trick. The second team went on to win the trophy for the first time that season, overwhelming Walsall Swifts 4-1 in the Final.

In 1900-01 Albion's second string participated again after

a long absence and were joint holders of the Cup after drawing 1-1 with Small Heath reserves. In 1903 Albion became Cup winners again on beating Brierley Hill Alliance 5-0 but in the following two years they lost in the Final, first to Small Heath by 5-0 (after a 0-0 draw) and in 1906 to Wolverhampton Wanderers (2-1).

WALSH, David

Irish international centre-forward Dave Walsh joined Albion for £3,500 in 1946 from Linfield – and he made a terrific start to his career at The Hawthorns by scoring in each of the first six League games at the start of the 1946-47 Second Division season. A player with an eye for goal, he continued to net regularly for Albion and was a key figure when promotion was gained in 1948-49. He went on to score exactly 100 goals in 174 games for the Baggies, up to 1950 when he signed for neighbours Aston Villa for £25,000 as a replacement for Trevor Ford. He did well at

Villa Park, notching a further 40 goals in 114 outings before rounding off his League career with Walsall (1955-56). After a brief spell with Worcester City he retired in 1957 to concentrate on running his sports outfitters shop and general store in Droitwich. He sold up in 1984 and moved to Thurlestone, near Plymouth where he still lives today. Born in Waterford in 1924, Walsh played for St Joseph's, the Corinthians, Shelbourne (Waterford), Glen

Albion line up before their 1-1 draw in Belgium with Anderlecht on 8 May 1946, the last season of 'wartime' football. Left to right are Billy Elliott, Frank Hodgetts, Len Millard, George Tranter, Ike Clarke, Doug Witcomb, Ray Barlow, Stan Butler, Reg Ryan, Harry Kinsell and Jim Sanders.

Rovers, Limerick and Shelbourne (Dublin) prior to joining Linfield in 1943. He netted 122 goals while playing in Ireland, including 73 with Linfield (61 in League and Cup) during the 1945-46 season when they won the Irish League championship and the Irish Cup, having earlier lifted the Irish Cup (1945). Capped 20 times by the Republic of Ireland, his record in English League football was 137 goals in 293 appearances.

WARTIME FOOTBALL (1914-18 & 1939-46)

Along with many other clubs Albion were forced to abandon their Football League programme between May 1915 and August 1919 and from September 1939 until August 1946.

On each occasion it was due, of course, to the wartime conditions in Europe.

In fact, World War One broke out officially in August 1914, but the Football League authorities resolved to play out the remainder of that season as the fixtures had already been prepared and the respective clubs were willing to continue.

In the enforced break which followed Albion played a total of only 19 matches; eight were won, four drawn and seven lost. Their goal-average was 42-30.

Six of these fixtures were in the Midland Victory League (played in March and April 1919) which Albion eventually won, pipping Derby County and Wolves on goal-average for the title.

Albion's best win in this first wartime period was 5-1 – achieved on two occasions against Aston Villa on Boxing Day 1916 (Jack Mann scored a hat-trick) and 19 April 1919, both at The Hawthorns.

One player who made his debut for Albion during World War One, and who later made such an impact at the club, was little Tommy Magee. He stepped out for the first time in an Albion jersey against Derby County (h) on 5 April 1919, lining up at inside-right. He later

occupied the right-half berth and became an England international.

Whenever possible Albion fielded their strongest team during that 1915-19 period and the players usually available were: Hubert Pearson (goal), Joe Smith, Jesse Pennington and Arthur Cook (full-backs), Frank Waterhouse, Sammy Richardson, Sid Bowser, Bobby McNeal, Fred Reed and Sam Hatton (half-backs) and Claude Jephcott, Harry Wright, Jack Crisp, Jack Mann, Alf Bentley, Fred Morris, Tommy Newall, Howard Gregory and Ben Shearman (forwards).

Other players made the odd appearance here and there, including veteran goalkeeper Ike Webb, who was aged 43 when he lined up against Wolves and Aston Villa in August 1918, Wally Arch, Walter Hackett, Bill Roberts, Cliff Sambrook, Albert Lindon (Barnsley), Sid Joyce and Magee.

Centre-forward Mann top-scored with eight goals; Gregory and Magee each netted six and Roberts claimed four.

In the second enforced lay-off Albion played 298 first-team games (266 in League and Cup competitions) and these figures include the three Second Division matches staged at the start of the 1939-40 campaign which were subsequently declared null and void.

Albion played in the Midland Regional League in 1939-40, in the Football League South Midland Group in 1940-41, in the Football League South in 1941-42 and the Football League North in 1942-43, 1943-44 and 1944-45. In the transitional season of 1945-46, when teams were slowly getting back into some sort of order after the hostilities, Albion reverted back to the Football League South.

Each season provided various Cup competitions and Albion were victorious in one – winning the Midland War Cup in 1943-44 when they beat Nottingham Forest 6-5 on aggregate in the two-legged Final. Albion's winning team in that vital second leg at the City Ground, where they triumphed 4-3 after extra-time, was: Norman Heath; Jim Southam, Jack Smith; Len Millard, Billy Gripton, 'Sandy'

Albion's Harry Kinsell (right) pictured with Wolves' Billy Wright (left) and Stoke's Neil Franklin.
All three played for England in wartime football.

McNab; Sammy Heaselgrave, Ike Clarke, Jack Acquaroff, Charlie Evans and Frank Hodgetts. Acquaroff (2), Hodgetts and Clarke scored the goals in front of 14,438 fans.

This second leg clash at Nottingham, is in fact, the longest football match an Albion team has ever played in – it lasted for 145 minutes – from 3pm until 5.25pm!

A grand total of 116 players appeared in those 298 games and 42 of them were guests (See appropriate section under PLAYERS).

Top appearance maker for Albion during that 1939-46 period was Billy Gripton (207, including 194 in League and Cup). Billy Elliott played in 169 matches, Len Millard in 157, 'Sandy' McNab 147, Jack Sankey 143, Cecil Shaw 141, Charlie Evans 135, goalkeeper Jimmy Adams 131, Sammy Heaselgrave 127, Ike Clarke 114, Frank Hodgetts 112, Idris Bassett 108, 'W.G.' Richardson 106 and Joe Johnson 102.

The honour of leading goalscorer went to outside-right Billy Elliott who totalled no fewer than 128 goals (117 in League and Cup). 'W.G.' Richardson netted 123, Ike Clarke 77, Harry 'Popeye' Jones 60, Sammy Heaselgrave 50, Robbie Newsome 34 and Charlie Evans 33. In all Albion scored 795 goals (673 in League and Cup).

Albion's 1939-46 wartime record (League and Cup):

Season	P	W	D	L	F	A
1939-40	37	23	5	9	107	67
1940-41	32	14	5	13	92	82
1941-42	31	18	4	9	115	69
1942-43	38	17	6	15	84	83
1943-44	39	14	11	14	90	93
1944-45	40	15	11	14	75	74
1945-46	46	23	9	14	110	74
Totals	263	124	51	88	673	542

War News

Albion utilised 54 players in their first team in 1942-43 – a club record.

Just four players played for Albion's first team in each of the wartime seasons: Ike Clarke, Billy Elliott, Sammy Heaselgrave and Billy Gripton.

The two Albion-Chelsea League games in 1945-46 produced 20 goals – Albion won 8-1 at home and lost 7-4 in London.

There was a penalty-kick awarded in each of Albion's first five matches at the start of the 1945-46 season – a club record.

A total of 45 hat-tricks were scored by Albion players during World War Two – 'W.G.' Richardson netted 12, Clarke 10, Harry Jones 8, Elliott 7. Albion had 40 trebles scored against them.

Jack Sankey, normally a wing-half and Robbie Newsome, a forward, both kept goal in wartime games for Albion, the former against Aston Villa at The Hawthorns (in 1941), the latter for the reserves at Molineux (in 1942).

In March 1942, Albion full-back Harold White was awarded the Military Medal – only the second professional footballer to be decorated during World War Two. The other was cricketer/footballer Bill Edrich.

When Albion beat Luton Town 10-1 at home on 22 November 1941, they scored eight of their goals inside 32 minutes.

Three goals were scored (two by Albion) in 90 seconds of the first half of a League game with Walsall in March 1941.

In 1941-42 Billy Elliott equalled Harry Jones's 1939-40 club record of scoring in 11 consecutive first-team games for Albion.

Four penalties were awarded during Albion's friendly match with Birmingham in May 1942 – two to each side.

Albion's best wartime wins were 10-1 over Luton Town in 1941 (see above), 8-0 v Swansea Town (October 1941), 8-1 against Notts County (January 1941) and against Chelsea (October 1945), 8-2 v Wolverhampton Wanderers (at Molineux, November 1941), 7-0 v Northampton Town (December 1941), 7-1 v Walsall (January 1944) and 7-2 v Walsall (January 1945). Their heaviest defeat was 10-3 at

Walsall in May 1941, and they also lost 9-0 at Leicester in January 1943, 8-0 at Coventry in December 1943 and 8-2 against Aston Villa in October 1942 and Stoke City (home) in February 1944.

'Sandy' McNab was Albion's regular captain during the war. Jack Sankey, Cecil Shaw and Harry Kinsell were all vice-captains who skippered the side occasionally.

The first guest player to appear for Albion was Billy Price (Huddersfield Town) and the last was Jimmy Jinks (Millwall). Both were centre-forwards.

Fifteen players scored on their debuts for Albion between September 1939 and April 1946 with Scotsman Peter 'Ma-Ba' McKennan netting a hat-trick on his first appearance against Northampton Town in 1941.

Eddie Connelly was sent-off twice while playing for Albion in wartime soccer (See SENDINGS OFF).

Albion lost £6,099.83 on the 1939-40 wartime season.

Three times in 1940-41 Albion played home games at The Hawthorns in front of crowds of less than a thousand.

Excluding the abandoned game against Sheffield Wednesday, Albion played 24 home matches in 1939-40 and they scored in every one.

Over 80 personnel connected with West Bromwich Albion Football Club served in HM Forces during World War Two.

Albion reserves beat a Smethwick League XI 17-0 in a friendly in January 1945. Tommy Bowen scored seven of the goals and Ray Barlow six.

WATERHOUSE, Frank

After winning a junior international cap for England in 1909, 'Puffer' Waterhouse never looked back. He went from strength to strength with Albion and appeared in 188 League and Cup games for the club as a solid defender, able to play at right-half or centre-half. Born in Oldbury in 1889, he joined Albion from Wednesbury Old Athletic in 1908 and made his senior debut the following year. He helped Albion win the Second Division title in 1910-11. He left The Hawthorns for Derby County in 1920 and later served with Leeds United (1921-22). He returned to the Black Country and played for Dudley Town before retiring in 1925. Waterhouse died in Smethwick in 1967.

WATFORD

Albion's record against Watford:

Football League

Venue	P	W	D	L	F	A	Pts
Home	10	5	2	3	19	13	17
Away	10	3	2	5	9	16	11
Totals	20	8	4	8	28	29	28

League Cup

Venue	P	W	D	L	F	A
Home	1	1	0	0	1	0
Away	1	0	0	1	1	4
Totals	2	1	0	1	2	4

Other Match

Venue	P	W	D	L	F	A
Away	1	0	1	0	1	1

Albion's first encounter with Watford saw them draw 1-1 in an away friendly on 30 April 1898.

Their paths did not cross again for 79 years until Watford visited The Hawthorns for a League Cup-tie in October 1977. Albion beat the Fourth Division champions-to-be 1-0 that night with a late goal from Tony Brown.

The first two League meetings between the clubs took place in season 1982-83 (Division One). Watford won them both, 3-1 on Albion soil and 3-0 at Vicarage Road.

Albion's best League win over the Hornets is 4-1 at home in October 1993, while Watford's best over Albion is 5-1 at Vicarage Road in August 1985. Future Albion centre-forward Colin West scored a hat-trick for Watford in this game.

Albion's Alistair Robertson and Watford's George Reilly (later to join Albion) were sent off for fighting in the tunnel at the end of the League game between the clubs at The Hawthorns in December 1984 (Albion won 2-1).

A terrific eight-goal relegation thriller between Albion and Watford at The Hawthorns in March 1996 ended in a 4-4 draw. Despite leading 3-0 and 4-2 with Bob Taylor scoring his first hat-trick for the club and Richard Sneekes netting on his debut, Albion were pegged back with two Watford goals in the last four minutes.

Albion League debutants v Watford: Mick Perry (1983), Gerry Armstrong (1985), Brian Rice (1989), Mark Barham 1989), Richard Sneekes (1996).

Players with both clubs: Gerry Armstrong, Luther Blissett, George Drury, George James, Billy Law, Jimmy Poxton, Mel Rees, George Reilly, Brian Talbot, Garry Thompson, Colin West.

Also associated with both clubs: Albion reserves Bobby Downes (1974-80) and Bill Hicklin (1947-48) both played League football for Watford; Ron Saunders scored 18 goals in 39 League games for Watford (1964-65) and was Albion's manager (1985-87); Gordon Clark managed Albion (1959-61) and was Watford's chief scout (1979-80); Tommy Jones played for Watford (1935-46) and became Albion physiotherapist in 1965 (until 1971). Goalkeeper Perry Digweed, an Albion loan player in 1993, was with Watford (1993-95).

Colin West, played for both Albion and Watford.

WATNEY CUP

Albion participated in this competition prior to the start of the 1971-72 season. They defeated Wrexham 2-1 (away) in the first round on 31 July (Tony Brown scoring twice), accounted for Halifax Town 2-0 at The Shay in the semi-final four days later (with two goals from Colin Suggett) and then met Colchester United at The Hawthorns in the Final on 7 August before a crowd of 19,009 (receipts £7,337). United were skippered by former Albion defender Bobby Cram and managed by Dick Graham who had been trainer at The Hawthorns in the 1950s. Also in their ranks were two players who later joined Albion – goalkeeper Graham Smith and left-half Phil Bloss.

Albion were held to a 4-4 draw by the Layer Road club who then went on to win the trophy by beating Albion 4-3 on penalties.

In normal outfield play Jeff Astle (2), Len Cantello and Suggett scored for Albion, while Astle, Tony Brown and Bobby Hope netted in the penalty shoot-out. Bloss hit the vital Cup-winning spot kick for United.

WEATHER

The hottest temperature in which Albion have played a Football League game has been 90 degrees F (in the shade) at Turf Moor, Burnley, on 1 September 1906.

It was 82 degrees for Albion's home League game with Sunderland on 28 August 1926.

When Albion played on tour in East Africa in 1968, temperatures of 102 degrees F were recorded at games in Kenya and Uganda.

Other 'hot spots' where Albion have played:

100 degrees F	(Arizona)	1990
95 degrees F	(Bahrain)	1980

93 degrees F	(Syria)	1978
93 degrees F	(Tunisia)	1989
92 degrees F	(Kuwait)	1981
92 degrees F	(Saudi Arabia)	1977
91 degrees F	(Cyprus)	1982
90 degrees F	(New York)	1965
90 degrees F	(Alicante, Spain)	1977, 1982

In contrast, there have been several instances whereby Albion have played games in bitterly cold temperatures.

Since 1946 Albion have, in fact, played three matches when the needle fell well below freezing point: v Dunfermline Athletic (h) European Cup-winners' Cup, 19 February 1969 (minus seven); v Chelsea (a) League Division Two , 31 January 1976 (five degrees below) and v Valencia (h) UEFA Cup, 6 December 1978 (four degrees below freezing).

WEBB, Isaac

A big, burly goalkeeper, quick off his line with outstanding reflexes, Ike Webb was spectacularly agile at times and always wore a cap on the field. Born in Worcester in 1874, he played his early football for St Clement's Rangers, Berwick Rangers (Worcester), Worcester Olympic, Evesham Town and Mansfield Town. He had a spell with Wellington Town prior to signing for Birmingham (Small Heath) in

1898. He was bought by Albion in 1901 (as a straight replacement for Joe Reader) and in his first season at The Hawthorns helped Albion win the Second Division title. He went on to appear in 101 games for Albion up to 1904, when he was transferred to Sunderland, later serving with Queen's Park Rangers. Webb retired in 1910 and joined the West Yorkshire Regiment as a catering orderly. He later made a comeback with Albion as a guest in 1918 at the age of 43. Towards the end of his playing career Webb suffered a

fractured skull but continued to play, not knowing the seriousness of the injury. He died in Birmingham in 1950.

WEDNESBURY CHARITY CUP

This was another short-lived competition which Albion entered twice – in 1882-83 and 1883-84.

By ousting Wednesbury Strollers and Aston Unity Albion qualified to meet Nottingham Forest in the 1883 Final. But after leading 2-1 and then having skipper John While taken off with a broken leg, Albion went down 5-3, Tinsley Lindley scoring four of the Forest goals.

The following season Albion were dismissed by St George's in the second round after beating Aston Unity 3-0.

Albion's reserve side were beaten Finalists in the 1890 Wednesbury Charity Cup Final but four years later they lifted the trophy after defeating Newport at Wellington 4-0 in the Final.

Albion's record in the Wednesbury Charity Cup (first team):

Venue	P	W	D	L	F	A
Home	1	1	0	0	7	1
Away	6	2	2	2	11	13
Totals	7	3	2	2	18	14

WEST BROMWICH CHARITY CUP

Albion's first team participated in the West Bromwich (Friendly Societies) Charity Cup for the first time in May 1888. Although the two ties which Albion contested were for the benefit of local charities, all was not particularly friendly for when Albion mastered Wednesbury Old Athletic in the semi-final there were skirmishes among rival supporters. And in the Final against Great Bridge United, which Albion won 10-1 ('Jem' Bayliss scored 4) a Unity defender was sent off for rough play – a very rare occurrence in those days.

In the 1890s Everton made regular visits to Stoney Lane to play Albion for the WBC Cup. Indeed, they met Albion on five occasions in West Bromwich and all told won three Finals: 2-0 in 1893, 2-1 in 1896 and 4-0 (on Merseyside in a replay after a 1-1 draw) in 1898. Albion were victorious in two Finals against Everton in 1895 (1-0) and 1897 (2-1). In 1889 Albion beat Wolverhampton Wanderers 2-0 to win the Cup and the club's first team also shared the trophy in 1890 (with Aston Villa). Albion's reserve side were victors in 1903, 1904, 1905, 1906, 1912, 1913, 1914, 1915, 1921, 1922 and 1923 – this being the last time Albion competed for this local prize.

Albion's record in the WBC Cup (first team):

Venue	P	W	D	L	F	A
Home	10	6	2	2	25	11
Away	1	0	0	1	0	4
Totals	11	6	2	3	25	15

WEST HAM UNITED

Albion's record against West Ham:

Football League

Venue	P	W	D	L	F	A	Pts
Home	33	20	5	8	65	35	47
Away	33	10	4	19	45	71	27
Totals	66	30	9	27	110	106	74

FA Cup

Home	3	0	2	1	2	4
Away	5	1	1	3	7	10
Totals	8	1	3	4	9	14

League Cup

Home	3	2	1	0	9	2
Away	4	1	2	1	6	6
Totals	7	3	3	1	15	8

Simod Cup

Away	1	0	0	1	2	5

Other Matches

Home	2	1	0	1	2	2
Away	2	1	1	0	5	3
Totals	4	2	1	1	7	5

West Ham United were known as Thames Ironworks when they met Albion for the first time in a friendly at Hermit Road (Canning Town, London) on 20 March 1896. The game was played under a primitive form of electric floodlighting and Albion won 4-2.

The first League meetings took place in 1923-24 (Division One), the Hammers winning 1-0 at home and drawing 0-0 at The Hawthorns.

In season 1912-13, West Ham (then a non-League side) knocked Albion out of the FA Cup, winning a first-round tie 3-0 at the third attempt (at Chelsea) after 1-1 and 2-2 draws.

Albion's best League win over West Ham is 7-1, achieved at The Hawthorns on 24 October 1925 when Welsh international Stan Davies scored a hat-trick.

Albion have also twice beaten the Hammers 5-1 – at Upton Park on 7 November 1931 when 'W.G.' Richardson equalled the League's scoring record by netting four goals in five minutes (5th to 9th) at the start of the game, and at The Hawthorns on 4 May 1985.

West Ham's best win over Albion is 6-1, at Upton Park on 16 April 1965, when Brian Dear scored five times in the space of 21 minutes (44-65). The Hammers also ran up 4-0 home victories over Albion in January 1966, August 1968 and November 1985.

Albion beat West Ham 5-3 on aggregate in the 1966 League Cup Final, winning their home leg 4-1 after having gone down 2-1 at Upton Park in the first game (See FOOTBALL LEAGUE CUP).

Jack Lovatt, made his Albion debut against West Ham.

The following season Albion again got the better of the Hammers in the same competition, ousting them in the semi-finals 6-2 on aggregate (4-0 at home, 2-2 in London).

West Ham's 2-1 win at The Hawthorns on 18 September 1982 ended a run of 16 visits there without a victory.

Leroy Rosenior scored four of West Ham's goals in their 5-2 Simod Cup win over Albion in November 1988.

Jeff Astle scored 16 goals for Albion in games against West Ham, including hat-tricks in that 4-0 League Cup semi-final victory in 1967 and in a 3-1 home win in the First Division match at The Hawthorns in May 1968.

Jack Vernon made his Albion debut against West Ham at Upton Park on 15 March 1947 and the man he marked – Frank Neary – scored a hat-trick in the Londoners' 3-2 victory.

Albion League debutants v West Ham: Joe Evans (1926), Stan Butler (1939), Jack Vernon (1947), Jack Haines (1948), Ray Potter (1958), Jack Lovatt (1961), Ronnie Fenton (1962).

Danny Campbell made his senior debut for Albion against West Ham United in the first leg of the 1966 League Cup Final and Darren Goodall made his only senior appearance for Albion against West Ham in the 1988 Simod Cup-tie at Upton Park.

Players with both clubs: Jeroen Boere, David Burrows, Peter Butler, David Cross, Alan Dickens, Fred Fenton, Bobby Gould, Tommy Green, Geoff Hurst, Harry Kinsell, Peter McManus, George Reid, Charlie Simmons, David Speedie, Gary Strodder, Steve Walford, Chris Whyte.

Associated with both clubs: Archie Macaulay played as a wing-half for West Ham (1940s) and was Albion's manager (1961-63); Stuart Pearson was a goalscorer with West Ham (1979-81) and Albion's coach and assistant manager (1987-92) and Tudor Martin played for the Hammers (1936-37) having earlier assisted Albion's second team. Current Albion first-team goalkeeper Nigel Spink had trials for West Ham's youth team in the 1970s.

WHITEHEAD, Clive Robert

Between 1981 and 1987 Clive Whitehead scored nine goals in 196 first-team appearances for Albion while occupying

seven different positions! Born in Birmingham in 1955, he had unsuccessful trials with Wolves in 1971 and two years later became a professional with Bristol City. He was mainly a left winger at Ashton Gate and was transferred to Albion for £100,000 in December 1981. During his six-year stay at The Hawthorns, Whitehead, an unselfish footballer, skippered the Baggies and generally performed with total commitment. He left Albion for Portsmouth after a loan spell at Molineux (1986), and later served with Exeter City and Yeovil Town (as player-manager for six months in 1990-91). He then went back to Bristol City as a senior coach and assistant manager until 1995.

WHYTE, Christopher Anderson

Strong in the air and timely with his on-the-ground interceptions, Chris Whyte made his League debut for Arsenal in 1979. Seventeen years later he helped Charlton Athletic reach the First Division promotion Play-offs and in between times he played for Crystal Palace (loan, 1984), New York Express (1986-87), Los Angeles Lazers (1987-88), Albion (from 1988 to 1990), Leeds United, Birmingham City, Coventry City (on loan) and West Ham United (on loan). He joined Charlton on the transfer deadline of 1996. Born in Islington, London in 1961, Whyte made 96 appearances for Albion (nine goals scored) during his two seasons at The Hawthorns and was then sold to Leeds for £400,000, the fee being fixed by a Tribunal. He helped the Elland Road side win the Premiership title in 1992 and was the back-bone of the Blues' defence when they carried off the Second Divis-

ion championship in 1995. Capped four times by England at Under-21 level with Arsenal, Whyte passed the milestone of 500 senior appearances in his career in 1996.

WIGAN ATHLETIC

Albion's record against Wigan:

Football League

Venue	P	W	D	L	F	A	Pts
Home	2	1	1	0	6	2	4
Away	2	1	0	1	1	1	3
Totals	4	2	1	1	7	3	7

League Cup

Home	1	1	0	0	3	1	
Away	1	0	1	0	0	0	
Totals	2	1	1	0	3	1	

Other match

Away	1	1	0	0	2	1	

Albion first opposed Wigan Athletic in a testimonial match for former Baggies' goalkeeper Bob Ward at Springfield Park in March 1983. A crowd of only 784 turned out to see Albion win 2-1 with Noel Luke and Romeo Zondervan on the scoresheet.

In 1984-85 the sides met in the second round of the League Cup, Albion going through 3-1 on aggregate after a goalless draw in the first leg at Wigan.

The first time the teams met in the Football League was in season 1991-92. It was 1-1 at The Hawthorns on 31 August and 1-0 to Albion at Wigan on Boxing Day when 5,068 fans saw Craig Shakespeare score the all-important goal from the penalty spot.

The following season, when Albion gained promotion to the First Division, Wigan won 1-0 at Springfield Road, but succumbed 5-1 in the return fixture at The Hawthorns on 24 April, when Bob Taylor (2) Micky Mellon, Paul Raven and Kevin Donovan were on target in front of a crowd of 14,867.

Wigan goalkeeper Bob Ward was granted a testimonial against Albion, his old club.

No player has made his League or Cup debut for Albion in games against Wigan, but reserve forward Peter Frain made his first senior appearance for the Baggies at Springfield Park in Bob Ward's testimonial match in 1983.

Players with both clubs: Ian Benjamin, Mark Grew, Tony Kelly, Bob Ward, Winston White.

Also associated with both clubs: John Deehan was a striker with Albion (1979-81) and Wigan Athletic manager in 1995-96; Kenny Swain had two spells on loan at The Hawthorns (1970s & 1980s) and in 1993-94 was manager of Wigan Athletic; Albion reserves Sid Glidden (1920s), Monty Wilson (1930s) and Darren Patterson (1980s) later played for Wigan, while David Campbell had trials with Albion (1993) and Wigan (1994).

WILE, John David

As centre-halves go, few were as uncompromising as Albion's rugged and inspirational skipper John Wile. Reliable, commanding, powerful and forthright, he was the backbone of the Baggies' defence for more than a decade. Epitomised by his astute reading of the game and never-say-die approach, he appeared in 715 first-team games for Albion (500 in the Football League) during his 13½ years at The Hawthorns, being an ever-present seven times (a club record). Wile will always be remembered for the way he battled on (head swathed in bandages) after receiving a

terrible wound early on in the 1978 FA Cup semi-final against Ipswich Town at Highbury. Albion lost the tie 3-1, but the big fellow's courage was admired by all that day. Born in Sherburn, County Durham in 1947, Wile played for Durham City and Sunderland before joining Peterborough United in 1967. He was transferred to Albion for £32,000 in 1970 and right up until the summer of 1983 when he returned to Posh as player-manager, he gave the Baggies tremendous service. Along with Alistair Robertson he formed a superb defensive partnership and, indeed, they played together in 404 League games – a club record – and in 573 senior matches. Sadly, Wile never won a major honour with Albion nor did he receive international recognition. He appeared in three losing Cup semi-finals while at The

Hawthorns and helped Albion win promotion to the First Division in 1975-76. He was player-manager for Peterborough (second time round) but resigned in 1986. Earlier, in 1982, he played for Vancouver Whitecaps and also served the Albion All Stars in charity matches. In later years Wile managed both the Solihull and Cradley Heath indoor cricket centres and even played briefly for Sutton United in 1987. He now lives in Shenstone, Staffs.

WILLIAMS, Graham Evan

Graham Williams spent 18 years at The Hawthorns, starting off as an orthodox left winger and finishing up as a Welsh international left-back. He played very few games on the wing but as a defender he was tough, resilient, determined and courageous. He skippered Albion in three major Cup Finals, leading them to success in two – the League Cup of 1966 and the FA Cup in 1968. Born in Hellan, North Wales in 1938, Williams joined Albion from Rhyl Athletic in 1954. He made his debut a year later and went on to amass a total of 360 appearances for the club, scoring 11 goals. He was capped 26 times by his country and also had two games for the Under-23 side. He left The Hawthorns in 1972 to

Graham Williams shows off the FA Cup to ecstatic Albion fans in 1968.

become player-manager of Weymouth. Later he coached in Kuwait, Greece, Nigeria, Finland, UAE and Dubai, and was also coach and then manager of Cardiff City (1981-82) and scout for Newport County (1983-84).

WILLIAMS, Stuart Grenville

One-time inside-right, then right-half, Stuart Williams developed into a fine Welsh international full-back who appeared in 246 League and Cup games for Albion, scoring nine goals. Born in Wrexham in 1930, he played for his home town club before joining Albion as an amateur in November 1950, turning professional in February 1951. He won a total of 43 caps during his career, 33 whilst at The Hawthorns, which makes him the most capped player in Albion's history. Williams, who was a full-back partner to Graham (above) for both Albion and Wales, left The Hawthorns for Southampton in a £15,000 deal in 1962. He stayed at The Dell until 1967, when he returned to Albion as trainer, taking a similar position with Aston Villa in 1970. Thereafter Williams managed Payhaan of Iran, was trainer-coach of Morton, coach and assistant manager at Southampton 1971-73, scout for Carlisle United in 1973 and manager of Stavanger, Norway, 1973-74. On quitting football he became a hotelier in Southampton where he lives today.

WILLIAMS, William

Billy Williams was a brilliant full-back, sure-footed under pressure, stylish and a strong kicker whose career ended abruptly in 1901 when he was forced to retire through injury at the age of 26. Born in Smethwick in 1875, Williams played local football for West Smethwick FC, Hawthorn Villa and Old Hill Wanderers, before joining Albion for only £20 in 1894. He went on to appear in 208 games for Albion, scoring 12 goals, one of which found the back of the Nottingham Forest net from fully 55 yards in an FA Cup-tie in 1898. He played in the 1895 FA Cup Final defeat by Aston

Villa and collected six England caps, also representing the Football League and the Professionals team. Williams, whose retirement came as a bitter blow to Albion, subsequently helped the club as a trainer and then coach before taking over a pub near to The Hawthorns. He died in West Bromwich in 1929.

WILSON, Charles

'Tug' Wilson, with his film star looks, was an opportunist striker who netted 45 goals in 133 games for Albion during the 1920s. A constant threat to defenders, he became the youngest player ever to appear in a League

Billy Williams, 208 games for Albion, scoring 12 goals.

Charlie Wilson, Albion's youngest League debutant.

match for Albion when making his debut at Oldham on 1 October 1921 at the age of 16 years, 63 days. Born in Sheffield in 1905, Wilson, who had trials with Chesterfield and Sheffield United, played his early football with Stonehouse FC and Hallam FC, joining Albion initially in 1920. He spent just over seven years at The Hawthorns, transferring to Sheffield Wednesday for £3,000 in 1928. Thereafter he played for Grimsby Town, Aston Villa,

Coventry City, Kidderminster Harriers (two spells), Charlton Athletic and Aldershot (as a wartime guest), Worcester City and Kidderminster Police before retiring in 1947. He became a publican in Kidderminster in 1971 and died in that town in 1985.

WILSON, Joseph James

Scorer of Albion's first ever Football League goal (against Stoke on 8 September 1888), Joe Wilson was a smart, aggressive outside-left who netted 20 goals in 53 senior appearances during a three-year stay at the club. Born in Handsworth in 1861, he played for Hamstead Swifts, Aston Unity, Stoke Works, Walsall Town and Aston Villa (trial) before joining Albion in 1887. He won an FA Cup winners medal at the end of his first season with the club and formed a fine left-wing partnership with Tom Pearson. Wilson left Albion for Kidderminster Harriers in 1890, and later served with Birmingham St George's before retiring to become a Football League linesman and then referee (1894-1910). A goldsmith by profession, he died in Birmingham in 1952, aged 91.

WILSON, Raymond Thomson

Ray Wilson started off as a dashing outside-left but was successfully converted into an aggressive, strong-tackling left-back who gave Albion wonderful service by appearing in 284 games and scoring three goals between 1965 and 1975. Born in Grangemouth in 1947, he joined Albion as an amateur from Woodburn Athletic in 1964, turning professional a year later. He won a regular place in the first team (at left-back) in 1969 and the following year gained a League Cup runners-up medal when Albion lost to Manchester City. He played in 19 League games during the first half of Albion's successful promotion-winning campaign of 1975-76 before suffering an injury at Luton which subsequently ended his career in 1977. Wilson was

granted a testimonial in 1975 and after leaving The Hawthorns he went into business in Birmingham. He was related by marriage to former Albion winger Clive Clark.

WIMBLEDON
Albion's record against Wimbledon:

FA Cup

Venue	P	W	D	L	F	A
Home	1	1	0	0	2	0
Away	1	0	0	1	1	4
Totals	2	1	0	1	3	4

Albion have yet to meet Wimbledon in League action, but they have met the Londoners twice in third-round FA Cup-ties.

At Plough Lane on 9 January 1988, Wimbledon, managed at the time by former Albion player Bobby Gould, beat Albion 4-1 on their way to Wembley glory. They beat Liverpool 1-0 in the Final with former Albion star Laurie Cunningham in their line-up.

Albion gained revenge for that defeat by knocking the Dons out of the same competition at The Hawthorns on 6 January 1990. That day, goals by Gary Robson and Kevin Bartlett gave Albion a 2-0 victory on a quagmire of a pitch before a crowd of almost 13,000.

Players with both clubs: Laurie Cunningham, Stewart Evans.

Also associated with both clubs: Bobby Gould (player and manager of Albion, also manager of Wimbledon); Don Howe (player and manager of Albion, coach at Wimbledon) and Phil Bloss (Albion reserve, 'Dons' non-League player). Albion coach Mike Kelly (1982-83) won England amateur international honours and an FA Amateur Cup winners medal as a Wimbledon goalkeeper. Another goalkeeper, Perry Digweed, had loan spells with Albion (1983) and Wimbledon (1993).

WITCOMB, Douglas Frederick
A highly-talented wing-half, quick and cunning, a fine passer of the ball, who tackled hard but fair, Doug Witcomb joined Albion from Enfield in 1937 and stayed at The Hawthorns for 10 years before transferring to Sheffield Wednesday for £6,500. Born near Ebbw Vale in 1918, he scored ten goals in 122 games for Albion whom he served before, during and after World War Two. In his career, he won ten caps for Wales (including Victory internationals) and also represented the All British XI in 1939. After leaving Hillsborough in 1953, he served with Newport County and Llandudno Town, retiring in 1956. He later assisted Alloys & Alkmatic FC (South Wales). During the 1939-46 hostilities he guested for Grimsby Town, Leicester City, Swansea Town, Lovells Athletic and Newport County. In all Witcomb made over 350 senior appearances (303 in the Football League) and he helped Wednesday win the Second Division title in 1952. He now lives in Redditch.

Doug Witcomb, joined Sheffield Wednesday for £6,500.

WOKING
Woking of the Vauxhall League stunned Albion by winning a fourth-round FA Cup-tie at The Hawthorns by 4-2 on 5 January 1991. Albion had not lost in this competition to a

Colin West's goal against Woking in the FA Cup.

non-League side since 1913 when West Ham United (Southern League) won a first-round tie at the third attempt. But they were humiliated in front of their own supporters in the 14,516 crowd as Tim Buzaglo stole the glory with a second-half hat-trick for Woking who had trailed 1-0 at the interval to a Colin West goal. Albion gave a senior debut to goalkeeper Mel Rees in this game. Brian Talbot, the Albion manager, was required to resign after this sensational defeat.

WOLVERHAMPTON WANDERERS
Albion's record against the Wolves:

Football League

Venue	P	W	D	L	F	A	Pts
Home	63	28	19	16	112	86	78
Away	63	17	15	31	89	122	51
Totals	126	45	34	47	201	208	129

FA Cup

Venue	P	W	D	L	F	A
Home	5	3	2	0	8	3
Away	5	4	0	1	8	4
Totals	10	7	2	1	16	7

FA Charity Shield

Venue	P	W	D	L	F	A
Away	1	0	1	0	4	4

United Counties League

Venue	P	W	D	L	F	A	Pts
Home	1	1	0	0	3	1	2
Away	1	0	0	1	2	4	0
Totals	2	1	0	1	5	5	2

Other matches

Venue	P	W	D	L	F	A
Home	41	19	10	12	85	62
Away	56	16	13	27	99	111
Totals	97	35	23	39	184	173

Albion and Wolves have now met each 236 times at first-team level, and surprisingly both teams have 88 wins to their credit.

The rivalry between the Black Country clubs commenced on 20 January 1883 when they met in the third round of the Birmingham Cup at Dudley Road (Wolverhampton). Albion took the honours, winning 4-2 and left winger George Bell had the pleasure of scoring Albion's first goal against Wolves – equalising on 52 minutes after the Wanderers had taken a 20th minute lead.

Albion knocked Wolves out of the Birmingham Cup in the semi-final the following season and they also defeated them twice in friendlies before the Wanderers finally gained their first victory over Albion. This came on 25 May 1885 when they won 2-0 in a friendly in Wolverhampton.

At League level, the first encounters took place in the inaugural season of 1888-89, and Wolves won them both, 2-1 at home and 3-1 on Albion territory.

The first time the clubs were paired together in the FA Cup was in season 1885-86 when Albion won a fourth-round tie 3-1 at Stoney Lane on 2 January before a crowd of 5,196.

In 1886-87 Albion and Wolves met each other seven times – the most important fixtures being the semi-final of the

Albion's Jim Pemberton gets in a tackle against Johnny Walker of Wolves at The Hawthorns in 1950 and the ball goes outside Jim Sanders' goal in the 1-1 draw.

Staffordshire Cup (which Albion won) and the semi-final of the Birmingham Charity Cup (which the Wanderers won at Stoney Lane after two replays).

The clubs opposed each other a further seven times in 1887-88; Albion beat Wolves 2-0 in a third-round FA Cup-tie and by the same score in the semi-final of the Birmingham Cup, but Wolves ousted Albion from the Staffordshire Cup in the semi-final at Stoney Lane, this being the Throstles only home defeat that season.

The first penalty kick ever awarded at Stoney Lane was missed by the Wolves defender Harry Allen against Albion in a League game on 19 September 1891. Albion won the match 4-3 after trailing 2-0 at one stage.

Albion's record win (in League and Cup) over Wolves is 8-0 – in a First Division game at Molineux on 27 December 1893. At the time Wolves were FA Cup holders, but Albion tore them apart with some devastating attacking play and they led 5-0 at half-time. Roddy McLeod (3), Charlie Perry, Billy Bassett (3) and Owen Williams scored the goals. This remains as Albion's best-ever away League win and it is also Wolves' heaviest home defeat.

On 2 March 1895, a classic FA Cup-tie was played at Stoney Lane which Albion won 1-0 before a record crowd of 20,977. McLeod scored the winning goal 13 minutes from time.

Wolves trounced Albion 6-1 in a home League game over Christmas 1896 and in mid-January 1899 they again thrashed Albion, this time by 7-0 in a second-round Birmingham Cup-tie at Stoney Lane.

The first clash between the two clubs in the Second Division took place on 29 September 1906 at Molineux – and it turned out to be a great day for four ex-Wanderers

players – Jim Stringer, Dick Betteley, Ted Pheasant and Adam Haywood – who helped Albion to a 3-0 victory.

From 1911 to 1926 Albion and Wolves did not meet in League action, but there was a tremendous confrontation in the third round of the FA Cup in February 1924. In the first game at The Hawthorns Albion of the First Division were held to a 1-1 draw by Wolves of the Third Division North before 53,649 spectators. But it was the Throstles who came out tops in the replay, winning 2-0 in front of a mid-week crowd of 40,283.

On 29 December 1929 Albion crushed Wolves 7-3 in a home Second Division match but the victory was marred when the Wanderers' goalkeeper, Billy Walker, making his debut, broke his leg just before half-time.

During Albion's double-winning season of 1930-31 they defeated Wolves twice in the League (2-1 at The Hawthorns and 4-1 at Molineux) and also knocked the Wanderers out of the FA Cup, winning a sixth-round replay 2-1 at Molineux after a 1-1 draw. These four matches were watched by a combined total of 175,264 spectators with over 99,000 witnessing the two Cup clashes.

During the 1930s Albion remained unbeaten in home games against Wolves while similarly the Wanderers never lost to Albion at Molineux! Albion's best wins during the period were those of 4-1 in October 1932 and 5-2 in February 1935 – both at The Hawthorns – while Wolves won 5-2 at Molineux in April 1937.

Jimmy Prew and centre-half Bill Richardson scored their only goals for Albion in a 2-1 home win over Wolves in October 1936.

In May 1940, Wolves beat Albion 5-4 to clinch the Midland Regional League championship.

Eighteen months later – in November 1941 – Albion ran out 8-2 winners over Wolves in a League South game. Billy Elliott and Charlie Evans both scored hat-tricks. But Wolves quickly gained revenge by knocking Albion out of the wartime League Cup, beating them 7-0 on aggregate in the two-legged semi-final in May 1942 (winning 4-0 at The Hawthorns, 3-0 at Molineux).

Albion's biggest wartime crowd at The Hawthorns – 38,077 – witnessed the 1-1 draw against Wolves in a Football League South game on 23 April 1946.

Albion and Wolves met for the first time after the restoration of League football in 1946 at Molineux on 26 February 1949 in the sixth round of the FA Cup. After a dogged affair Wolves eventually scraped through 1-0 with a goal by Jimmy Mullen. This is Wolves' only FA Cup victory over Albion – and they went on to win the trophy at Wembley.

A record League crowd at The Hawthorns – 60,945 – saw Albion held to a 1-1 draw by Wolves on 4 March 1950. This game also marked Ronnie Allen's debut for the Baggies following his £20,000 transfer from Port Vale – and he scored to celebrate the occasion.

Allen scored a total of 10 goals against Wolves, including two hat-tricks – the first at Molineux in a 4-1 League victory there in April 1952.

Albion and Wolves were involved in a titanic battle for the League championship in 1953-54 – and it was Wolves who finally took the star prize. They beat Albion twice (1-0 on both occasions), the vital victory coming at The Hawthorns on 3 April which virtually ended Albion's chances of taking the title.

Wolves (the League champions) and Albion (the FA Cup holders) played out a tremendous 4-4 draw at Molineux in the FA Charity Shield in September 1954. Over 45,000 fans saw Ronnie Allen score a hat-trick for the Baggies who trailed by two goals with 14 minutes remaining.

Over a period of 10 years – from 1953 to 1963 – Albion lost eight times in ten League visits to Molineux, winning one and drawing the other. That victory was a thrilling 5-1 triumph under floodlights in March 1962 when wing-halves Chuck Drury and Bobby Robson scored with 25 yard drives and Derek Kevan netted with a 20 yard header! Earlier in the season Albion knocked Wolves out of the FA Cup, winning 2-1 at Molineux in the fourth round, thanks to two fine goals by Clive Clark. Six years previous Albion had won by the same score in a third-round tie on the same ground.

In December 1962 snow caused the Wolves-Albion League game at Molineux to be abandoned at half-time with the home side 2-0 ahead. The re-arranged fixture was played in March 1963 and this time Wolves romped to a 7-0 victory, outside-right Terry Wharton netting a hat-trick. Albion's 'keeper in this game was Tony Millington who had played earlier in a Central League game on the same ground and let in eight goals!

When Albion easily beat Wolves 5-1 at The Hawthorns in a First Division game in October 1964, Jeff Astle scored twice on his home debut for the Baggies.

The 100th League meeting between the clubs took place at The Hawthorns on 20 March 1971. Wolves came out on top, winning 4-2 with Bobby Gould (soon to join Albion) among their scorers.

One of Albion's best performances over Wolves in the 1970s came at Molineux in December 1978 when they won 3-0 with Alistair Brown scoring twice.

Cyrille Regis scored twice when Albion eased to a comfortable 3-0 home win over Wolves in a First Division fixture in December 1981, but two seasons later Wolves, without a win in 14 starts and propping up the table, came to The Hawthorns and beat a frustrating Albion side 3-1, winger Danny Crainie netting two fine goals.

Wolves did the League 'double' over Albion in 1989-90

(winning both games 2-1), but Albion gained sweet revenge by twice beating Wolves in 1993-94 – 3-2 at The Hawthorns and 2-1 at Molineux.

The first Second Division fixture Albion and Wolves since 1931 resulted in a 2-1 win for the Wanderers on 15 October 1989. Both their goals (obtained in the last minute of each half) were scored by former Albion forwards Robbie Dennison and Steve Bull.

Albion, battling for points to pull clear from the relegation zone, beat Wolves 2-0 at The Hawthorns on 15 March 1995, Lee Ashcroft and Bob Taylor both on target with superb headed goals.

When holding Wolves to a 0-0 draw at home on 13 January 1996, Albion ended a sequence of 11 successive League defeats – the worst run in the club's history.

Albion League debutants v Wolves: Jimmy Nicholls (1889), Seth Powell (1889), Willie Groves (1890), Ernie Fellows (1892), Billy Richards (1894), John Paddock (1894),

Steve Bull, wearing an England shirt, was sold to Wolves for a mere £65,000 by manager Ron Saunders.

Jim Spooner (1895), Sam Brett (1898), Isaiah Turner (1898), Tom Pickering (1900), Fred Wheldon (1900), Tommy Broad (1906), George Garratt (1906), David Walker (1906), Joe Brooks (1907), Frank Cresswell (1929), Billy Light (1936), Idris Bassett (1938), Cyril Davies (1938), Gordon Inwood (1949), Ronnie Allen (1950), George Corbett (1952), Alan Merrick (1968), Allan Glover (1970), Paul Holmes (1995).

Players with both clubs: Harry Aston, Dicky Baugh, Dick Betteley, Paul Bradshaw, Steve Bull, Davey Burnside John Chadburn, Sid Corfield, Ray Crawford, Robbie Dennison, Peter Eastoe, Paul Edwards, Don Goodman, Bobby Gould, Andy Gray, Adam Haywood, Danny Hegan, Eric Jones, Billy Jordan, Andy King, Tony Lange, Stacey North, Dan Nurse, John Paskin, Walter Perry, Ted Pheasant, Cyrille Regis, Alistair Robertson, Cecil Shaw, Jimmy Stringer, Andy Thompson, David Walker, Clive Whitehead, George Woodhall, Tom Worton, Harry Wright.

Bull went on to become Wolves' record marksman of all-time, netting over 275 goals for the Molineux club (up to 1996). Also associated with both clubs: outside-right Billy

Elliott left Wolves for Bournemouth in 1937 and joined Albion in 1938. Meynell Burgin had a spell with Wolves in 1933 before joining Albion in 1938. Handsworth-born defender Bill Morris began his career as a junior at The Hawthorns in 1932 and went on to make over 250 appearances for Wolves (1933-47). He also won three England caps and an FA Cup runners-up medal in 1939, and made his debut for Wolves at centre-forward against Albion in a First Division match at The Hawthorns in February 1934. Goal-ace Arthur Rowley was an amateur at Molineux in 1942-43. He joined Albion in 1944, and scored the first four of his record-breaking 434 League goals with the Baggies before transferring to Fulham in 1948. Don Howe was also on amateur forms at Molineux in 1949 before making the grade with Albion and England. Joe Butcher gained an FA Cup winners medal with Wolves in 1893 and was transferred to Albion for £25 in 1895. Unfortunately before he could make his debut for the Throstles, a crippling knee injury was diagnosed and he was forced to quit the game at the age of 21.

Tudor Martin was released by Albion in June 1929. He joined Wolves from Newport County in 1930 and stayed at Molineux until 1937. Inside/centre-forward Ronnie Stockin was an amateur with the Albion before playing for Walsall then Wolves. Republic of Ireland international midfielder Mick Martin was on loan to Wolves in 1984 (from Newcastle) having earlier played for Albion (1975-78). Mark Jones, an apprentice at The Hawthorns in the 1980s, had a brief spell with Wolves in 1987-88. Goalkeeper Vince Bartram, an ardent Albion fan as a boy, played for Wolves (1985-91) and was on loan at Albion in 1991. Mel Eves, scorer of 53 goals in 214 games for Wolves (1977-84) played for Albion in a first-team friendly in 1988. Former Wolves striker Paul Dougherty (1983-88) was a trialist in Albion's reserve team in 1992-93 and another former Wolves youngster, Cavan Chapman, was also at The Hawthorns for a brief spell in 1985. His brother, Campbell, released by Wolves in 1986, played for Albion in a first-team friendly in 1989. Jimmy Dunn, who played for Wolves, 1942-52, winning an FA Cup winners medal in 1949, was an Albion trainer 1965-71. Ronnie Allen, an Albion player (1950-61), then manager (1977 & 1981-82) and coach (1990s), was also a coach and in charge at Molineux (1965-68). Ron Bradley was an Albion player, 1956-64, who later held a coaching position with Wolves (1966-68) under Allen's management. Garry Pendrey had two seasons as a player with Albion (1979-81) and was coach at Wolves in 1986-87, returning to Molineux as coach 1989-94. Jack Screen played full-back for Albion before World War Two and after the hostilities was trainer at Molineux. Jack Smith was a player with Wolves before and during World War Two and was appointed Albion's first-ever team manager in 1948. John Jarman was trainer-coach at both clubs in the 1960's (Albion 1961-65, Wolves 1977 onwards). Gordon Dimbleby was commercial Manager at The Hawthorns (late 1970s) and then at Molineux (mid-eighties). He was also secretary at Albion following his brief spell with Wolves. Kim Wassall and Bobby Downes were in Albion's second team in 1966-67 and 1975-77 respectively and both later served Wolves, Wassall as a player in 1985 and Downes as assistant manager to Graham Taylor from 1994 to 1995. Jesse Pennington, who had spent almost 20 years as a player with Albion from 1903, became a Wolves scout in 1938-39. Bobby Hope, an Albion player from 1959-72, had a brief coaching spell at Wolves in the 1990s. Two future Albion managers, Ron Atkinson (1954) and Keith Burkinshaw (late 1940s), were both amateurs with Wolves. Fred Pedley was physiotherapist at The Hawthorns and Molineux. and groundsman Bob Burton also served with both clubs.

Guests

Twelve players guested for both Albion and Wolves during World War Two whilst already registered with other Football League clubs. They were: Jack Acquaroff, George Billingsley, Lester Finch (an England amateur international), Jimmy Jinks, Jimmy McCormick, John McDonald, England international full-back Laurie Scott (Arsenal), Jack Shelton (Walsall), Tom Smalley (Norwich) who gained one England cap against Wales in 1936, Jack Smith, later to manage Albion , Les Smith, who played outside-left for England, and Tom Wood.

Full back Charlie Mason, who played over 100 games for Wolves in the late 1800s, guested for Albion (the FA Cup winners) v Renton (the Scottish Cup winners) in the 'Championship of the World' game at Hampden Park in 1888. Charlie won three caps for England and appeared in the 1889 FA Cup Final for Wolves.

Derek Dougan turned out – and scored – for Albion in Johnny Giles' testimonial match (Albion v Leeds) at The Hawthorns in October 1975.

WOOD, Stanley George

An enterprising left winger with good skill and a strong shot, Stan 'Splinter' Wood was a key figure in Albion's attack when they achieved the Cup and promotion double in 1930-31. He made scores of openings for his colleagues and weighed in with 17 goals himself (13 in the League). Born in Cheshire in 1905, Wood joined Albion in 1928 from his home-town club Winsford United, and he remained at The Hawthorns for ten years, during which time he netted 66 goals in 281 first-team appearances. He represented the Football League and was an England reserve. He lost his place in the side to Wally Boyes and eventually left Albion for Halifax Town in 1938, taking over as trainer at The Shay in 1946, a position he held for three years. He played for Halifax in every season during the war as well as guesting for Huddersfield Town. Wood died in Halifax in 1967.

WOODHALL, George

'Spry' Woodhall was indeed a sprightly footballer who occupied a number of forward positions for Albion whom he served from 1883 to 1892, appearing in 74 competitive games and scoring 20 goals. As a winger he could centre with true accuracy; as an inside-forward he was smart and elusive on the ball and when he played as a centre-forward he was quick and alert. Born in West Bromwich in 1863, Woodhall played for All

Saints and Churchfield Foresters prior to joining Albion. He appeared in three successive FA Cup Finals (1886-87-88) gaining a winners' medal in the latter when, as partner to Billy Bassett, he scored the deciding goal against Preston North End. Woodhall, capped twice by England, left Albion for neighbours Wolves and later played for Berwick Rangers and Oldbury Town in the Birmingham League. He died in West Bromwich in 1924.

NB: Richie Woodhall, the British and European boxing champion of the 1990s is a distant relative of the former Albion footballer.

WORKINGTON

Albion have never met Workington (a League club from 1951 to 1977) but over the years several players have been associated with both clubs, namely Dave Butler, Barry Donaghy, George Corbett, Bobby Dixon, John Honour, Jock Wallace and Brian Wood. Alan Ashman managed both clubs: Albion 1967-71 and Town 1975-77, and Tommy Jones was physiotherapist at The Hawthorns (1965) and trainer at Borough Park (1953). Bob Crone, Albion's full-back of the 1890s, became Workington's trainer in 1909. Keith Burkinshaw, Albion manager (1993-94) was a Workington defender (1957-64) and then player-manager at the club for four months until March 1965.

WREXHAM

Albion's record against Wrexham:

FA Cup

Venue	P	W	D	L	F	A
Away	1	0	0	1	0	1

Watney Cup

Away	1	1	0	0	2	1

Other Matches

Home	2	2	0	0	9	5
Away	5	3	2	0	17	10
Totals	7	5	2	0	26	15

Albion first played Wrexham as long ago as Boxing Day 1882 when they won 5-2 in a friendly in North Wales. Later in the season they defeated the Welsh side 3-1 at The Four Acres.

The first competitive game between the clubs was a third-round FA Cup-tie at The Racecourse Ground in January 1930 when, in front of a near full-house of 16,570, Third Division North Wrexham caused an upset by beating Albion 1-0.

In 1941-42 two Football League Cup clashes between the two sides produced 20 goals. After 25 minutes of the first game at The Hawthorns on 27 December, Albion were 2-0 down to the Welsh club, but they rallied splendidly and eventually won 6-4. A week later when the teams met for the return fixture, ten goals were shared in a thrilling 5-5 draw. Wrexham, who lagged behind three times, were denied victory by a last minute equaliser. 'W.G.' Richardson netted twice in each game for Albion.

On 31 July 1971 two goals by Tony Brown (one a penalty) gave Albion a 2-1 win before an 11,218 crowd at Wrexham in the Watney Cup.

Players with both clubs: Peter Barnes, Arthur Cook, Sid Corfield, Shaun Cunnington, Arthur Davies, Llewellyn Davies, Ian Edwards, Elfed Evans, Grenville Jones, Craig Madden, Andrew Marriott, John Paskin, Stewart Phillips, David Powell, Bruce Rankin, George Savage, Jack Screen, Archie Styles, Mickey Thomas, Bill Tudor, Brian Whitehouse, George Williams, Stuart Williams.

Also associated with both clubs: Charlie Hewitt, an Albion player for two seasons (1908-10) was Wrexham manager, 1924-26; Tony Rance was secretary at both clubs in the 1980s. Albion reserves Rolf Lenney (1923-24) and Eli Postin (1935-36) later featured in Wrexham's first team.

WRIGHT, Harold Fereday

Harry Wright had two spells with Albion – the first from

1906-09, the second from 1910-19. Although only 5ft 8ins. tall, he was an energetic, purposeful inside-forward, who scored a combined total of 20 goals in 105 appearances for the club. He helped Albion win the Second Division championship in 1911 and reach the FA Cup Final the following year. Born in West Bromwich in 1888, he joined Albion initially from West Bromwich Wednesbury Athletic and played for Stourbridge before returning to The Hawthorns. A guest for Oldbury Town and Bilston during World War One, he left for Wolves at the end of his second spell with Albion and later served with Newport County, retiring in 1922. Wright died in 1950.

WYCOMBE WANDERERS

Albion's record against Wycombe:

FA Cup

Venue	P	W	D	L	F	A
Home	1	1	0	0	1	0
Away	1	0	1	0	2	2
Totals	2	1	1	0	3	2

Other Match

Away	1	1	0	0	4	1

The first time Albion met Wycombe Wanderers was in a friendly in Buckinghamshire on 21 March 1896 (won 4-1).

The two Cup-ties were second-round affairs played in 1992. Albion held a 2-0 lead at Adams Park before a near 7,000 crowd on 6 December, but Wycombe fought back after the break to earn a replay. This took place nine days later at The Hawthorns and in front of 17,640 fans, Bob Taylor scored a late winner for Albion.

Nicky Reid (later to join Wycombe) made his debut for Albion in the Cup match at Adams Park.

Players with both clubs: Simon Garner, Cyrille Regis, Nicky Reid, Darren Rogers, Fred Rouse, Steve Walford. Albion trialist Paul Kerr (1994) played for Wycombe's first team in 1995-96.

YORK CITY

Albion's record against York:

Football League

Venue	P	W	D	L	F	A	Pts
Home	2	1	1	0	4	2	3
Away	2	2	0	0	4	1	4
Totals	4	3	1	0	8	3	7

FA Cup

Away	1	0	0	1	2	3

Albion's first game against York City ended in disaster when they lost a fourth-round FA Cup-tie at Bootham Crescent by 3-2 on 22 January 1938. City's centre-forward Reg Baines scored a hat-trick to the delight of the home supporters in a crowd of 18,795.

City were in the Third Division North at the time,

Craig Madden, played for both York and Albion.

while Albion were members of the First Division.

The first of the four League meetings between the clubs was played at The Hawthorns on 5 October 1974 (Division Two). Albion won 2-0 with goals from Willie Johnston and Alan Merrick.

In the return game at York that season (12 April) Joe Mayo scored twice in Albion's 3-1 win.

Albion League debutant v City: Bryan Robson (1975).

Players with both clubs: George Lee, Craig Madden, Jack Mahon.

Also associated with both clubs: Albion reserves Arnold Charlesworth (1950s) and Sid Glidden (1920s) later joined York. Another reserve, Derek Hood, left Albion in 1977 and played 301 League games (13 goals) for York between 1981 and 1988. Colin Addison, who was twice Albion's assistant manager, was a York City forward (1956-61).

YOUTH FOOTBALL
Development
As early as 1886-87 Albion fielded a third team but it was not until after World War Two had ended that the real strides were made in the development of young talent at The Hawthorns.

In 1950-51 the maximum wage was £12 per week and Albion could afford to have some 40 professionals signed up, although not all of them were available owing to National Service commitments.

Albion had seven teams in those days: in the League Division One, Central League, the Midland Mid-Week League, Birmingham Combination, the Walsall Senior League, the Birmingham & West Midland Alliance and the Handsworth League. In addition, the club's nursery side, Erdington Albion, participated in the Birmingham Youth Committee. And by the mid-1950s, Albion were putting out as many as fifteen teams (at various levels).

Starting in 1952, Albion's Under-18 team participated in the FA Youth Cup – and they reached the Final for the first time in 1955 when they lost to Manchester United over two legs. They also had a fine record in the Amsterdam Youth International Tournament, which they won three times: in 1956 when they beat Everton 4-2, in 1957 when they were 2-0 victors over Racing Club of Paris and in 1960 when they triumphed 2-1 over Nottingham Forest.

In 1958 they lost in the Final to Ajax Amsterdam 1-0.

The Midland Intermediate League was formed in 1960 with Albion secretary 'Eph' Smith as its first honorary secretary.

At the start of the 1960-61 season, however, Albion were parading only four teams – in the League Division One, the Central League, the Warwickshire Combination and the new Intermediate League, and by 1964 they had withdrawn from the Combination. The reduction of Albion's playing strength and consequently their youth football activities, had been brought about by the abolition of the maximum wage in 1961 which meant that football clubs could no longer afford such a large pay-roll.

As the 1970s approached, Albion's youth team were still competing in the FA Youth Cup (and still do today) and they were also playing regularly in overseas tournaments, losing in the Final of the Bremen Youth International Tournament in 1969 to Ajax by 3-1.

In 1972 the club's youth policy was re-organised with trainer Albert McPherson (the former Walsall centre-half) and scout Roy Horobin (an ex-Albion left winger who became the club's first youth development officer) taking an increasing interest in affairs of the youngsters.

The foreign trips continued – to Yugoslavia in 1972 and Augsburg (Germany) in 1973, 1974, 1975, 1977. Albion, in fact, won the tournament in 1974 under the expert eye of director and former player Cliff Edwards. The team also reached the quarter-finals of the Southern Junior Floodlit Cup in 1973.

In 1979 Albion won the Rheinfelden International Youth Tournament in Germany, taking maximum points from their four matches, two of which were played on the same day – 3 June.

Further occasional summer excursions were made by Albion's youngsters during the 1980s. In 1981 Albion's youth squad won the Duisburg International Tournament and in 1982 the Phorzheim Youth Tournament. The only recent success has been the winning of the youth competition in Amsterdam in the spring of 1996.

Scouting System
At the present time Albion have eighteen authorised scouts who are based all over Great Britain, including one in the extreme Scottish Highlands, another in the hot-bed of English soccer, the North-East (John Allan in Washington, Tyne and Wear), a couple scanning the Southern coastline from Devon and Cornwall through to Dorset and Hampshire, and representatives in Wales and Ireland. There are also a dozen local scouts serving the Midlands region who work mainly with coaches Richard O'Kelly and John Trewick.

The Albion scouting system is now under the close supervision of chief scout Ronnie Mann, who took over the role from Norman Bodell in 1994, Bodell having held the position since 1986

If a youngster looks as if he could make the grade, he is cordially invited to The Hawthorns for a trial, usually during the summer holidays. Most clubs these days (Albion included) have a 'School of Excellence' which caters for boys aged 10 to 15 and if there is anyone who looks the part during his scheduled period of training at the school, then his name is put forward too. Normally a youngster is taken on initially as an associate schoolboy, and is encouraged to attend weekly coaching sessions organised by Albion. The parents and, indeed, head teachers of the boy are all kept informed as to his progress and at the same time they are given details of what could be in store for the youngster if he does make the grade and is taken on as a trainee. 'Digs' have to be vetted and arranged for those boys who live well outside the Hawthorns catchment area and further education is discussed just in case the boy fails to progress as a footballer.

Apprentice/Trainee Footballers
The apprentice professional scheme was first introduced in 1960; it became known later as the Youth Training Scheme (YTS).

A player must be 17 years of age before he can be signed as a full-time professional by any club under the jurisdiction of the FA but youths between the ages of 15 and 17 may be registered as apprentices/trainees, and they have until their 18th birthday to decide whether or not they want to join the senior professional ranks if invited to do so by their club.

Albion have been quite successful with their scheme, although not always as shown in the close season of 1974!

At that time eleven new apprentices were engaged under manager Don Howe, but only one (Wayne Hughes) played for Albion's League side, although Steve Lynex subsequently made the grade as a professional with Shamrock Rovers, Leicester City and Birmingham and later returned to The Hawthorns to play in first-team football.

Winger Dick Krzywicki was the first Albion apprentice to play in the Football League, making his debut at Fulham on 19 December 1964.

In more recent years a number of players have made the grade having joined Albion virtually straight from school and developed through the club's junior ranks, among them: Martyn Bennett, Tony Brown, Daryl Burgess, David Burrows, Len Cantello, Gary Childs, Ian Collard, Nicky Cross, Ian Edwards, Ray Fairfax, Mickey Forsyth, Asa

Hartford, Jim Holton, Gerry Howshall, Lyndon Hughes, Kevin Kent, Krzywicki, Peter Latchford, Mickey Lewis, Graham Lovett, Alan Merrick, Gordon Nisbet, Carlton Palmer, Alistair Robertson, Mark Robinson, Gary and Bryan Robson, Dick Sheppard, Derek Statham, Kenny Stephens, Kevin Summerfield, Andy Thompson, Trevor Thompson, Ray Treacy, John Trewick and Ray Wilson.

Honours
Apart from winning the aforementioned international youth tournaments, Albion have acquired several more honours in youth team football as shown here:
FA Youth Cup winners: 1975-76, runners-up 1954-55, 1968-69.
Midland Mid-Week League champions: 1937-38, 1938-39
Midland Intermediate League champions: 1971-72, 1973-74, 1976-77; runners-up: 1968-69.
Midland Intermediate League Cup winners: 1969-70, 1973-74; runners-up: 1971-72.
Midland Youth League champions: 1977-78, 1981-82.
Midland Youth League Cup runners-up: 1981-82.

Albion in the FA Youth Cup:
Albion's record in the FA Youth Cup (1952-96) is:

Venue	P	W	D	L	F	A
Home	78	44	19	15	184	88
Away	76	35	10	31	140	122
Totals	154	79	29	46	324	210

Albion won their first game 10-1 away against Brush Sports (Loughborough) on 4 October 1952. This is their best victory in the competition to date.

On 7 November 1988 Albion beat Scunthorpe United 9-0 at The Hawthorns in a second-round tie. Adrian Foster (3), Daryl Burgess (2), Adrian Littlejohn (2) were the prominent marksmen.

A disconsolate Albion team are comforted by trainer Jimmy Dunn after losing to Sunderland in the 1969 two-legged FA Youth Cup Final.

6-0 against Wolverhampton Wanderers at home on 15 October 1955 and in the second leg of the Final at Sunderland in May 1969 have been Albion's worst defeats in the competition.

Albion's second heaviest home defeat in the competition is 6-3 against Leicester City in 1985-86.

In 1963-64 Albion beat Coventry City 6-4 in a thrilling cup-tie at Highfield Road and a season later Albion were held to a 4-4 draw at The Hawthorns by Birmingham City.

Albion beat Wolves 5-0 on aggregate (2-0 away, 3-0 at home) to win the 1975-76 Youth Cup Final – their team (for the second leg) being: Mark Grew; Tony Cooper, Derek Statham; John Loveridge, Brian Clarke, Martyn Davies; Steve Lynex, Colin Gregson, Mark Tranter, Wayne Hughes, Kevin Summerfield. Subs: Derek Monaghan, Derek Hood.

Manchester United and Sunderland beat Albion in the 1955 and 1969 Youth Cup Finals respectively, Sunderland coming back from a 3-0 first-leg deficit to win the tie 6-3 on aggregate. Jim Holton and Asa Hartford were both sent off in the second leg at Roker Park by referee Tommy Dawes.

Albion lost in the semi-finals of the competition in 1953-54 (beaten by Manchester United), in 1973-74 (eclipsed by Huddersfield Town) and in 1977-78 (ousted by Crystal Palace).

Two players have scored six goals in a Youth Cup-tie for Albion – Dick McCartney in a 7-0 victory over Aston Villa (away) in 1954 and Ray Wilson in a 7-1 home win against Northampton Town ten years later.

Youth International honours:
The following players won Under-16 and Under-18 caps for their country while with Albion:
England – Ian Benjamin (1979), Ron Bradley (1955), Tony Brown (1964), Peter Bunch (1956), Davey Burnside (1956, 1957), Len Cantello (1970), Gary Childs (1981, 1982), Barry Cooke (1955, 1956), John Crosby (1959), Neil Cutler (1992, 1993, 1994), Barry Donaghy (1973, 1974), Chuck Drury (1955), Mickey Forsyth (1984), Peter Frain (1982), Mike Gibson (1956), Lyndon Hughes (1970), Alan Jones (1961), Grenville Jones (1947), Mickey Lewis (1982), Alan Merrick (1968), Derek Monaghan (1976, 1977), Bryan Robson (1975), Jeff Rumjahn (1974), Maurice Setters (1956), Derek Statham (1976, 1977), Kevin Summerfield (1976, 1977), John Trewick (1975), Alan Wileman (1957, 1958).
Northern Ireland – Darren Patterson (1986, 1987, 1988).
Scotland – Gary Germaine (1994), Asa Hartford (1968, 1969), Mike McCartney (1973), Stewart McLaren (1971), Hughie Reed (1968), Alistair Robertson (1968, 1970).
Wales – Wayne Hughes (1976), Mark Tranter (1976).
Republic of Ireland – John Anderson (1977), Ray Treacy (1964).

Schoolboy Internationals:
The following all won British and Irish schoolboy international honours and subsequently played League football for Albion:
England – Martyn Bennett, Stan Butler, Len Cantello, Harry Chambers, Frank Cresswell, Joe Evans, Tommy Glidden, Lyndon Hughes, John Osborne, George McVitie, Steve Parkin, Paul Raven, Colin Suggett, John Talbut, John Trewick, Bill Williams.
Scotland – Arthur Albiston, Campbell Crawford, Kenny Foggo, Bobby Hope, Bobby Murray, Alistair Robertson.
Wales – Andy Dibble, Michael Lee, Jimmy Murphy, Tony Rees, Bill Tudor.
Northern Ireland – Paul Agnew, Alan Fettis, Billy Lunn
Republic of Ireland – Johnny Giles, Ray Treacy.
NB: Fred Horne (England) also played for England schoolboys, but never made Albion's first team. He later became the club's assistant secretary (1959-74).

ZENITH DATA SYSTEMS CUP
Albion conceded 10 goals in two home matches in two seasons (1989-90 & 1990-91) of this short-lived competition, their record being:

Venue	P	W	D	L	F	A
Home	2	0	0	2	3	10

Derby County beat Albion 5-0 at The Hawthorns on 29 November 1989, four of their goals coming in a five minute second-half spell. Welsh international striker Dean

Saunders scored three times for the Rams.

In the following season, Barnsley inflicted a 5-3 defeat on Albion at The Hawthorns with former Baggies' midfielder Ian Banks netting a second-half hat-trick in the space of 12 minutes for the Tykes. Barnsley's first goal was also scored by an former Baggies player, Mark Robinson.

ZONDERVAN, Romeo

Zondervan, a Dutch international at three levels, schoolboy, Under-21 and senior (capped against Cyprus in 1981), was voted Albion's Player of the Year at the end of his first full season at The Hawthorns (May 1983). A versatile footballer, able to play at left-back, in midfield or on the wing, he was born in Paramaribo, Surinam in 1959, and served with Postalia (1975), Den Haag (1976) and FC Twente Enschede before joining Albion for £225,000 in 1982, teaming up with his fellow Dutchman, Maarten Jol. He spent two years at The Hawthorns, scoring five goals in 95 appearances, before leaving for Ipswich Town for £70,000 in 1984 when Johnny Giles became Albion's manager for a second time. He quit first-class football in 1994, later scouted for Ipswich and Bradford City and returned to Holland to become youth team coach of his former club, FC Twente in 1995-96. Zondervan is a qualified pilot.